UNDERWORLD WORK

CLASS 200 NEW STUDIES IN RELIGION

A SERIES EDITED BY Kathryn Lofton and John Lardas Modern

ALSO PUBLISHED IN THE SERIES

Life in Language: Mission Feminists and the Emergence of a New Protestant Subject
Ingie Hovland

Fraternal Critique: The Politics of Muslim Community in France
Kirsten Wesselhoeft

Promiscuous Grace: Imagining Beauty and Holiness with Saint Mary of Egypt
Sonia Velázquez

Slandering the Sacred: Blasphemy Law and Religious Affect in Colonial India
J. Barton Scott

Earthquakes and Gardens: Saint Hilarion's Cyprus
Virginia Burrus

Awkward Rituals: Sensations of Governance in Protestant America
Dana Logan

Sincerely Held: American Secularism and Its Believers
Charles McCrary

Unbridled: Studying Religion in Performance
William Robert

Profaning Paul
Cavan W. Concannon

Making a Mantra: Tantric Ritual and Renunciation on the Jain Path to Liberation
Ellen Gough

Neuromatic: Or, A Particular History of Religion and the Brain
John Lardas Modern

Kindred Spirits: Friendship and Resistance at the Edges of Modern Catholicism
Brenna Moore

UNDERWORLD WORK

Black Atlantic Religion Making
in Jim Crow New Orleans

AHMAD GREENE-HAYES

The University of Chicago Press
Chicago and London

The University of Chicago Press, Chicago 60637
The University of Chicago Press, Ltd., London
© 2025 by The University of Chicago
All rights reserved. No part of this book may be used or reproduced in any manner whatsoever without written permission, except in the case of brief quotations in critical articles and reviews. For more information, contact the University of Chicago Press, 1427 E. 60th St., Chicago, IL 60637.
Published 2025
Printed in the United States of America

34 33 32 31 30 29 28 27 26 25   1 2 3 4 5

ISBN-13: 978-0-226-83884-7 (cloth)
ISBN-13: 978-0-226-83886-1 (paper)
ISBN-13: 978-0-226-83885-4 (e-book)
DOI: https://doi.org/10.7208/chicago/9780226838854.001.0001

Visitation 1 reproduces material from *Tell My Horse* by Zora Neale Hurston. Copyright © 1938 by Zora Neale Hurston. Renewed 1966 by Joel Hurston and John C. Hurston. Used by permission of HarperCollins Publishers.

Visitation 4 reproduces material from *Mules and Men* by Zora Neale Hurston. Copyright © 1935 by Zora Neale Hurston. Renewed 1963 by John C. Hurston and Joel Hurston. Used by permission of HarperCollins Publishers.

Library of Congress Cataloging-in-Publication Data

Names: Greene-Hayes, Ahmad, author.
Title: Underworld work : Black Atlantic religion making in Jim Crow New Orleans / Ahmad Greene-Hayes.
Other titles: Black Atlantic religion making in Jim Crow New Orleans | Class 200, new studies in religion.
Description: Chicago ; London : The University of Chicago Press, 2025. | Series: Class 200: new studies in religion | Includes bibliographical references and index.
Identifiers: LCCN 2024042375 | ISBN 9780226838847 (cloth) | ISBN 9780226838861 (paperback) | ISBN 9780226838854 (ebook)
Subjects: LCSH: Hurston, Zora Neale. | African Americans—Louisiana—New Orleans—Religion. | African Americans—Louisiana—New Orleans—Social life and customs. | African Americans—Louisiana—New Orleans—Social conditions. | Vodou—Louisiana—New Orleans. | New Orleans (La.)—History.
Classification: LCC F380.B53 G74 2025 | DDC 305.896/073076335—dc23/eng/20241204
LC record available at https://lccn.loc.gov/2024042375

♾ This paper meets the requirements of ANSI/NISO Z39.48-1992 (Permanence of Paper).

In memory of my great-grandmother,
Louise Johnson, and grandmother, Gean
Evette Greene, who had me on their minds,
and took the time and prayed for me.

This the kind of world . . . that makes fools of the living and saints of them once they dead. And devils them throughout.

JESMYN WARD, *Sing, Unburied Sing*

The Christian faith provided a language for the meaning of religion, but not all the religious meanings of the black communities were encompassed by the Christian forms of religion. I have been as interested in other forms of religion in the history of black communities—as those forms are contained in their folklore, music, style of life, and so on. Some tensions have existed between these forms of orientation and those of the Christian churches, but some of these extra-church orientations have had great critical and creative power. They have often touched deeper religious issues regarding the true situation of black communities than those of the church leaders of their time. The religion of any people is more than a structure of thought; it is experience, expression, motivations, intentions, behaviors, styles, and rhythms. Its first and fundamental expression is not on the level of thought. It gives rise to thought, but a form of thought that embodies the precision and nuances of its source.

CHARLES H. LONG, *Significations*

Gods always behave like the people who make them.

ZORA NEALE HURSTON, *Tell My Horse: Voodoo and Life in Haiti and Jamaica*

CONTENTS

List of Abbreviations   xi

Introduction   1

VISITATION 1   *Zora on "Voodoo"*   29

1   "Midnight Orgies": Voudou and the Problem of Possessed
Black Flesh from Haiti to Louisiana   31

VISITATION 2   *Zora on Lynching*   57

2   "Smoke Out the Negro Devils": Black Cosmopolitan Eclecticism
in the New Century and the Terror of Lynching   59

VISITATION 3   *Zora Eats the Salt*   87

3   "Making a Place for Negro Untouchables": Black Sexual
Victorianism and Its Counterconducts   89

VISITATION 4   *Zora Talks "Hoodoo in America" and Elsewhere*   117

4   "Dangerous and Suspicious": Hoodoo, Faith Healing, and Sex
Work in the Black Slum   119

VISITATION 5   *Zora's Unpublished Satire on Marcus Garvey:*
"The Emperor Effaces Himself"   147

5   "The Right Idea of God": Sinners and Saints in the New Orleans
Division of the Universal Negro Improvement Association   149

VISITATION 6 *Zora Worships with the Sanctified* 179

6 "We Ain't Spiritualists, We's the Sanctified Church":
Black Pentecostals and the Politics of Distinction 181

Coda: Black New Orleans on the Move 213

Acknowledgments 219
Notes 223
Index 273

ABBREVIATIONS

AFS	American Folklore Society
AME	African Methodist Episcopal
COG	Council of God
COGIC	Church of God in Christ
FWP	Federal Writers' Project
LWP	Louisiana Writers' Project
NAACP	National Association for the Advancement of Colored People
NOD	New Orleans Division of the Universal Negro Improvement Association
WPA	Works Progress Administration
UNIA	Universal Negro Improvement Association

FIGURE I.1. Zora Neale Hurston in the underworld doing fieldwork, late 1930s. Zora Neale Hurston Papers, box 2, folder 14, image 27. Courtesy of the University of Florida.

INTRODUCTION

Zora Neale Hurston descended into the underworld in New Orleans and the Black Atlantic in the late 1920s and early 1930s and never came back. Nearly thirty years later, in 1960, she died alone at age sixty-nine in the St. Lucie County Welfare Home in Ft. Pierce, Florida, from hypertensive heart disease and a stroke before finally being buried in an unmarked grave. Newspaper headlines read: "Negro Authoress Dies Impoverished."[1] It was there in the underworld that, before her passing and unceremonious burial, she communed with and interviewed sinners and saints, took copious notes, created complex recordings, and bore witness to the sights and sounds of Black Atlantic religion making in the deepest depths of *the Black slums*—a place maligned by the government and social scientists but celebrated by Black people as a site of "beautiful anarchy," where one made feasts out of scraps and dreamed of a better life amid confinement.[2] No one else cared about the underworld and its inhabitants quite like Hurston; in fact, Hurston found sanctuary and fellowship there. The writer, filmmaker, and ethnographer always kept a pen and notepad nearby, and then there were matters of the heart and spirit that she held close, seemingly away from the eyes and ears of her white philanthropic supporters and academic advisers. She repeatedly reminds us through a host of significations that some things were just too sacred to be written in letters to be sent up North for white public consumption, and then there were other things that she gifted us, seeking to make legible the seemingly illegible and to make known the unknowable.

After first visiting the city in 1928, she wrote, "New Orleans is now and has ever been the Hoodoo capital of America. Great names in rites that vie with those of Haiti in deeds that keep alive the powers of Africa . . . It has thousands of secret adherents."[3] It was there in New Orleans that this daughter of an Eatonville Baptist preacher spent more than six months immersed in the city's Voudou, Hoodoo, Spiritualist, Sanctified, and other religious communities, observing, watching, and eventually becoming initiated at several Hoodoo and Voudou ceremonies. While Hurston never officially described herself as a religious practitioner, her regard for the sacred and the traditions of the African diaspora is both apparent and undeniable. After New Orleanian Hoodoo doctor Leon Turner lit a candle for her during one of her initiations, Hurston confessed, "But from then on I might be a candle-lighter myself" and in another instance, she affirmed, "Hoodoo is private."[4]

In line with the methodological commitments of Africana religious studies, I regard Hurston "as an undisclosed spiritist" who inserted "a politics of purpose where racialized spirituality [bled] into the process of ethnographic capturing," and as a Hurstonian, I follow in the ethnographer's footsteps to recover the stories, voices, and innovations of the people whom she communed with in New Orleans.[5] Hurston's archive of Hoodoo, Conjure, and Voudou and her ethical imperative are guiding forces for this book's structure and analysis. This book would not be possible without Hurston, who had "five psychic experiences" while in the city and across the banks of the Mississippi River in Algiers.[6] Hurston knew that the Mississippi River valley had a cultural distinctiveness that Black people preserved by venerating their ancestors iconographically through the Catholic saints. It was there in the valley that Hoodoo and Voudou thrived in the Black South with New Orleans at its center, and a seeking Hurston journeyed there, yearning to know for herself.[7] She wrote her friend and fellow writer Langston Hughes on August 6, 1928, "I have landed here in the kingdom of Marie Laveau and expect to wear her crown someday—Conjure Queen as you have suggested."[8] Writing again about New Orleans in two separate letters to her adviser, Dr. Franz Boas at Columbia University, Hurston expressed the merits behind her ethnographic dive into the city. In one exchange dated October 20, 1929, she noted while visiting Miami, Florida, "New Orleans is the womb of cults and there I find the Protestant churches being as individual as one can imagine. Pagan."[9] Two months later, on December 10, 1929, she confessed her ethical commitments for her fieldwork, noting, "I want to make this conjure work very thorough and inclusive."[10]

In the pages that follow, I grapple with Hurston's desire for thoroughness and inclusivity in my own research and writing. Just shy of a century later, as I sorted through a diverse array of archival sources, Hurston and her contemporaries manifested themselves as archival ancestors and urged me

INTRODUCTION   3

to work through scarce, unassuming, and often neglected social scientific, governmental, census, police, church, and other public sources. In doing so, I recover an Africana demimonde as a metaphorical and material space that was constituted by the spiritual "work" of marginalized and dispossessed religion makers in Jim Crow–era New Orleans who have been otherwise pejoratively rendered cultists, fanatics, and criminal others in American religious histories.[11] In this vein, Hurston's ethnographic capturing was underworld work, as she went into the deepest depths of criminalized Black religious communities in the slums as "introspection into the mystery," and through her critical analyses, we encounter Black (queer) under/worlding as method.[12] Hurston, a daughter of the rural South and an urban migrant, most assuredly employed her own "Black queer urbanism" in her ethnographic spiritism (not necessarily in regard to her sexual identity, though possibly), and through her and the people she studied, we come to know other and alternative modes of being and religious experimentation in the wake of slavery.[13]

Yet, despite the magnitude of Hurston's literary and ethnographic archive, we are faced with a conundrum: her descent into the underworld had grave consequences for her work as a Black (queer) woman writer and ethnographer, in that she was maligned, dismissed, and not taken seriously by many of her contemporaries because of her proximity to criminalized peoples and their religious practices.[14] Consequently, Hurston's archive of Black Atlantic religion making has mysteriously also not been fully taken up by later scholars in African American religious history, and much of that has to do with a northern, Protestant, heterosexual, male hegemony that has historically shaped some of the field's political and ethical obligations, despite significant interventions by Black women historians, theologians, and ethicists to move the field beyond the Protestant pew and male-dominated pulpit.

UNDERWORLD WORK

When we look to Hurston and her contemporaries who bore witness to the underworld, we can tell new stories and return to forgotten stories about how Black people cultivated religions in slavery's wake. Many of these criminalized religions fell into the category of "underworld work," which Hurston's colleague Harry Middleton Hyatt, a white Anglican minister and self-taught fieldworker, described in detail in his five-volume collection, *Hoodoo—Conjuration—Witchcraft—Rootwork: Beliefs Adopted by Many Negroes and White Persons*. He further characterized these practices as "concealed, low-class, or dirty works" of a spiritual nature, having to do with "turning de law away [from yo' door]."[15] It is abundantly clear that Hyatt gleaned this language from the Black religious practitioners he encountered in New Orleans and throughout the Black South in the early twentieth century, like Madame Collins in Memphis, who described using "Hindu weed" in her Hoodoo practice "tuh turn de law off any business."[16] He wrote, "After all, the work I was seeking to record *was called* underworld work" (emphasis added).[17] Underworld work had already been called such before Hyatt encountered its existence; he merely reiterated what Southern Black people had already been saying about themselves for decades.[18] Such a distinction reveals how Black religious practitioners conceived of their own subjectivity and practice as working counter to the world as they knew and experienced it. I recover the term "underworld work" from the archive as a theoretical framework for understanding the Black religious innovation of the people at the center of this book's concerns, without jettisoning an analysis of Jim Crow governmentality.[19] To quote critical theorist Saidiya Hartman, "The state of emergency was the norm not the exception," and underworld work emerged within the enclosures of gratuitous anti-Black violence.[20]

In this vein, the term "underworld" has historically referred to "the abode of the departed, imagined as being under the earth; the nether world" and "the world of criminals or of organized crime."[21] In *An American Dilemma: The Negro Problem and Modern Democracy* (1944), sociologist Gunnar Myrdal confirmed the significance of the latter definition in a section entitled "Note on Shady Occupations." He wrote, "In the cities, particularly in the big cities, there is a Negro 'underworld.' To it belong not only petty thieves and racketeers, prostitutes and pimps, bootleggers, dope addicts, and so on, but also a number of 'big shots' organizing and controlling crime, vice, and racketeering, as well as other more innocent forms of illegal activity such as gambling."[22] While Myrdal's assessment aligned with many of his contemporaries who theorized and often pathologized "the Negro problem," the underworld was far more capacious than Myrdal could have ever imagined or anticipated.[23] In Jim Crow–era New Orleans, the underworld was a site for communication with the spirits and with ancestors, and it was also a site for religious, sexual, economic, and political practices and gatherings criminalized by the white Christian hegemonic state.

Given the abundance of public discourse about underworlds, it is no sur-

INTRODUCTION

prise that they piqued the interest of scholars of Black Atlantic religious and cultural expressions, like Hurston, seeking to understand the people who had been criminalized within them.[24] Take for instance the work of cultural anthropologist and art historian Daniel J. Crawley, who in his 1956 article "The Traditional Masques of Carnival," published in the *Caribbean Quarterly*, commented on the Jamèt Carnival in Trinidad and its suppression due to "obscenity." He wrote, "'Jamèt' [comes] from French *diametre*, the underworld or 'other hand.' The term currently signifies a prostitute, but as used in Carnival it meant the underworld in general. Jamèt women, who were said to be 'matadors' or retired prostitutes gone respectable, were understandably always masked." He went on, observing, "Their most startling characteristic . . . was their habit of throwing open their bodies and exposing their breasts." Similarly, their counterpart, the Jamèt man—otherwise referred to as "sweet man" as a play on his perceived queer sexuality—"had trousers of serge or flannel worn low over the hips and held up by two belts of rope or leather from which hung multicolored silk kerchiefs and ribbons."[25] Both the Jamèt woman and the Jamèt man—otherwise understood as underworld persons—embodied an unrestrained Black sexuality. They did so in exaggerated form through the Carnival's vibrant, flamboyant ancestral celebration and its use of the spirits—both that of deities and of alcohol—as the diasporic still for surviving postslavery Trinidad, as was also the case with Carnival in New Orleans in the late nineteenth and early twentieth centuries.[26]

The inhabitants of the underworld, with their elaborate gestures and spiritual powers, conceived of themselves and their social contexts in terms and on registers of their own making. Mother Catherine Seals, who appears in chapter 3, told Hurston in the late 1920s, for instance, "There is no hell beneath this earth. God wouldn't build a hell to burn His breath. There is no heaven beyond [that] blue globe. There is a between-world between this brown earth and the blue above. So says the beautiful spirit."[27] I take Seals's sacred geology as an articulation of the underworld as she understood it. A prophet and faith healer, Seals was known to communicate with the spirits and to convey divine messages to her followers. For her, the underworld was her brown earth. In fact, she dwelled there at the Temple of the Innocent Blood. Outside the literal space of her temple and house church was the "between-world" where everyone else dwelled; both, however, were shaped by anti-Blackness as the governing apparatus, such that Seals dwelled there insofar as Jim Crow confined her there. Seals, like so many of the other religious practitioners examined, *did underworld work*, and so, she was an *underworld worker*. As Elizabeth Pérez reminds us, the "work" or "works" that practitioners did and continue to do in Black Atlantic religions refers not only to labor but also to "something that is done," typically a transformative ritual or assemblage (as in *trabajo*); it is a root metaphor of Black Atlantic religious practice.[28] In this way, the underworld was a terrain in which practitioners did "work" or labor as religious practice and also for economic survival.

For clarity, however, underworld work was not monolithic or ubiquitous in its character. It looked different in varying temporal, theological, and cultural contexts in the city of New Orleans and throughout the Black Atlantic world. Although Hyatt used "underworld work" interchangeably with "Hoodoo work," his assessment of this diversity is instructive. He wrote, "Many other pursuits are found in association with Hoodoo work: magicians, patent medicine salesmen, fortunetellers, healers, numerologists, and spiritualists in addition to rootworkers. This amorphous conglomeration that forms Hoodoo work also has connection with other *underworld* activities, such as bootlegging, gambling and prostitution as connections to various religious sects, including Protestantism and Catholicism."[29] In his assessment of this "variation," as he called it, Hyatt concluded, "As for academic theories concerning Hoodoo and related practices: I leave that for the scholars who use these volumes."[30] I respond to Hyatt's call, but cautiously and prayerfully at the bidding of my own blood, archival, and intellectual ancestors—who sit in that great cloud of witnesses—such that this book ultimately embodies "the religious histories revealed by the dead."[31]

Underworld Work: Black Atlantic Religion Making in Jim Crow New Orleans is an interdisciplinary, historical study or "history as theory and theory as history" and it grapples with a rich array of spiritual modalities cultivated by practitioners in and around the Black slum.[32] This book is ultimately about the beauty and complexity of Black religious innovation in the afterlife of slavery, amid the horrid period of Jim Crow segregation and racial violence. It is about how people of African descent utilized their religious imaginations to conjure new "under/worlds" in the face of the ever-present and inescapable anti-Black world, all the while communing with worlds of times past and worlds yet to come. Many of the individuals at the center of this book's analysis were unchurched or antichurch, or they ultimately created their own house churches and religious institutions, or they reinvented other public and private spaces like bars, hotels, and the slums for their religious services and offerings. In the face of gratuitous state violence—lynching, poverty, surveillance, policing, and social scien-

INTRODUCTION   7

tific voyeurism—they embraced a wide array of Africana esotericisms, such as the production of mystical knowledges, ancestral veneration, dancing, conjuring, rootworking, tarrying, faith healing, and spiritualized sex work.[33] Through these practices, they stretched beyond the enclosures of this world, into the depths of the underworld, and there they revered covert gatherings and economies, spirits and hauntings, ancestors and afterlives. There, their practices also operated on registers at odds with the American grammar book, in that its grammatologists wrote their own scripts for living beyond the human—a fraught category of which they were ultimately excluded.[34]

RELIGION, SLAVERY, AND UN/FREEDOM

Considering the interconnectedness of race and religion in the Americas, this work joins a long genealogy of Black religious studies scholarship that has endeavored to think about the structural antagonisms and systems of domination surrounding Black religious practitioners, evident in the work of such scholars as Charles H. Long, Delores Williams, James H. Cone, Joseph Washington, Jacquelyn Grant, Gayraud Wilmore, Albert Raboteau, Kelly Brown Douglas, and many more. This list is by no means exhaustive (nor is it intended to be), but it serves as a representative framing for a discourse in Black theology, ethics, and history regarding the political sensibilities of Black religious practitioners during slavery and in the afterlife of slavery. Contrary to the reductionist framings often offered by secular historians and theorists of Black life and culture, Black religionists have conjured and cultivated critiques of domination and anti-Blackness. The individuals discussed in this book were targeted by state actors, and their religions—across the political spectrum—were subject to hyperbolic ridicule by press writers, policemen, and state-employed researchers. It is true that these individuals were able to nonetheless cultivate Black religious innovation in the face of this governmentality, but before we can fully tell and appreciate that part of the story, we must render the conditions in which they innovated legible for our understanding—a political imperative guided by the myriad contributions of my forebears.

   In this way, the methods by which Black actors made "religion" in slavery and its afterlives often emerged in response to the violent procedures utilized by white race makers to demonize and criminalize them.[35] Thus, I contend that any celebrations of Black creativity or Black progressive political empowerment cannot be understood without appreciation of underworld work—or the political and spiritual maneuvers cultivated by Black people to mitigate the effects of white ritualization. Through this framework, it becomes clear that underworld work influenced and formed what could be in the above ground (so to speak) as legible, legal religious activity that largely worked in concert with, or at times as critique of, white ritual violence and anti-Blackness.

Black people were encircled by a world of ritualized policing and surveillance during Jim Crow, a period in which "policing" included the jail cell and the state-sanctioned court of the lynch mob. Black neighborhoods, homes, storefront churches, botanicas, and recreational spaces were always subject to the threat of white racial-sexual terrorism, whether the burned cross on a lawn, the Klan waiting outside of a revival meeting, or the white social scientist sitting in a Black church pew. No Black space was always Black space; there was always the intrusion of white eyes and the white gaze of social scientists, tourists, and policemen into the lives of Black Atlantic religious practitioners. Many Black people were also cordoned off as "undesirables" who were forced to live in shacks on unpaved roads, sometimes funded by predatory loans from largely white-owned banks, in the poorest wards of New Orleans. Marcus Christian, the director of the Dillard History Unit (the all-Black wing of the Louisiana Writers' Project [LWP]), captures Black Protestants' sense of desperation, writing in the 1930s, "Although primarily interested in, and devoted to the gaining of, complete freedom in the world to come, the Negro church is becoming increasingly cognizant of the inadequacy of such aims under present world conditions."[36] No matter what Black people did, white ritual violence loomed large, like an enormous gray cloud hovering over the swamps and the banks of the Mississippi River wherein they held baptisms and Voudou ceremonies.

No other scene of subjection confirms this sentiment quite like the "Ghost Map of Louisiana" by Roland Duvernet (fig. I.2), which was included in the opening pages of the LWP's popular 1945 book *Gumbo Ya-Ya*. The map depicts lynched African American men hanging from Southern trees as part of the geography of the underworld, which only confirms the quotidian reality of policing, surveillance, and gratuitous violence in the social and religious (under)worlds of Black life and culture. Even in the spaces in which Black people sought respite, anti-Blackness consumed them, such that they cultivated spiritual practices to manage the ever-present threat of death and dying.[37] Roots, herbs, spells, prayers, hymns, and other material objects were coupled with a variety of Africana esoteric rituals as a means

FIGURE I.2. "The Ghost Map of Louisiana," by Roland Duvernet, from *Gumbo Ya-Ya* by Robert Tallant, Lyle Saxon, and Edward Dreyer. Copyright © 1945 by the Louisiana Library Commission. Used by permission of HarperCollins Publishers.

of making it from minute to minute, hour to hour, and day to day. There was no guarantee that one could be "saved," but many practitioners believed that they might as well die trying. Others relied on the Negro spiritual—"Before I'll be a slave, I'll be buried in my grave and go home to my Lord and be free"—in which self-defense and ritual harming practices were their "salvation" in a world that called for Negroes to be docile, meek, and lowly. This complex continuum of religious practice to stave off the impermeability of anti-Blackness's effects is of principal concern to my analysis in the pages that follow.

Indeed, there was no escaping the need for Black suffering and Black death in the maintenance of the category of the human—from which the slave, the Negro, and the Black are excluded.[38] In other words, we cannot sidestep this crucial point to recover joy, play, or religious ecstasy. We must, as June Jordan long admonished, tarry in "the graveyard and the groin of our experience."[39] We cannot understand what the underworld is and how Black people navigated it if we will not reckon with why it was created in the first place. Duvernet certainly conceived of the need for the specter of violence as the (under)grounds upon which Louisiana's geopolitics were structured through his investment in and recapitulation of the scene of Jim Crow subjection—lynching—as an extension of the white, American Christian hegemonic state. Forty-five years before Duvernet's depiction, the antilynching crusader Ida Bell Wells-Barnett had observed in her 1900 book *Mob Rule in New Orleans*, "The mob in New Orleans . . . despising all law, roamed the streets day and night, searching for colored men and women, whom they beat, shot and killed at will."[40] Duvernet's "Ghost Map" recapitulated the Southern horror that Wells-Barnett and others had long bemoaned.

In Louisiana, a land of creolization, cultural hybridity, and blood mixing among Spanish, French, Portuguese, Asian, Mediterranean, Native American, West African, and Caribbean peoples for centuries—with the slave trade and a series of forced migrations and acts of violence at its center—a legacy of anti-Blackness undoubtedly structured the very grounds upon which "Blackness" was constructed in the late nineteenth and early twentieth centuries.[41] To be Black in Louisiana meant that one was of enslaved ancestry or that one's social and material condition in slavery's afterlife mirrored that of the slave—quotidian, unrelenting violence and surveillance by whites and all who aspired to be white or to be in social, classed, religious, or geographic proximity to whites.

During Jim Crow modernity, the heirs to this European legacy in Louisiana, by way of violent processes of creolization and Americanization vis-à-vis slavery, enforced proper ways of being "religious." They also challenged African, Afro-Creole, and Black denunciations of the diabolical, which were based on racist ideologies of the white Christian as human and the slave as nonhuman. This reinterpretation and queering of "the diabolical" was a central feature of underworld work in that practitioners understood themselves to work on spiritual registers at odds with white Christianity as the modus operandi of all religious belief and practice. Moreover, in their relegation to the underworld as a site of/for survival, many Black religious practitioners understood themselves to embody subjectivities that denounced the category of the human; in fact, all were not vying for recognition of personhood. Many Black people deified themselves, reconstituted new ideas about their religious and racial identities, or altogether embraced and inverted Jim Crow grammars by reinterpreting fraught labels such as "queer" and "freak."

Thus, setting out to fully understand underworld work is a complex theoretical and archival undertaking, especially given the fact that American

INTRODUCTION

religious studies, developed during the era of Jim Crow modernity, have largely maintained this European theocentric legacy and have historically positioned Blackness, Black people, and Black religion in the space of "the unthought," and therefore, the field has ultimately failed to fully understand the contours of Black Atlantic religious life and innovation.[42] Anthropologist of religion Marla Frederick extends this idea in *Colored Television*, in which she writes, "Too often white religious practice by default has been categorized as 'American religion' while the study of African American religious practitioners sits solely under the category 'black religious studies.'"[43] The same can be said for Black studies regarding Black religions, as scholars often privilege secularized narratives of Black social life, wherein "Black religion" is only understood to be a feature of the monolithic plantation church and its antecedents, such that the multifaceted manifestations of Black religions across time and varying geographies have not been thoroughly examined or regarded as legitimate sources of study in Black studies.[44]

This is especially evident in the astounding correspondence between Hurston and Dr. W. E. B. Du Bois, who is championed as one of the fathers of Black studies. Hurston penned,

Dear Dr. DuBois,

As Dean of American Negro Artists, I think that it is about time that you take steps towards an important project which you have neglected up to this time. Why do you not propose a cemetery for the illustrious Negro dead? Something like Pere la Chaise in Paris. If you like the idea, may I make a few suggestions to you?

1. That you secure about one hundred acres for the site in Florida. I am not saying this because this is my birth-state, but because it lends itself to decoration easier than any other part of the United States. . . .

2. That there be no regular chapel, unless a tremendous amount of money be secured. Let there be a hall of meetings, and let the Negro sculptors and painters decorate it with scenes from our own literature and life. Mythology and all. Funerals can be held from there as well. . . .

3. As far as possible, remove the bones of our dead celebrities to this spot.

4. Let no Negro celebrity, no matter what financial condition they might be in at death, lie in inconspicuous forgetfulness. We must assume the responsibility of their graves being known and honored. You must see what a rallying spot that would be for all that we want to

accomplish and do. There one ought also to see the tomb of Nat Turner. Naturally, his bones have long since gone to dust, but that should not prevent his tomb being among us. Fred Douglas and all the rest. . . .

I feel strongly that the thing should be done. I think the lack of such a tangible thing allows our people to forget, and their spirits evaporate. But I shall not mention the matter to anyone else until you accept or refuse.[45]

Hurston's plea to the heralded leader of the Negro race went largely unheard as Du Bois bemoaned a month later, "The idea of the cemetery for illustrious Negroes has its attractions but I am afraid that the practical difficulties are too great, and I regret to say I have not the enthusiasm for Florida that you have, naturally. I do know of its magnificent weather and vegetation, but in other matters more spiritual it is not so rich."[46] Exchanges between the two waned. Fifteen years later, Hurston died lonely and poor and was later buried in an unmarked grave thanks to donations from her friends and neighbors. "Let no Negro celebrity, no matter what financial condition they might be in at death, lie in inconspicuous forgetfulness," she had written, almost prophetically. And there she was, all but forgotten. Hurston's plea and her subsequent unceremonious burial following her journeys in the underworld stand as indictments of the historical and historiographical prioritizing of largely political and social issues by Black scholars at the expense of the sacred, specifically, the veneration of ancestors and communication with the Negro dead. Hurston's plea functions as counter to the salvage ethnographers examined in chapter 1, in that she offers ethnography against "the colonial desires in ethnographic exoticism and [she] refuses to reproduce ethnographic porn" as her approach to the Black study of religions in the Atlantic world.[47] Hurston, as ethnographer and underworld worker, beckons us to visit the graveyards and institutional archives that house the remains of religious practitioners of African descent because "the lack of such a tangible thing"—in her eyes a "cemetery"—"allows people to forget, and their spirits evaporate."

Conversant with and a student of Hoodoo, Hurston's call for the Negro cemetery in 1945 built upon her observation in her 1931 article in the *Journal of American Folklore*, "Hoodoo in America," in which she observed, "The dead, and communication with the dead, play traditionally a large part in Negro religions."[48] Hurston's cemetery proposal, as an extension of her underworld ethnography in New Orleans—a city of the dead, where the dead are entombed above ground, always among the living—instructs us as

INTRODUCTION

scholars of Black Atlantic religions to communicate with the dead, in earnest and with deep respect, as a critical Black (religious) studies methodology.[49] A deceased Hurston herself would speak to the writer Alice Walker as she searched for Hurston in that Eatonville cemetery in 1973, authenticating the Black womanist literary tradition. Walker found the ethnographer's unmarked grave obscured by weeds and hurried to purchase a headstone "as majestic as Zora herself must have been when she was learning voodoo from those root doctors down in New Orleans."[50] Like Walker, critical theorist Christina Sharpe, in her work on the state-sanctioned murders of Black people, asks similarly, "What does it mean to defend the dead? To tend to the Black dead and dying: to tend to the Black person, to Black people, always living in the push toward our death? It means work."[51] Drawing from her analysis of "the wake"—an event and funerary practice in Black communities—Sharpe names this practice "wake work," a mode of attending to Black life and Black suffering in the wake of chattel slavery. Sharpe's meditative intervention has theological and religious implications, though they are not explicitly stated. Indeed, the wake is "a watching practiced as a religious observance."[52] It is not only a significant theoretical entry; it is a sacred practice of deep introspective care conjured and saged into the pages to follow, as I have communed with the archives of the dead with Hurston as my underworld guide.[53]

The literary journey that awaits us is one charted by Black spatial, theological, and topographical mapping, and *Underworld Work* posits that Black people contrived and plotted these maps for racial, sexual, and religious identity and meaning during the era of Jim Crow, decades after "the nonevent of emancipation," in their own personal quests for "freedoms" amid widespread unfreedom.[54] In this way, I am refusing to reify the Protestant hegemony of African American religious historiography—with the narrative victory and triumphalism of the Negro church in the face of white supremacy at its crux as an extension of the Exodus biblical account.[55] Instead, I wish to tarry in the space of chronological and historical disorientation, endeavoring to recover a story about Black religious actors who charted these maps precisely because they did not feel "free" or "emancipated" following the legal emancipation of the enslaved. Here, I invoke the words of Du Bois from his 1935 classic *Black Reconstruction*, "The slave went free; stood a brief moment in the sun; then moved back again toward slavery."[56] Likewise, one ex-slave in Louisiana, Henrietta Butler, recounted in 1940, "My damn old missis was mean as hell. You see dis finger here? Dere is where she bit it [the] day us was set free. Never will forget how she said,

'Come here, you little black bitch, you!' and grabbed my finger [and] almost bit it off . . . When she found out we was goin' to be free, she raised all kind of hell. De Boss could do nothin' at all with her."[57] Butler went on to note the parallels between life in slavery and "post"-slavery, writing, "After I was free, I . . . washed and ironed for [the] white folk."[58] Another ex-slave Rebecca Fletcher, who was born in 1842, lamented to LWP writer Zoe Posey, "After Freedom when we were on our own account, we had a hard time."[59]

While historians often mark the Louisiana Purchase of 1803 as a "nation-building tale" and as a "triumphal" event in the shaping of "freedom" in the US empire, as Paul Christopher Johnson has also observed, the post-1865 period was one of the most harrowing moments in American history for Black people—the latter portion (roughly 1877 to 1915) often referred to as "the Nadir"—and Black practitioners of non-Christian and quasi-Christian religions felt the wrath.[60] Sorting through LWP interviews and police records confirms that underworld workers lived with their third eyes open wide both day and night, and that they used rituals to keep the police and the law away from their door, in constant fear of violent captivity or death. To them, this was not "freedom."

In this vein, *Underworld Work* is conversant with the theoretical scaffolding offered by Afropessimists and the nihilist philosopher Calvin Warren, for instance, who has described this unfreedom as "ontological terror." Warren writes, "Our metaphysical notions of freedom . . . reduce antiblackness to social, political, and legal understandings, and we miss the ontological function of antiblackness—to deny the ontological ground of freedom by severing the (non)relation between blackness and Being."[61] For many historians of African American life and culture, the retort to largely US nationalist and imperialist chronologies of "progress" and "freedom" when confronted with the persistence and pervasiveness of anti-Blackness *before*, *during*, and *"post"*-slavery confirms Warren's assessment. Warren insightfully observes, "our metaphysical conceptions of freedom neglect the ontological horrors of antiblackness by assuming freedom can be attained through political, social, or legal action. This is a humanist fantasy, one that masks subjection in emancipatory rhetoric."[62] *Underworld Work* builds on Warren's contention by asserting that religious innovation—while significant as a means of preserving and passing on African cultural inheritances amid colonial, white Christian attempts to cast out "the African"—cannot be a catalyst for "freedom" in an anti-Black world. This, I know, may be upsetting to many humanist scholars and theologians of the Black religious experience, but we must tarry here, albeit uncomfortably.

INTRODUCTION

We must tarry here precisely because this is why the *under*world exists; it is outside of the Western world's purview and comprehension, and its practitioners cannot access recognition in the world as we know it, nor do many of them want to access it precisely because of the very ontological terror of their existence as Black practitioners of criminalized religions. In this way, we might consider how Afropessimist theory converges with Charles H. Long's notion of "opacity," which emerged out of his critique in the 1970s of Black religious studies' overarching Christian hegemony, in which he wrote, "The slave had to come to terms with the opaqueness of his condition and at the same time oppose it. He had to experience *the truth of his negativity* and at the same time transform and create *an-other* reality" (emphasis added).[63] Underworld work is that "*an-other* reality," a product of nonbeing as opacity, and as Long admonishes, "Not only did this transformation produce new cultural forms, but its significance must be understood from the point of view of the creativity of the transforming process itself."[64] This book examines the "transforming process" of New Orleans in the afterlife of chattel slavery, during the long postemancipation period, and in the face of Jim Crow modernity. Indeed, this *an-other* reality, as criminalized religion, existed in the anti-Black enclosures of the underworld.

AFRICA, MIGRATION, AND THE
CRIMINALIZING OF BLACK RELIGION

Consistent with most terrorized people of enslaved ancestry in the United States, Black New Orleanians forged connections with Africa using a variety of complex methods, some of which functioned in ways similar to but also distinct from the descendants of enslaved Africans in the Caribbean and Latin America due largely to distinct histories of Christianization.[65] In this way, many scholars of Black Atlantic and African diasporic religions tend to read African Americans out of the historical frame, implying that African Americans embody a superficial or essentialist connection to African indigenous and African-derived religions, all while marking religious practitioners in the Caribbean and Latin America as "more genuine" or "more African" in their approach to matters of religious practice and connection to the African continent. *Underworld Work* complicates this reductionist binary, especially as the underworld workers examined understood themselves to be communing with the spirits of the African diaspora, both past and present. Anthropologist Brendan James Thornton also reminds us that "stressing the notion of Africanness, per se, is not always or even a key reference point in everyday articulations of [practitioners], nor does it feature prominently in the strategies of self-definitions that [some] employ when asked to describe their own beliefs."[66] In this way, scholars should be less quick to jettison Africanisms in the United States context, thus upending the disconnectedness between the study of "African American religions" and the study of "Black Atlantic religions." The latter is typically regarded as an umbrella category for all of the religions of the African diaspora in the Caribbean and in Latin America (excluding Afro-Caribbean Christians, as Thornton also argues). In contrast, the religions of the African diaspora, as embodied and practiced in the United States, are typically excluded from this category, and have often fallen solely into the category of "African American religions." *Underworld Work* and its unruly subjects disrupt this historiographical impasse and represent New Orleans's rich African heritage.

Relatedly, this book intervenes in African American religious historiographies on migration, transnationalism, and "Negro cults and sects" in the early to mid-twentieth century.[67] To date, much of this literature is situated in the period of the Great Migration and focuses on the urban North and Midwest. Sociologist E. Franklin Frazier observed in 1940, however, "The imperceptible drift of a million rural black folk to over eight hundred small towns and cities of the South has attracted little attention. By 1930 nearly three million Negroes were city dwellers in the South."[68] To paraphrase the words of one Black Southerner, historians can learn much about the "new South" even as they are interested in the "new Negro" in the urban North and out West during the era of the Great Migration.[69] Thus, this is where my work departs from the existing literature using New Orleans as a case study, in order to center the place of the Black South and the role of Black Southerners who remained in the South during the era of the Great Migration, as the project's sources demonstrate the network of circum-Caribbean migration and South-to-South movement in the Black Atlantic underworld of New Orleans.[70] Thus, *Underworld Work* engages circum-Caribbean migration within the Atlantic Ocean (or what Joseph R. Roach calls "the circum-Atlantic"), and I use "Black Atlantic religions" as it prioritizes the complex terrain of New Orleans as a "heavily traveled transgeographical complex" with a religiously inflected migration to and from such countries as Ethiopia, Nicaragua, Jamaica, and Cuba—a central feature of the work of the Universal Negro Improvement Association, the subject of chapter 5.[71] To this end, "Black Atlantic religions" captures the indigeneity

INTRODUCTION   17

of Black Louisianans (along with Native and Afro-Creole peoples), and it underlines the migratory and the geospatial as pivotal to the cultivation of Black religions in urban centers and port cities like New Orleans, where Black people from the US South and the Caribbean cocreated sacred gatherings. Given the confluence of these cultures, Hurston observed in 1931, "Shreds of Hoodoo beliefs and practices are found wherever any number of Negroes are found in America but Conjure has had its highest development along the Gulf coast, particularly in the city of New Orleans and in the surrounding country."[72] This "highest development," I argue, was due to the cross-pollination of religions and politics among Black Atlantic migrants, as practitioners of different beliefs, practices, and creeds opened new house churches and temples, often on the same streets and in the same Black neighborhoods.[73]

The diversity of religious services and communities confirm the fact that underworld work was widespread, and that its workers differed in terms of their spiritual efficacy and legitimacy. "There are too many crooks in the business and there isn't enough known about the true Spiritualist church," lamented Althea Morris, an African American Spiritualist, to LWP worker Robert McKinney in the late 1930s. She later noted, "As for Spiritualism and voodooism, well, there is no connection between [them]. There are a lot of people practicing voodooism under the Spiritualist banner but they are fakes and that is what I am going to try and stop . . . I'll admit it is a hard job but we are going to tackle it." In another instance, she drew a sharp distinction between Spiritualism and fortune telling, claiming, "In fortune telling you use something, cards or the palm of the hands and you do not seek the aid of the spirits. Fortune telling is purely an intellectual thing. But in Spiritualism you seek the aid of spirits."[74] Morris's words are textured and replete with a spiritual grammar that beckons our attention, especially as she references the various conflicts and tense relationships among Black religious practitioners in the city—Christian, quasi-Christian, and non-Christian. Black practitioners were committed to being seen and regarded as individuals with their own unique beliefs and practices, and much of their rhetoric centered on how they were different from other practitioners in the complex Black Atlantic religious world of New Orleans, where week after week, a new house church or spiritual center emerged.

Complex intraracial relationships and conflicts formed as a result and were exacerbated by policing and surveillance by white leaders and city officials—Catholic, Protestant, and Jewish—who legally and socially enforced anti-African sentiment vis-à-vis the demonization of Black Atlantic religions, sexualities, and cultural expressions. In their attempts to navigate this racial climate, many Black religious practitioners, like Morris, publicly distanced themselves from criminalized rituals and practices most commonly characterized by white people as "voodooism." In this way, an intraracial hierarchy formed with Black Catholics followed by Black Protestants at the top, wielding social control and dominance over and against non-Christian and quasi-Christian practitioners of other Black Atlantic religions, like Spiritualism, Conjure, rootwork, and Hoodoo, all practices criminalized by the overlap between Jim Crow law and laws against certain religious practices in the late nineteenth and early twentieth centuries.[75] On May 12, 1897, for example, Mayor Walter Chew Flower, the Catholic son of a planter and cotton factor, signed the following, "Be it ordained by the Council of the City of New Orleans, that any and all persons known as mediums, clairvoyants, fortune tellers and others who may carry on for a monied consideration the business of telling or pretending to tell fortunes, either with cards, hands, water, letters or other devices or methods . . . shall be arrested."[76] Given these kinds of Jim Crow laws, individuals like Morris found themselves between two ends of the same continuum of Black Atlantic religious expression in New Orleans, specifically that of "the Negro church" and the racialized and sexualized category of "the Negro cult and sect." Black religious practitioners would all fall victim to white supremacist terrorism, however, and their negotiations of racial and religious identity were intimately connected to their proximity to white American Christianity and economic privilege.

BLACK ATLANTIC RELIGION MAKING

Bearing in mind these social conditions, I offer the theoretical concept "Black Atlantic religion making" to interpret Black Atlantic religious processes of differentiation as a series of intentional choices cultivated to legitimize emergent Black Atlantic religions in the face of state-sanctioned policing in the afterlife of slavery. My use of "religion making" differs from the term as it appears in Markus Dressler and Arvind-pal Singh Mandair's *Secularism and Religion-Making* (2011), in which they define religion making as "the reification and institutionalization of certain ideas, social formations, and practices as 'religious' in the conventional Western meaning of the term, thereby subordinating them to a particular knowledge regime of religion and its political, cultural, philosophical, and historical interven-

INTRODUCTION

tions."[77] My invocation of Black Atlantic religion making refers to strategic and intentional methods articulated and crafted by practitioners of African descent to literally make their own religions—not in "the conventional Western meaning" but on their own terms and in defiance to Western Christianity. For Dressler and Mandair, "the politics of religion-making" work in response to the secularization thesis, and they offer religion making as a stand-in for "the thoroughly intertwined natures of religion and secularism in the modern period." My formulation of religion making challenges the secularization of non-Christian and quasi-Christian Black Atlantic religions and deconstructs the West as the central object of study and as the starting point for religion making. For Dressler and Mandair, however, religion making is dependent on the notion of "the religio-secular." However, the sources examined here show how non-Christian, quasi-Christian, and Christian Black Atlantic religions were deemed "secular," unreligious, and "fanatic," and yet Black religious practitioners understood their practices to be a part of their religions and carried themselves accordingly as religious subjects. Finally, for Dressler and Mandair, religion making serves as a bridge between the religious and the secular, and as a theoretical tool for attending to regulation of religious practices and the convergence of religion and politics. They contend, "Religion-making works, sometimes more and sometimes less explicitly, by means of normalizing and often functionalist discourses centered around certain taken for granted notions, such as the religion/secular binary."[78]

In this way, through my focus on "processes of differentiation," I examine how Black religious practitioners articulated their unique individual identities using language that set them apart from their competitors in the larger religious economy of early twentieth-century New Orleans. Given the variety of spiritual merchants in the city, whenever a new street preacher, rootworker, movement leader, or storefront church came on the scene, it was their duty to demonstrate how their services, offerings, or political strivings differed from those down on South Rampart or Canal Streets in the tourist and entertainment area of the city. For instance, Hyatt observed in the mid-1930s while talking to a New Orleanian practitioner, "So today there's too much competition—too many of them? And you can't get them organized anymore?" The informant replied, "The same as churches—too many churches to be any good."[79] Thus, the clients and congregants who attended these practitioners' revival meetings or sought them out for root tinctures or faith healing were integral to the process of legitimizing Black Atlantic religion making. To attend a service at a house church or seek Hoodoo recipes week after week ultimately confirmed the spiritual efficacy of the practitioner in question. To not have a substantial listing of followers, clients, or congregants suggested that one did not have the approval of the spirits or that one was one of the "fakes" or "crooks" that Althea Morris had alluded to in her conversation with Robert McKinney.

In this way, "Black Atlantic religion making" differs from such terms as "religion," "religious practice," and "religious expression," because it captures *the methods by which* Black institutions, gatherings, practices, and expressions ultimately become Black Atlantic religions considering these marketing and legitimizing strategies. I use "Black Atlantic religion making" to show how Black religious practitioners were invested in self-authenticity, rather than the religion/secular binary—that is, Black religious practitioners were more concerned with the fact of having a religion known for its efficacy, with core tenets, underground economies, and alternative ethical systems and sources of authority, that was held in high regard in the context of intraracial community. These Black Atlantic religions, as products of Black Atlantic religion making, were authentic even if said authenticity was not recognized or legally protected during the era of Jim Crow segregation and racial violence.

The individuals surveyed in this book—conjurers, Hoodoo practitioners, rootworkers, healers, preachers, church mothers, faith healers, and sex workers—were "knowledge makers" of their own religions who "healed, assuaged, and birthed new realities while simultaneously lying, scheming, and killing."[80] They were self-taught theologians and intellectuals who drew upon several schools of thought and religious orientations, including but not limited to Ethiopianism, Pan-Africanism, New Thought, Christianity, Judaism, and Spiritualism, to cultivate their own unique practices. Some of those practices did require that they lie to police to avoid incarceration or death, gossip about one another to attract and steal each other's followers, scheme their own followers out of money to pay their bills, and kill their enemies to do away with harmful theologies and practices. Other belief systems relied on the guidance of the spirits, the Spirit, and ancestors. These religions, however, have each weathered their own storms of colonial encounter and rupture within the Black Atlantic world, and have stood tall like firmly rooted trees on Jordan's stormy banks.

The archives included evidence of how Black Atlantic religions embody ingenuity and creative genius. Yet the white American Christian hegemonic state—a unified body of lawmakers, journalists, social scientists, police, and vigilantes—has historically and contemporaneously demonized the

INTRODUCTION

religions of Black people. Collectively, they have relegated these religions to the monolithic, racist, and sexualized category of the "negro cult," such that Black people are at once "too religious" and innately given to "emotionalism" and "fanaticism." Under these circumstances, Black people are always demonized and are always sinners, and sometimes Black Christians do the work of demonizing on behalf of the white Christian hegemonic state. White race makers, or the individuals who have since the precolonial period philosophized, theologized, and enacted racist and racialized discourse onto Blackened sentient beings, joined forces with some Black Protestant and Catholic authorities to deem non-Christian Black Atlantic religious practitioners sinners.[81] On the converse, those regarded as saints, specifically white Christians and their allies, demonstrated the enduring legacy of white American Christian hegemony as they were the arbitrators of who was deemed a sinner and who a saint, who was consigned to hell and who was not, and most prominently, who lived and who was lynched on Southern crosses.

Social scientists and government-employed researchers reinforced this binary in their analysis of Black religiosities in the city. According to an unpublished chapter from the LWP's work *The Negro in Louisiana*, written by Marcus Christian, "Spiritual cults of every possible description are found here and there in Negro sections of New Orleans. They range from Sanctified and Holy Rollers cults under 'Bishops' to many large and small Spiritual cults under 'Mothers' and 'Fathers' whose names run the list of nearly all of the saints."[82] Christian's use of "cults" was set in stark contrast to the earlier portions of the chapter where he described Baptists, Roman Catholics, the African Methodist Episcopals, the Colored Methodist Episcopals, the African Methodist Episcopal Zion Church, and the Congregational Church as "churches" and "denominations" given their large numbers, substantial financial statuses, and the class and education ranks of members and leaders. "Cults," in the words of Christian, ranged "from Sanctified and Holy Rollers" to "Spiritual"—thus, he efficaciously set two different groups of Black Atlantic religious formations in concert to comment on their distinction from "churches" and "denominations," and to emphasize their racialized and classed peculiarity as noninstitutional religions among the poor and uneducated, many of whom were migrants from the rural South and the circum-Atlantic world.

Christian's categorization of Black Atlantic religions in the city, specifically those cultivated by people of African descent from numerous geographical backgrounds, spoke to a larger (white) American Christian hegemonic binary between normative American Christianity and the "cults" (or non-Christian and quasi-Christian Black Atlantic religious practices). In the context of Jim Crow New Orleans, white Christianity—both Protestant and Catholic—was *the* only American religion. Black Atlantic practices were considered un-Christian, and therefore, un-American. Black Protestants and Catholics negotiated their acceptance into the category of American religion often by aligning themselves with white state actors and colluding with them to surveil, police, and criminalize non-Christian practitioners. The LWP's Marcus Christian, who was also a member of the African Methodist Episcopal Church, expressed disdain for such practices as Conjure, rootwork, and Hoodoo, collapsing their differences and pejoratively describing them as "Voodoo quackery."[83]

With knowledge of the historically Catholic New Orleans's ever-growing Black Protestantism in the early twentieth century, Christian was ultimately concerned with how African American Christianities had been affected by the social and cultural transformations caused by circum-Caribbean migration, or the Black Atlantic movement of West Indian and Central American migrants to and from the United States. Indeed, Christian's analysis of the variety of Black Atlantic religions in Black New Orleans in the early twentieth century suggests that these "cults" emerged in response to larger global and political migratory transformations. It is unclear if Christian thought of these "cults" as reinventions of the denominations, or more specifically of "the Negro church" as understood in the parlance of many African American leaders of the day.[84] Yet what is most significant about Christian's observations as part of the LWP was his framing of New Orleans as an exceptional place where "Spiritual cults of every possible description are found." Many of these "spiritual cults" were not only esoteric, but they also had express political aims, in which their religious gatherings were organizing sites for the cultivation of Black racial consciousness.

NEW ORLEANS "VOODOO"

Pejorative language has been a fixture of how Africana religions have historically and historiographically been discussed in American religious history. Specifically, scholars who have written on Black Atlantic religions in the city of New Orleans have all too often simplistically categorized them all as "Hoodoo," "Conjure," and most frequently "Voodoo" without attending to

INTRODUCTION

the differences articulated by Black religious practitioners.[85] The wide array of sources consulted in conversation with the papers of the LWP significantly challenge us to reexamine the synonymizing between "voodoo" and New Orleans, and also between "voodoo" and all Black Atlantic religions. Robert Tallant, LWP writer and author of *Voodoo in New Orleans*, wrote in 1946, "Voodoo is a sort of nerve that runs mostly in the dark meat, but sometimes gets into the white meat, too."[86] Hurston took issue with Tallant's problematic characterization, writing in her 1947 review of the book published in the *Journal of American Folklore*, "*Voodoo in New Orleans* is totally exterior so far as Hoodoo is concerned. There is no revelation of any new facts, nor any analysis of what is already known. It is rather a collection of the popular beliefs about Hoodoo from the outside." She continued, holding back nothing, "It offers no opportunity for serious study, and should be considered for just what it is, a creative-journalistic appeal to popular fancy."[87]

The historical actors examined emphasized their differences, even as they often embodied similarities and points of convergence in their rituals and aesthetics. In 1920, Charles M. Melden, president of New Orleans University, published "Religion and the Negro" included in the anthology *Progress of a Race*, in which he took issue with the reductionist characterization of Black religious life by his white contemporaries. "Too often no attempt is made to differentiate, and all Negroes are grouped indiscriminately together," he wrote. "The man of culture, of high ideals, of upright life, of polished manners is confounded with the lowest and most ignorant, the most degraded and brutal. This works a grave injustice to the aspiring and advanced members of the race."[88] Some Black religious practitioners deployed similar rhetoric as Melden summarizes to distance themselves from poor and working-class practitioners. Others emphasized their differences from each other to lay claim to a sense of legitimacy in the eyes of the state and middle-class and educated Black Christian practitioners. Much of this tension was a product of the period of sexual Victorianism and social respectability, such that many Black people in the new century sought out ways to shed the residue of the plantation church, disavow slave religions often simplistically troped as "voodoo," and claim Christian morality to articulate or show worthiness of American citizenship. Blackness, Black sexuality, and Black religions were shaped and policed by the Jim Crow legal system and by white Christian state actors and their allies, including multigenerational white ethnic Jewish residents in New Orleans, who enforced anti-Voudou sentiment as enactments of Jim Crow modernity.

The LWP, and subsequent historical texts engaging with the records of the LWP, was responsible for cultivating voyeuristic imaginings of the city and of the Gulf states to aid the local tourist economy during the 1930s up until the demise of the LWP in 1943.[89] The LWP, of course, was part of the Works Progress Administration (WPA), which deployed similar methods and characterizations of Black people in cities and towns across the United States. In the 1938 *New Orleans City Guide*, which also included advertisements for "some Negro cults," for instance, the LWP staff wrote, "It's a nation of a queer place; day and night a show!"[90] Consequently, religious practitioners fell victim to reporters, LWP staff, and other social scientists who caricatured their Black Atlantic religions, sexualities, and cultural expressions, such that LWP and WPA records essentially functioned as an archive or treasure trove of documents, photographs, and interviews showcasing those deemed "nutty," "queer," "crazy," or "strange."

This is perhaps why Althea Morris told LWP writer Robert McKinney, "Don't ever publish this because every church in New Orleans will be on my head."[91] Morris was reticent about sharing her religious practices with McKinney and having the details of them published by the LWP due to the kinds of mental institutionalization, criminalization, and policing enforced by white American Christians against Black religious practitioners. She knew that someone like her who said that she saw and heard spirits, received dreams and visions from the Spirit, and challenged the hegemony of Catholics and Protestants could ultimately end up behind bars, in an insane asylum, or lynched. Hurston captured this climate when she wrote about Samuel Thompson, "a Hoodoo Catholic doctor of New Orleans," observing, "When I first went to his aging pink stucco house, he received me very reluctantly. When I told him that I wanted to become a disciple of his, he grew even more aloof. I could see distrust in his eyes. The city of New Orleans has a law against fortune-tellers, Hoodoo doctors, and the like."[92] McKinney and the LWP, unlike Hurston, did not care about Black religious practitioners' reticence, however, and they published certain details without Moore's express consent and against her wishes. Their dismissal of her request sits at the crux of this project's chief concerns. Indeed, what does it mean that we come to know about the policed and surveilled practices of Black Atlantic religious practitioners and underworld workers through the nonconsensually published interviews crafted by the LWP, who partnered with Jim Crow police and sorted through and edited their files?[93] Moreover, how do we do justice to Morris and other religious practitioners like her

INTRODUCTION

who were wronged and mischaracterized while they were alive and have arguably been maligned and forgotten in the canon of American religious history? These questions guide *Underworld Work* and are productive queries for embodying an ethic of care and integrity while sorting through archives of violent dismemberment, coercion, and erasure.

In figure I.3, for instance, LWP writers sort through police records as part of their editorial process, further evidencing the conjoined relationship between the social scientific enterprise and policing. White men and women, the descendants of Louisianan slaveholders and European immigrants to the Jim Crow South, gaze upon fingerprints, mug shots, and police reports. As we look at these images nearly a century later, I am certain that they probably never envisioned themselves being the subject of the gaze that they enacted in their work—work that they garnered most likely because they had been unemployed and were seeking employment during the period of the Great Depression. Yet their despised contemporary Ida B. Wells-Barnett had already been "turning the light of truth upon them" in her investigative reports, which read against the social scientific and mainstream press depictions of Black victims of racial-sexual terrorism.

With attention to the problems at play in the LWP's reports, I read with and against the grain of these white supremacist depictions while listening deeply, and to the best of my ability, for the voices of Black people held captive, literally and on the page, during the era of Jim Crow. Much of my process for research and writing involves sorting through piles of newspaper scraps; sitting with and listening to images; tracking individuals through census, police, and other government records; and speculating and theorizing in the gaps between what the archive, a site of dismemberment, reveals to us about Black people and what we know to be true by way of intuition and ancestral and other Black religious ways of knowing.[94] I also "take care" in the way that Christina Sharpe encourages, by engaging in my own practice of "Black annotation" and "Black redaction," asking questions of sources that recapitulate anti-Blackness in their original form and troubling the means by which we cite and engage them.[95] At times, this search for truth—a Black truth—led me into extensive analyses of the social and economic motivations undergirding practitioners' cultivation and development of a diverse array of Black Atlantic religions in the city of New Orleans. Other times, I struggled to fully bear witness to the unique contours of Black Atlantic religion making in different contexts because those who constructed these violent archives were more invested in caricature than they

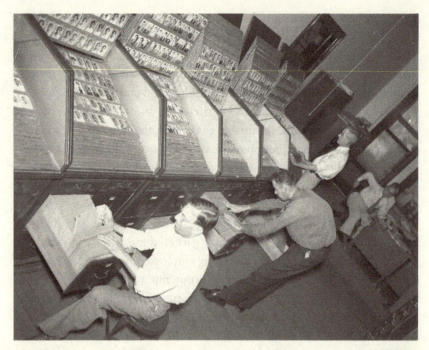

FIGURE 1.3. Louisiana Writers' Project staff members sort through police records, 1939–40. From WPA Records. Courtesy of the City Archives & Special Collections, New Orleans Public Library.

INTRODUCTION

were in truthfully characterizing diverse Black religious subjects. As you traverse these archival dilemmas with me, I also urge you to take care.

Notwithstanding these challenges, my attention to their religious diversity is intentional. New Orleans poet Thomas Dent conveyed this sentiment by encouraging storytellers in the city to "begin with a series of gods, gods who are not the christian god, not the deity of charity, for the city was not built with that, no matter how much evoked. Supernatural deities make it possible for the abandoned people of the city to survive the everyday mundane, the backwash of progress."[96] Given Dent's characterization of the city during the period and his directive, the chapters in *Underworld Work* are arranged both thematically and chronologically. Beginning with the gods in Congo Square along with Lake Pontchartrain and Bayou St. John, chapter 1 traces the surveillance and criminalization of the Voudou ceremony of the nineteenth century alongside the emergence of salvage ethnography and folklore. Chapter 2 examines the Council of God, a new religious movement founded in the late 1890s in Algiers that drew upon Black Israelite, Christian, Hindu, New Thought, and other traditions to cultivate its religion, and it challenges readers to think beyond the categories of Christian, non-Christian, and quasi-Christian with respect to Black religious formations in the face of state-sanctioned policing and lynching. Chapter 3 extends the discussion to the competing forms of social reform and rehabilitation offered by Black religious practitioners in the "cults" and in Protestant institutions, with an eye toward gender, reproductive justice, and social respectability. Situating sex work as religious commerce for women, queer, and gender nonconforming religionists, chapter 4 interrogates the boundaries of Black sexuality and Black religion during Jim Crow. In a slight departure from earlier examinations on individuals within burgeoning religious institutions, chapters 5 and 6 examines how Protestant-adjacent institutions, namely the Universal Negro Improvement Association and the Church of God in Christ, utilized the tools of Black Protestantism to substantiate and legitimize their own identities while distancing themselves from the maligned conjurers, Hoodoo practitioners, and Spiritualists examined in earlier chapters. Before each chapter, I present an ethnographic account or musing from Hurston related to the subject of that chapter to guide readers through the underworld as Hurston guided me through its different components. Rather than analyze these ethnographic snapshots, they function as interludes or "Visitations." In this way, Hurston as underworld worker deciphers hieroglyphics for our collective understanding, and we must read them through an embodied mediumship that earnestly trusts her expertise.[97]

In line with the sensory turn in the humanities, each chapter also considers how the policing of Black Atlantic religions in the slum had much to do with white racial concerns about Black touch, hearing, sight, smell, and taste as markers of counterhegemonic regimes of religious value, sensory hierarchies of power, and affective registers in the underworld. Whether it be the smell of sweat or of bodies in motion during a Voudou ceremony; Pentecostals' and Spiritualists' emphasis on touch through the laying on of hands and ritual healings with blessed oils; mystics and churchwomen's ability to see into the spirit world things imperceivable to the Western eye; the moanings and groanings of pleasure and ecstasy in the bedrooms and house churches of sex workers; or the raucous call and response of practitioners conjuring the Spirit, spirits, or ancestors, all of these sensory experiences frightened white Americans precisely because of long-held ideas circulating in the Black Atlantic world that cast Black religions as diabolical and as social contagions. White race makers used the law, policing, and surveillance as tools to drive out the disruptive capacity of Black sensory religious experiences and Black religious noise, while also engaging in their own sensory regime of power—the lynching of Black flesh chief among them. Yet to fully grasp the true disruptive force of Black Atlantic religion making, we must first descend chapter by chapter into the underworld for ourselves as its inhabitants bid us to commune with them and with their gods.

VISITATION 1

ZORA ON "VOODOO"

[Voodoo] is the old, old mysticism of the world in African terms. Voodoo is a religion of creation and life. It is the worship of the sun, the water and other natural forces, but the symbolism is no better understood than that of other religions and consequently is taken too literally . . . Some of the other men of education in Haiti who have given time to the study of Voodoo esoterics do not see such deep meanings in Voodoo practices. They see only a pagan religion with an African pantheon. And right here, let it be said that the Haitian gods, mysteries, or loa are not the Catholic calendar of saints done over in black as has been stated by casual observers. This has been said over and over in print because the adepts have been buying the lithographs of saints, but this is done because they wish some visual representation of the invisible ones, and as yet no Haitian artist has given them an interpretation or concept of the loa. But even the most illiterate peasant knows that the picture of the saint is only an approximation of the loa.[1]

* * *

The Negroes fleeing Hayti and Santo Domingo brought to New Orleans and Louisiana, African rituals long since lost to their continental brothers. This transplanted hoodoo worship was not uninfluenced by its surroundings. It took on characteristics of the prevailing religious practices of its immediate vicinity. In New Orleans in addition to herbs, reptiles, insects, it makes use of the altar, the candles, the incense, the holy water, and blessed oil of the Catholic church—that being the dominant religion of the city and state.[2]

ZORA NEALE HURSTON

"MIDNIGHT ORGIES"

Voudou and the Problem of Possessed Black Flesh from Haiti to Louisiana

> orgies (plural),
>> from 1560s. "secret rites, revels, or ceremonies in the worship of certain Greek and Roman gods"
>> from 1660s. "any licentious revelry, a wild carousal"

They gathered at night, away from *some* white eyes. There, they danced in counterclockwise fashion; it was often the ring shout, and at other times it was the bamboula, the carabiné, the juba, the calinda, or the congo, all with rhythmic chants to the beat of the drum. With loud voices and deep, soulful cries, they invoked the spirits to mount or pass through them. Foot stomping, hand clapping, and chanting filled the night air. Soon they became "occupied bodies" and "spoken-through persons," moving intensely and making divine utterances.[1] They were possessed by African gods whom they now called by new names.[2] At times, they fell to the ground, rolling to and fro, moving their bodies as the spirits deemed necessary. Other times they would speak in their native tongues, standing in the gap between the above world and the underworld of their ancestors, unraveling spiritual mysteries and communicating prophecies to the edification of all present.

These spirit possessions took place precisely because those gathered consecrated the grounds collectively, albeit surreptitiously, to properly receive the spirits.[3] They assembled dressed candles, alcohol bottles, flowers, foods, and a host of other elements to make an altar, around which they would dance. Congo Square along with Lake Pontchartrain and Bayou St. John were their own Black geographies of religious life in New Orleans, and these spaces were also havens for Haitian refugees who had migrated to Louisiana during the late eighteenth and nineteenth centuries, joining the descendants of Africans who had been brought to Louisiana during the slave trade and had already cultivated their own distinct religious culture.[4] Some of those refugees came as a result of the Haitian Revolution, which had been engineered by many Vodouists led by the spirits, and all who heard of their underworld work feared the spread of Black rebellion with the aid of the spirits.[5] Charles Dudley Warner, a New England writer of Puritan heritage, observed while gazing upon a Voudou ceremony in New Orleans in 1889, "The barbaric rites of Voudooism originated with the Congo and Guinea negroes, were brought to San Domingo, and thence to Louisiana. In Hayti the sect is in full vigor, and its midnight orgies have reverted more and more to the barbaric original in the last twenty-five years."[6] In Haiti, as would later be the case in Louisiana, Vodou had also been criminalized and policed, due largely to the Catholic Church and the Haitian Code Pénal, which linked the success of the revolution with the ritual assembly of Vodouists.[7]

White race makers posited that *Haitian Vodou* and its cousin *Louisiana Voudou* were "primitive" retentions from Africa and worked tirelessly during the postemancipation and Reconstruction periods to Christianize all people of African descent.[8] Even as Voudouists in Louisiana "frequently borrow[ed] rituals and customs from the Christian religions" (i.e., Catholicism), their Black Atlantic religion making in the afterlife of chattel slavery ultimately challenged the supremacy of white American Christian hegemony and fueled white racial anxieties about religiously motivated Black rebellion, especially in the wake of both the Haitian Revolution and Nat Turner's Rebellion.[9] The Louisiana Writers' Project staff reported in the 1930s that during Reconstruction, "large groups of [refugees] in concentration camps supervised by the Freedman's Bureau were converted to the Baptist and Methodist beliefs. This wholesale conversion, along with the emotional appeal of revivals, account for the great majority of adherents to these creeds among the Negroes."[10] Despite these efforts, however, Voudou persisted. Spirits from the Haitian Revolution would also often visit Afro-Creole practitioners of Spiritualism and Voudou during their ceremonies, critiquing white supremacy and calling for resistance from their descendants.[11] As a result, white race makers imagined Afro-Creole ceremonial rituals as "orgies" such that people of African descent were believed to be performing occult, sexualized acts in the service of non-Christian, foreign gods, thus tapping into an invented, yet supposedly innate, Black hypersexuality and African barbarism.

The policing of Voudou in slavery persisted during what I am referring to as the long postemancipation period—1865 to 1896 (the latter marking *Plessy v. Ferguson*, a case of immense importance in both Louisiana and the nation). This chapter analyzes this policing in order to narrate the pre-1900 religious, political, and racial discourse that developed, effectively setting the stage for the policing of Black Atlantic religions in the early twentieth century—the social context within which practitioners' Black Atlantic religion making took shape as a practice of survival on the one hand, and as counter to white Christian hegemonic authority on the other. I begin by tracking how Voudou was misrepresented, weaponized, and wielded as a trope within the New Orleanian and national presses, with a particular focus on the writings of white New Orleanian George Washington Cable. While he was just one writer in a larger constellation of press writers and writers of amateur ethnography and fiction deploying similar racialized themes, he was also the most prominently known and widely read Southern writer during the period. In 1900, Charleston's *Evening Post* maintained, "There has at no time arisen in the South a stronger novelist than George Washington Cable."[12] Because he was a native of the city, his portrayal of New Orleans and its inhabitants undoubtedly held weight and shaped outsider perceptions of the city in and beyond the South. In the next section, I discuss the Louisiana Association of the American Folklore Society, which flourished between 1892 and 1896, to show how this division's work in the city became a blueprint for later studies at the center of early twentieth-century discourses on the problem of Black Atlantic religions. Folklorists in New Orleans and in the broader American Folklore Society (AFS), founded in 1888, deployed a particularly troubling methodological apparatus to collect as one of its primary missions "the fast-vanishing remains of . . . Lore of Negroes in the Southern States of the Union," as described by the society's founder William Wells Newell, and people of African descent in New Orleans and Louisiana were viewed as rich material for white folkloric consumption.[13] Finally, the chapter ends with a brief examination of *The Picayune's Guide to New Orleans* (which had roughly thirteen editions between 1892 and 1918) to elucidate how local imaginings of the city and of Black religions within its bounds prompted a national discourse about the problems of Black religious gathering—an extension of Jim Crow Black Codes that criminalized idle Black folk who failed to use their bodies in the service of the Southern labor economy.[14] Voudou most assuredly fell within the bounds of folk religion as the formerly enslaved and the poor were its captive devotees, alongside wealthy Afro-Creoles and white New Orleanians who stood solidly in the religion's minority in the late nineteenth century. Moreover, "dramas of possession" caused religious practitioners to be "beside oneself": these religious performances and enactments of spirit power "[marked] the self as fundamentally (not incidentally) social, necessarily constituted by what lies outside or beside it."[15] Put differently, Voudouists embraced "being beside oneself" as a mode of difference from the Jim Crow apparatus that criminalized and policed them, which troubled the making and unmaking of the Negro "self" in the afterlife of the slave self.[16]

In this regard, it is important to note that much of the disconcertment among many white Louisianans concerning Voudou also had to do with their own racial anxieties about the supposed primitivity of the formerly enslaved and free Black and Afro-Creole persons during the long postemancipation period. These individuals also held similar anxieties directed at Native Americans and other nonwhite immigrants to the United States. White Louisianans, like white Americans throughout the nation, saw it as their responsibility to modernize "primitive" populations and exorcise them of their "fetishes." As Jim Crow developed in the aftermath of Reconstruction, white supremacist technologies of the human also crystallized and were built firmly on the interconnected relationships among race, religion, gender, sexuality, and the modern.[17] In the face of this modernizing discourse, salvage ethnography developed as an enterprise during the nineteenth century. As Brian Hochman puts it, "the architects of the salvage paradigm insisted that certain populations were incapable of progressing beyond the primitive social state. It was the duty of the civilized to record primitive life in the face of its certain demise."[18] These populations happened to largely be of African and Indigenous heritages, and the architects of this Jim Crow modernizing apparatus utilized the phonograph, the pen, the photograph, and other technologies in concert with troubling ethics (or no ethics at all) to procure African and Indigenous religious knowledges, cultural traditions, dialects, recipes, folk stories, and communal secrets. This chapter focuses on just a snippet of this history of exploitation: the salvage ethnography of Voudou in Black and Afro-Creole communities, and the problem of possessed devotees in the afterlife of slavery. In their attempts to "salvage" this "vanishing" religion from this "vanishing" people in light of the burgeoning eugenics movement, white Louisianans had also attempted to salvage the plantation.

VOUDOU, POSSESSION, AND ITS MISREPRESENTATIONS

With the emancipation of the enslaved in the rearview, white spectators' misrepresentations of the Voudou ceremony continued to crystallize alongside the development of Carnival culture by Mardi Gras Indians in the city of New Orleans during the 1880s.[19] White writer Henry Rightor rightly observed in his 1900 historical account of the city, "There are enemies of this Carnival; not those chill-hearted, shrivel-skins who frown it down as a device of the devil; not the clergy, nor any overt opposition. It is the innovators who are to be feared, they who do not understand the carnival spirit, and seek to have it new."[20] Rightor later described Carnival culture as "gay and mad and rollicking, and over it all broods the ghost of the grotesque."[21] Negroes in masks paying homage to Indian and Indigenous spirits, with faces and limbs adorned in war paint, feathers, and animal skin affixed on their bodies, gyrating in the streets, drunk with wine and spirits, and loudly uttering proclamations of ancestral veneration and joy prompted both fear and titillation in many white spectators. In the nineteenth century, Afro-Creole and Caribbean practitioners of myriad religious and cultural practices blurred the lines between the private and the public, and their performances were deemed excessive and in need of taming.[22]

While it is true that Black religion has been described by Europeans in erotic, sexualized terms, ever since the Europeans first made contact with Africans and their indigenous religions during the colonial period, sources from the long postemancipation period demonstrate the development of a "post-slavery" discourse about the maintenance and control of Black flesh and Black religions.[23] Moreover, white race makers ultimately debated their perceived proprietary rights over the *when, where,* and *how* of Black gathering through staunch critiques of the Voudou ceremony, often found in travel accounts, folklore studies, anthropological narratives, and the local and national press. Drawing connections between Haiti and Louisiana, the *Times-Picayune* reported on June 22, 1891, in an article entitled, "The Voudou Dance: Described by the Eye-Witness of a Crazy Orgy Near Port-au-Prince," for example, that "Voudouism is practiced quite generally in Hayti, but with such secrecy, especially in the cities, that few except the natives ever witness its rites."[24] In many respects, the surveillance of and ordinances against Voudou in New Orleans mirrored those in Haiti in the preceding century.

As mentioned in this book's introduction, in 1897, the year after *Plessy*, the city of New Orleans issued an official ordinance forbidding mediumship, clairvoyance, fortune telling, and practices largely relating to Voudou, which ultimately forced them underground into the underworld. This ordinance would not have been possible without the racialized and sexualized discourse cultivated by white race makers and some Black Christian commentators regarding the problems of the Voudou ceremony, held at night, in the public square, and across the color line, in the decades preceding *Plessy v. Ferguson*. While Louisiana has a unique history of interracial engagement given the vast ethnic and racial diversity within its bounds, white supremacist attitudes shaped and determined the terms upon which Black and Afro-Creole persons navigated this complex social terrain, especially as the French colonial regime had structured the tripartite racialized system, as opposed to the later English binary, and this largely accounted for the city's interraciality.[25] Relatedly, the historian John W. Blassingame contended, while writing about the antebellum period in his now classic text *Black New Orleans*, "An anomaly in Louisiana, the free Negro was neither bound nor free."[26] In this vein, white race makers remained concerned about interracial ritual ceremonies and sexual intercourse across the color line.[27] However, these white racial anxieties were not only about Black sexuality and interracial sex; they were also about postemancipation apprehensions concerning *possession*—that of Black flesh by the spirits, specifically non-Christian, African spirits, as shown in figure 1.1, a caricatured image of spirit possession entitled "Night Voodoo Scene" published in *The Caucasian* in 1903.[28]

In the United States, the Southern sons and daughters of planters and colonists were also deeply disturbed, yet titillated, by the idea that people of African descent could be possessed—not by white race makers, but by gods whom those same white race makers did not know or revere. They ultimately wondered if the formerly enslaved and other free Afro-Creole persons had quite literally changed masters or been repossessed by entities who had never legally owned them.[29] Spirit possession posed problems for white planters seeking insight into the future of their plantations in the afterlife of emancipation. Concerns about civil disorder, Black rebellion, and interracial sex were also precipitated by how the Voudou ceremony was imagined, and how a sexualized grammar emerged among white race makers to describe Black religions and spirit possession. The "Voudou orgy" was Negro licentiousness en masse, albeit "religious." As Elizabeth Pérez reminds us, "Whether in Yorùbá, Spanish, Portuguese, Creole, or English, the term used to describe possession phenomena, *mounting*, retains its double meaning,

FIGURE 1.1. "Night Voodoo Scene," from *The Caucasian* (Shreveport, LA), February 8, 1903, 2.

with the gods consistently compared to husbands penetrating their wives in sexual congress."[30] In light of *mounting*'s double meaning, two questions undoubtedly animated the minds of those surveilling the Voudou ceremony of the long postemancipation period: First, did white people still own Black and Afro-Creole persons, or had the spirits subsumed extralegal ownership over these Black bodies? Second, had white practitioners of Voudou—especially curious white women—been possessed and mounted by Black (male) gods bearing Black phalluses?

New Orleans attorney and judge Henry C. Castellanos pondered a similar line of inquiry in *New Orleans as It Was*, published in 1895: "Blacks and whites were circling round promiscuously, writhing in muscular contractions, panting, raving and frothing at the mouth. But the most degrading and infamous feature of this scene was the presence of a very large number of ladies (?), moving in the highest walks of society, rich and hitherto supposed respectable, that were caught in the drag net."[31] The "(?)" following "ladies"—a term used during the Victorian era to describe white women committed to Christian social respectability, sexual chastity, and ultimately, marriage—signified that, for Castellanos and his contemporaries, white women who participated in the Voudou ceremony had somehow become dishonorable women, having no sexual discipline and rejecting their identities as "ladies." Castellanos even went on to describe a situation in which a husband, "unable to survive the disgrace of his wife, deliberately took his life on the following day," demonstrating how anxious white patriarchs relied on white women's social respectability.[32] In comparison, Black and Afro-Creole women were denied access to the category of "womanhood" and were thus not given the honor of being called "ladies," such that the disdain for white women's participation in the Voudou ceremony further cemented white patriarchal ideas about Black and Afro-Creole women and men as contagions, capable of sullying the honor of white womanhood. Black feminist scholar Hortense Spillers has described this as a process of "ungendering," in which Black women were *dis*/regarded as "the materialized scene of unprotected female flesh" and were considered non-"ladies" undeserving of "protection" in the white patriarchal imaginary.[33] It is important to note, however, that these racist and sexist ideas about Black women also circulated on the African continent and in the Caribbean and Latin America for centuries, and the notion of the fallen woman being penetrated by a Black (if not) foreign, diabolical presence had strong resonances with accusations of witchcraft in both Inquisition trials of the seventeenth century and the annals of slave trial records in the American South and throughout the Black Atlantic world.[34] In the New Orleans context, white race makers—who fully embraced their roles as planters or former planters—drew upon long-standing conceptions about Black women's supposed inferiority, sexual degeneracy, and maleficent spiritual power as a means of maligning Voudou as a potent force of evil that sought to terrorize the lives of white religious authorities and all who sided with them.

Black women, however, cultivated other modes of self-definition and honor, relying largely on the ancestral wisdoms and African matrilineal heritages of their foremothers as a site of power.[35] Despite these resistance strategies to white patriarchal imaginaries, white commentators' paranoia about Voudou as a gendered and sexualized site continued. Indeed, these anxieties were of central importance to white race makers, and they sit at the center of this chapter's analysis, especially as these concerns set the stage for the policing of Black Atlantic religions in New Orleans during the early twentieth century.[36] During the era of slavery, Voudou ceremonies in the United States fell under the category of "Unlawful Assemblies," as was characteristic of all Black religious gatherings in the absence of white authority in the city of New Orleans. According to Ordinance No. 3847, which went into effect on April 7, 1858, the mayoralty stated, "Be it ordained, that each and every Congregation of persons of color and each and every assemblage or gatherings of persons of color, which is now or may hereafter exist within the incorporated limits of the city of New Orleans for worship, the same shall be under the supervision and control of some recognized white congregation or church."[37] Voudou, as a non-Christian religion, most assuredly fell outside of the parameters of acceptable religious practice on two counts: its insistence on secret or privatized worship and its worship of non-Christian deities. New Orleans's *Times-Picayune* further clarified this legality, noting, "The public may have partly learned from the Voudou disclosures about what takes place at such meetings, the mystic ceremonies, wild orgies, dancing, songs, &c. All meetings are not dens of vice; this would be asserting more than is just, but there is nothing to show that any of them have ever been productive of good to the habits or morals of the slave population."[38] As a result, police officers frequently broke up these meetings, and in their reports, they often described finding women in the nude. In July 1863, for instance, two police officers claimed to have "found about forty naked women—all colored except for two—who were dancing the Voudou dance and performing rites and incantations pertaining to that ancient African superstition yclept Voudoism."[39] In October of the same year, more Black women were arrested "who were engaged in practicing the fetish rites known as the Voudou Mysteries." The *New York Day-Book* continued, citing the New Orleans *Era*, "There were some thirty of them in a small room, all as nude as Venus new risen from the sea, engaged in the wild African dance around a pot filled with all sorts of charms."[40] Police and white spectators read these enactments and celebrations of nude Afro-Creole flesh as inevitably sexual and erotic, even as Afro-Creole Voudouists might not have viewed them in that way or even been naked for that matter, further revealing the machinations of the white Christian imagination.

THE "VANISHING" AND TRANSFORMATION
OF NEW ORLEANS VOUDOU

In contrast, George Washington Cable enjoyed gazing upon Voudou cere-monies, and he published a few of his observations in the evangelical Chris-tian, illustrated monthly publication the *Century Magazine*, which had been founded by the Century Company of New York City in 1881. Cable, who was once described by press writers as a "celebrated novelist" and "the historian of a peculiar and unique people with a past at once pathetic and roman-tic," dedicated much of his writing to capturing the customs, dialects, and superstitions of Afro-Creole people in the late nineteenth century.[41] In line with the development of salvage ethnography both inside and outside of the nation's universities, Cable pondered, "Did [the Voodoo dance] ever reach Louisiana?" following the criminalization and policing of Vodou in Haiti, since "the best efforts of police had . . . only partially suppressed it."[42] Answering his own question, he noted, "Let us, at a venture, say no." A closer look at his own salvage ethnography of Voudou in the late nine-teenth century, however, suggests that Voudou was prominently alive in New Orleans, and white race makers deemed its devotees a problem people. Cable opined, "The negro was the most despised of human creatures and the Congo the plebeian among negroes."[43] It is no surprise that Voudouists were Place Congo's most frequent visitors, building elaborate altars and calling upon the spirits to mount them while doing what Cable called "the Voodoo Dance" (see fig. 1.2).

Although Cable based both of his two well-known articles, "The Dance in Place Congo" and "Creole Slave Songs" in 1886, on his own amateur ethnographic encounters around the same time, he situated Voudou in the slave past, denying its late nineteenth-century prevalence despite his own attendance at Voudou ceremonies as a spectator. While writing about the vast array of dances performed at the Voudou ceremony, Cable confessed, for instance, "Only a few years ago I was honored with an invitation, which I had to decline."[44] While it is unclear who "invited" Cable, his appearance at late nineteenth-century Voudou ceremonies in New Orleans is well docu-mented. He had even been accused by Creole writer Adrienne Rouquette of supposedly joining "in voodoo dances with Marie Laveau, the black voodoo queen," because of his proximity to Voudou ceremonies as a spectator and amateur ethnographer.[45] Yet, in the spirit of the period, Cable nonetheless joined commentators in demonizing and attempting to "salvage" the alleged

FIGURE 1.2. "The Voodoo Dance," from Cable, "Creole Slave Songs," *Century Magazine* 31, no. 6 (1886): 816.

vanishing remnants of formerly enslaved, Afro-Creole religions. Following the death of renowned Voudou queen Marie Laveau on June 15, 1881, Cable reasoned, for example, "It is pleasant to say that [Voudou] worship, in Louisiana, at least, and in comparison, with what it once was, has grown to be a rather trivial affair."[46] His commentary on the "vanishing" of Voudou in the 1880s had less to do with the religion's decline, however, and more to do with the policing of Voudou and white racial anxieties about possessed Afro-Creole persons in the afterlife of slavery. Indeed, Cable rightly asserts, "In Louisiana it is written Voudou and Voodoo, and is often changed on the negro's lips to Hoodoo," confirming Voudou's existence and robust transformation in the city of New Orleans.[47]

Nonetheless, in his use of both past and present tense to describe the Voudou ceremony, Cable gave voice to persisting concerns among white Americans about their perceived proprietary rights over Black people's bodies, beliefs, and gatherings. For Cable, the Voudou ceremony during slavery and the Voudou ceremony during the long postemancipation period were both a problem because they both afforded Afro-Creole persons the time and space to be effectively undisciplined and unruly. He wrote, "The hour was the slave's term of momentary liberty, and his simple, savage, musical and superstitious nature dedicated it to amatory song and dance tinctured with his rude notions of supernatural influences." While observing a Voudou ceremony around the time of his publication in 1886, Cable described devotees and their rituals as "a queer thing."[48] For Cable, the Voudou ceremony's queerness had to do with its celebration of excess and his inability to control its devotees.[49] The spirits possessed Afro-Creole persons in Place Congo, in the woods, and often at night in cabins, intentionally away from white intrusion notwithstanding white surveillance, and these possessions were not always carceral; they were sometimes liberating.[50] The same caution remained in the long postemancipation period as Afro-Creole persons navigated the policing and criminalization of their assemblies and communion with the spirits. Their intentional movement outside of the purview of white onlookers served a dual function. It was as much about practicing illicit religious activities deemed sexual as it was about finding pleasure in the idea of self-possession on the one hand, and possession by the spirits on the other. These instances of bodily excess and sacred informational safeguarding situated Afro-Creole persons outside of the bounds of white control, even if these moments were transient and fleeting.[51] Even Cable exclaimed, "What wild—what terrible delight! The ecstasy rises to madness."[52] Later he described spirit possession as "a frightful triumph of body over mind," implying that formerly enslaved and free Afro-Creole persons had internal values that exceeded bodily commodification and white ethnographic consumption.[53]

Writing nearly twenty years later, Harvard-trained sociologist W. E. B. Du Bois described spirit possession in terms like, yet distinct from, Cable's, in that Du Bois centered what he called "the religious feeling of the slave," an idea that viewed Black religious expression as much more than performance material for amateur ethnography. Referring to Black Protestant revivals—which he argued "[vary] according to time and place, from the West Indies in the sixteenth century to New England in the nineteenth, and from the Mississippi bottoms to cities like New Orleans or New York"—he observed, "The Frenzy of 'Shouting,' when the Spirit of the Lord passed by, and, seizing the devotee, made him mad with supernatural joy, was the last essential of Negro religion and the one more devoutly believed in than all the rest." Du Bois continued, "It varied in expression from the silent rapt countenance or the low murmur and moan to the mad abandon of physical fervor,—the stamping, shrieking, and shouting, the rushing to and fro and wild waving of arms, the weeping and laughing, the vision and the trance."[54] Du Bois's thick description situated spirit possession in terms that adjudicated devotees, showing its normative power and its diverse manifestations among people of African descent across various time periods and geographical locations. Moreover, his attention to Black people's "supernatural joy" while possessed stood in stark contrast to the demoralizing observations of Cable, which deemed devotees excessive, unruly, and perverse. Du Bois's relationship with and proximity to Afro-Protestantism certainly shaped his sociological sensibilities and his inner sensitivity to the moving of the Spirit among the faithful.[55]

Contrastingly, it is through Cable's use of Jim Crow grammar to describe spirit possession that we see how he had also largely relied on a normative white American Christianity upheld through biblical fundamentalism to demonize Voudou and its practitioners, even as many of those same white Christians would come to rely on Voudou's powerful influence. Cable observed, "There are swoonings and ravings, nervous tremblings beyond control, incessant writhings and turnings, tearing of garments, even biting of the flesh—every imaginable invention of the devil."[56] For Cable, Voudouists who were possessed by the spirits—specifically, non-Christian, African spirits—were like those in the New Testament who had been possessed by demons in need of Jesus's and the disciples' exorcising power, and Cable described through a host of sensory registers his discomfort with Black bodies in ecstasy.[57] It was one thing for Afro-Creole persons to be possessed by "the devil," but it was an entirely different ordeal for white women to be possessed by the devil through the ritual workings of Black people. Cable and his contemporaries, however, often failed to acknowledge that white planters and their families would often look to Voudouists for ritual healing when ailed by a variety of bodily afflictions—a long tradition that dates back to the early Atlantic context.[58] James W. Buel, who includes an image (shown here as fig. 1.3) of a white woman being "exorcised" by Black women Voudouists, glosses over the fact that the white woman pictured had come to those same Black women for assistance because she had allegedly been "Voudoued" by "an old black witch who resided within a short distance of the plantation" who had "laid a charm upon her." The Voudou that had allegedly caused her harm was the same Voudou expected to save her.[59] He writes that in January 1882, "The daughter of a wealthy planter fell ill of a strange disease, that at first assumed the nature of extreme nervousness, but this partly subsiding, a marasmus succeeded that created great alarm in the family. From a fleshy, plump, and beautiful girl, in a few weeks she was reduced to the frailest proportions and was apparently upon the point of death."

The Black women Voudouists pictured, who had, in other instances, been demonized by the planter class, did the work to save the young woman from

FIGURE 1.3. "Voudous Curing a Possessed Girl by Exorcism," from Buel, *Mysteries and Miseries of America's Great Cities*, 541.

death. Buel writes, "It was decided by the planter to place his daughter under conditions prescribed by the old obi negro and thus test a power which he had heard so much of but never saw exercised."[60] Upon successful completion of this ritual by the elder Black woman who had been accompanied by seven other women, Buel confessed, "Planters [also] pay Voudou queens large sums of money for their influence in preserving peace and satisfaction among their hands. Politicians also use this occult agency to further their ends and find it exceedingly potential."[61] In addition to the burgeoning field of salvage ethnography, white political interest and planter class reliance on Black ritual healing through Voudou were motivating factors for wealthy white people's engagement with the vilified religion, which raises additional questions about whether Afro-Creole practitioners engaged in performativity for voyeurs and tourists looking for the exotic, as a means of furthering economic stability, racialized interests, or legal protection vis-à-vis white presence. Alexis Wells-Oghoghomeh has also observed in her account of enslaved women's religious cultures in Georgia that "for some Whites, the ecstatic performances, melodic singing, and evocative utterances of Black religious spaces and rites served as an unconventional form of entertainment."[62] Whether political interest, the need for healing, or white spectatorship as entertainment, white engagement varied, and Afro-Creole practitioners seized the opportunity.[63]

Despite the complex relationship white planters had with Voudou, many continued to surveil Afro-Creole persons on their plantations and in surrounding towns during the long postemancipation period. In "Creole Slave Songs," Cable included an image with the caption "Planter and Voodoo Charm" (fig. 1.4) following a brief discussion of the uses of alcohol among Voudouists, in which he placed an emphasis on Afro-Creole sound, movement, and eating: "There was frenzy and a circling march, wild shouts, delirious gesticulations and posturings, drinking, and amongst other frightful nonsense the old trick of making fire blaze from the mouth by spraying alcohol from it upon the flame of a candle." While it is unclear whether Cable had issues with alcohol use, considering the growing Temperance movement of the nineteenth century, it is certainly clear that the celebrated novelist took notice of how alcohol intensified the effects of spirit possession, such that practitioners produced "delirious gesticulations and posturings" uncommon to the sober minded. If Voudouists could so easily go into a "frenzy" by way of the spirits—inclusive of deities and alcohol—Cable along with many planters believed that Voudou charms could also potentially spread the effects of spirit possession, from Afro-Creole persons to white Louisianans. He continued, noting, "But whatever may be the quantity of the Voodoo *worship* left in Louisiana, its superstitions are many and are everywhere. Its charms are resorted to by the malicious, the jealous, the revengeful, or the avaricious, or held in terror, not by the timorous only, but by the strong, the courageous, the desperate."[64] In figure 1.4, however, three Black men cower in fear of punishment, or worse, death, as a planter holds a "Voodoo charm" and stares them down, most likely shaming them for their beliefs and the presence of said object in their living quarters.

One is left to ponder if the planter even considered the possibility of his being "Voudoued" by touching the charm, signifying white deference to the potent power of Black religious material culture and the efficacy of Black ritual practices.[65] Moreover, the planter's posture in relation to the three Black men demonstrates how plantation society persisted in the long postemancipation period, such that Afro-Creole persons were always subject to white authorities, having to overexplain their Black religious ways of knowing and worldview. In Cable's 1880 historical romance *The Grandissimes: A Story of Creole Life*, a "Congo slave-woman" named Clemence, an accomplice of Palmyre, a healer, is killed after similarly being caught hiding Voudou charms near the Grandissimes' uncle Agricola Fusilier's estate. She is then taken into nearby woods for what would be an interrupted lynching, set "free," and then shot to death by an unknown gunman, following

FIGURE 1.4. "Planter and Voodoo Charm," from Cable, "Creole Slave Songs," 821.

one of the Fusilier kin's call to "shoot the black devils without mercy!"[66] Even though it was commonly said among planters that "all the blacks are voudous, more or less," this particular killing was deemed a public exorcism, an attempt to rid the plantation of Voudou.[67] It is worth noting, too, that some formerly enslaved people who had been Christianized and later self-identified as Black Christians took offense to being grouped together with "voudous" and "Hoodoos" by white planters. Marie Brown, an ex-slave, told LWP interviewer Zoe Posey in June 1940, "Marie Laveau, that hellcat, that she-devil! I never went with Hoodoo peoples, but once saw them dance at Congo Square. Look, that's it at the corner. You wouldn't believe the devilment that went on there. For music they made drums outer pork barrels and knocked out both ends which they [covered] with deer skins, and took the jaw-bone of a mule—maybe a hoss—and drew it across, and they danced until they dropt."[68] Brown distanced herself from Voudouists precisely because of the threat of danger that affiliation with Voudou and Place des Negres caused Black people in Jim Crow modernity.

FOLKLORE, PLANTATION SOCIETY, AND VOUDOU

As planters attempted to destroy the material remnants of Voudou on their plantations during the long postemancipation period, folklorists and salvage ethnographers sought to preserve the supposed "vanishing" of "Negro superstitions." In this regard, the Louisiana Association of the American Society of Folklore was perhaps the most prescient example of this attempt to recapture Afro-Creole persons, cultures, and religions otherwise seeking to flee carceral confinement in New Orleans. The Louisiana Association was founded at Tulane University on February 8, 1892, after Professor Alcée Fortier, scholar of Romance languages, convened a group of white intellectuals, writers, and artists from New Orleans to collect folklore. In the minutes from the first meeting, it was noted that "Prof. Fortier informed the society that the book on Louisiana folk-lore would be the first one issued by the American Folk-Lore Society, and asked permission to incorporate the contributions of members. This was agreed to."[69] The group's findings would make their way into what would later become Fortier's *Louisiana Studies: Literature, Customs and Dialects, History and Education*, published in 1894, and *Louisiana Folk Tales: In French Dialect and English Translation*, published in 1895. The group, as noted by Rosan Augusta Jordan, a scholar of folklore, comprised "members . . . mostly from 'society' (but not necessarily from families with money); many had connections with plantation families; their names appeared often in the society columns of the local newspapers. Some were the wives of prominent businessmen, particularly cotton brokers and bankers."[70] One of the original twenty-four members of the Louisiana Association was George Washington Cable, who, as Jordan argues, "helped create and publicize a romantic image of New Orleans, with its lush semitropical climate and its culturally distinctive inhabitants, especially the Creoles and Creoles of color."[71] Similar to Cable's prominence as one of the most prolific Southern writers during the period, "The Louisiana Association was the only branch of the American Folklore Society located in the South, and it was active in the early 1890s. Most of its members had actually lived through the Civil War, the Emancipation of slaves, and Reconstruction, events which brought about drastic changes in their lives, often including economic ruin."[72] In their work as folklorists, members nostalgically longed for the days of old, harkening back to times not long ago when the Afro-Creole people they studied were their or their parents' slaves.

During its four-year run, the Louisiana Association grew to a total of sixty-nine people—fifty-six women and thirteen men—and their meeting minutes and published writings in the *Journal of American Folklore* include, as Jordan and Frank De Caro have also observed, "repeated connection made between folklore and plantation life and servants."[73] Moreover, "the plantation *is* 'folk-lore land' and its (Black) residents are the 'folk-lore people' who teem there. The plantation is where folklore exists."[74] Upon further examination of the Louisiana Association's records, however, I argue that in this literal and imagined plantation society, folklorists posited that Afro-Creole persons were the *possessors of folklore* meant solely for scholarly consumption and commodification, and that those same possessors of folklore were to be disallowed *possession by the spirits* that mounted them during Voudou ceremonies and sat at the crux of their oral traditions. As Paul Christopher Johnson reminds us, "Possession served as a fulcrum for modern discourses about freedom and autonomy, thrown into relief through split images of the possessed—those who are like things—and the possessors—those who own things."[75] We might think of this postemancipation enigma as yet another example of Black dispossession, such that all that Black people possessed, even their own religious knowledges and experiences, were to be consumed by white eaters.[76] Indeed, Johnson's poignant question "Of what is *possession* possessed?" raises a host of questions about how spirit possession was, at once, despised by white race makers and also of central importance to their anthropological and folkloric accounts during the period.[77] This possession of Afro-Creole spirit possessions, otherwise described as "Negro Folk-lore," only intensified as the AFS grew in membership and spread throughout the United States.[78]

Prior to the Louisiana Association's founding in 1892, for example, Haitian Vodou and Louisiana Voudou had already been captive topics of interest for the members of the national AFS, which had been founded in 1888 in Cambridge, Massachusetts, by Harvard College and Harvard Divinity School graduate William Wells Newell.[79] The same year of the AFS's founding, Newell published in the journal's first issue "Myths of Voodoo Worship and Child Sacrifice in Hayti," an article in which he responded to *The English in the West Indies* (1888), a book written by Mr. J. A. Froude in which

Froude "makes incidental reference to the existence of certain superstitious practices in Hayti," specifically "the serpent worship, the child sacrifice, and the cannibalism." Newell attempted to trace Vodou both etymologically and historically, relying largely on sources written by European missionaries, and he regurgitated missionary eyewitness accounts about the perceived dangers of the Vodou ceremony.[80] In the following issue of the journal, Fortier published "Customs and Superstitions in Louisiana." He began his reflection with a misrepresentation of the violent system of slavery, commenting, "The planters lived in the greatest opulence and possessed many slaves. These were, as a rule, well treated by their masters, and, in spite of their slavery, they were contented and happy." While describing parties held by enslaved people on New Year's Day, Fortier added, "Very different is this scene from those described in 'Uncle Tom's Cabin,' for the slaves were certainly not unhappy on the plantations. The proof of this is, that, although our equals politically and citizens of the United States, they often refer to the time of slavery, and speak willingly to those bygone days."[81] Yet it was not the enslaved who waxed poetic about their enslavement and the evils and terrors of it, but it was Fortier harkening back to a time when the subjects of his study were captive to the whims of the planter class. In his attempt to preserve this horrid time in American history, Fortier had also misrepresented the system of slavery, positioning powerless subjects deemed nonhuman by enslavers as "equals" and "citizens."

These sorts of distortions went together with the demonization and caricature of Voudou in the early days of the AFS's journal. In the same piece, Fortier went on to write, "The negroes, as all ignorant people, are very superstitious. The celebrated sect of the Voudoux, of which so much has been said, was the best proof of the credulity and superstition of the blacks, as well as of the barbarity of their nature."[82] He insisted that Afro-Creole people lacked mental dexterity and intelligence, and that Voudou was a result of an innate intellectual deficiency on the part of the descendants of Africa. Yet, like many of his contemporaries, Fortier deemed Afro-Creole people's superstitions legitimate, worthwhile material for the AFS's readers, especially as he tapped into members' concerns about the alleged vanishing folklore of people of African descent. "This sect is nearly extinct," he claimed, and continued by outlining "superstitions among the common people in Louisiana."[83] Although all of Fortier's research subjects were not Voudou practitioners, for the purposes of his AFS article, Voudou was inherently synonymous with all "Negro superstitions." The following year, 1889, Newell cited Fortier's article (1888) and Cable's "Creole Slave Songs" (1886) along with correspondence with the United States Minister Resident to Haiti, Mr. Benjamin F. Whidden, in "Reports of Voodoo Worship in Hayti and Louisiana." Although Newell noted, "The orgies of the Vaudoux are represented as taking place in secret, and in remote places," he also questioned the sensibilities of many of his contemporaries who claimed that Vodouists practiced human sacrifice or cannibalism, writing, "That intelligent and trustworthy persons thoroughly familiar with the island have been unable to discover any trace of cannibal or Voodooistic rites is in itself a very strong ground for believing that these have their seat only in the imagination of a credulous people."[84] To his credit, Newell effectively called on AFS's readers to produce "evidence," or in contemporary parlance, to produce receipts and methodologically show their math.

Contributors answered the call, providing "evidence" in their submissions to the AFS. One such example is found in white ethnographer Stewart Culin's "Reports concerning Voodooism," in which he relayed a secondhand account noting that "the following was related to [him] last summer (1888) by Rev. R. E. Gammon, for several years of missionary of the London Baptist Missionary Society at Port-au-Prince."[85] Gammon's account, by way of Culin, recapitulated much of the anti-Vodou rhetoric of his contemporaries, though he prefaced his remarks with qualifying phrases such as, "*It is popularly asserted* in Hayti and San Domingo that the negroes perpetuate Voodoo orgies, and that cannibalism is still practiced" (emphasis added). In another instance, he wrote, "*It is said* that meetings are held in the mountains, and that the members of the fraternity are compelled to attend at the sound of the drum, notwithstanding their efforts to resist the call" (emphasis added). At the time of publication, Cullin had never actually been to Haiti, but he presented "ethnographic" data by way of a secondhand account from a missionary to the island, no less, yet folklorists considered this material evidentiary of cannibalism in Haitian Vodou. Gammon continued, "The negroes in Hayti and San Domingo are very superstitious and make use of spells and resort to conjurers." In this account, AFS's readers are not afforded the privilege of hearing Haitian people's voices; instead, Gammon speaks for them, centering his own Eurocentric understanding of the religion and its devotees, and Culin publishes the material without any analysis of its contents—a pattern evident in many of the AFS's queries, notes, and short articles published in the late nineteenth century. The secreting of Haitian people's voices further confirms that Black Atlantic religion making occurred in the deepest depths of the underworld, and Black religious subjects occasionally let white people in.

Nonetheless, white folklorists often forced their way into Black religious spaces to which they had not been formally invited. On this point, by 1892, the Louisiana Association had convened and seemed to form a consensus on the question of ethical folklore methodology, even if said consensus had not been fully articulated or named. Their local mission read, "The object of Folk-lore Society should be the accumulation of correctly reported stories and the discovery of their relationships."[86] The politics of procurement, however, were far less clear. What exactly constituted a "correctly reported story," and how did the identities and biases of folklorists color how these stories were constructed and narrated, and how they were ultimately interpreted? In an article published by the *Times-Picayune* entitled "Folk-Lore Studies," the press summarized one meeting of the Louisiana Association, noting, "Prof. Fortier stated that the principal object of the association being the accumulation and collection of ancient folk-lore stories which have never been published, but handed down from generation to generation through old people and nurses, he respectfully requested any member of the society who could furnish such valuable contributions to the society to do so."[87] The fact that the association's meeting minutes were reprinted and summarized in the *Times-Picayune* provides insight into the association's recruitment efforts. Many of the Louisiana Association's members were not academically trained as folklorists, but were often high-society commoners, who had no expertise in the burgeoning field but were instead novices developing and shaping a field built largely on the backs of those most harmed by the plantation—the enslaved and their descendants, and Indigenous peoples whose lands had been overrun by plantations. For example, three of the Louisiana Association's members included Professor Fortier's cousin's widow, Mrs. (Louise) Augustin Fortier, along with her two sisters, Aimée Beugnot and Marie Augustin.

Moreover, in his plea for "accumulation and collection," Fortier prioritized quantity over ethics and quality. For the Louisiana Association to make its mark, he ultimately argued that it had to rapidly produce a vast collection of materials to compete with other chapters and to center New Orleans in the emergent field of folklore studies, especially as the cultures and superstitions of its research subjects were believed to be "vanishing." That said, questions about *how* a society member collected a story never made it into meeting minutes, and instead, members often emphasized aspects of plantation society and its antecedents in their narrative accounts. One such example of this can be found in the meeting minutes dated May 1892, in which "Dr. Buchner . . . gave members a most interesting lecture on what he had seen amongst the African tribes, and, in opening, remarked that he had hoped, that instead of giving a lecture, to have had the pleasure of hearing one, and in the absence of any notes, his memory would have to serve him." Following Buchner's "lecture," Fortier thanked the professor and "mentioned that the national society placed much stress upon the value of the folk lore of the African races."[88] Members answered the call again and published "findings"—without sources, citations, or explanation of their methods—recapitulating much of the aforementioned anti-Voudou sentiment and disdain for Black religions of the period in such AFS journal publications as "Superstition of Negroes in New Orleans" (October–December 1892), "Conjuring and Conjure-Doctors in the Southern United States" (April–June 1896), and "A Voodoo Festival near New Orleans" (January–March 1897), just to name a few. Indeed, questions about ethics and method within the field seem to have been critical in causing the ultimate demise of the Louisiana Association in 1896, especially as the New Orleans group comprised mostly literary folklorists whose work veered from Newell's call for the AFS to do anthropological folklore, "a scientific discipline with high professional standards," as Rosan Augusta Jordan has observed.[89]

CONCLUSION: VOUDOU AS LOCAL TOURIST ATTRACTION *AND* NATIONAL PROBLEM

The legacy of the Louisiana Association, however, continued in other ways as their literary folklore cemented the romanticization of the New Orleans underworld by residents and tourists during the late nineteenth and early twentieth centuries. Just as "tourists to New Orleans clutched volumes by Cable in their hands in the 19th century," they also clutched such volumes as *The Picayune's Guide to New Orleans*, which had roughly thirteen editions between 1892 and 1918.[90] Echoing much of the plantation nostalgia of amateur ethnographers and literary folklorists in the decades prior, guide writers zoned in on Congo Square as a Black religious geographical site where people of African descent would gather and do "the Voudou dance." Tourists were encouraged to visit this site precisely because it was a known, public space where the vilified religion had once been practiced, fortifying the idea that Voudou was, in fact, a "vanishing" religion as suggested by Cable and other members of the Louisiana Association. The fourth edition of *The*

Picayune's Guide to New Orleans, published in 1900, seems to be the most relevant in this regard, as it was the first time that guide writers dedicated an entire section to the topic, titling the sixth chapter "Rampart Street and Its Vicinity—The St. Louis Cemeteries—Congo Square—The Voudous—The Barefooted Nuns—St. Roch's Cemetery." The 1892, 1896, and 1897 editions make little to no reference to people of African descent or to Voudou and Black Atlantic religions, which suggests that press writers were catching up to the work of salvage ethnographers and literary folklorists who had published material in the decade prior, but also concurrently with the publication of the guides, as evident in the work of the Louisiana Association between 1892 and 1896. Later iterations of the guide post-1900 revised the contents of the 1900 edition. Some versions expanded its attention to Voudou, usually with more content relating to Afro-Creole Voudou queen Marie Laveau—crystallizing her name in a particular touristic mythology and mystifying the truth of her biography and religious practices.[91] Other editions contracted the section on Congo Square, as evident in the 1913 edition, which only included about a paragraph on the subject, while maintaining the anti-Voudou sentiment of previous versions.

Alongside historical narratives and directions to the city's famous streets, churches, statues, monuments, and cemeteries, guide writers also pointed tourists to Congo Square, otherwise called Place des Negres or Negro Square—as the symbolic marker of the city's slave past and the legacy of the Voudou ceremony within its quarters. They wrote, "In the center of the square stood a canon, which was fired promptly at 9 o'clock. After that hour any negro found on the streets without his master, or a written permit from him, was arrested. Sunday was no exception to this rule."[92] During slavery and during the long postemancipation period, it was the rule of the day that if Afro-Creole persons—free or slave—were not working in the service of the Southern economy, they were to be away from the public square and out of white people's sight, confirming white Southerners' belief that Voudou, like other components of folk religion, distracted Black people from labor, and ultimately, capital exploitation. In line with much of the anti-Voudou rhetoric discussed in this chapter, the *Picayune* stressed that Black people had "many queer and terrible superstitions, not the least of which were the 'voudoo rites,' remnants of which still secretly exist in the city today."[93] To drive the point home, commentators cited George Washington Cable's literary folklore and amateur ethnography and drew connections between Voudou and devil worship. They wrote, "'Voudouism,' it has been said, had its origin in the bosom of hell itself, and raged so fiercely there that, unable to contain itself within bounds, it forced the spirits who were most under its influence to roam at large through the world, until they found a habitation in the bosoms of mortals."[94] What guide writers failed to comprehend was that the underworld became a gathering space for the spirits of the African diaspora in the late nineteenth century, and people of African descent journeyed there, allowing the spirits to possess their bodies in ways that ultimately disrupted Jim Crow modernity.

Of central concern to these guide writers, however, was the denunciation of spirit possession among Voudou devotees, linking their practices to a colonial, Christian demonology that read the spirits of the African diaspora as diabolical, "strange," and "so awful," tapping into a long genealogy of white writers reading Black Atlantic religions as "a mysterious fetish worship" in the service of non-Christian gods. It was through these imaginings and this constructed narrative about Voudou that guide writers, in concert with salvage ethnographers and folklorists, equated Voudou with "the terrible and malignant evils which Satan himself seeks to propagate."[95] The Voudou ceremony, then, was the means by which African spirits—from Satan and from hell—corrupted Afro-Creole persons, taking them captive and possessing their bodies and minds in slavery and well into the long postemancipation period. As this chapter has argued, the policing and criminalization of Voudou was a state-sanctioned project in concert with salvage ethnography that attempted to drive Voudou out while simultaneously preserving the lore of it for white folkloric consumption.

In turn, a tourist economy developed in the city of New Orleans built in large part on other misrepresentations of Black Atlantic religions, even as those same Black Atlantic religions, and the religious practitioners at the helm of them, were subject to legal scrutiny and humiliation by press writers and staff members of the LWP.[96] In many ways, the LWP was the direct institutional descendant of the Louisiana Association of the American Folklore Society, especially as Lyle Saxon, its director and a journalist for the *Times-Picayune*, was the grandson of Louisiana Association member Mrs. Elizabeth Lyle Saxon. Mr. Lyle Saxon had also befriended Mrs. Cammie Henry, the owner of the Melrose Plantation near Natchitoches, Louisiana, where he owned a cabin, and where Henry housed ex-slaves.[97] Saxon, along with Catherine Dillon, a staff member of the LWP, collaborated with Benjamin A. Botkin, Federal Writers' Project (FWP) folklore editor, and several others, to host the folklore meeting of the FWP of Louisiana in 1938 in New

Orleans. The group built upon the aims of the Louisiana Association, and Botkin called upon Saxon and his staff to collect "legendary stories—local stories of real life rather than what we call supernatural."[98]

The LWP—like its folklorist forebears—was attentive to the supernatural, paying particular attention to Voudou and its afterlives in both the American imaginary and in the lives of Black people in New Orleans. However, Saxon, who was a peer and colleague of Zora Neale Hurston as they both worked as employees of the FWP during the late 1930s, reified the salvage ethnography of his forebears while Hurston engaged in a process of spiritist ethnography in that her research and writing *sought to accurately* portray the potent supernatural powers embedded in Black people's diverse beliefs. To this end, she clarified the misrepresentations offered by her white colleagues, writing, "Veaudeau is the European term for African magic practices and beliefs, but it is unknown to the American Negro. His own name for his practices is hoodoo, both terms being related to the West African term *juju*. 'Conjure' is also freely used by the American Negro for these practices. In the Bahamas as on the West Coast of Africa the term is obeah. 'Roots' is the Southern Negro's term for folk-doctoring by herbs prescriptions, and by extension, and because all hoodoo doctors cure roots, it may be used as a synonym for hoodoo."[99] Saxon, on the other hand, relied on tropes of the Negro's inferiority, collapsed the differences articulated by Black religious practitioners, and implicitly questioned the lucidity of Black people's mental capacities given the pantheon of spirits, deities, folktales, conjuring remedies, and supernatural beliefs at the helm of Southern Black religious culture during the period of Jim Crow.

Yet it is also true that the FWP's massive archive is a treasure trove of these competing and complex approaches. It was through Saxon's relationship with Cammie Henry, who was a benefactor of many artists and writers during the 1930s and 1940s, that Henry later acquired some of the LWP's papers, specifically interviews related to ex-slaves in Louisiana. The religious and cultural experiences of the enslaved had been "salvaged" by the wealthy plantation owner before she eventually donated them to Northwestern State University of Louisiana, where they are now included in the Melrose Collection at the Cammie G. Henry Research Center in the Watson Memorial Library—a collection that this book largely grapples with and critically assesses using the tools of Africana religious studies.[100] To contend with these historical legacies and contingencies, the next chapter turns to the organizing of a group of Black religious practitioners who were politically

56   CHAPTER 1

and theologically radicalized at Congo Square. It considers the threat of lynching encircling their religious beliefs during the 1910s as a result, and how LWP staff writer Catherine Dillon invoked the anti-Voudou sentiment of the long postemancipation period in her 1930s report on these Black religious practitioners and their criminalized practices.

VISITATION 2

ZORA ON LYNCHING

When I suggest to our "leaders" that the white man is not going to surrender for mere words what he has fought and died for, and that if we want anything substantial we must speak with the same weapons, immediately they object that I am not practical.

No, no indeed. The time is not ripe, etc. etc. Just point out that we are suffering injustices and denied our rights, as if the white people did not know that already! Why don't I put something about lynchings in my books? As if all the world did not know about Negroes being lynched! My stand is this: either we must do something about it that the white man will understand and respect, or shut up. No whiner ever got any respect or relief. If some of us must die for human justice, then let us die. For my own part, this poor body of mine is not so precious that I would not be willing to give it up for a good cause. But my own self-respect refuses to let me go to the mourner's bench. Our position is like a man sitting on a tack and crying that it hurts, when all he needs to do is to get up off it. A hundred Negroes killed in the streets of Washington right now could wipe out Jim Crow in the nation so far as the law is concerned, and abate it at least 60% in actuality. If any of our leaders start something like that then I will be in it body and soul. But I shall never join the cry-babies.[1]

ZORA NEALE HURSTON

"SMOKE OUT THE NEGRO DEVILS"

Black Cosmopolitan Eclecticism in the New Century and the Terror of Lynching

The Reverend Albert Leon Antoine (also known as Abaline Antoine) was no stranger to the underworld as he had been a frequent visitor of the Voudou ceremonies so prevalent in Congo Square during the long postemancipation period. Some sources note that Antoine had been radicalized there at "the ancient camp of the negro," the area in the Tremé neighborhood of New Orleans where enslaved Africans gathered to practice slave religions and would perform the ring shout and other diasporic dances to the sound of African drums, banjos, marimbas, and gourds, as discussed in the previous chapter.[1] Antoine's religious commitments were not limited to the Voudou ceremony, however, and he would eventually become an ordained Methodist minister. He led a small storefront church on Carrollton Avenue for about four years, between 1899 and 1903 roughly, until local developers demolished the building to establish a railroad—a common feature of industrialization in many American cities during the Gilded Age. Given the policing and criminalization of Voudou and of spirit possession in the long postemancipation period, it is apparent that Antoine had strategically found ways to circumvent legal retribution for his non-Christian and quasi-Christian religious beliefs. Zora Neale Hurston's observation in the 1930s that "the Negro has not been christianized as extensively as is generally believed" reverberates as one consults the scarcity of sources related to Antoine and his practices.[2] Likewise, the historian Nicole Myers Turner rightly reminds us that during the nineteenth century, "Black religious folks found themselves negotiating with government agents and missionaries to undo the culture of surveillance initiated after Turner's rebellion," and they did so in many predominantly white denominations.[3]

It is likely that this sentiment resonated with Antoine, as it did with "gifted clairvoyant" Madam McNairdee-Moore, an African American woman who lived in New Orleans and gained popularity in the Black press during the period for her religious offerings even as she consistently described herself as "strictly a Christian lady [who] depends entirely on her heavenly gift."[4] One is left to speculate if McNairdee-Moore's Christianity, like that of Rev. Antoine's, functioned as a spiritual caul against police and authorities, especially as those "who [were] painful or ailing [or] think [they] have been witchcrafted" were encouraged to see her. As Antoine's ministry began in the Place des Negres, McNairdee-Moore is said to have "spent eight years in the jungles of Africa and [to have] traveled through 34 states doing good wherever she went . . . She reunite[d] the separated, [made] peace where there [was] confusion." Like his contemporary, Antoine was attentive to a world beyond the confines of Jim Crow New Orleans, one that connected him to the children of Africa—a connection he worked hard to maintain through his Black Atlantic religion making.

A Negro living in one of the most turbulent eras in American history in the afterlife of chattel slavery, Antoine, however, would not stay long in the white Methodist Church. While it is true that Baptists and Methodists often encouraged and licensed African American male ministers, these denominations historically opposed the abolition movement and supported white supremacy. As early as the late eighteenth century, for example, Bishop Richard Allen and his faithful followers left the white Methodist Church and formed their own independent Black denomination, the African Methodist Episcopal (AME) Church, to function on their own, absent of white authority.[5] By the late nineteenth century, many more Black Methodists would leave the denomination due largely to Jim Crow segregation and racial and sexual terrorism in the South.[6] Antoine was one of these Black Methodists, but he would not remain a traditional Christian, or at least his Black Atlantic religion making, like the Spiritual Baptists in Brendan Jamal Thornton's work, "challenged conventional articulations of Christian orthodoxy and Black Atlantic religiosity by reconciling a 'fundamentalist' Christian identity with an especially fluid cosmopolitan eclecticism."[7] In fact, Antoine began preaching a different kind of gospel, one that deemed white American Christians "devils" given their enactments of racial-sexual terrorism.

During the early 1900s, Reverend Antoine founded the Council of God (COG) in Algiers, the town across the Mississippi River from New Orleans. It was an underworld religious movement among people of African descent situated in the first major period of Black Israelite religious formation in the 1890s and into the first decade of the twentieth century, led primarily by members of the Holiness-Pentecostal movement (some of whom had also been Methodists).[8] In New Orleans, the COG engaged in a practice of "fluid cosmopolitan eclecticism" that firmly upheld their Black Atlantic religion making, or the combining of various theological, political, and philosophical schools of thought to engender their own definitions of race and racialization just a few years after *Plessy*. In her consultation of press writings about the COG, LWP writer Catherine Dillon, an Irish Catholic, concluded in her report, "Racial equality was the goal at which the cult aimed, but, as in the case of their conception of God and Eternity, their definition of equality was highly inconsistent. They merely wished to change places with the white people," and "eventually [wipe them] out."[9] Without question, the COG was a Black separatist religion charting its own racial destiny, and its practices call to mind the emergence of similar Afro-Caribbean religions, such as Revival Zion and Rastafarianism, that also creolized conventional biblical articulations and reconciled multiple racial, ethnic, and spiritual identities, including but not limited to Hindu traditions and New Thought. This chapter examines these developments and the subsequent policing, surveillance, and criminalization of those beliefs, which led to the lynching of the COG's members by white Christians during the early twentieth century, to further elucidate how the policing of Voudou in the previous century morphed into the policing of other non-Christian and quasi-Christian religions and the death of Black religious practitioners. In the process, many African American Christian actors colluded with state entities to survive during this period, which often meant that intercommunal conflict emerged at the intersections of race, class, and religion.

THE "QUEER" COUNCIL OF GOD

In its attempt to theologize its freedom, the COG looked to ancient Israelite rituals and practices along with emerging discourses among people of African descent in the Americas concerning race and the violence of white

Christianity in the afterlife of chattel slavery.[10] Indeed, its own conception of Black religious nationalism, or the Blackening of God vis-à-vis a theologized connection to the sacred geography of continental Africa—and the demonization of whiteness, white Jesus, and the white man—was a component of intentional attempts to cultivate and legitimize their own religion in the new century.[11] The group did not travel outside of the United States, but its theological purview regarded the gathering spaces of people of African descent as sacred geographies, in which its nationalism worked outside of the logics of "the nation" as conceived by white race makers.[12] By way of its Black religious nationalism, the COG also worked against Christianization by looking to other religious heritages, especially the symbols, theologies, and material cultures of ancient Judaism.[13] Relatedly, the COG's members regarded each day of the week as a feast day: "First Day, Feast of Canaanites; Second Day, Feast of Hittites; Third Day, Feast of Amonites; Fourth Day, Feast of Perizzites; Fifth Day, Feast of Hevites; Sixth Day, Feast of Jebusites; Seventh Day, Feast of Israelites."[14] Like other Black Israelite religions, the COG also rejected the racial designation "Negro" and called themselves "Hebrew," participating in what Judith Weisenfeld has described as "religioracial movements," though in an earlier period before the Great Migration, in which they endowed their Blackness with spiritual significance.[15] Sylvester Johnson also describes this period as marking "the rise of the black ethnics," which resulted in "a new religious order that asserted blacks were a people with peoplehood, with history and heritage that transcended the space and time of the American experience of slavery and racism."[16] With their religio-racial identities, the COG also challenged American historical chronology and reconceptualized the length of chattel slavery. Antoine preached, "The nigger has been praying for one thousand years and look how much they have gotten in return."[17] In his appeal to Judaic history and theology, Antoine was referring to the enslavement of the Israelites by the Egyptians.[18] To confirm the COG's religio-racial heritage, they declared "that the negro was the true Israelite, the real Jew, in whom all promises are fulfilled," and they performed circumcisions as a result.[19] In response to the Jewish Mayor Martin Behrman's public takedown of the group, the COG's members reasoned, "The negro's birthright had been taken from him by these persons professing to be Jews, who bought the name from the Pope of Rome at a time when he ruled the world! The black man labored under the curse of slavery because he had rejected and killed Christ," further supporting, in their Black religious nationalism, their heritage as Black Jews.[20]

European Jewish immigrants who emigrated to the city in the early nineteenth century, however, did not take kindly to these assertations, and they often partnered with white Christian state actors, as they "enjoyed a considerable degree of social assimilation and financial success and were extremely lax in religious observance."[21] Thus, the COG's criticisms of European Jews in the city and their claim to an ancient Hebrew identity was also a critique of the socioeconomic power ethnic Jews, like Mayor Behrman, wielded against religious practitioners of African descent, despite their own experiences of anti-Semitism.[22] Much of the tension between ethnic Jews and people of African descent in New Orleans also had to do with "the violent acts of incensed [whites] who were displeased with Jewish businessmen who hired black laborers or fellow Jews instead of whites."[23] Jews navigated these racialized and classed dynamics as they struggled to assimilate into white American culture, as they attempted to cultivate a uniquely American Jewish identity in light of their European heritages, and as they were often banned from exclusively white establishments. In light of these challenges, European Jews formulated their own high-class society, in which they created their own clubs, committed themselves to philanthropy, built schools, and developed international business networks in the pharmaceutical, fruit, and cargo industries in New Orleans, the West Indies, and Central America.[24] By the 1920s, these European immigrants would become "established Jews" living uptown, propagating an "authentic" American Judaism, occupying local political offices, and controlling a significant portion of the city's business district.[25] For people of African descent, many of whom had migrated to New Orleans from the US South, the West Indies, and Central America for new opportunities, jobs, and financial security, European Jews had begun holding their Black financial futures in their Americanized (white) Jewish hands.

These religious, racial, and class politics notwithstanding, Rev. Albert Antoine and the COG materialized their own movement in Algiers right alongside the Mississippi River, somewhere off Verrett and Lamarque Streets, and it took root "in the shacks of the congested negro sections and the shanties of the thinly populated areas."[26] The women were the COG's primary evangelists, spreading their message throughout New Orleans's Black neighborhoods. They would go from house to house telling of their dreams and visions. "They would say that they dreamed of a new life, full of all the beautiful things which the prophets had promised them. Some of the women would get out on the street and dance for hours at a time."[27] Like their Pentecostal sisters, the women of the COG used their charisma and the power of their testimonies to draw the masses. As members joined the COG, they took on the names of biblical characters, in which "the souls of the patriarchs of old [were] transmigrated into their bodies," and in their use of the language of "transmigration of souls," or the belief in a cycle of birth and rebirth, the COG drew upon Hindu theology in its Black Atlantic religion making.[28] Taking note of their cosmopolitan eclecticism, Dillon and other writers listed the following as members of the COG, in which they drew from the Hebrew Bible, the Christian scriptures, and the New Thought movement of the nineteenth century to rename themselves: Samuel E. Davis (High Priest Aaron), Edward Honore (Chief Butler), Marie Honore (Mother Superior), Jacques Pierre (Prophet Ezekiel), Ferdinand Boyd (Prophet Joel), Daniel Latimore (Apostle Paul), Robert Slaughter (Prophet Daniel), Alfred Zenon (Prophet Job), Thomas Manson (Apostle Peter), Mamie Graves (Sister Eve), Lottie Boyd (Sister Rhodia), David Major (Prophet Melanchia), Joseph Gaspar (Prophet Amos), Henry Boyd (Father Abraham), Sarah Randall (Mother Seriah), and Louise Woods ("claimed to be a Creole Catholic").[29] These names, along with their sexual ethics, ritual practices, and Black religious nationalism, confirmed their religio-racial identities as they continued working as laborers in the local economy and as active community members, according to the 1910 census. Weisenfeld contends, "Such performative assertions . . . disrupted the expected relationship between the surface of the body and race."[30] Through their religion making, COG's members refused white America's racializing processes and situated themselves as race makers.

Through their articulation of their religio-racial identities, the COG's members' Black religious nationalism took root in the underworld, and they contested all forms of white Christian supremacy, both Catholic and Protestant. Dillon observed, "After the singing, the negroes stood around discussing religion among themselves. Blasphemy against the white race, the Catholics, the protestants, Christians in general and wholesale profanity characterized the assemblies."[31] In her 1930s purview, she conceived of "the white race" as having divine sanction, making blasphemy possible and further upholding the sacralized color line between "the white race" and "negro devils." It is significant that Dillon, a woman of Irish Catholic ancestry, made such an assertion, resembling the rhetoric and hate speech of the predominantly Anglo-Protestant and anti-Catholic Ku Klux Klan.[32] In her use of such language, she effectively modeled white American Christian solidarities against Black people, despite various attacks on her own white ethnic ancestors by white Protestants. Intraracial allegiances in the service of white supremacy crystallized the white American Christian hegemonic state as the sons and daughters of planters, police officers, government officials, politicians, and the press collectively demonized and criminalized religious practitioners of African descent. Dillon and her white contemporaries co-constructed the color line and imbued it with religious and theological meaning. As the COG's members navigated this white supremacist terrain, they viewed the white Christian race makers as true devils and so-called gods and the world in which they dwelled as the Negroes' hell and the white man's heaven.[33] Dillon observed that for the COG's members, "heaven and hell were not places in the hereafter; heaven, occupied by the white man, consisted of earthly pleasure, wealth, ease and power; hell, inhabited by the negro, was comprised of the world's misery, poverty, labor and slavery."[34] The *Times-Picayune* also noted that COG leader Edward Honore had a "profound contempt for the whites and negroes of other religions."[35] Honore's "contempt" was due largely to Black Protestant collusion with white Christian race makers who also policed, surveilled, and violated Black Protestant church communities. The COG's members were surrounded by enemies on every side. The *Times-Picayune* noted, "The white people laughed at the preachings of the Council and looked upon the 'prophets' as schemers whose only object was to fleece the ignorant negroes of their spare nickels and dimes. The children in the neighborhood delighted in throwing stones against the house when the Council was in session, the black boys joining in with the whites in the fun."[36] Like most non-Christians of African descent, the COG's members did not feel safe, and armed self-defense was their salvation during a period of incessant anti-Black violence in which many African Americans kept guns in their homes.[37]

While the voices of the COG's members were often stifled by white supremacist caricature of their beliefs and practices in press, police, and popular accounts, the question remains: *What exactly did the Council of God believe?* One source entitled "Remarkable Creed of Queer Council of God" (fig. 2.1), published in 1907, appears to be the most reliable reprinting of the group's beliefs as they are said to have been found in documents seized by police from the COG's headquarters. The headline's invocation of the term "remarkable" and "queer" confirms Black feminist historian Sarah Haley's observation that white race makers invoked such language to describe Black embodiments and practices deemed unruly and excessive.[38] Moreover, press writers and the police were stunned by the group's bold and impudent "performed biblicism," or what Seth Perry describes as "biblically-scripted activity that is not repeatable nor defined by its notational repeatability. It is

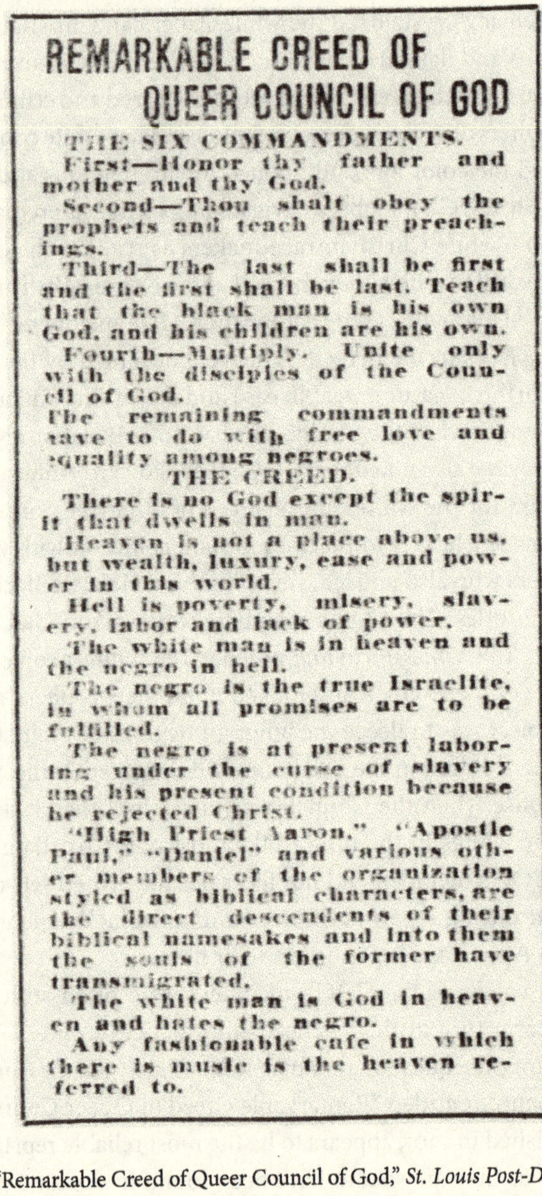

REMARKABLE CREED OF QUEER COUNCIL OF GOD

THE SIX COMMANDMENTS.

First—Honor thy father and mother and thy God.

Second—Thou shalt obey the prophets and teach their preachings.

Third—The last shall be first and the first shall be last. Teach that the black man is his own God, and his children are his own.

Fourth—Multiply. Unite only with the disciples of the Council of God.

The remaining commandments have to do with free love and equality among negroes.

THE CREED.

There is no God except the spirit that dwells in man.

Heaven is not a place above us, but wealth, luxury, ease and power in this world.

Hell is poverty, misery, slavery, labor and lack of power.

The white man is in heaven and the negro in hell.

The negro is the true Israelite, in whom all promises are to be fulfilled.

The negro is at present laboring under the curse of slavery and his present condition because he rejected Christ.

"High Priest Aaron," "Apostle Paul," "Daniel" and various other members of the organization styled as biblical characters, are the direct descendents of their biblical namesakes and into them the souls of the former have transmigrated.

The white man is God in heaven and hates the negro.

Any fashionable cafe in which there is music is the heaven referred to.

FIGURE 2.1. "Remarkable Creed of Queer Council of God," *St. Louis Post-Dispatch*, October 27, 1907, 7.

social, contextual, provisional, and, most importantly, ad hoc—behavior in lived circumstances that accords with an assumed biblical identity."[39] Drawing from "bibles," specifically the Hebrew Bible and other sacred texts, Black Jews in the COG theologized their own racial and religious identity, and did so in direct opposition to white American Christian authority.

"SMOKE OUT THE NEGRO DEVILS" 67

Albeit deemed "queer," the COG's guiding principles included "The Six Commandments," which mirrored the biblical Ten Commandments, along with "The Creed," which included nine statements further elucidating the COG's religious ideology and racial theology. The first commandment, "Honor thy father and they mother and thy God," combined the tenth and first commandments from the Hebrew Bible: "Honour thy father and thy mother" and "Thou shalt have no other gods before Me" (Exod. 20:2, 11). The COG's second commandment, "Thou shalt obey the prophets and teach their preachings," revised 2 Chronicles 20:20, which reads, "Believe his prophets, so shall ye prosper." The third commandment—"The last shall be first and the first shall be last. Teach that the Black man is his own God, and his children are his own"—drew upon the words of Jesus from the New Testament, and the COG's fourth commandment, "Multiply," aligned with God's command to Adam and Eve "to be fruitful and multiply and fill the Earth" as recorded in Genesis 1:28. The press did not reprint the COG's fifth and sixth commandments but claimed "the remaining commandments have to do with free love and equality among the negroes," thus mocking the COG's sexual ethics and their demand for equal rights during Jim Crow segregation.

The COG's "Creed" expanded upon the group's Black religious nationalism. "Heaven" was a social construction, "not above us" but rather on/in the Earth and it represented white people's experience of "wealth, luxury, ease, and power in the world." "Hell," on the other hand, "is poverty, misery, slavery, labor, and lack of power." They continued, "The white man is in heaven and the Negro is in hell." Given this lived, rather than soteriological experience, "The negro is the true Israelite" because "the Negro is at present laboring under the curse of slavery and his present condition because he rejected Christ." Although successionist in their approach to Judaic history, the COG's members believed wholeheartedly that according to white Christian belief, "the white man is God in heaven and hates the negro." In a world system where some individuals experienced hell on Earth, while others lived in heaven, the COG's members felt it their divine right to cultivate their own heaven on Earth through the demise of "the white devil" in their underworld work. These theological and political beliefs ostensibly situated the COG as a terrorist organization in the minds of state actors, even though it was Black folk who had effectively been terrorized by white racists.

Yet this one document, "Remarkable Creed of Queer Council of God," invites us to listen closely to the voices of the COG's members, even as the white supremacist press attempted to suppress and caricature their beliefs.

But what exactly did the members look like? *Who were they, really?* To date, I have recovered just one photograph of what the COG's members looked like—of their sacred, Black personhood in flesh (fig. 2.2). We are privy to this sole image, like we are to the COG's commandments and creeds, by way of Jim Crow capture and surveillance. Within this photograph, taken inside of the Fifth Precinct station in New Orleans, jail cell at rear, the COG's members speak back to us—through their stares and their postures and beneath the haze of over one hundred years. Here, Black feminist scholar Tina M. Campt's provocations in *Listening to Images* serve as a guide to ethnographic photos of rural Africans in the Eastern Cape and South Africa. She writes, "Their tense expressions of self-fashioning register quotidian practices of refusal—a refusal to engage the colonial, ethnographic, and missionary gazes that produced these photos and to allow those gazes to subsume their black subjects."[40] Moreover, in the same way that Saidiya Hartman has described early twentieth-century wayward women and girls, the COG's members likewise "refused the terms of visibility imposed on them."[41] Indeed, in the photo of the COG's members, their eyes stare back at their captors. They tell us that they are persons of African descent, the descendants of slaves, Negroes turned Hebrews living in New Orleans. According

FIGURE 2.2. Some members of the Council of God, from the *Daily Picayune*, October 20, 1907, 4.

to the 1910 census, some of them are migrants from Mississippi and other parts of the rural South. They emote from the space of carceral confinement theologies of survival during Jim Crow. Some wear long skirts or dress shirts and suit jackets, while others wear turbans. They tell us that their knives for self-defense, found at the COG headquarters—their underworld—were what the conjure bag meant to the rootworker.[42] Hurston observed as much, "Take an old razor, break the handle with dust and wrap it up. Bury the razor sideways with the blade up, and the police will never cross your gate."[43] All in all, they acknowledge, as many African Americans have, that they only do harm to those who have harmed them. One member says, "We don't believe in hurting anyone. Every person is alike to us. We want to follow our religion, that is all."[44]

THE CUTTING ROOM FLOOR
OF THE LOUISIANA WRITERS' PROJECT

In my attempt to find their voices and to see what they looked like—to revere them as persons who lived despite carcerality—the pens of their captors nonetheless hold them hostage. In their written assessment of the COG, for instance, the LWP staff—led primarily by Catherine Dillon with regard to many of their reports on Black religions—invoked white supremacist tropes to malign the group in their report written in the 1930s, in which they drew upon newspaper clippings and police reports from twenty years prior.[45] This section of the chapter uses the edits that went into their report to consider how Black Atlantic religions have historically been imagined and constructed in the white mind and in the minds of African American Protestants as part of legally sanctioned policing and surveillance during the period.[46] In images evidencing the report editing process, discussions about how to exactly characterize the COG filled the margins, crammed the lines between sentences, and sat in the spaces and marks underneath crossed-out words, phrases, and observations deemed inappropriate, question-able, or lacking substantial evidence. The LWP staff largely relied on white supremacist mainstream newspapers from the 1900s to 1910s, often to the point of plagiarism, to articulate their own deep-seated concerns about non-Christian and quasi-Christian Black Atlantic religions in the 1930s.[47] The result essentially authenticated the press and its white supremacist depictions and misrepresentations as a site for legitimate information concerning practitioners of African descent. Editors wrote in the margins, for instance, "Do the newspapers say this? If so, we should quote them. We cannot say so ourselves."[48] Ultimately, the parts that remained in the document and the parts that were crossed out each demonstrate the extent to which white observers of Black religions relied on the exaggerated form in their descriptions, even as the crossed-out portions show the LWP's reticence about publishing some of its ideas about people of African descent and the religions of Black people in the Americas.

While many of the actors discussed in this book who policed Black Atlantic religions in New Orleans were white Protestants, many of the white actors in this chapter were Catholic or of Catholic heritage.[49] Dillon and the individuals who would eventually lynch the COG's members were white Catholics living in New Orleans, a city uniquely known and recognized for its Old and New World Catholicity, within the greater Anglo-Protestant American South. Black Catholics also experienced racism in their local Catholic parishes.[50] Practitioners of African descent who were not Catholic or Christian identified faced immense challenges in practicing their religions in the context of this white Christian majority. The Catholic Church in New Orleans worked with government agencies, the press, and other non-Catholic Christian denominations to criminalize "negro cults and sects," specifically in their attempts to commercialize voodoo while demonizing Voudou's Black Atlantic origins.[51] Even as it appears that the COG did not practice Voudou and rootwork, its members did confess "the power to cure diseases and resist opposition," and their religious practices were nonetheless demonized in much the same way as Voudouists and rootworkers. In response, the city's officials "issued orders . . . to break up any [of their] gatherings which may be held in the city," deeming the COG "highly immoral and the teachings inimical to the public peace."[52] Despite the COG's creed and practices, the LWP's mischaracterizations are a central entry point into understanding how, on the one hand, they were titillated by the COG's Black Atlantic religion-making processes as Black Jews in the early twentieth century, and on the other hand, how "unthinkable"—in the Michel-Rolph Trouillot sense—it was and has been for the white American Christian hegemonic state and its actors to truly see Black religions as legitimate religions, as white race makers "devise[d] formulas to repress the unthinkable and to bring it back within the realm of accepted discourse" through hyperbolic ridicule.[53] Such a perspective negates the innovations undergirding these new religious formations among working-class migrants of African descent. For instance, one white reporter boldly confessed that the COG was an "alleged religion."[54]

Catherine Dillon followed in these press writers' footsteps. She maintained that this "new religion" enticed "a small group of followers, mostly free thinkers, easy dupes, and those who wanted soft jobs."[55] It was in the COG that many of these poor and working-class individuals found honor and recognition, however—whether it was through their newfound biblical names or in their ability to work within the COG's headquarters. Indeed, "despite the fact that Antoine had been evicted from an established church, and several times hauled into court for swindling and separating couples," as Dillon claimed, as noted in the below image from her essay drafts:

his strange sect, which was antagonistic towards all branches of Christianity, spread throughout the city.

The distinction Dillon drew in the 1930s between "an established church" and Antoine's "strange sect" aligned with the ways the police and other state actors of the early 1900s viewed Black Atlantic religions in the city. Antoine's constantly being "hauled into court" for allegedly "swindling" followers and "separating couples" who were encouraged to commit themselves to the COG's tenets around sex and marriage—specifically Antoine's call for all followers to forsake nonmembers as lovers and partners and to marry within the COG—stand as evidence. Dillon claimed, "The doctrine was a good thing, it dispensed with the usual necessary procedure in ridding one of an unwanted wife and was very liberal in its privileges."[56] It is highly likely that the COG, like many new religious movements such as the Oneida Community before it, engaged in "free love."[57] The *Daily Picayune* stated similarly, "The preachers advised members of the congregation to live in open adultery. They were allowed to discard one wife and unite with another. Polygamy was even practiced by the high priests."[58] One Creole man took the COG to court as the prophet's teachings allegedly "alienated the affections of his wife, causing her to desert him and permit his house to go to rack." The man claimed that "she sold the household effects and spent all of her and his money with the high priest."[59] Other doctrines of the COG were published, often in flippant ways, in newspapers following the arrest of several of its members, to portray them as licentious and hypersexual. Many Black religious practitioners during the early twentieth century were accused of founding "sex cults" and their followers confined to the same jail cells as queer people and sex workers.[60] These racialized and sexualized tropes were byproducts of the color line constructed in the long post-emancipation period and were also a result of New South plantation erotics.

Nonetheless, despite the COG's clear and concise articulation of its underworld religious beliefs, the LWP, the press, and the police maintained that the COG went about "having no creed." In her assessment of the afore-mentioned "creed," however, Dillon even wrote, and then crossed out,

> The Council of God's ~~had~~ six commandments, ~~were vulgar desecrations of estab-lished religious precepts.~~

She noted earlier, "Antoine established a church which was indiscriminately called Christ Hebrew Church, the Christian Jewish Church, and Christ's Council, but was listed officially under the Baptist sect, as Christ Church. Out of this Hebrew-Baptist congregation, about 1903, sprang a branch organization of ruthless, illiterate, unscrupulous negro fanatics, known as the Council of God."[61] Dillon's historicizing here, however, is replete with factual errors. The most significant one worth noting is that she conflated several different religious organizations—which had emerged in the late nineteenth and early twentieth centuries—with the COG. Antoine was also formerly a Methodist, not a Baptist. The second part of this book includes discussions about how these sorts of conflations were commonly made by actors employed by and invested in the white American Christian hegemonic state, and about how Black religious actors worked to distinguish their beliefs and practices from each other as a result. In her dismissal of the COG's own unique religious beliefs as a new religious institution, Dillon also mocked Black religious modes of communal honor and leadership. "One of the earliest officials of the Council of God must have been a disgruntled, minor house servant, who felt his inferiority keenly," she wrote. "The position of head butler seems to have been an enviable rank, higher than a prophet or an apostle."[62] Moreover, Dillon, like many of her contemporaries, recapitulated colonial, paternalistic ideologies of the Negro's supposed innate inferiority and of the Negro's inability to think critically for herself. For Dillon and the LWP, like the journalists of Antoine's era, Black people, especially poor and working-class Black people, were not a thinking people who could make their own decisions. These ideas were also common among middle-class Black Protestants—many of them Baptists and Methodists, who partnered with authorities to terminate the COG and to legitimize their own religions in the face of state violence.

Dillon described the COG's members as "diabolical" and as "devils," and her own white Christian belief that people of African descent were biologically inferior and lacking intelligence supported her wholesale demonization of the group. She stated, and again crossed out,

> ~~Not knowing the harm they were doing to themselves, they readily fell for the prophet's teachings.~~ The spread of the cult's dogma was such that black people from other sections of the Nation applied for instructions in the art of branch establishment. Soon three hundred or more members were actively at work gathering followers and disseminating the diabolical doctrines of Abaline Antoine.

In another instance, she noted, "Weird incantations burst upon the nocturnal air—shrieks ~~that seemed~~ born of a Satanic origin. The negroes seemed possessed of countless devils," a holdover idea from the long postemancipation period in which the formerly enslaved were said to be possessed by devils, as discussed in the previous chapter.[63] Ironically, in her attempt to malign the organization, Dillon proved Antoine's theological conviction that Negroes were living in hell on Earth through the routinized violence they experienced at the hands of white supremacists—whether by pen or by the lynching rope in the presence of the mob. To the COG's members, the very white devils they sought to confront were now calling them "negro devils."

These supposed "negro devils," like the Voudouists in the century before them, were like social contagions spreading a bad Black religion. In this regard, Dillon's sources note that Antoine's tenure as the group's leader had ended sometime around 1907 and that Edward Honore, "an elderly man, [with] a short-stubby, gray mustache" took over as the church's high priest, spreading a radical racial theology that challenged white authority. Honore "had a stand at the corner of North Rampart and Canal Streets"—New Orleans's booming market and entertainment area—where he "frequently held discourses and discussions with the colored people who visited him. He sometimes mounted the driver's box of his wagon and preached to limited congregations, but his addresses were short and terse."[64] Honore was just one of many street preachers in the underworld, peddling his own gospel and articulating his own Black Atlantic religion making on his own terms, and this prophetic tradition of street preaching can be traced back to slavery in which street preachers were accused of "trying to incite slave rebellions in New Orleans," as one press writer put it in 1850.[65]

To further explicate the supposed barbarism of the COG, writers also often penned vile descriptions of members' bodies and physical traits, deeming them "black ruffians."[66] The *Times-Picayune* described Honore as "the great, black negro, who has a head shaped like an ape."[67] In one instance, Dillon even wrote, "All of these fellows were desperate looking, brutal types, and while some of them were worse that they looked, and others not as hard as they seemed, altogether, they were a dangerous, menacing lot."[68] Dillon never saw these individuals from the 1900s to the 1910s with her own eyes, and twenty years later, in the 1930s, she exaggerated their features and depicted them as monstrous fanatic beings. These depictions were in line with the trope of the Black brute and were also rooted in Victorian notions of respectability. Moreover, they were directly connected to the hypersexualization of Black Atlantic religions, especially non-Christian religions, in the new century. White supremacists depicted religious practitioners like the COG as having "queer beliefs" and as performing "hectic orgies" during their religious services held at night.[69] Dillon went as far as writing, "When sickness prevailed in a home, the prophet would perform a wild orgy by the patient's bedside, shouting incoherently," echoing much of the white racial anxiety about the Voudou ceremony in the previous century.[70] And in her own inability to understand Africana funerary rituals, she wrote, "The solemnity of death was lost [in sensuality] in the wild orgy attending a Council of God wake and its uncanny [burial] ceremony. When a member died, his body was wrapped in a sheet and at midnight handed out the door to the undertaker."[71]

Although the press had already proliferated erroneous depictions of the COG and other Black religious actors across Louisiana and the nation twenty years before Dillon, the LWP's writers would exacerbate these descriptions in the 1930s. Indeed, in later portions of their report, they would use the murder of one white New Orleans police officer by COG members to exaggerate the COG's beliefs and to further portray the COG as a "black fanatic religion." Dillon drew upon a copy of the *New Orleans Telegram* of July 28, 1900, that the police found at Antoine's house, which "contained an account of the killing of Robert Charles, a negro desperado, who was stopped by a bullet after he had murdered and wounded several officers," further confirming white Christian anxieties from the 1900s to the 1930s about "the Black Jews' campaign of race hatred." State actors also used this "evidence" to support their claims about "negro religious fanaticism."[72]

THE MURDER OF ROBERT CAMBIAS
AND BLACK SELF-DEFENSE

No other event brings to light the extent to which the white American Christian hegemonic state actively demonized the COG than the racialized discourse that circulated following the murder of a white police officer by a few of the group's members. On the evening of October 18, 1907, at about 8:30 p.m., patrolman Robert J. Cambias responded to local reports of a "general disturbance [which] took place at #1906 Allen Street between Drier and Johnson Streets, occupied by Edward Honore and his wife Marie Honore, colored, where a religious council was being held by a crowd of negroes."[73] Dillon noted that prior to Cambias's visit to the Honores' home, the New Orleans police department had been surveilling the COG and its members, along with other Black Atlantic religious actors in the city, and generally approached these individuals with skepticism, due largely to the white supremacist belief that no good could come from people of African descent gathering in secret, let alone at night. Keenly aware of the inherent dangers of being approached by white men for such gatherings, the COG's members were alarmed and frightened by Cambias, who was "called upon to quell the disturbance and on reaching the premises . . . attempted to place one of the negroes under arrest." Honore, along with the other men, grabbed the officer, threw him down, and while one of the men "was holding him down, officer Cambias was cut across the throat, severing his neck and killing him instantly."[74] The police station somehow caught wind of what had just taken place at the Honores' house and dispatched several officers to the scene of the crime. "The officers ordered all negroes to surrender, the High Priest, as he is called by his Element Samuel Davis who had a revolver in his hand refused to surrender, saying that it would take a hundred policemen to take him to jail, after which a general shooting took place from the inside."[75] More officers were shot, as were some of the COG's members, yet the COG's members continued to stand their ground in self-defense. Some escaped, while others "remained and barricaded themselves" in the closets and crawlspaces of the house and continued to shoot back.[76]

To overpower their opponents, the police lit the house church on fire. "Smoke out the negro devils," they exclaimed. Dillon narrated the arson as follows: "A bucket of coal oil, paper and matches were brought and a torch was applied to a little shack on the Allen Street side, where some officers had been placed. It failed to burn, so a flame was set to the feather-edged fence near the Honore's gate. This burned slowly, but it put fear into the fanatic minds. A hole was [burned] in the fence between the little hut that was fired and the negroes' stronghold."[77] Once subdued, some of the injured members of the COG were taken to Charity Hospital for treatment, while others were carried to jail. "As the wagons dashed at break-neck speed through the surging throngs that filled the streets and sidewalks of downtown New Orleans," wrote Dillon, "the police [did] all they could do to prevent the mob from halting their progress and lynching the negroes."[78] Dillon fabricated the series of events, based on lies and old anti-Voudou tropes embedded in the press features she consulted from 1907. In this way, the police were actively supported by white race makers in attacking the COG. On the day of their capture, "the shots attracted the attention of a number of citizens, who hastened to the aid of the police with shotguns and revolvers," emboldened by their commitments to white supremacy.[79] One COG member, Dave Major, who hid in the crawlspace of the COG's temple, stated, "I was beaten by the crowd, and before the God of the white folks I was beaten for no cause whatsoever."[80] White race makers used their guns and the lynching rope in much the same way their forebears used the Bible to routinize Black submissiveness to white supremacist authority. "Shoot the nigger! Lynch him!" they exclaimed through the streets from their wagons.[81] This, they reasoned, was their divine right and duty as white Christian citizens in the Jim Crow South.

In the days following the COG members' arrest, the press and the police framed the COG as a cult that engaged in human sacrifice and used "the butchery of Cambias" as evidence. The *Courier-Journal*, for instance, wrote, "From the amount of cutlery in evidence it seems that while the colored brothers differed as to the efficacy of prayer, they agreed as to the efficacy of razors."[82] The *Indianapolis Star* stated, "The 'Council of God,' an order of negro fanatics, slashed Cambias with razors and held his would-be rescuers at bay."[83] The *St. Tammany Farmer* wrote, "While Cambias was struggling with his prisoner two negroes came up behind him, and knives or razors flashed in the moonlight. Cambias sank to the sidewalk, the blood gushing from a wound which severed the carotid artery, as well as the jugular vein."[84] The *Nashville Tennessean* went as far as to describe the COG as follows, drawing upon age-old, colonial tropes: "The religious fanaticism of the race, when at fever heat, takes on the savagery of its African origin, and constitutes a peculiar menace in the far South. It 'maddens to crime' with little difficulty."[85] Dillon joined the chorus, writing, "The Chief Butler wiped the blood from the crimson stained knife," and in her description of Cambias's body at the morgue, she noted, "The autopsy showed that the boy had died from a cut that had almost severed his head from his body, muscles, arteries and tendons having been slashed in the most horrible way that the coroner had ever beheld. Death had been only a matter of moments."[86] Notwithstanding the COG's denial of performing human sacrifice in their statements to police, the white American Christian hegemonic state continued to link the group to such allegations, and one newspaper even cited "fanaticism [as] the cause."[87] While it is true that Cambias was killed by the COG, he was not killed as part of a human sacrificial rite, but in self-defense. White commentators often made such claims against Black religious practitioners. Even observers of the case indicated that authorities noted the fact that "the murderers made no attempt to cover up their crime, but went calmly back into the yard, leaving the dead man on the sidewalk."[88]

Despite the plurality of practitioners' Black Atlantic religious practices, Dillon, while plagiarizing an article from the *Daily Picayune*, tried to make sense of Cambias's murder by re-presenting the same fictitious account of the group's sacrificial rituals found in a 1907 article. In the process, she recapitulated widespread anti-Voudou tropes for readers, writing, "The 'Burning of the Blood of the Dragon' was a curious custom of an especially dubious nature. 'The blood of the dragon' was supposed to be 'the blood of all non-believers.' The ceremony was usually 'performed' after the death of an enemy. None but the Council of God members were permitted to witness these rites."[89] Dillon's invocation of Voudou here aligned with mischaracterizations of many different Black Atlantic religions in New Orleans and throughout the South and the Caribbean more broadly in the early twentieth century. In another instance, she wrote, "The tactics of the old-time voodoo doctors were mild compared with the performances of the Council of God."[90] In light of these white American Christian imaginaries that painted the COG as a "cult" that performed human sacrifice and used "the dragon's blood of voodoo," we must consider the other conditions that led people of African descent to ultimately choose to kill white vigilantes and the police.

Given the pervasive reality of Jim Crow racial terror, the COG killed Cambias for fear that he would take their lives either by gunfire or with the lynching rope. In the early twentieth century, it was common for policemen and Klan members to lynch people of African descent, so much so that there was constant panic among African Americans regarding interracial engagement or confrontation across the color line. In 1897, for example, three African American men were lynched by a mob not far from the COG's meetings. John Johnson, Arch Joiner, and Gus Williams were killed by over 250 white men. "The latter they hung to a tree near the colored church . . . while Johnson and Joiner were carried back to the scene of their awful crime to be burned at the stake."[91] The men were accused of murder, assumed guilty, and never stepped foot in court. This lynching, and the thousands of other lynchings that occurred throughout the United States, served as intimidation tactics in Black communities, and as quotidian practice they instilled in African Americans a constant state of fear. Historian Grace Elizabeth Hale has contended, "As separation of the races became the foundation for white racial identity, black homes, businesses, churches, and bodies threatened to provide a ground of black autonomy that could challenge white supremacy. Yet lynchings denied that any space was black space; even the very bodies of African Americans were subject to invasion by whites."[92] Despite this context, some African Americans, like members of the COG, practiced and theologized self-defense and the taking up of arms, and so on that October evening in 1907, they chose to kill patrolman Robert Cambias.[93]

By killing Cambias, the COG effectively issued a warning to the New Orleans police department, and they spoke back to a culture of white supremacy where white people killed Black people with impunity. Antilynching crusader Ida B. Wells-Barnett observed in 1893, "Those who commit the murders write the reports, and hence these lasting blots upon the honor of a nation cause but a faint ripple on the outside world."[94] The New Orleans police department's characterization of the COG supported Wells-Barnett's claim. Indeed, Cambias, like so many patrolmen, was the son and grandson of Irish police officers and slavecatchers, who policed Black people and upheld white supremacy as a means of becoming white.[95] Cambias's maternal grandfather, John Crofton, was noted as "one of the most fearless men of the old police set" and "had [also] been shot in the discharge of his duty. His paternal grandfather, George Cambias . . . had attained the rank of captain [and] figured in countless thrilling incidents."[96] The night before his murder, Cambias had allegedly dreamed of "the terrifying sensation of being cornered by a band of desperate negroes," further evidencing his own internalized ideas of the Black people as violent, aggressive, and antagonistic to white men, especially the police.[97] Dillon noted, "His strange dream should have been sufficient to make a young policemen steer clear of dangerous negroes, and even avoid the most harmless black people, at least for a while. But with his indomitable will, Robert Cambias combined the fierceness of the French and a spirit of reckless daring handed down from his Irish ancestors, he could not be expected to let a little thing like a dream, quell his sense of the adventurous."[98] In similar fashion to Dillon's report, journalists heralded Cambias as a "hero" across the nation. The *Daily Picayune* described the officer as a "martyr" who died "in the religious war planned by the high priests of the Council of God."[99] At his funeral at the St. Peter and Paul's Church in New Orleans, Father Hanrahan conducted the service, the mayor gave words, and police officers served as pall bearers.[100] In the months following Cambias's death, a benefit ball was scheduled by the police department in his honor at Woodmen of the World's Hall.[101]

AFRICAN AMERICAN PROTESTANT COLLUSION WITH THE POLICE

African American Protestant clergy aided local authorities in their efforts to heroize Cambias and the New Orleans police department.[102] These ministers joined together to form ministerial alliances and worked with the police and other state actors in their mission to eradicate the COG and all other non-Christian inhabitants of the underworld. One journalist observed, "The police have been receiving information from the colored people of the neighborhood, and much of it has helped to make out a case against the blacks. The same feeling prevails all over the city. The respectable colored churches of the city are holding indignation meetings and adopting resolutions denouncing the teachings of the council and condemning the high priests and apostles."[103] By aiding government authorities, these ministers further developed their own process of Black Atlantic religion making and attempted to authenticate their African American religions—denominational differences notwithstanding—as legitimate in the eyes of the white Christian hegemonic state. It seems, too, that the ministers deemed the COG "blacks" and themselves "colored," further evidencing their attempts to distinguish themselves in ways not at all distinct from colorist politics in the Caribbean and Latin America. The historian John W. Blassingame has contended that distinctions along the lines of "color" or complexion among people of African descent in New Orleans had to do with "the association of color with a certain social class," with "most of the educated, refined, wealthy, and skilled Negroes in New Orleans [being] mulattoes" and "Creole Negroes" who spoke French, and often used the language barrier to distance themselves from darker-skinned, English-speaking people of African descent.[104] Moreover, as Walter O. Pitts has contended, Baptists and Methodists separated themselves from "working-class fundamentalist churches" and did not entertain non-Christian practitioners.[105] These colorist and classist distinctions played out in the lines drawn between Black religions in the city. To many African American Protestants, "darkies" were involved in the "cults and sects," while lighter-skinned Black people were among the Black Christian managerial class, policing dark-skinned Black people regarding their religious practices and their social and cultural behaviors. These lines were arbitrary, however, given the numbers of Afro-Creoles in the COG, and the numbers of dark-skinned African Americans in Protestant churches. Contradictions notwithstanding, mainline African American Protestantism was largely committed to preserving itself by upholding colorist, elitist, and anti-African sentiment in the United States.

Interdenominational meetings were the spaces in which these politics crystallized. The press noted, "Vitriol denunciation, untinged by Christian charity, was the keynote of a mass meeting of colored Methodists, Baptists, Congregationalists, Presbyterians . . . to warn the colored people against the heretical sects such as the 'Council of God.'"[106] At one of their meetings, for example, the AME Church presented its disdain for the COG in a resolution also presented at a widely attended meeting held at the Central Congregational Church in New Orleans.[107] They stated, "These fanatics do not represent the sentiments of our best people, but the lower element . . . We deplore their presence in our midst, for our best people stand for law and order and for peace and harmony between the races throughout the country. We stand for God for humanity. The motto of our religion is God our Father, Christ our Redeemer, Man our Brother." They continued, "We extend to the officers of the law our heartfelt thanks for their vigilance in upholding the law and in seeing that the offenders be dealt with according to law. We, as ministers of New Orleans, stand unalterably opposed to crime and will do all in our power to uplift the masses of our people and to banish ignorance darkness and superstition from our race."[108] The Colored Baptist Ministers' Conference of New Orleans resolved, "A dangerous and pernicious doctrine, under the guise of religion, has been inculcated in the minds of certain band of ignorant colored people . . . We condemn such a wicked movement, and call upon the various churches and Christian people of our city to take an active part in the dispersion of such a band of fanatics."[109] In line with the accommodationist leanings of other educated, upper-middle-class African Americans like Booker T. Washington (see chapter 3), the ministers "[invited] the co-operation of Christian teachers, ministers and workers of the dominant race," to aid them in the destruction of the COG and groups like it, effectively colluding with the white American Christian hegemonic state.[110]

In their maligning of the COG, Black Protestant clergy confessed their own anti-African and colonial theological commitments. Dr. C. V. Edwards, pastor of the First Baptist Church of New Orleans, went as far as preaching, "I believe the negroes had the help of the devil in working out the diabolical system. It teaches the negro that the white man is his everlasting enemy. The white man who lifted the negro up from the jungles of Africa, where he was eating with the monkeys, and gave him an equal position with him in the land. It teaches this man is his mortal enemy. You see how easy it would be to get one of this cult to cut the throat of a white man."[111] Edwards had actually also volunteered himself as an informant to the New Orleans police department and requested that he be allowed to listen to the statements of the COG's incarcerated members.[112] Another pastor even exclaimed, "This black man must look to the white man for aid. The blows of the infidels have not only been aimed at the negroes, but also at every intelligent and enlightened religion on the face of God's green earth," further evidencing the true motivations for the Protestant clergy's denouncement of the COG and the inhabitants of the underworld.

In some instances, these Protestants joined forces with Black Catholics to also demonize the COG, writing, "Resolved, That we, the colored citizens of Catholic, Methodist, Presbyterian, Baptist and Congregational denominations, in mass meeting assembled, do denounce said Council of God and his deluded followers as a menace to the community and our people and we do hereby pledge ourselves to support and assist the authorities by all lawful means in securing the suppression of said sect."[113] The ministers deployed an "us" (Christians) versus "them" (Negro fanatics) strategy to legitimize themselves in the eyes of the state. Dillon noted, "Black people gave some of the most damning evidence against the willy prophets."[114] In his work on Elder Lightfoot Solomon Michaux's collusion with the Federal Bureau of Investigation in its takedown of the Rev. Dr. Martin Luther King Jr. in the 1950s, historian Lerone Martin contends, "The Elder substantiated the Bureau's labor while authenticating his own status as the prophet of black Protestantism."[115] Black clergy in New Orleans used similar methods and were largely successful in securing their place in the rising Protestant frontier in the city. Indeed, historian James Bennett has similarly observed, "Black church members wanted to assure their denomination that they were orthodox, despite living in a city that teemed with Catholics and practitioners of voodoo and suffered from a reputation for moral laxity."[116] While Bennett is referring to African American Protestants' use of anti-Catholicism to validate their identities as American citizens living in New Orleans, it is important to note that these same clergy were particularly invested in eradicating the cults and sects in the Crescent City in order to safeguard their own Protestant churches. Many of them understood themselves to be fighting in the service of their civil rights amid Jim Crow segregation, by working with white officials and distancing themselves from "the cults and sects."[117]

Much of their success had to do with how the press and the police characterized Black Protestants, specifically Baptists and Methodists, as "intelligent negroes" and the COG as "some bad negroes," "a band of desperate negroes," "unlettered blacks" and "illiterate darkies."[118] This framing was about ethnicity, complexion, class, education, and socioeconomic status, but it was also about who was allowed to think intellectually about religion, or more pointedly, who was allowed to be theologians or theorists of American religion vis-à-vis Christianity. During the late nineteenth and early twentieth centuries, many middle-class and upwardly mobile African American men were afforded the opportunity to attend the nation's largely white-funded colleges, universities, seminaries and divinity schools—a privilege that set them apart from the unlearned and uneducated Southern Black preacher.[119] In 1902, for instance, the *Afro-American* reported that a "theological teacher" was sent from New York to "reach a larger number of preachers by systematic work in all the Southern States." The plan was for a meeting to be "called by circular addressed to the colored preachers, Sunday School teachers and officers of churches," in which they would collectively discuss sermons, scriptures, and doctrine at the guidance of the northern instructor, bringing about "a quickening of intelligence."[120] Such "instructors" would have certainly tried to reach the likes of Antoine and many of the Black church leaders throughout New Orleans.

Dillon, writing about this moment, favored the learned Black preacher over Antoine and the members of the COG, stating, "The warped mentalities of its degenerate leaders, throw-backs to or hang-overs from the tragic Reconstruction Era, directed the minds of their misguided followers towards the ultimate annihilation of the white race."[121] For Dillon, and her white forebears, education was thought of as a means by which they could tame Black people and unite them with whites. Of course, individuals like Mary McLeod Bethune, W. E. B. Du Bois, and Anna Julia Cooper contested these ideas through their roles in higher education as either school founders

"SMOKE OUT THE NEGRO DEVILS" 83

or teachers. What is striking, however, is that the COG engaged in critical debate about race and religion. The *Daily Picayune* noted, "Volumes of infamous literature used to excite and inflame the feeble minds of ignorant negro converts against the teachings and doctrines of enlightened religion were unearthed by District . . . There is no doubt in the minds of the police that the Council sent out missionaries to work among the lowliest negroes of the country and spread the teachings of the cult."[122] Despite tangible evidence of the group's intellectual practice, including its use of historical, philosophical, and sociological texts to understand "the social conditions of the negro race," the press, the police, and the LWP maintained that the group was made up of "the lowliest negroes" devoid of the ability to think for themselves or to engage in theological conversations among themselves. To these white spectators, only white people, and the Black people they shared intellectual space with, were capable of being a part of these discourses. The irony lay in the fact that even learned Black people's religious institutions were also policed by the state, and they, too, were victims of church bombings, lynchings, and other forms of white supremacist violence.

The lynching of religious practitioners of African descent, in the name of white Christian supremacy, was deemed a legally sanctioned antidote to "negro fanaticism." On October 18, 1909, the *Washington Post* published an article entitled "Why Divinity Student Became a Hangman." The article began, "Who has not at one time or another formed in their imagination some idea of how a hangman would look if they should meet one face to face? Yet how few have really ever seen a hangman, to know him for one." Such a query was quite absurd, given the prevalence of mobocracy in the American South in the early twentieth century. Nonetheless, the article featured Frank E. Johnston, a former Catholic priest and an executioner, widely known as "The Hangman of New Orleans." A native of Waveland, Mississippi, "a quiet seaside resort 50 miles from New Orleans," Johnston was known for "[inventing] a new kind of gallows—a kind that would not require a human hand to spring the trap." By 1909, Johnston had put forty-three men to death, two of whom were members of the COG: Jacques Pierre and street preacher Edward Honore.[123] Prior to their lynchings, the *St. Mary Banner* printed, "The negroes heard the news without tremor and said they were glad of it; that this was the white man's heaven and the negro's hell. When the execution comes off it will be the riddance of bad rubbish, and a few more like this one would not hurt."[124] Speaking of his execution method, Johnston noted, "I was successful in every case except that of Jack Pierre, the negro who styled himself 'prophet' of that organization of negro fanatics in New Orleans who called themselves the 'Council of God.' You will recall his case—convicted as one of the murderers of Policeman Cambias about two years ago . . . Pierre, you know, held the officer's arms behind his back while Honore, another 'saint' of the 'council' cut his throat."[125]

In his attempt to maintain law and order, Johnston sacrificed many lives to the state that employed him. He was not only an executioner, but a performer of human sacrifice.[126] Johnston, rather than the COG's members, was the true human sacrifice ritualist, evidenced by the press features of him boasting about his participation in lynching culture across the American South. Johnston was celebrated for murdering religious practitioners of African descent, while the COG's members were demonized for killing Cambias in defense of their lives.

Indeed, these conflations and hypocrisies undergirded Jim Crow, and white race makers deified themselves and demonized Black underworld workers, evident in the LWP's process of exhumation, in which they reopened a case from decades earlier and further sensationalized it utilizing anti-Voudou sentiment. By focusing in on how Dillon and her colleagues falsified information about the COG, this chapter has rendered visible the white American Christian hegemonic imagination, unpacking it as not only a furtive ideology but as a tangible entity and active force in the Jim Crow South. Sifting through the LWP writers' editorial process—with Dillon, a white Catholic, at its helm—not only exposes the inner logics of the social scientific enterprise as an extension of the police state, but it further confirms how white Christians—Protestant and Catholic—joined forces, together with European Jewish immigrants in the service of white supremacy.

Moreover, by assessing both the press and popular sources from the 1900s to the 1910s that were available to and ultimately plagiarized by Dillon and her colleagues during the 1930s, we can fully come to terms with the enduring legacy of the white American Christian hegemonic imagination and its pervasive mischaracterization of Black Atlantic religious practitioners like the Black Jews in the COG. For the COG, the plantation was only about fifty years at its rear, yet in the press features about their practices prior to their incarceration and lynching in the 1910s and also in the LWP's report in the 1930s, plantation nostalgia persisted, such that white Christians, like slaveholders, situated themselves as white citizens, and Black Jews as "negro devils" needing to be "smoked out," eradicated, and consigned to the gates of hell. These white state actors and vigilantes, however, would not only engage in these anti-African racializing discourses about practitioners of African descent, but they also simultaneously policed Black sexualities while sexualizing Black Atlantic religions and practitioners. By the 1920s, non-Christian and quasi-Christian practitioners of the underworld would have to reckon with this troubled legacy as they navigated a new frontier: Black sexual Victorianism and the politics of social respectability both marked by largely Black Protestants and white elites as a solution to the presumed urban crises of poverty, crime, and sexual passion in the Black slum.

VISITATION 3

ZORA EATS THE SALT

One must go straight out St. Claude below the Industrial Canal and turn south on Flood Street and go almost to the Florida Walk. Looking to the right one sees a large enclosure walled round with a high board fence. A half-dozen flags fly bravely from eminences. A Greek cross tops the chapel. A large American flag flies from the huge tent.

A marsh lies between Flood Street and that flag-flying enclosure, and one must walk. As one approaches, the personality of the place comes out to meet one. No ordinary person created this thing.

At the gate there is a rusty wire sticking out through a hole. That is the bell. But a painted notice on the gate itself reads: "Mother Seal is a holy spirit and must not be disturbed."

One does not go straight into the tent, into the presence of Mother Catherine (Mother Seal). One is conducted into the chapel to pray until the spirit tells her to send for you. A place of barbaric splendor, of banners, of embroideries, of images bought and images created by Mother Catherine herself; of an altar glittering with polished brass and kerosene lamps. There are 356 lamps in this building, but not all are upon the main altar.

The walls and ceilings are decorated throughout in red, white and blue. The ceiling and floor in the room of the Sacred Heart are striped in three colors and the walls are panelled. The panels contain a snake design. This is not due to Hoodoo influence but to African background. I note that the African loves to depict the grace of reptiles.

On a placard: *Speak so you can speak again.*

It would take a volume to describe in detail all of the things in and about this chapel under its Greek cross. But we are summoned by a white-robed saint to the presence.

Mother Catherine holds court in the huge tent. On a raised platform is her bed, a piano, instruments for a ten-piece orchestra, a huge coffee urn, a wood stove, a heater, chairs and rockers and tables. Backless benches fill the tent.

Catherine of Russia could not have been more impressive upon her throne than was this black Catherine sitting upon an ordinary chair at the edge of the platform within the entrance to the tent. Her face and manner are impressive. There is nothing cheap and theatrical about her. She does things and arranges her dwelling as no occidental would. But it is not for effect. It is for feeling. She might have been the matriarchal ruler of some nomadic tribe as she sat there with the blue band about her head like a coronet; a white robe and a gorgeous red cape falling away from her broad shoulders, and the box of shaker salt in her hand like a rod of office. I know this reads incongruous, but it did not look so. It seemed perfectly natural for me to go to my knees upon the gravel floor, and when she signaled to me to extend my right hand, palm up for the dab of blessed salt, I hurried to obey because she made me feel that way.

She laid her hand upon my head.

"Daughter, why have you come here?"

"Mother, I come seeking knowledge."

"Thank God. Do y'all hear her? She come here lookin for wisdom. Eat de salt, daughter, and get yo mind with God and me. You shall know what you come to find out. I feel you. I felt you while you was sittin in de chapel. Bring her a veil."

The veil was brought and with a fervent prayer placed upon my head. I did not tell Mother then that I wanted to write about her. That came much later, after many visits. When I did speak of it she was very gracious and let me photograph her and everything behind the walls of her Manger.[1]

ZORA NEALE HURSTON

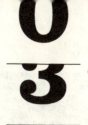

"MAKING A PLACE FOR NEGRO UNTOUCHABLES"

Black Sexual Victorianism and Its Counterconducts

In 1924, one press writer for the *Chicago Defender* exclaimed, "New Orleans Gets Dancing Religion," noting that a new "religious sect" had been founded in the Lower Ninth Ward by Mother Catherine Seals, formerly a cook and washerwoman, who called upon her new followers to perform "various forms of dancing, singing and shouting with an accompaniment of drums, bells, tambourines and guitars comingling simultaneously in an effort to 'make a joyful noise unto the Lord.'" These rituals, within Seals's "newly organized sacred order"—of which dance was a central feature—were described by perturbed neighbors as a "voodoo ceremony," and those same neighbors called upon the city police to ban Seals's crowded, loud services at the Temple of the Innocent Blood, also referred to as "the Manger," which commenced most Thursday and Sunday evenings at 8:30 p.m. and continued until the crack of dawn.[1] Other nights as Mother Catherine slept in "the Manger in an ornate brass bed . . . she conversed with spirits," as "an array of weaponless bodyguards watched over [her] as she slept. At midnight, as in the blaze of day, persons came to her to be prayed over and blessed."[2] The fact that those drawn to Seals were people of the underworld—sex workers, unwed mothers, pregnant girls, the homeless, and other discarded persons—did not help her cause.[3] Seals drew those who had been rejected by mainline churches, their families, and society writ large.

In many ways, the complaints about Seals's temple mirrored similar

FIGURE 3.1. Mother Catherine Seals leading her congregation, circa 1920s. Courtesy of Xavier University of Louisiana.

concerns expressed by African American Protestants in the infamous red-light district of the city—Storyville—regarding their proximity to the underworld and concerns about what said proximity might mean for their social respectability. For instance, Union Chapel AME Church's members contested the placement of the district bounded by North Robertson, Iberville, Basin, and St. Louis Streets between 1897 and 1915, and "Storyville was designed as a segregated district that would serve to quarantine the city's undesirable population of prostitutes."[4] Union Chapel's members felt that it was a particularly racist statement on the part of city officials to place "undesirables" in the vicinity of their Black Protestant middle-class community. Mother Seals's neighbors were no different. They were troubled by the idea that a haven, or as Seals described it, "a religious meeting of sinners," had been created near their homes and churches that affirmed "sinners," especially if the temple's ritualists reenacted the infamous Voudou ceremony with its spirit possessions, communication with African gods, and its reverence for the snake.[5] Writer Edward Laroque Tinker, who visited Seals's temple, joined the chorus, describing her services as having "the sound of whining sing-song voices, accentuated by rhythmic drum-beats having all the savage insistence of a Haitian *bamboula* calling votaries to Voodoo worship."[6]

Despite these sensationalist accounts and criticisms, Seals gathered anyway, and in her gathering she drew the masses. Among the many faith healers listed in the LWP papers and in the press in the 1920s and 1930s, Mother Catherine was featured most prominently. Observers took note of the aesthetics of her temple, the diverse people who followed her, her influence in New Orleans's Lower Ninth Ward and the ways she healed thousands, and the litany of criticisms of her by other faith healers who were often envious of her prominence. In the 1938 *New Orleans City Guide,* a book compiled and written by the FWP, Seals is not the only faith healer listed under "Some Negro Cults," but her feature is the only to cover over four detailed pages.[7] Nearly a century later, scholars have recently returned to her religious contributions, including Africana religious studies scholar Margarita Simon Guillory, and archaeologists like Danny Ryan Gray, who have simulated reconstructions of her temple or "Manger."[8]

This chapter situates Seals's underworld work as a counter experiment to Black sexual Victorianism, a social phenomenon of the early twentieth century, in which, "African American reformers, led first by women, addressed questions of sexuality in order to advance their own standing and, by association, that of the entire race," notes historian Christina Simmons. "To defend themselves and to demand resources from whites, they had to critique the original subjects of Victorian ideology—whites with power—to point out white oppression and moral hypocrisy, thus defining whites as 'other' while claiming a place for themselves as subjects within the Victorian framework."[9] The women that Mother Catherine ministered to were often on the receiving end of Black bourgeoise women's chastising in their efforts to clean up the race as a challenge to white racist ideas about alleged Black moral and social depravity. Thus, in her own way, Mother Catherine offered, as Saidiya Hartman observes of the women in her book, "different ways of conducting the self, directed at challenging the hierarchy of life produced by the colored line and enforced by the state."[10] This counter experiment, as Tinker also observed, required that all men be searched for guns and knives, so that she could keep the Temple of the Innocent Blood safe from all forms of intimate partner violence.[11] Seals provided shelter for women and children abandoned by unsupportive and abusive male partners and fathers, and she believed in protecting women and girls at all costs. The materials at the temple, including but not limited to Epsom salts, copious amounts of blessed castor oil, chicken bones, headbands with the inscription "M.C.S." (short for "Mother Catherine's Saints"), and various statues had been envisioned as defenses against the knives and guns used by men and the police as objects of patriarchal domination and racial-sexual violence.[12] The women knew to go to Mother Catherine's Manger, and their ways of knowing reveal women's interracial and intraracial networks of care and intimacy, and they also demonstrate how women faith healers centered motherhood, birth, and reproductive justice in their practices.

As Mother Catherine Seals—herself a survivor of domestic violence—taught a gospel that centered the lived experiences of those abandoned by the institutional church, other African American social reformers championed Black sexual Victorianism, which as Simmons has argued, "favored 'high' moral standards, sexual continence, the provision of basic venereal disease information, and the leadership of professional experts."[13] This chapter examines the development of Black sexual Victorianism in the afterlife of the long postemancipation period and considers the contours and nuances of this initially Anglo-American crusade led by sexual reformers in New Orleans, and eventually reinterpreted by middle-class Black Protestants, who attacked premarital sex, prostitution, and venereal disease, and associated these sexual practices and sexual health risks with the immigration of ethnic Jewish and Catholic Europeans into urban centers, and the presumed social debauchery of the Black poor and working class. Black sexual Victorianism was a Black Christian movement rooted in the demonization of non-Christian and quasi-Christian Black Atlantic religions such as Voudou, Hoodoo, Conjure, and rootwork in the new century. It was also a strategy developed among middle-class, mostly educated Black Christians to be regarded as American citizens in the afterlife of slavery. In New Orleans, the champions of Black sexual Victorianism included but were certainly not limited to the likes of Tuskegee Normal and Industrial Institute founder Booker T. Washington, who visited the city several times between 1898 and 1915; Washington's third wife, Mrs. Margaret Murray Washington, a writer and orator; and their close friend, Mrs. Sylvanie F. Williams, the president of the Phyllis Wheatley Club in New Orleans, a local chapter of the National Association of Colored Women (NACW). Each led the charge in proliferating Black sexual Victorianism as a Protestant evangelizing project and did so in opposition to the wayward evangelizing of faith healers like Mother Catherine Seals and the women and girls she healed, mothered, and protected. This chapter elucidates the competing interests of these different social experiments conjured by people of African descent by uncovering the implications of them for early twentieth-century racial, religious, and sexual politics in New Orleans and the New South. This is a significant intervention, in part, because Mother Catherine's "feats [were] discredited only by the negro unbelievers, the orthodox brethren who [relied] upon Sunday collections for church income."[14] Moreover, the underworld work of individuals caricatured as cultists is rarely engaged in conversation with hegemonic Christianity, even as Mother Catherine's work reveals that she was always conversant with Christianity—critiquing it and utilizing it to theologize her own religion.

MOTHER TO ALL KINDS OF CHILDREN

Born Nanny Cowans in Lexington, Kentucky, in 1887, Seals knew well the pain of violence at the hands of a patriarchal man. She had migrated to New Orleans at the turn of the century, and by the early 1920s, she was fleeing her third husband, an abuser, who beat her so terribly that he caused her to have a paralytic stroke, in which "one eye drooped shut, her mouth was pulled askew and she dragged one leg painfully."[15] In another account, "Physicking Priestess," published in *Time* magazine in 1931, the author went further into detail about Mother Catherine's assault, writing, "Some nine years ago [Mother Catherine] remonstrated with her third husband for his philandering. He kicked her in the stomach. The kick caused a partial paralysis."[16] In search of healing, Seals sought out famed white faith healer Brother Isaiah at the Levee who turned her away because she was Black, stating that he "was not treating colored folk that day."[17] She cried out, "Oh, Jehoviah, hear me! Sweet Jesus help me! Only [give] me [the] power [to] heal and I'll help [colored] an' white, jes de same."[18] After having received a vision from the Spirit, Seals was healed, received her own gift of healing, and was instructed by the Spirit "to exercise her power to cure people by touching them with her finger, by blowing her breath into their faces, and by permitting them to touch the hem of her skirt."[19] Seals had apprenticed with famed Spiritualist Mother Leafy Anderson, the founder of the Spiritual Church Movement in New Orleans, who utilized Protestant, Catholic, African and Indigenous religious traditions, especially her relationship with the spirit of the Native American war chief "Black Hawk," in her practice.[20] Seals split from Anderson, in part, due to theological differences and leadership tensions, and opened the Temple of the Innocent Blood in late 1922 at 2420 Charbonnet

Street, as a haven for Black and white women and their children. One fellow classmate of Seals at Anderson's church recalled, as noted by Margarita Simon Guillory, "Under Leaf Anderson we were supposed to wear white in class. But Catherine came into class one day wearing a middy blouse [loose fitting sailor-type top] with a red collar, which was against the laws, and they had a little misunderstanding. Then Mother Catherine left Bishop Anderson."[21] Seals, like many new religious leaders, came to the knowledge of her spiritual authority by way of a schism.

Before Seals's temple officially opened and before she accrued a massive following, the *New Orleans Item* interviewed her in March 1922 and published their findings in a piece entitled "Negro Woman Healer Plans Retreat for Life," in which Seals noted that she wanted to build "a specially prepared place—to which the afflicted of body and spirit may come, regardless of race or creed: for manifestation of her . . . power."[22] Seals had been conducting underworld work in her home at 2533 Jackson Avenue prior to opening the Temple of the Innocent Blood, and reporters observed, "She has a bale of testimonials from persons, including many white people, she says, who have consulted her and found her effected. She treated, she says, as many as 1,180 people in one day."[23] By the time she opened the temple, it was rumored, according to the LWP, that Mother Catherine had a following of ten thousand. According to the 1930 census, many of the members of Seals's temple, children included, lived with her or in the surrounding neighborhood, which substantiates Seals's claim that her followers not only looked to her for religious guidance, but they also looked to her as a mother.[24] She healed them by "touching them with her finger, by blowing her breath into their faces, and by permitting them to touch the hem of her skirt."[25] Another writer observed, "To her come whole colonies of negroes tormented by evil spirits which vanish at the laying on of her hands," confirming the efficacy of Seals's underworld work in that she knew how to discern a variety of evil spirits and command them to go or pass, and the spirits ultimately obeyed her.[26]

Seals's identity as a spiritual mother was central to this work. It was just as much a part of her Black Atlantic religion making as her drawing from myriad practices and traditions in her faith healing at the Temple of the Innocent Blood. In his description of Mother Catherine, editor of the LWP Robert Tallant wrote, "To enliven her performances, this woman preacher borrowed from the Baptists and Holy Rollers. The result of this pot-pouri was Mother Catherine's own special brand of religion."[27] The LWP's Catherine Dillon condescendingly described the faith healer's practice as "com-

"MAKING A PLACE FOR NEGRO UNTOUCHABLES"

bining freak religion, the hocus-pocus gestures of a tent show magician and the horse and buggy medicine man, with the forms that lay nearest her, [such that] Mother Catherine imitated Brother Isaiah, Mother Anderson, and some of the ceremonials of the Roman Catholic Church, which appealed to the black prophetess."[28] Tinker likewise commented, "Credulity in large doses entered into this weird blend of castor oil and Catholic ritual, but I sensed still another element. Certain details, hitherto overlooked, persuaded me that someone's 'blind faith,' probably Mother Catherine's, had been leavened with a healthy ad-mixture of shrewd foresight."[29] In stark contrast, Hurston, who had actually "spent two weeks with [Mother Catherine] and attended nightly and Sunday services continuously at [the Temple of the Innocent Blood]," observed, "There is a Catholic flavor about the place, but it is certainly not Catholic. She has taken from all the religions she knows anything about any feature that pleases her."[30] Hurston, a self-described agnostic who had been initiated into Hoodoo and Voudou by several practitioners in Algiers around 1928, confessed that in Mother Catherine's presence, "it seemed perfectly natural for me to go to my knees upon the gravel floor, and when she signaled me to extend my right hand, palm up for the dab of blessed salt, I hurried to obey because she made me feel that way."[31]

Matriarchal in her orientation and a healer woman who used the laying on of hands, blessed castor oil, and Epsom salts in her ritualistic practice, Mother Catherine believed that "it is right that a woman should lead. A womb was what God made in the beginning, and out of that womb was born Time, and all that fills up space. So says the beautiful spirit."[32] Seals, who had been kicked in her stomach by her ex-husband, centered women, wombs, and children in her theologizing and in her temple's cultivation of values, which nurtured sex workers, survivors of domestic and sexual violence, and women who needed help recovering from "coat-hanger abortions" or what Seals described as "the shedding of innocent blood"—hence her temple's name.[33] Mother Catherine preferred that women avoid abortions, or as Hurston observed, "Her compound is called the Manger, and is dedicated to the birth of children in or out of wedlock. Over and over she lauds the bringing forth. *There is no sinful birth.* And the woman who avoids it by abortion is called 'damnable extrate.'"[34] The fact that women who had or desired abortions still came to Mother Catherine for guidance suggests, however, that even in her personal disdain for the illegal procedure due to her theological beliefs, Seals cared about them and honored their reproductive choices.

While Seals's underworld work was prolific, she has for the most part been eclipsed by largely Black Protestant religious and social institutions in the history of social reform in New Orleans. Both historically and historiographically, African American Christian churches have been portrayed as successful institutions given how they encouraged Black men and women to be champions of Black sexual Victorianism during the era of Jim Crow. Yet this heteropatriarchal, class-based, and largely Protestant-centered metric of success often worked against institutions such as the Temple of the Innocent Blood and religious leaders such as Mother Catherine Seals. Even Hurston reasoned in her ethnographic account that Seals's faith healing "had no inner meaning to an agnostic but it did drive the dull monotony of the usual Christian service away. It was something, too, to watch the faith it aroused in her followers."[35] Women and men experienced spirit manifestation at the laying on of Mother Catherine's hands, and some even had visions, or were healed of various ailments—internal and external to the eye. It was through the Spirit that Mother Catherine Seals healed, and she admonished her seeking followers and other curious spectators, "Don't doubt me. Go home in faith and pray," that they might cultivate their own personal religious practices.[36]

In figure 3.2, most likely taken by celebrated Afro-Creole photographer Arthur Bedou (a working-class man who often failed to receive credit for his work), Mother Catherine Seals stands flat footed, staring into the distance, and adorned with a colorful, self-designed robe affixed with an image of Jesus that intentionally resembled the stylized Vodou *drapo*, evidencing her myriad, diasporic influences and her relation to New Orleans's vibrant Haitian community.[37] The image mirrors the stylistic choice of Bedou's other photographs for Booker T. Washington and Tuskegee, in which he skillfully depicted "scenic, sepia-toned vistas of a tranquil campus."[38] While Bedou often depicted "Washington's power as orator" in which the school founder wore "a business suit as a secular foil for religious dress," here he depicts Mother Catherine as the messianic embodiment of the rehabilitation her women followers sought and ultimately received, in that Seals is quite literally wearing Black Jesus on her body as she preaches, embodying the Divine.[39] Indeed, her robe bears the face of Black Jesus with "hair like lamb's wool," confirming as Hurston observed, "that Mother Catherine takes her stand as an equal with Christ."[40] Moreover as one *Time* press writer observed, her women followers "prayed to a vast, crudely carved Jesus, who was black because the Scriptures did not say that he was not black."[41] Indeed, "Mother Catherine was not converted by anyone. Like Christ, Mohammed, Buddha, the call just came. No one stands between her and God."[42] At the

FIGURE 3.2. Mother Catherine Seals, circa 1920s, presumably by Arthur Bedou. Courtesy of Xavier University of Louisiana.

same time, however, Seals's faith healing was not in competition with Jesus, but she viewed Jesus as a spiritual ally. Tinker recorded her as saying in one of her sermons, "De Lawd Jehoviah done tole Mother Catherine Seals a secret, an' she done pray over dis oil. I ain't goin' tell yer what de Lawd tole me to say, cause den you know as much as me. But de spirit of sweet Jesus done enter [into] dis oil an wid de he'p of de Lawd it sho' goin' chase yo' misery."[43] Likewise, LWP workers observed that Mother Catherine told her followers that when she received her call to the ministry, the Spirit told her, "Great things I am doing, but greater things you shall do," echoing the words of Jesus found in John 14:12, which reads, "Verily, verily, I say unto you, He that believeth on me, the works that I do shall he do also; and greater works than these shall he do; because I go unto my Father."[44] Mother Catherine's religious artistry, especially her "Jehovah God" statue, her "Key to Heaven" sculpture ("a large, gilded key, decorated with a bow of ribbon"), and her inclusion of the Roman Station Liturgy creatively etched on the walls of her temple, as shown in figure 3.4 below, also encapsulated her meticulous engagement with the Christian faith.[45] In this vein, Mother Catherine embraced a hermeneutical approach to the Bible, especially the words of Jesus, in her cultivation of her own ministry, even as Christianity was not the singular ordering apparatus of her theological belief or of her preaching, ministering, and healing in the underworld.

In fact, Seals spent a great deal of time church hopping and exploring the diverse religious marketplace of the city before she founded the Manger. In 1927, she told press writer Marguerite Young, for example, "Oh, I was pert when I was young, I joined all the churches, but none of 'em used to like me, cause I used to teach them. I wasn't studying 'bout Sweet Jesus then; I belonged to the world. But just the same I used to tell the people in the churches, 'I'se going to build me my own church one of these days.' I used to be a hairdresser too, and a massager."[46] Seals's mention of herself as a hairdresser may have called to mind for her listeners the memory of Marie Laveau and signaled that she was a kind of spiritual descendant of the famed Voudou queen as many other women practitioners did in the early twentieth century.[47] By self-authenticating her own spiritual gifting through a rhetoric of legitimation and legacy, Seals also self-identified herself as a wayward woman who spoke back to powerful religious institutions and asked questions that Negro women were not supposed to ask. Her waywardness was "a practice of possibility at a time when all roads, except the ones created by *smashing out*, [were] foreclosed. It [obeyed] no rules and [abided] by no authorities. It [was] unrepentant. It [trafficked] in occult visions of other worlds and [dreamed] of a different kind of life."[48] Seals opened her Manger in the cypress swamps on the outskirts of the city and beckoned those seeking "a different kind of life" to be healed in order to conjure a world where women were not subject to heteropatriarchal domination, where Black people were not the slaves of white people, and where children were honored as life forces, upon which this new world would ultimately thrive. The faith healer and reverend mother told Hurston, "I got all kinds of children, but I am they mother. Some of 'em are saints; some of 'em are conzempts (convicts) and jailbirds; some of 'em kills babies in their bodies; some of 'em walks the streets at night—but they's all my children. God got all kinds, how come I cain't love all of mine? So says the beautiful spirit."[49] Seals's underworld work was a direct counter to the objectives of Black social reformers like the Washingtons who often demeaned and chided Seals's wayward children, ultimately maligning her as an unfit Black mother who glorified the underworld.

MOTHER CATHERINE'S COMPETING INDUSTRIALISM

Before Afro-Creole photographer Arthur Bedou met Mother Catherine Seals in the Industrial Canal, however, he had been commissioned by Booker T. Washington to be one of the official photographers for the Tuskegee Normal and Industrial Institute in 1903, just after Washington had reviewed photographs Bedou took at a conference held at the school that same year. A native New Orleanian, Bedou had most likely been following Washington, who began visiting the city in 1898, and used his association with the leader to gain visibility. After all, wherever and whenever Booker T. Washington lectured, there was a packed house with every pew filled and all eyes on him. In advance of one of his visits in 1899, organized by the Longshoremen's Protective Union Benevolent Association, for example, the *Times-Picayune* publicized his lecture, noting, "[Washington] has been speaking, lecturing, and earnestly trying to promote the advancement, in a dignified, conservative way, of the colored race in this country. He is called the Moses of the negro race and he is idolized by his congeners, besides being very favorably looked upon by the white people."[50] In what would be one of many appearances in the Crescent City between 1899 and 1915, Washington reemphasized ideas from his highly contested 1895 Atlanta Compromise Address, in which he called for African Americans, northern white capitalists, and the white leaders of the New South to form an alliance. To crystallize this relationship, Washington argued that African Americans should accept disenfranchisement temporarily with the hope of eventually benefiting from northern investments in Southern life and culture at the dawn of the new century. Canadian American writer James Creelman, correspondent for the *New York World*, wrote of Washington, "A Negro Moses stood before a great audience of white people and delivered an oration that marks a new epoch in the history of the South, and a body of Negro troops marched in a procession with the citizen soldiery of Georgia and Louisiana." Washington's face, he noted, was "lit up with the fire of prophecy."[51]

At his address in New Orleans just four years later, Washington shifted the tenor of his speech. He was no longer talking to an audience of white men and women, but to Black New Orleanians who had invited him to share his philosophy on race, theology, and politics. The press observed, "The central idea of his address last night was, 'The negro problem in the south; his solution [included] teaching the negro to be self-supporting before aspiring to become an individuality in the community in which he lives.'" New Orleans's white mayor, Walter C. Flower, endorsed Washington's lecture, exclaiming to the mostly all-Black Protestant audience, "He has done the most earnest work on behalf of his people, and the seeds he has sown will live, teaching the colored people the lessons of thrift and industry, inculcating the principles of true citizenship."[52] The white mayor's endorsement of Washington, a guest of the city, stood in stark contrast to his disdain for and policing of the humanitarian and healing work of members of the "Negro cults and sects," like Mother Catherine and the Council of God, who had committed their lives to a different kind of rehabilitation.

In this vein, given the nature of Washington's complicated interracial class politics, he has been characterized by historians and in popular discourse as either an accommodationist to white leaders or as an integrationist, begging for whites and African Americans to come together, and debates concerning these categorizations have prevented in-depth analysis of Washington's complexities or of the ideas he believed and espoused. Washington was at once respected and despised by individuals across the color line. Michael Scott Bieze and Marybeth Gasman have observed in *Booker T. Washington Rediscovered*, "That he is simultaneously well known and completely unknown should raise questions about how we have judged him. Today, few people remember why he is famous, and he suffers the unenviable fate of being spoken for by a long list of detractors who cherry-pick from a mountain of writings."[53] Moving away from this tendency, the sources examined here show Washington as a Black Atlantic religion maker who wove together a conservative diagnostic assessment of Black sexuality and Black religion in the early twentieth century, ultimately influencing other Black Atlantic religion makers in the greater New Orleans region and the New South.[54] As a result, Washington effectively developed a network of Black social reformers committed to the Protestant work ethic and in professional relationships with white philanthropists, reformers, and politicians in both the New South and the urban North.[55] While historians have been obsessed with trying to solve the mystery of Washington as a singular authoritative figure in concert with other Black male leaders and white politicians, in order to truly make sense of his complexities and understand the larger implications of Washington as both an idealogue and an ideology, we must pay attention to his network—friends and enemies alike. Thus, the focus here is on Black club women who sought professional partnerships with him and non-Christian and quasi-Christian religious practitioners, whose lives and institutions served as direct counternarratives to Washington's totalizing mischaracterizations of Black people living in urban centers such as New Orleans.

For example, Hurston, who spent time documenting Mother Catherine's religious interventions and whom literary scholar Farah Jasmine Griffin has described as "occup[ying] a unique position that eschews social conservatism while embracing political conservatism even as she advance[d] a protofeminist and anticolonial politics," embraced Washington's political complexity.[56] In her encyclopedic 1947 entry, "The Negro in the United States," for example, Hurston praised Washington for "making a place for 'Negro untouchables,'" in ways that W. E. B. Du Bois—who denied her request for a Negro cemetery—had not.[57] In some sense, Hurston saw connective tissue between herself, Mother Catherine Seals, and Washington—suggesting that the complexities of Black social life necessitated careful and critical engagement and consideration, and that ultimately, the lived experiences of the Black poor and working class demanded coexistent methods on a spectrum of reform to conjure and materialize societal transformation, healing, and communal protection in and beyond the underworld. After all it was Mother Catherine who told Hurston, just as she had told her followers, "Don't teach what the apostles and prophets say. Go to the tree and get the pure sap and find out whether they were right."[58] Taking seriously Mother Catherine's admonition, especially as Washington has been valorized as one of many Black messiahs or political voices in African American history, we must get to the heart of how Black social reformers like him and faith healers like Mother Catherine Seals offered competing, though at times overlapping, solutions to Black social depravity, thus underscoring how the "rightness" of these respective social experiments depended largely on the constituents engaged and the respective needs met.

In this regard, the political and religious landscape of New Orleans was certainly fitting for Hurston's ethnographic inquiries, just as it was for Washington's political project in the city center and Seals's underworld work in the swamps. In fact, New Orleans was arguably one of the professor's favorite destinations. Washington, who emphasized "harmony between the races" in 1899, called upon African Americans in the city to "lay the foundation of the negro in education, property, thrift, skill and Christian character and in the friendship of those among whom he lives, and all the needs and rights of the race will, in due time, adjust themselves about these essentials in a logical and natural order."[59] Using Tuskegee as a model and explicating the school's founding and successes since 1881, the famed orator went on to name the stakes of his political worldview. "As a race we want to do everything in our power to see that the moral and educational status of the race is raised so high," he claimed, "as to make impossible many of the brutal crimes charged against us, and the best white people should make an effort to see that all persons charged with crime are given a fair and legal trial."[60] Washington was immensely optimistic of white Southerners' ability to align with the Black freedom struggle, even as antilynching crusader Ida B. Wells-Barnett's *The Red Record* (1895) stood as evidence of what she called an "awful barbarism ignored" by Southern whites. By 1904, however, Washington would pen "A Protest against the Burning and Lynching of Negroes," following the murder of three African Americans. He observed, "All of these burnings took place in broad daylight and two of them occurred on Sunday afternoon in sight of a Christian church."[61]

Reflecting his lecturing, or more aptly, his preaching to Black Southerners about respectability, race pride, industry, property, and the importance of theological education and sexual purity, the *Times-Picayune* described the professor as "Rev. Booker. T. Washington" on two separate occasions, the *Southwestern Christian Advocate* styled him the "Apostle of Industrial Education," and William Anthony Aery of the Hampton Institute called Washington "a missionary junket carrying the gospel of co-operation, educational and economic, to black folk and white."[62] As his observers noted, Washington was invested in "Christian morality," and it undergirded his lecturing to Black people throughout the American South. In 1905, for example, Washington penned, "The Religious Life of the Negro," in which he described Black Atlantic religions as "primitive" manifestations of "fetichism." The famed orator continued, "The Negro came to America with the pagan idea of his African ancestors; he acquired under slavery a number of Christian ideas, and at the present time he is slowly learning what those ideas mean in practical life. He is learning, not merely what Christians believe, but what they must do to be Christians."[63] In his theologizing, Washington minimized Black religious survival strategies during the era of Jim Crow and signaled his familiarity with the discourse on "fetichism" circulating during the period as a means of authenticating his own modernism and asserting himself as an equal to other intellectuals debating "world religions" in the early twentieth century, largely through the exclusion of Black and Indigenous peoples.[64] In this way, Washington was concerned with what it would take for Black people "to be Christians" in light of the pressing "Negro problem," or the insistence by whites and Black elites that Black people were *a problem people*, and not necessarily *a people with problems* caused by enslavement, white supremacy, poverty, and racialized sexual terrorism. Mother Catherine took a different approach. She reckoned that *people with problems* who had been deemed *a problem people* came to her seeking solutions and healing from those social problems and that the Spirit had anointed her to heal and provide solutions. Hurston rightly observed, "unlike most religious dictators [she did] not crush the individual. She [encouraged] originality" and her Manger "had an air of gaiety."[65] Moreover, while Washington and other Black social reformers would have reprimanded young, unwed women and girls for having premarital sex or becoming pregnant, one of Mother Catherine's followers observed, "She was always taking people in who had no place to go and no one to help them . . . She always had girls who had babies, or were going to have babies, and had no place to go, or their husbands had left them."[66]

In figure 3.3, for instance, Mother Catherine is adorned in a white-and-black robe holding a trombone. As a spiritual mother and trombonist, she stands bidding those in the underworld singing and playing jazz, the then-maligned musical genre, to come worship at her temple, and they did. As noted by New Orleans native Kristina Kay Robinson, "Early jazz musicians like Ernie Joseph Cagnolatti, Harold 'Duke' Dejan, and Frank Lastie all played in the Temple of Innocent Blood's services. Lastie, who also played with Louis Armstrong in the Waif's Home band, went on in the early 1940s to become a deacon for another congregation, that of the Guiding Star Spiritual Church, where multiple jazz musicians would find their footing while pursuing professional careers in music."[67] A noted jazz musician herself—who had one of the largest jazz funerals in the city's history in 1930 and had been inspired by Mother Anderson's jazz services—Mother Catherine stared into the photographer's lens, almost as if she was preparing to lift up her voice as a trumpet, to cry aloud against the sins of social reformers like Booker T. Washington, who had spent decades demonizing the practices of underworld workers like her and her children.[68]

In contrast to Washington's industrial institution and its contradictions, the Temple of the Innocent Blood was an industrial masterpiece in its own right. One writer described it as "an inexplicable freak of geography."[69] It was couched in the Industrial Canal, offering women and children an architectural covering away from patriarchal hands so often meant to beat and afflict them. Mother Catherine, who had experienced the pain of being hit by a

FIGURE 3.3. Mother Catherine with her trombone, circa late 1920s. Courtesy of Xavier University of Louisiana.

man, enlisted the help of trusted male followers to build the Manger, and she was its chief architect, mapping out the blueprint for its construction. She recalled, "De Lawd tol' me to have a twelve boarded fence round ma Manger but de contractors give me only ten. Ah's been gypped."[70] LWP writers elaborated in the *New Orleans City Guide* that "Each 'boad' represented a nation. The extraordinary height of the church fence was intended to keep curious persons off the grounds. The Manger is sixty feet long, fifty feet wide, and can accommodate 300 people . . . It was planned in minute detail by Mother Catherine herself. She even made most of its statues and painted the pictures that adorned its walls."[71] A follower of Mother Catherine by the name of Mrs. G. LeGallais confirmed the above to a LWP staff member in May 1940, noting in detail, "Mother Catherine's foundation sprawled in unattractive unity of bare grounds and ugly buildings. Once woods crowded

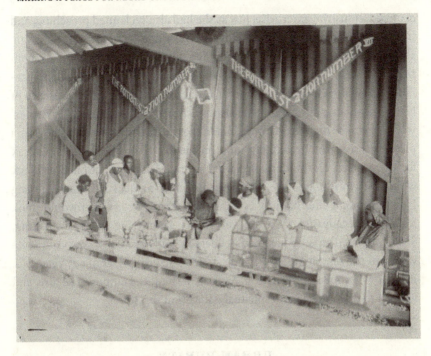

FIGURE 3.4. Mother Catherine Seals (at center left) performing underworld work, circa 1920s. Courtesy of Xavier University of Louisiana.

in luxuriant verdancy to river's edge, where now a few scrub trees shrugged gnarled branches disdainful of environment. Recently put on the market, this section lacked the picturesque disorder of the older negro centers ... These crude buildings erected with one end in view, utility, straggled without location, plan, or grace of architectural design. This experiment in miracles was in outward semblance twin to experiment in some new industrial enterprise."[72]

Mother Catherine, like so many Black women religion makers and underworld workers of her generation, built beauty amid desolation and created a feast for all with the scraps left for Negroes in the slums. Unlike Washington's Tuskegee, her industrial project was in the service of building spaces of communal wholeness and safety—a Black New Orleanian Spiritualist ritual of social reform.[73] Seals countered Washington's call to use the head and hands to prevent the judgment of whites, who would judge all Negroes the same, leaving select seats at the proverbial table for just a few Negroes who dressed and sounded like Washington in that they had distanced themselves from the slums. Moreover, Seals had reclaimed the male-centered industrial enterprise, just as she had also reclaimed preaching, and in so doing, she offered an alternative to Washington's industrial campaign, situating working-class women as architectural diviners "making a way in the wilderness, and rivers in the desert," as told by the biblical prophet Isaiah. And while it is said that Mother Catherine declared in the presence of New Orleanian elites, whom she also welcomed at the Manger, "In de nex' worl' Ah will be high up in things, but in the things of dis worl', Ah knows ma place," she asserted herself as a mouthpiece for those who could not speak for themselves. Her underworld work at the Manger functioned as Black womanist worlding before such practice had a name, such that a seeking Hurston sought after her just as womanist writer Alice Walker would "look for Zora" decades later.[74] Moreover, in her sanctifying and placemaking, Seals cultivated girls' and women's leadership and spiritual power. One white visitor to the temple noted, "Inside stands a negro girl, about 15 years old. It is she who opened the gate."[75] As Seals healed, she empowered girls and women to open the gate to spiritual edification for others.

URBAN PURITY

Mother Catherine's Manger as an industrial, Black Atlantic religion making project brought together those on the literal and imagined outskirts of New Orleans society. In contrast, Washington, a sought-after leader of the elites, drew those seeking the same kind of political power and public recognition he held. Indeed, Washington's moralizing and his investments in Black sexual Victorianism colored his leadership and his recruitment efforts and engagement with Black working-class urbanites in cities across the United States, where he thought that the "moral weakness of the race" was the result of idleness, the lack of a Protestant work ethic. In an evening talk to Tuskegee students on May 13, 1900, Washington stated, for instance, "Too large a proportion of our men, as you will see in such cities as Washington, Atlanta, New Orleans, are idle people and making a dishonest living. A large number of these men get their living by women working and feeding them."[76] Washington's conception of "idleness" invoked images of the underworld and was connected with his ideas about agriculture and industrial education, but it was also about Victorian ideas concerning manliness, manhood, womanliness, womanhood, and the civilizing processes undergirding each of these social constructions.[77] Black queer theorist Roderick Ferguson deftly characterizes Washington's patriarchally informed moralizing and its class inferences in his discussion of racialized sexuality as a form of Foucauldian governmentality. He writes, "The black middle class, as Washington avers, would inherit modernity by adhering to gender and sexual propriety. That is, the black middle class would be the first U.S. model minority, championing civic ideals around industry, citizenship, and morality."[78] These commitments, imbricated in their Victorian racialized sexuality and moralizing discourse, were also attempts to routinize the Black heteropatriarchal family at a time when white Americans considered Black women "jezebels" and "mammies" (holdovers from the plantation's "nasty wench"), and they considered Black men "black brutes" and rapists lusting after white women. In this vein, Ferguson rightly underscores how, for Washington, "industrial education [w]as the name of an alliance between sexual normativity and citizenship," in which young Black women and men were trained to use their hands in the service of gendered roles and to evidence their Christian morality.[79] Moreover, in Washington's and other sexual Victorian crusaders' purview, Black men were expected to be providers, and Black women were supposed to solely be concerned with the domestic sphere as good wives and good mothers. As the men heralded their own industrial education, Mother Catherine kept proclaiming again and again, "It is right that a woman should lead."

The image of National Urban League (NUL) members in New Orleans captured by Arthur Bedou around 1919 (fig. 3.5), four years after Washington's death, confirms the racialized gender training inherent in the project of Black sexual Victorianism. Suit-and-tie-wearing Black men were the majority in cultivating ideas of respectability and Christian morality. Many of these same men were theologically trained, like Washington, serving in Protestant churches or beyond the four walls of the church in civic, political, educational, and social organizations, such as the NUL and the National Association for the Advancement of Colored People. While holding a banner bearing the words "Overcome evil with good," they understood themselves to be doing the work of the Christian church by ministering to and galvanizing people of African descent in urban centers toward upright living. In 1919, for instance, Tuskegee alumnus, Washington's protégé, and NUL's field secretary Jessie O. Thomas visited New Orleans from Atlanta and expressed how the NUL, like Tuskegee, was committed to "co-operating with the municipal officials and other white people in assisting the negro."[80]

Times-Picayune reporters confirmed Thomas's sentiments, observing, "Negroes of New Orleans are preparing to organizing a branch of the National Negro Urban League. The purpose of the league is to cooperate with the white people of the community where branches are established for the betterment of the economic and industrial conditions of the negro race."[81] At this meeting, the race relations committee of the Association of Commerce approved the establishment of the NUL in New Orleans, and "several teachers, doctors and ministers of New Orleans spoke at [the] meeting."[82]

Through their vested interests in collaborating with white people, largely white men, Black men of the NUL in New Orleans and outside of the city had further situated themselves as race men chasing after the same patriarchal power wielded by the white men to whom they sought professional partnerships and allyship on the behalf of "the race." As a result, as figure 3.5 shows, Black women's concerns often remained marginal to Black male social reformers. As "providers" and "protectors," they dominated the discourse on race, sexuality, and religion during the era of Jim Crow. The sole woman, whose name escapes the historical record, is in the minority in the photograph—representative of the larger gender politics at play in popularized Black civil rights organizing in the early twentieth century. The men are all wearing dark-colored suits, and she is wearing all white—the color of sexual purity. She is outnumbered, her function in the organization unclear. What thoughts coursed through her mind as Bedou's flash filled the room? What purpose did she find in the National Urban League's work, as a young Black woman living in the Jim Crow South?[83] Without her name or her voice, we are left to speculate how her life's course would have been altered or influenced had she crossed paths with the likes of Mother Catherine Seals, who told a seeking Hurston around 1928, "Eat de salt, daughter, and get yo mind with God and me. You shall know what you came to find out. I feel you. I felt you while you was [sitting] in [the] chapel. Bring her a veil."[84] Veils were important material artifacts at the Manger, and young women adorned their heads with them. During his visit, Edward Tinker came across "a young Negress dressed in a white robe. A green veil, covering her head and falling to her shoulders, was kept in place by a white fillet, on which was embroidered I AM HOLTED."[85] "Holt," according to the *Oxford English Dictionary*, can refer to "A place of refuge or abode, a lurking-space, an animal's lair or den" suggesting that "I AM HOLTED" can best be translated as "I am safe" among the temple's livestock. It is worth contemplating, then, whether the white that Mother Catherine and the women at the Temple of

FIGURE 3.5. National Urban League, New Orleans, ca. 1919, by Arthur Bedou. Library of Congress, LC-DIG-ppmsca-24952.

the Innocent Blood wore symbolized something different from the white that the NUL member wore. Might the former have been in homage to the spirits at work at the temple ("white being the color associated with the dead, with protection from the dead, and with mourning"[86]) or a representation of the cleansing, healing, and birthing so central to many Black Atlantic religious rituals, and the latter a sole representation of sexual purity—the hallmark and prize of Black sexual Victorianism and Black Protestantism despite its often anti-Black and anti-African undercurrents?[87]

BLACK CLUB WOMEN AND THE EVANGELIZING PROJECT OF BLACK SEXUAL VICTORIANISM

Differing approaches to Black social issues sat at the crux of Black religious institution building in the early twentieth century. For many Black middle-class women, such as Mrs. Sylvanie Francoz Williams, a New Orleanian and friend of Washington, Black sexual Victorianism was the guiding force in their calls for racial and women's equality. Williams was the president of the NACW-affiliated Phyllis Wheatley Club of New Orleans, she ran the Fisk School Girls' Department from 1883 to 1896, and she was the principal of the Thomy Lafon School in the city from 1898 until her death in 1921.[88] In these roles, she perfected the art of women's professionalization, and her lessons ranged from how to properly dress to how to be a good wife. In 1902, Fannie Barrier Williams even described Williams as "a fine example of the resource-fulness and noble influence that a cultivated woman can and will give to the uplift of her race."[89] Much like the National Baptist Convention (NBC), the NACW's conventions provided space for educated African American Christian women to train and professionalize working-class women.[90] Williams, a devout member of the Blessed Sacrament Catholic Church at Constance and Sonia Streets in New Orleans, was not only "rank[ed] highest as an essayist and newspaper correspondent," but she was also a regular delegate of the NACW and a widely sought-after public speaker.[91] Moreover, her passing privilege as a light-skinned Black woman, her Catholic identity, and her involvement with a largely Black Protestant middle-class community of social reformers effectively positioned her as a bridge between the histori-cally Catholic New Orleans and the rising Black Protestant frontier in the city. Her voice, reach, and influence on these fronts cannot be denied. For example, she was the Louisiana delegate at the World's Columbian Exposition in Chicago in 1893, for which she prepared a substantive report on the state of education among people of African descent in the city, based on her own fieldwork experiences as an educator.[92]

In 1904, Williams published "The Social Status of the Negro Woman" in the African American literary journal *The Voice of the Negro*, in which she riffed on the New Testament query "Can anything good come out of Nazareth?" and rephrased a question asked consistently by white race makers: "Can anything good come from the Negro race?" In her meditation, Williams, a race woman, reasoned, "the educated Negro woman has been reserved the hardest blow, the darkest shadow, and the deepest wound. A wound so painful that her detractors rely upon her not voluntarily reopening it, even to probe it for its cure."[93] As Williams wrestled with these theological inquiries, Mother Catherine Seals responded to a different divine call, heeding the Spirit's voice to "put down here [in New Orleans] the Pool of Gethsemane so that the believers may have holy water to drink."[94] Williams's insistence that there was something wrong with the Negro race differed quite substantially from Seals's diagnostic assessment of the Negro race as lacking essential and vital resources and in need of "holy water to drink." Their differing assessments confirm the distinctive spiritual sensibilities of club women in relation to the reverend mother, whose work ultimately disrupted the unsettling ethos of Black sexual Victorianism.

Williams and Seals, however, both agreed on the necessity of Black women's leadership, even if the sexual politics undergirding their respective leadership practices differed. For instance, Williams had called for Black and white men to look to "the educated Negro woman" to uplift African Americans, and her words were printed alongside the likes of notable club women Mary Church Terrell and Nannie Helen Burroughs. Williams's call, however, distinguished between two classes of African American women— that of the educated or "the better class" and "the pauperized and brutalized members of the race." In her defense of the former, Williams distanced herself from the latter, arguing that white race makers had staged a "broad condemnation without exception; that uncharitableness of thought and deed that casts a shadow of distrust over the women of an entire race." To prove Black women's sexual Victorianism, Williams emphasized the numbers of Black children conceived within heterosexual marriages and challenged the trope of the absent Black father that emerged during the Civil War era as Black men went off to war.[95] She wrote, "As a proof of the moral progress of the colored woman all down the line is the fact that we find families of six and seven children who are the offsprings of the same father, and the celebrations of silver weddings among the lowly are quite frequent."[96] In contrast, Mother Catherine effectively queered the Negro family, in which she created a sanctuary for sex workers, unwed mothers, women who loved other women, men who believed Black women's claims of violation, and children without fathers. Seals allowed her wealthy followers to support her mission, buying land for her ministry, as children ran around the Industrial Canal in the company of animals. Mother Catherine had that effect; all were welcome. "Come just as you are" was a constant refrain. And by calling her temple a Manger, she sought to remind all that Jesus—the savior of the world and the bright and morning star of the Negro church—was born in a manger in the ghetto. She took her theologizing one step further and preached in the presence of a seeking Hurston "that Joseph was [Jesus's] foster father as all men are foster fathers, in that all children are of God and all fathers are merely the means."[97]

While Mother Catherine's theology appealed to the lowly, Williams and other Black social reformers distanced themselves from her and others like her. For club women like Williams, education, socioeconomic status, sexual chastity, and religious conviction were markers of difference as part of club women's own religion-making strategies in the new century, which ultimately separated poor, uneducated, and often, non-Christian and quasi-Christian Black women from club women. As historian Evelyn Brooks Higginbotham contends in her examination of "the politics of respectability" embodied by Black Baptist women, "The zealous efforts of black women's religious organizations to transform certain behavioral patterns of their people disavowed and opposed the culture of the 'folk'—the expressive culture of many poor, uneducated, and 'unassimilated' black men and women dispersed throughout the rural South or newly huddled in urban centers." Higginbotham goes further, noting that these Black Protestants "rejected conjuring, belief in ghosts, voodoo, and practices of 'superstition' that carried over from slave religion."[98] Booker T. Washington confirmed these ideas, writing in 1906, "No less repulsive to me than the negative Christian is the one who is always using his religion as a means of escape from something, from hell fire or brimstone or some less remote punishment. This class of Christians use religion as people use the conjurer's bag or a disinfectant to ward off evil. They are not drawn to any vital thing in religion; they simply use it as a cloak to shield them from harm."[99] Mrs. Fannie Barrier Williams raised similar concerns when she wrote in 1900 about African American women as ex-slaves "left to grope their way unassisted toward a realization of those domestic virtues, moral impulses and standards of family and social life that are badges of race respectability. They have had no special teachers to instruct them."[100] Club women and their male counterparts in New Orleans considered it their duty to Christianize those still wading in swamps just steps away from plantations in the rural parishes of Louisiana, or in the city's Industrial Canal where Mother Catherine had created "a religious meeting of sinners." So they became "special teachers" to the uneducated with the help of the American Missionary Association, spreading the Christian gospel undergirded by the demonization of non-Christian and quasi-Christian Black Atlantic religions, especially Voudou, Conjure, rootwork, non-Victorian sexualities—mainly premarital and nonheterosexual sex—and wayward cultural expressions within the cabaret, bars, jazz lounges, and New Orleans nightlife.

Williams and the other women of the NACW saw themselves as uniquely situated, in terms of education, religious convictions, and class, to uplift "the plantation woman," such that their rhetorical endeavors and philanthropic projects created on the behalf of poor and working-class Black women were often dreadfully paternalistic, condescending, and infantilizing.[101] For example, in 1903, Williams visited the Tuskegee Institute and in the same issue in which Williams published the aforementioned essay, Margaret Murray Washington penned "Social Improvement of the Plantation Woman," in which she likened educated African American women to "the condition of the white races of women ripening under favorable circumstances." At the heart of Mrs. Washington's essay, however, was an attempt to make sense of her identity in relationship to "plantation colored women," or women living on farms and participating in the Southern agricultural economy during the period. In this vein, Washington continued to look down upon the "thousands of these women whose souls are as white and clean as their fairer sisters who can boast of a line of ancestry that may have descended from the savagery of the Britons."[102] Mrs. Washington, however, did not mention how many white and Black women could boast of the same ancestral lines because of the "savagery of the Britons" on slave plantations, in which Black women were often raped and sexually abused by both planters and their mistresses. Club women attempted to salvage the image of "white and clean" souls of poor and working-class Black women in the face of largely white race makers and social reformers suggesting that their own middle-class souls did not stand in need of saving. As Williams and her colaborers worked to wash off the stench of the plantation, Mother Catherine Seals instead revered the land, the animals, and the great outdoors so central to Black life as she held court under a tent. Hurston observed, "All during her sermons two parrots were crying from their cages. A white cockatoo would scream when the shouting grew loud. Three canary birds were singing and chirping happily all through the service. Four mongrel dogs strolled about. A donkey, a mother goat with her kid, numbers of hens, a sheep—all wandered in and out of the service without seeming out of place. A Methodist or Baptist church—or one of any denomination whatever—would have been demoralized by any one of these animals."[103]

Unlike Seals, Williams used the proliferation of socially reformist ideas to uplift herself, thus effectively rising in popularity. In a 1911 essay, "An Open Letter to Mothers of the Race," for example, she wrote on behalf of the NACW's Mothers' Department, calling for mothers to come together "to demand one law of morality for your boys and girls, thus proving to your children that honest labor is nobler than gilded sin. Your open discussion of these vital questions will help your boys to be more manly, and your girls to be more womanly and develop a much needed respect for each other."[104] Much like Booker T. Washington's words about "idle" men making a "dishonest" living, Williams confirmed her own Black middle-class anxiety about a generation of young urbanites failing to adhere to the doctrine of Black sexual Victorianism, which called for the sanctity of the heterosexual family and for gender roles (women in the domestic sphere and men in the professional, theological, business, and political spheres). On this point, the Black middle class worked to end "Negro crime," alcoholism, and "passion" experienced by unwed men and women in the city. They were concerned with the growing number of African Americans held in penitentiaries across the nation, and reasoned that the incarcerated were confined largely due to their own inferiority, or because of their unwillingness to fully come "up from slavery."[105]

Washington confirmed the efforts of his wife, Margaret, along with Williams and the NACW, and even sent letters out to the chiefs of police and recorder of courts in various counties in Alabama and throughout the South, asking them, "What in your opinion are the chief causes of Negro crime? What effect does strong drink have in making the Negro a criminal? Since the prohibition law has gone into effect has there been any decrease in the crimes committed by Negroes in your County, especially rape, murder and other serious offenses?" White race makers responded, noting that Negro crime was the result of the excessive use of alcohol, specifically whiskey, combined with "the drug habit (cocaine)," along with such things as gambling and vagrancy. One sheriff went as far as arguing, "Strong drink tends to make the Negro vicious and to have less regard for themselves and for the laws of the country."[106] Washington and other state actors confirmed that excessive alcohol caused high rates of homicide in Black communities and that Black people's supposed propensity toward aggression and crime, rather than white supremacy and poverty, were the cause of their criminalization. In contrast, Du Bois, who regularly enjoyed wine and whiskey, argued in 1924, while citing the widespread use of alcohol among all races: "It seems very well established that the excessive use of alcohol liquors is one of the lesser faults of the American Negro."[107]

In many of their critiques of state pathologization of Black people, Black social reformers reified much of that same pathology. Sarah Haley has rightly noted that while the NACW engineered a movement against convict leasing, its leaders and members also used a highly religious discourse to demonize the very women they sought to save from the penal system. Haley contends, "If clubwomen were embroiled in a contested ideological battle with their working-class sisters in the city, they were also engaged in an intense confrontation with the state, whose violent oppression of poor black women they would not tolerate. The complexity and messiness of black women's institutional, intellectual, and political histories must be acknowledged."[108] Outside of their anti-convict-leasing activism, however, club women's moralizing discourse had grave consequences. Indeed, by consulting the archives of their work at the intersections of policing, state violence, and Black Atlantic religious history, we necessarily come to see their collusion with state entities that policed and surveilled poor and working-class Black women, their gender and sexual nonconforming identities, and their religion making strategies during the early twentieth century.

Club women's disdain for such practices as Hoodoo, Conjure, and rootwork and their demonization of sex outside of heterosexual marriage worked against the religious sensibilities and healing work of such faith healers as Mother Catherine, who believed that "Our brains is trying to make something out of us. Everybody can be something good."[109] Seals, who died in 1930 after she had promised her followers that she would rise from the dead in three days like Jesus, offered another way of being in the world that directly challenged Black social reformers and their accomplices. Though she was not resurrected in the literal sense, her followers worked tirelessly to keep her memory alive, erecting a life-size statue in her honor, commemorating the counterconduct to Black sexual Victorianism so central to the haven that was the Temple of the Innocent Blood. By the mid-1930s, amid the Great Depression, scores of other faith healers had entered the spiritual marketplace in New Orleans, and the policing of Black Atlantic religious and sexual cultures by white race makers and Black social reformers took a different form, enveloping many on the fringes of communal survival in an inescapable cycle of debt and confinement in the underworld.

VISITATION 4

ZORA TALKS "HOODOO IN AMERICA" AND ELSEWHERE

Nobody knows for sure how many thousands in America are warmed by the fire of Hoodoo, because the worship is bound in secrecy. It is not the accepted theology of the Nation and so believers conceal their faith. Brother from sister, husband from wife. Nobody can say where it begins or ends. Mouths don't empty themselves unless the ears are sympathetic and knowing. This is why these voodoo ritualistic orgies of Broadway and popular fiction are so laughable. The profound silence of the initiated remains what it is. Hoodoo is not drum beating and dancing. There are no moon-worshippers among the Negroes in America. . . .

When I found out about [Luke] Turner, I had already studied under five two-headed doctors and had gone thru an initiation ceremony with each. So I asked Turner to take me as a pupil. He was very cold. In fact he showed no eagerness even to talk with me. He feels sure of his powers and seeks no one. He refused to take me as a pupil and in addition to his habitual indifference I could see he had no faith in my sincerity. I could see him searching my face for whatever was behind what I said. The City of New Orleans has a law against fortune tellers, Hoodoo doctors and the like, and Turner did not know me. He asked me to excuse him as he was waiting upon someone in the inner room. I let him go but I sat right there and waited. When he returned, he tried to shoo me away by being rude. I stayed on. Finally he named an impossible price for tuition. I stayed and dickered. He all but threw me out, but I stayed and urged him. I made three more trips before he would talk to me in any way that I could feel encouraged.[1]

* * *

VISITATION 4

Dear Langston [Hughes],

New Orleans again. I was expecting to go to Nassau, but my look out over there warned me not to come for a few weeks. You see the Govt. is prosecuting obear [obeah] men (hoodoo doctors) pretty strenuously at present and my man found he was under suspicion, so he went to one of the outer islands to lie low till things calm down.[2]

ZORA NEALE HURSTON

"DANGEROUS AND SUSPICIOUS"

Hoodoo, Faith Healing, and Sex Work in the Black Slum

Men have combined preaching and healing with a little Hoodoo.

HARRY MIDDLETON HYATT[1]

Ain't you heard that whores is the most superstitious women in the world. They put pennies in their piss water to bring men.

JERRY COLEMAN TO LWP WORKER ROBERT MCKINNEY[2]

On March 3, 1938, the *Clarion-News* in Opelousas, Louisiana, reported, "Stories of snake oil and divining rods [and] 'treatments' for various human ills and wants, ranging from claims to grow hair to obtaining and guaranteeing retention of jobs figured in charges against 'Professor' Joseph Rajah Lyons." With a bond set at $800, Lyons, "a negro flaunting a green cape with a goatee," was in violation of Louisiana law, which criminalized "practicing medicine without a license and obtaining money under false pretenses." He was subsequently taken into custody. At the time of arrest, the faith healer and rootworker had snake oil and a divining rod in his possession and warned the jailer, "Be careful and don't hold that before your face. It will put you in a trance." The sheriff who had allegedly been "Hoodooed" by Lyons, exclaimed, "this is no man to have around," echoing the long-standing moral panic expressed by the police, state actors, and some Black constituencies against practitioners of non-Christian and quasi-Christian

Black Atlantic religions in the Black South, specifically Conjure, rootwork, Hoodoo, and other forms of Africana esotericism.[3] In 1912, for example, "a negro Hoodoo doctor," known throughout Baton Rouge and neighboring parishes by the name of "Doctor Green Watkins," was arrested for possessing "powders, herbs and pills of every description, medicines under the ban of law, dirty rags, a clothes brush, an old sweater and various tools . . . found in a hand satchel which the 'doctor' carried at all times." The press described him as an "old negro [who had] been in the 'trade' for many years" and "a colossal fake in several parishes" in whom "the negroes place[d] implicit confidence."[4] Watkins and Lyons were just two of the many faith healers arrested during the period, and they were confined to the same jail cells as sex workers, hustlers, queers, sissies, murderers, thieves, and gamblers.

Culling through the records of the New Orleans police department's mugshot and Bertillon card collections from the early twentieth century reveal "crimes" of poverty, of Blackness, and of survival.[5] Policemen characterized Black people's crimes as "dangerous and suspicious": breaking and entering, carrying a concealed weapon, petty and grand larceny, assault, armed robbery, using mails to defraud, having stolen property, taking auto without consent of owner, and prostitution. Out of the hundreds of cards related to the "Negro" archived at the New Orleans Public Library, roughly 50 percent of those jailed between 1910 and 1920 were charged with being "dangerous and suspicious." The specifics of what exactly made one "dangerous" or "suspicious" were not detailed in police records, but upon further review of press features related to the policing and incarceration of Black people in the slum, many of these individuals were believed to be "dangerous" and "suspicious" due largely to their spiritual powers, beliefs, and ways of moving through the world. The *Times-Picayune* reported on September 11, 1915, for example, that "the police [were] holding a tall, dark negro who gives his name as Tom Lee, on suspicion." Lee, presumably Afro-Creole given his claim to French heritage and his ability to speak French, "slipped into the Jackson suburbs barefooted, wearing two pairs of pants, a couple of shirts and two murderous-looking pistols girded about his waist." Lee's "suspicion" had much to do with his appearance and with his "[posing] as a Hoodoo doctor," suggesting that he was armed, in addition to the two pistols, with a spiritual power that threatened the commands of Jim Crow modernity and white Christian hegemony.[6] Religious practitioners like Lee often utilized the streets, back alleys, sidewalks, and their homes to peddle their services, and it was there that policemen also surveilled, harassed, and arrested them.

The street, much like the jail cell, was a unifying space and place for many of these individuals (see fig. 4.1). One writer once observed that "this city is famous for its gamblers, prostitutes, exhibitionists, anti-Christs, alcoholics, sodomites, drug addicts, fetishists, onanists, pornographers, frauds, jades, litterbugs, and lesbians, all of whom are only too well protected by graft."[7] All of these individuals largely gathered in the streets, in alleyways, and in crowded shotgun houses. Historian LaShawn Harris contends, "City streets served multiple functions for early-twentieth-century black [urbanities]. Crowded street corners and pathways were colorful backdrops for leisure and work as well as for political and religious activism." She goes further, "Using the streets to escape their cramped apartments, ordinary black men and women fraternized on city sidewalks and on their apartment building stoops, in doorways, and on fire escapes."[8] The street corner, the tenement, and the jail cell were sites of Black survival cultivated under intense state surveillance, and within these spaces of enclosure, migrants in the early twentieth-century Black slum developed a rich culture, deeply shaped by various religions and the burgeoning world of entertainment and amusements.[9]

FIGURE 4.1. "New Orleans Negro Street," 1935, by Walker Evans. Farm Security Administration, Office of War Information Photograph Collection, Library of Congress.

Just as street preachers sold the gospel for change and sex workers sold access to certain kinds of intimacy and pleasure to pay rent and feed their families, prophets, faith healers, mystics, conjurers, and rootworkers peddled their services from the corner as part of the larger religious, sexual, and economic geography of the Black slum. Thinking about all these different people as cohabitants of the Black slum allows us to disrupt the assumed secularization of urban centers and illuminates the intentional identities and practices articulated by African American, Caribbean, and Central American migrants. Indeed, the white supremacist Christian hegemonic state and its partners have historically policed Black sexualities, and they have also policed Black religions. This chapter argues that both forms of policing happened concomitantly as part of state and white supremacist efforts to regulate the lives of the children and grandchildren of the formerly enslaved amid multiple mass migrations in the early twentieth century. Without question, Protestants and Catholics villainized these practices in the press and inside of traditional churches as an extension of state legal sanctions. As discussed in the previous chapter, both Black and white Christians often upheld these distinctions, and by the 1920s and 1930s, the government and its allies would continue to distinguish between "good" versus "bad" forms of American religion. For instance, in 1924, Father Albert, an African American Catholic priest from Breaux Bridge preached "Is God Superior to the Influence of Hoodooism?" before the St. Teresa's Colored Catholic Church in Crowley, Louisiana. The priest, who "invite[d] white friends to join in hearing the sermon, announcing that he [had] reserved a special section of the church for the white visitors," questioned "the so-called spirits and Hoodoos that infested the imagination of the world's people."[10] These public criticisms worked to further marginalize an already vulnerable population of migrants employing their own underworld works while trying to survive using their own constellation of Black Atlantic religious practices.

These persons deemed criminal by the state and the church insisted on religious pluralism, freedom of religion, and the convergence of religious and sexual nonconformity as part of a larger community of migrants articulating a Black religious identity that fused together transgressive religious and sexual politics in and around New Orleans.[11] In this way, Black Atlantic religions, and the sexual politics of those religions, countered white American Christian hegemony by discursively and materially sacralizing sexual practices demonized by church and state. Moreover, by drawing again from Hartman's notion of "waywardness," which she defines as "the avid longing for a world not ruled by master, man or the police," this chapter theorizes wayward Negro religions and sexualities together as a facet of Black Atlantic religion making and underworld work, given how some migrants and local New Orleanians used the underworld to legitimize their religious and sexual labor, often by drawing upon spiritual genealogies with people of African descent in other places.[12] While most Black social and political historians ultimately ignore Black Atlantic religions and at times prioritize it as a particular kind of Black Protestantism positioned against "the wayward," this chapter underscores how Black Atlantic religions— beyond Protestantism—have historically been conduits for wayward living and social experimentation.[13] By attempting to create and legitimize their own religions and by drawing upon their connection to the sex economy in New Orleans, religious practitioners' homes and churches were not just sites for religious practice and ritual, but for sexual discourses, which have historically been cordoned off into the realm of "the secular" by both dominant historical actors and by scholars interested in uncovering and recovering queer sexual and religious histories.

Given the scope of this chapter, the case studies examined help us to understand how a sexual discourse about Black Atlantic religions—founded in plantocratic sexual terrorism, the mutilation of Black flesh, and lynching culture—undergirded the criminalization of Hoodoo in the early twentieth century. The white American Christian hegemonic state also often misinterpreted the diverse religious practices of people of African descent, collapsing critical differences under the umbrella terms "Hoodoo" and "Voodoo" and grouping together individuals who believed in cultivating their own unique identities and practices as a mode of Black Atlantic religion making to survive economic precarity and to respond to, obey, and carry out the wishes of spiritual powers that compelled them to do so. Some of these religious actors also articulated differences as a means of solely gaining followers, challenging dominant theological stances, and building their own religious institutions. Others drew upon long-standing Black Atlantic religions, including but not limited to Santería, Vodou, and Catholicism. In their attempts to prevent imprisonment, however, these actors, again, as Hurston wrote in the late 1930s, "[stood] before their pagan altars and [called] old gods by new names."[14] In their attempts to create new worlds as migrants braving Jim Crow and the threat of racial and sexual violence, Black religious practitioners charted new terrain by innovatively intellectualizing, theologizing, and defending their own unique religious rituals and services. Some of these innovations, however, had dangerous consequences, such as being sentenced to jail by the police for performing Hoodoo rituals to harm one's enemies. Through a careful examination of their words and articulated theologies, this chapter renders the contours of their queer religious worlding—sexual and otherwise—visible for our collective consideration.

INFORMANT 864: A NONBINARY HOODOO'S SEX WORK

In the 1930s, white Episcopal priest and self-taught ethnographer Harry Middleton Hyatt traveled to New Orleans with his wife as part of his Southern research tour. There, he met many religious practitioners of Hoodoo, Conjure, and Voudou, and he often described these practitioners as "strange-world believers."[15] They were strange for myriad reasons—"queer" even. One Black practitioner said to Hyatt, while being interviewed at the Patterson Hotel, a frequent gathering space for African American performers and socialites, in March 1938, "I'm what you call a freak. I guess you know that." They were identified as "informant 864"—their name escapes Hyatt's transcription and thus the historical record, perhaps intentionally so, as many practitioners feared legal retribution and police harassment for their practices and their spiritual businesses. In another instance, Hyatt writes, "I knew informant 864 was a *boy-girl* only because my contact man Edward through our local man Mack told me before bringing in *him-her*." He went on to speculate whether individuals like the informant were called "boy-girls" because they were "hermaphrodites" who "wore slacks and pretended to be men" or if it "meant [they were] dress-wearers." He concluded, "I do not know." Hyatt also noted "the belief that *he-she* before birth had been *fixed* like that by Hoodoo." He further clarified, "God was not accused of sending the deformity as a punishment of the parents."[16] In this vein, community members understood that informant 864's possible intersex or trans identity was the result of Hoodoo. Indeed, informant 864 was a person with an ambiguous gender that exceeded Jim Crow grammar, and their gender, sexual, and racial identification coalesced in their formation of their religious practice. Rather than reify the inherent intersexphobia, transphobia, and ethnographic voyeurism within Hyatt's preface to their interview, I use "they" pronouns to recognize that we do not know how exactly they may have identified, but we do know that they existed. I do not use "boy-girl" but instead describe them as "informant 864" and consider them to be a nonbinary Hoodoo in line with other queer and trans theorists of race thinking about the illegibility and refusal of binary categorization performed and demanded by gender nonconforming individuals in the archives of Black life and culture.[17] In this way, informant 864's existence and the religious hermeneutics undergirding their survival is of central importance to this chapter, especially in their own articulation of their religiously informed and inflected sexual ethics and practices.

Moreover, informant 864 was just one presumably queer, transgender, nonbinary, or gender nonconforming practitioner in the larger constellation of the Black Atlantic world, especially as many Black Atlantic religions are traditionally "female normative" and comparatively more "gay friendly" in relation to those traditions elevated to the status of "world religions."[18] For example, among Lucumí religious ancestors there have been not only many queer and transgender people but also sex workers and a documented brothel owner, Aurora Lamar (also known as Obá Tolá, Ibae), whose religious practices and gendered embodiment embraced "ambiguity" and "fluidity."[19] In the US context, Alexis Wells-Oghoghomeh writes about "trans-sense entities of, beyond, and between the sense and spirit worlds" among enslaved Africans in the Lower South "[that] represented dangerous excesses of feminine power, or rather the lethal potentialities of women's power should they choose to harm in their roles as mothers, nurses, midwives, and cooks."[20] This "power," as Wells-Oghoghomeh demonstrates, was available to both men and women, as some "men" identified as witches, a category that has largely referred to woman-identified individuals. Moreover, the idea of "trans-sense" occupies "the unclassified entities that inhabited the interstitial space between human and spirit, embodying characteristics of both yet resisting primary classification as either."[21] In this way, we might read informant 864 as embodying a trans-sense, or a refusal to be categorized while cultivating a religion deemed maleficent in 1930s New Orleans, and we might interpret that trans-sense as an underworld quintessence of something yet to be named.

In addition, other scholars have long documented the presence of gender variance and gender nonconformity in Black Atlantic religious life in the United States. Folklorist Mary A. Owens documented a cross-dressing Hoodoo practitioner in Missouri in the late nineteenth century, writing, "Alexander expressly states that a man's teacher should be a woman, and a woman's should be a man. His instructor was a man, but one night he dressed in woman's garb, and the next his master assumed the undivided raiment."[22] In 1895, Hampton Normal and Agricultural Institute employee

Leonora Herron, a librarian, published "Conjuring and Conjure-Doctors" in the *Southern Workman*, an essay based on research from Hampton students from 1878, in which Herron summarized their findings, and in one section on personal features, wrote, "Another calls them 'singular and queer, seeming always in a deep study, looking at some distant object.'" Of course, the observer's use of "queer" aligned with others during the period, in which they characterized strange and nonnormative social behaviors, including Africana esoterisms, as "queer" or challenging the normative as construed by Jim Crow modernity. In this vein, the historian Yvonne Chireau also contends, "Some supernatural specialists were also known to dress in styles that suggested sexual inversion. One account from the post-Emancipation period tells of 'Reverend Dr. H.' in Virginia, a conjurer who 'had his hair braided like a woman, and [had] rings in his ears.' Gender mutability may have been a dramatic means by which Conjure practitioners exploited their reputations as eccentric individuals."[23] By drawing upon informant 864's Black Atlantic religion making, however, this chapter argues that some gender nonconforming and nonbinary people were conjurers and Hoodoo practitioners who were disinterested in "exploiting their reputations as eccentric individuals," but were instead invested in garnering societal respect for their religious beliefs and services as gender and sexually transgressive practitioners of criminalized religions. Moreover, informant 864's claim, "I'm what you call a freak," suggests that queerness, at times, functioned less as a strategy or as a political identity, but as an ontological category, such that practitioners' queerness was a feature of their nonbeing as Black people who, in the afterlife of slavery, would always exist outside the bounds of acceptable or normative sexual behavior or gender performance.

To fully grapple with their "enfreakment," or "the process by which individual difference becomes stylized as cultural otherness" as theorized by Ellen Samuels, we must contend with this particular nonbinary Hoodoo's spiritual formation as outlined in their own words.[24] At the time of their interview with Hyatt, informant 864 was twenty-five years old, suggesting that they were born around 1913, and they shared with Hyatt that their "grandmother was a *spiritualist woman*."[25] One is left to speculate if informant 864's grandmother had been associated with the likes of Mother Leafy Anderson or Mother Catherine Seals.[26] Had informant 864 also seen their grandmother communicate with the spirits, heal the sick, or even raise the dead? After all, they conveyed in great detail how their grandmother's practices informed their own performances of ritual work involving eggs, grave dirt, the Holy Bible, burning candles, and lodestone. "I don't know what this lodestone is made out of, but my grandmother always used it," they noted.[27] Informant 864's grandmother even taught them "to go out to the road before the sunrise in the morning and make the sign of the cross three times . . . before yourself and throw dirt over your shoulder—left side, three times and make a wish and your wish will be granted."[28] Informant 864's grandmother's name was Henrietta Joseph (or Madame Joseph), and she lived at 611 Drive Street, where she performed ritual work for her seeking clients in the Girard Park Drive area of the city. While informant 864 does not mention their parents, their relationship to and spiritual apprenticeship under their grandmother demonstrates Hoodoo's intergenerational nature, as recipes and ritual instructions were taught and passed down.[29]

Informant 864, like many Spiritualists and Hoodoo practitioners in New Orleans, relied on these ancestral knowledges as a means of spiritual and physical protection from harm doers and the law. "[Hoodoo is] a way to protect yourself from anything people *plant down* for you to walk in, and if you walk in it, it means injury to yourself. You take saltpeter and sugar and crumble it up in your shoes and wear it in both shoes and no harm will befall from the evil that they have planted for you."[30] Informant 864 also recounted several rituals for returning evil to senders and for conjuring the death of an enemy, elucidating how practitioners utilized the underworld as a sphere of power in order to manipulate and control the course of events in the lived, material world of Jim Crow America. Informant 864's Hoodoo practice also relied on the Catholic saints in this regard, showing some regard and reverence for the relics of the church—St. Rita, St. Expedite, and St. Anthony—in which they prayed, "O, St. Anthony, bless me. Keep all danger and evils and away from me."[31] For informant 864, like many African Americans, Hoodoo and Christianity both had utility.[32]

In addition to their articulation of their and their grandmother's Hoodoo practices, informant 864 self-identified as a sex worker, whose clients included Black and white men. "When you *throw* white men or colored men—doesn't matter 'bout the nationality—that is no cause you no fuss. You take the holy water after the last one out the door, you throw it and you say, 'Go—go—go—and don't come back,' and sprinkle your house with holy water. Holy water will not permit the men of the law to enter the house."[33] By "throwing a man," informant 864 meant the same as "jazzing a woman," which they further clarified by adding, "Jazzing is fucking."[34] In the throes of sexual passion and distracted by informant 864's skills, their clients would often be robbed by other sex workers who would enter the room and "steal [their] money out of [their] pockets." To prevent legal retribution, "holy water [kept] the law away." Informant 864 reasoned that holy water could also protect bootleggers, too, as sex workers and bootleggers often coexisted in the Black slum, utilizing crimes of survival to stave off poverty and homelessness. In addition, holy water was used to "keep anyone from coming into your house," if sprinkled before leaving one's home; and it could prevent "any of kind of evil at all" if sprinkled before inviting someone inside one's living space. Holy water, when combined with a candlelit altar, was a potent force of spiritual protection in the homes of "most all of the Louisiana people," informant 864 reckoned.[35]

In their Hoodoo practice, informant 864 created tinctures, teas, and coffees for myriad purposes. They helped those addicted to drugs and alcohol drop their habits, and they also aided pregnant women with their abortions.[36] "You buys the powder and you put it in anything they eating or drinking and when you gives them nine drops of it—it's a dose each day—they'll have no more desire [to] be [a] dope addict at all, [and won't have] any desire for alcoholic drink."[37] In another instance, informant 864 explained to Hyatt that to "kill a baby before it's born," one should "take a herb, it's called *ammonia herb* . . . and make it into a tea or either coffee . . . Have them to drink some; and if they don't get to drink any, have some cooked up in some kind of food that they might get the [essence] of that herb, and the baby will be born dead."[38] A speculative reading of informant 864's account suggests that the Hoodoo practitioner and sex worker had used the spiritual knowledge they had gleaned from their grandmother to assist the community of bootleggers, alcoholics, sex workers, and underground economists in their orbit who suffered from a drug habit too far gone or grappled with the reality of being pregnant with a fetus that they did not want to bring into the anti-Black world of Jim Crow. Indeed, Black gender diverse underworld workers of intersex, transgender, and queer experience along with women, sex workers, and faith healers were subject to death-dealing legal scrutiny and punitive violence.

In the face of these threats to their survival, informant 864 still managed to find love through their relationship with an Italian man named Salvador C. Informant 864 recounted how "[their] grandmother worked the *trick* for [them]," meaning she fixed Salvador such that he would ultimately do right by informant 864. In a world where intersex, transgender, and gender nonconforming people are often the victims of gratuitous violence and medical voyeurism, it is striking that informant 864 was solidly and lovingly nurtured and protected by the ritual science of grandmother's rootwork and prayers, and that their partner, Salvador, under the spell of grandma's spiri-

"DANGEROUS AND SUSPICIOUS"

tual covering, could not help but fall in line. The historian Kodi Roberts, while writing about other faith healers in the city of New Orleans during this period, has observed, "Workers used their power to help men and women target each other, their power seemingly not mitigated by gender loyalty but by the ebb and flow of commerce and the needs of their customer base."[39] Informant 864's grandmother disavowed an express commitment to cis-heteronormativity in her spiritual work, disrupted the gender binary as conveyed by Roberts, and carved out a space for informant 864's rejection of and cultivation of their own gender. In this way, Henrietta Joseph (informant 864's grandmother) had effectively christened her grandchild's Hoodoo sex work, covering them in prayer and ensuring that their partner would do them no harm.[40]

PROPHET JOSEPH RAJAH LYONS

Despite the risks associated with opening temples and running businesses for the purposes of faith healing, rootwork, and sex work, other African Americans joined informant 864 in the spiritual marketplace. One such person was Prophet Joseph Rajah Lyons, whose arrest and capture in 1938 opened this chapter, and who had founded the Emperor Haile Selassie Nu-Way Ethiopia Mystic Light Baptist and Spiritual and Kingdom Church in New Orleans, located at 2228 Conti Street, in the years prior. Born in Sorrell, Louisiana, on October 7, 1899, with the name Joseph Lyons, he would later spend most of his spiritual career claiming that he was from India and had been imbued with a "heavenly gift that [he] got when [he] was a little boy."[41] In fact, his chosen middle name, Rajah, translated to Indian king or prince.[42] Like the COG's members in chapter 2, Lyons engaged in religio-racial self-fashioning, in which he imbued his Blackness "with meaning derived from histories other than those of enslavement and oppression."[43] We might also consider how Lyons invoked a certain kind of exoticism that functioned as an alluring and powerful label, especially given the familiarity many Black Atlantic migrants may have had with Ethiopia and Hinduism—significant points of reference in the circum-Caribbean during the period, considering the prominence of Emperor Haile Selassie. In this way, Lyons, like many of his contemporaries, sought out ways to rebrand himself in terms of racial designation and as social and economic currency as part of a larger project of asserting his own religious autonomy in the white American Christian privileging society of New Orleans.[44] In order to establish the legitimacy of his temple, on one occasion Lyons also went as far as to discredit Father Divine of the Peace Mission in the North, asserting that "there ain't nothing to him," and he encouraged the LWP workers who interviewed him in the late 1930s to "keep [their] eye on [him]."

The characteristics of Lyons's church were certainly worthy of critical observation. Addressing the peculiar nature of his church's long name, Lyons stated, "If the name seems unusual it is because all churches will have long names soon, names like 'The Mohammed Ally Christian Catholic Church.' It's the most important thing about a church. People will come to see what its like: they will think there is something strange about it."[45] Certainly, his church's name carried a Black transnational sentiment in tune with Ethiopia coupled with Southern Baptist and Spiritualist roots, and he claimed explicitly that he "[taught] all of the religions and [gave] all [his] customers anything they want[ed], from baptism to voodoo paraphernalia." Moreover, the name of Lyons's church was an homage to Selassie, a Coptic Christian, who stood with African Americans in the fight for civil and human rights as he drew connections between Jim Crow and the colonial desolation caused by the Italo-Ethiopian War.[46] Like many other Black men during the 1930s, Lyons found guidance and inspiration from Selassie's political message. In his June 1936 appeal to the United Nations, Selassie stated, "I, Haile Selassie I, Emperor of Ethiopia, am here today to claim that justice which is due to my people, and the assistance promised to it eight months ago, when fifty nations asserted that aggression had been committed in violation of international treaties." Citing the numerous harms caused to the Ethiopian people by the Italian government, he continued, "The very refinement of barbarism consisted in carrying ravage and terror into the most densely populated parts of the territory, the points farthest removed from the scene of hostilities. The object was to scatter fear and death over a great part of the Ethiopian territory."[47] To people of African descent in the United States who encountered Selassie's words over the airwaves, the Italians were no different from white Americans who lynched and brutalized Black people in the United States. In effect, Black people across the diaspora were under attack and Black male religious and political leaders developed masculinist revolutionary politics which, as Keisha Blain has observed, differed from the efforts of Black nationalist women.[48] Literary critic Hazel Carby contends that this time period was a moment in which "a modernist racial consciousness was produced out of the dissecting gaze [of white Americans]," such that "a number of male intellectuals, both black and white, created historical discourses of black manhood in the service of a revolutionary politics which argued for the violent overthrow of all racialized social formations."[49] Lyons's church and the racial and sexual transgressive politics theologized inside of it were rooted in this larger historical context, and he opened his house church to both Black and white people in an effort to challenge Jim Crow segregation and to survive the 1930s financially. Whether Black or white, in Prophet Lyons's eyes, all money was green.[50]

While the sources are unclear about exactly how successful Lyons's ministry was or about how many men he radicalized, Lyons stated that he founded his church for "healing purposes, reading, calling and entertaining the spirits." In another instance, he claimed, "I don't know exactly what kind of church this is but it is one that is established," given that "[his] congregation number[ed] fifty . . . both white and Black." Like many storefront and house church founders in cities across the US in the early twentieth century, Lyons also lived in his church and "[slept] on a castoff cot, which [was] under a group of colored lights, rags and cardboard pictures hanging from a wire that resembles a clothesline."[51] Two LWP writers, Robert McKinney, an African American journalist whose writings often appeared in the *Chicago Defender*, and another worker only identified by the surname Lemelle, described the prophet's home as "unsanitary" and "[encouraging] rats, roaches and the very popular bed bugs to show themselves without regard for his congregation or visitors." Given this description, it is difficult to imagine how fifty members squeezed into Lyons's house twice per week to attend services or to receive spiritual counsel. It is worth pondering, however, whether Lyons exaggerated those numbers to garner more support and to gain a larger clientele, with hopes that the LWP might ultimately include him in one of its many publications, such as the *New Orleans City Guide*, which included church advertisements in a section called "Some Negro Cults."[52]

Nonetheless, Lyons conveyed to LWP workers McKinney and Lemelle that "this is a democratic country" and "all men have the right to build their own churches." The interviewers then described Lyons as a "self-styled voodoo doctor, the South Rampart Street conception of Haile Selassie, poet, Christian Science teacher, master of 'spiritology,' ex-jail bird, adventurist and soap-box orator." They also used immensely racialized language to describe Lyons's body, depicting him as "the boogey-man looking prophet . . . a tall young man of twenty-nine with long beads and a black ruft face." Indeed, the hegemonic white Christian imaginary prefigured in the LWP's characterizations of Black religious actors in New Orleans, and the LWP actively sought out discursive ways to depict Black Atlantic religious actors as "crazy," "unkempt," and even "dirty."[53] For example, McKinney and Lemelle wrote that "two nervy rats alarmed them by running over [their] shoes without shivering." Lyons is quoted as saying, in response, "Y'all must excuse dem rats. But they won't harm you. They is religious rats." Not only were rats supposedly a feature of Lyons's church, but so were mosquitoes. Lyons, however, believed that "mosquitoes [didn't] bother [him]" and that "they [couldn't] bite a holy man like [him]." McKinney and Lemelle thought and asserted that they had observed differently, and by their characterizations, Lyons's home was less of a church and more of a zoo. It is significant, however, that Lyons included rodents and insects—two types of creatures that have historically been characteristic of the slum—as part of his religion-making project, calling them "religious" and regarding them as members of his 1930s house church.[54]

Lyons also used his transnational religious imaginary not only to draw connections between African Americans and Ethiopians, but to use pornography as a sacred material object for his clients in his house church, similarly to how Catholics and Spiritualists included pictures of the saints in their ritual practices.[55] LWP workers observed, "Strangely, there are very few saintly pictures in the church, but there are many suggestive pictures of women at leisure, the kind that are synonymous with certain places for men only." In response, Lyons explained that he used the images during his spiritual work, "Many men come in to see me who have had no contact and what they need is to be worked up."[56] Lyons's various run-ins with the police, his long list of arrests, and the presence of these images in his church indicate that Lyons was not only a faith healer but also a male sex worker, or perhaps both identities were collapsed into one—a faith healer who performed sex work, or a sex worker who did faith healing. While historian Kodi Roberts has described Lyons as "helping men deal with sexual dysfunction," Lyons "helped" his followers or "customers" achieve sexual satisfaction.[57] One historian has noted that "many histories of prostitution tend to replicate early twentieth-century experts in relation to male youth sex work, describing it, when at all, in passing."[58] In the parlance of the Negro spiritual, Black male sex workers from the early twentieth century are begging for the historian to "not pass [them] by." Rather than reify this historiographical tendency, assessing Lyons's religion making—specifically what he describes as his right to practice his religion—allows us to pause and to critically think about the intersections between faith healing and male sex work. Lyons conceptualized himself as offering services—religious and sexual—to men, both Black

"DANGEROUS AND SUSPICIOUS"

and white, who "needed to be worked up." As men entered brothels, they also entered Lyons's home for religious and sexual pleasure.

While some scholars might immediately situate pornography and sex work into the realm of the profane given its presumed oppositional nature to white American Christian markers of piety, sexual morality, and chastity—which have historically been upheld by quotidian legal regulations around the proliferation of pornography and sex in the spiritual marketplace—it is significant that these images are present *inside* and not outside of a church. As the historiography on religion and sexuality has shown, the very thought of pornography and sex work in traditional religious spaces was known to raise eyebrows, rile faithful congregants, and upset devout Christians. Consider, for instance, the issues that plagued both Catholic and Protestant churches in the early Americas concerning erotic poetry, letters, and images that were exchanged among Christians—heterosexual, homosexual, and otherwise.[59] To think of Lyons as being aware of this cultural history and the unique politics of it in the geographic space of 1930s New Orleans, which had only recently banned prostitution, allows us to contemplate and to fully grasp his intention for the inclusion, use, and sacralization of pornography inside of the sacred space of his house church.[60] It also opens up conversation about how faith healing and sex work functioned as crimes of survival in New Orleans.

Lyons's house church and his altar were for both private and public consumption. Surely, Lyons could have only used the pornographic images for his own private sexual and religious purposes, but he also used them with and for his clients and followers. To this point, historian Colleen McDannell's observations about how meanings are read onto objects deemed sacred or religious is especially prescient. She writes, "Religious objects function within complicated networks of beliefs, values, myths, and social structures. Clerical elites articulate the proper use of objects based on their understanding of scripture and religious traditions. People relate to objects as if they were sacred characters, in spite of warnings against idolatry."[61] Lyons created his own church. He was not a "clerical elite," but he was the founder and leader of his own new religious institution. The mode in which he theologized his religion and how he applied religious significance to the objects in his home do, however, align with McDannell's claim about "complicated networks." In other words, pornography was just one piece in a larger constellation of Lyons's religion-making process. Put differently, as McDannell notes, "Religious artifacts . . . also function like tools."[62] Pornography was one tool that Lyons employed within the space of his house church.

Notwithstanding the religious significance of pornography for Lyons, his sex work inside of his house church was informed by the economic precarity caused by the Great Depression. Roberts has contended, "Employment and money were scarce, and professional practitioners devoted a great deal of their effort and power to obtaining jobs for clients and attempting to help them improve their economic circumstances. In addition to dealing with clients so that they could practice within the constrictions of city ordinances and state and federal law enforcement."[63] Lyons used pornographic materials to draw men into the Emperor Haile Selassie Nu-Way Ethiopia Mystic Light Baptist and Spiritual and Kingdom Church. Once the men were drawn to Lyons's temple, they were "worked up," which in the vernacular of early twentieth-century sex work meant that these men most likely masturbated to the images or engaged in sexual acts with each other, with Lyons, or with the nonmen who may have also found themselves there.

While the sources do not substantiate Lyons or his clients publicly identifying as homosexual, his church provided space for the articulation of sexual desire among and between men. The extent to which said desire was queer-identified or homosexual is less significant. Lyons's male clients' coming to him to be "worked up" to pornographic images of women was already queer in the sense that the sexual act of being "worked up" happened among and between men. Nonetheless, these men's evasiveness or lack of explicit commentary on their assumed queer sexuality situates them within "down-low" (DL) discourse in Black queer studies about men who sleep with men but identify as heterosexual. As Jeffrey McCune has brilliantly argued, "DL men are new bodies dancing to an old song: the complex rhythms of sexual discretion."[64] Lyons and the men in his church were certainly doing their own version of the holy dance. They holistically merged the sexual and the sacred.

While most histories of sexuality in the twentieth century rarely look to religious spaces as sites of queer sexuality, the presence of pornographic materials, DL sexual culture, and queer sex in Lyons's church suggest that men who had sex with other men also used religious spaces to subvert state surveillance of homosexuality in the early twentieth century.[65] Religious spaces were sites for male solicitation, and they allowed practitioners to conceal their queer sexualities while presenting themselves as devout religious subjects.[66] Indeed, the early twentieth century was a historical moment in which gays, lesbians, and sex workers across genders and racial identities were criminalized and deemed monstrous, and as historian George Chauncey has contended, in the 1930s the police began to heavily crack down on urban gay spaces in light of "anti-pansy" legislation, causing queer and DL men to "[find] other places to meet their friends and to continue their participation in gay society."[67] In light of this history, Lyons's ministry and his use of pornography for male clients reveals that the Emperor Haile Selassie Nu-Way Ethiopia Mystic Light Baptist and Spiritual and Kingdom Church became yet another site for "gay society," and specifically, for "cruising" for potential sexual partners. To his credit, then, Lyons skillfully created a haven for Black and white men seeking sexual services under the auspices of "church."[68] His comfort with talking about pornography to McKinney and Lemelle also served as another means of encouraging men to attend his church for its religious and sexual rituals.

Beyond Lyons's transgressive sexual politics, some of his contemporaries took note of the larger message behind the establishment of his church during the Depression. In chapter 11 of his unpublished manuscript, *The Negro in Louisiana*, LWP worker Marcus Christian noted that Lyons's ministry was "reminiscent of Huey P. Long's Share-the-Wealth Plan."[69] Long, who was the fortieth governor of Louisiana from 1928 to 1932 and a member of the United States Senate from 1932 until he was assassinated in 1935, delivered his "Share Our Wealth: Every Man a King" speech on CBS radio to an estimated twenty-five million listeners on February 23, 1934. Lyons was most likely one of those listeners, especially as he had described his in-house ministry as a "radio church." A proponent of helping impoverished African Americans and whites, Senator Long's critiques of capitalism were especially poignant considering the Depression, a historical moment in which those who were fairly well off joined the ranks of those who were already poor. Much of Long's political message drew from the Bible and his Catholic upbringing. Long biographer Richard D. White Jr. has observed, "He would preach to the crowd, holding a Bible in hand in holy uplift and quoting from memory lengthy passages of the Scriptures."[70] Like many New Orleanians, Lyons was inspired by Long's message and sought ways to democratize his own religious practice. Christian quoted Lyons as saying, regarding his temple, "This League is asking only 3 Questions, but answers any of Past, Present, and Future, Regardless of color or creed: Every man a King. 3 Classes: A B and C."[71] Lyons resisted Jim Crow racial politics and made it a priority to open his church to both Black and white followers and customers. Regardless of their race or class, Lyons serviced them. "I ain't prejudice, all color people can come to my church," he said. "I expect to have five hundred members soon."

With no acknowledgment of prominent markers of Protestant and Catholic Christianities, specifically the theological notion that Jesus died on the cross for the sins of the world, Lyons effectively institutionalized a new conception of "church"—because "this is a democratic country [and] all men have the right to build their own churches"—inside of his home and held services, requesting "small change to the spirits."[72] In one newspaper clipping (fig. 4.2), he used the words "To Know. To Dare. And to Keep Silent," echoing the maxim "To know, to will, to dare, and to keep silent" (*Scire, velle, audere, tacere*), known as the "witches' pyramid" or the "four pillars" or "the four words of the Magus." These words are associated with French magician, esotericist, and author of more than twenty books on magic and the occult Eliphas Lévi, further demonstrating the breadth of Lyons's reading of metaphysical texts in the cultivation of his Black Atlantic religion making, specifically his incorporation of Rosicrucianism, Masonry, and Rastafarianism, among other esoteric texts.[73]

Modernity, and symbols of it like the radio, along with critiques of capitalism, loomed large in Lyons's underworld work. For instance, he also "[had] wires extending from his cot to the ceiling of his home-church." As McKinney and Lemelle noted, "he called these electric wires from the spirits" that had the power to give followers anything they had asked for, or to cleanse them of their sins. "These electric wires you see around here is electric wires from the spirits," Lyons would exclaim repeatedly. "They got electricity in them that is greater than worldly electricity. They give you power." In Black Atlantic religions, the image of electricity is a root metaphor for the movement of sacred energy through ritual activity and religious travel in many different places. Anthropologist Aisha M. Beliso-De Jesús contends in her contemporary ethnography *Electric Santería*, "Practitioners describe how they feel the strength of currents, meaning that the copresences manifest in ranges of their electricity."[74] Beliso-De Jesús's assessment complements Andrew Apter's earlier insights from the 1990s regarding Yorùbá rites of investiture as ceremonially "recharging" the battery of the reigning monarch's body. Apter has observed, "Ritual paraphernalia . . . transform, transmit, and store ritual power much as do electric condensers, cables, and batteries . . . Ritual power, like electricity, is 'hot,' highly charged, and dangerous. Unbridled, it can kill. It must be contained, limited, and properly regulated to work productively for human society. Finally, ritual power, like electricity, possesses both positive and negative values."[75] For Lyons, the electric currents from the spirits made him "a curer of disease and a man who [could] tell you your troubles by looking you in your eyes."[76] Similarly, in her discussion of Father

FIGURE 4.2. Lyons's advertisement in an unknown newspaper, circa 1930s. Howard C. McEwen Papers, folder 8, Amistad Research Center, New Orleans.

Divine's Peace Mission during the period, Weisenfeld includes the words of one Emma Wells, "a fifty-three-year-old African American domestic worker who had migrated from Virginia to Atlantic City, [and] used the metaphor of electricity to characterize Divine's healing from a distance, writing, 'I was sick for ten years and the doctor said that I had to have an operation, but Father Divine healed me with power like an electric shock. He cleaned me up from all sins, and I thank him for new life.'"[77] It is unsurprising that much of Lyons's language mirrors that of one of Divine's followers, as Lyons himself confessed to the LWP workers that he followed Divine's ministry to distinguish his healing ministry from that of Divine's. In the process, both relied on a vast Black Atlantic heritage in their religion making.

Despite his drawing from a variety of religious traditions, including Voudou, Lyons claimed that his source for "the principles of this religion" came from the spirits and the Psalms in the Hebrew Bible, along with first and second Corinthians and the letter to the Hebrews in the New Testament. In his cultivation of this unique religion, he told the LWP "Y'know I'm not crazy," directly addressing white American beliefs about "negro religious fanaticism." McKinney and Lemelle responded, "And this is very true. Anytime a man can make a living with a church like this he is definitely not crazy; he is lucky. What his congregation may be called is something else." This "something else"—or the underworld work and Black Atlantic religion making inside of Lyons's church—allowed for sexual acts otherwise policed by the state, and it also created space for the veneration of the spirits, faith healing, biblical teaching, and economic security during the Great Depression. "The police will not stop me because my work is legitimate," he told the LWP writers. "They can't do you anything for helping the people. Can they?" Although Lyons would be arrested several times following this interview with the LWP, his commitment to religion making and the democratization of his services set him apart from many of his contemporaries, so much so that his white neighbor, the local grocer who had recently moved to the neighborhood, told McKinney and Lemelle, "This man cured me of my ear disease . . . He made me hold his wires and passed a rod over my ears."

Whereas much of Lyons's biographical information remains a mystery beyond the LWP's interview, his name did appear in many prominent publications over the course of the twentieth century in various cities across the United States. In 1938 and 1939, the *Pittsburgh Courier* reported that he had been arrested again for loitering outside of the Jolly theater in New Orleans, while hosting a feature, despite having a local police press pass signed by the superintendent of police and being the local representative of the *Tampa*

"DANGEROUS AND SUSPICIOUS" 139

Bulletin.[78] By 1941, Lyons had moved briefly to Oklahoma and was listed as a representative of the *Black Dispatch*, the first African American newspaper in Oklahoma City founded by civil rights activist Roscoe Dunjee in 1915. He had also been named a delegate for the city, as part of the National Council for the Fair Employment Practice Committee (FEPC) cochaired by A. Philip Randolph, which was created to implement President Franklin D. Roosevelt's Executive Order 8802, in order to "ban discriminatory employment practices by Federal agencies and all unions and companies engaged in war-related work."[79] In 1945, Lyons lived in Starke, Bradford County, Florida, and was drafted into World War II.[80] In 1952, the Secret Service refused him access to press row to cover Howard University's commencement as a journalist, and he was described as "a lanky gent who sports whiskers."[81]

During the last couple of decades of his life, Lyons continued to reshape his religio-racial identity. In 1957, the *Chicago Defender* called him "a follower of Mahatma Ghandi" and included an image of Lyons praying outside a funeral home in Washington, DC, after "paying respects" to the late Senator Joseph R. McCarthy, an ironic move given McCarthy's racism and persecution of Communists, gays, and lesbians.[82] By the late 1950s, it is worth pondering whether Lyons had reinvented himself yet again such that he may have hidden his possible queer sexuality and his past as a male sex worker, or if the *Chicago Defender* had actually misrepresented Lyons's posture of prayer as revering McCarthy, such that he could have actually been praying for those most harmed by the late senator. A little more than a decade later, however, Lyons died on December 30, 1971 at the age of seventy-two, having outlived many of the faith healers of his generation, though it is unclear when, and if, his faith healing career ever ended.[83] Although he appears, disappears, and reappears in the archive, his words about the politics of naming Black Atlantic religions in 1930s New Orleans—"The name is the most important thing about a church. People will come to see what it's like: they will think there is something strange about it"—is especially poignant, as it speaks to a larger culture of intentional and strategic religion making, self-fashioning, and the political intonations embedded in early twentieth-century Black Atlantic religions in New Orleans.[84] Lyons's consistent movement throughout the United States during the twentieth century also confirmed Hartman's observation, "Negroes were drifters, nomads, fugitives, not settlers. They had not been allowed 'me' and 'mine.'"[85] Lyons constantly reinvented himself due largely to the dangers of fully actualizing as queer, faith healer, and sex worker in any given space due to the constraints of Jim Crow law.

LOVE, SEX, AND MARRIAGE

Despite these prohibitions, Prophet Joseph Rajah Lyons was not the only male faith healer to espouse nontraditional sexual politics as a form of Black Atlantic religion making in the underworld. His contemporary Bishop Jeff Horn did the same, but in another way. The founder of the Jeff Horn Spiritual Catholic Church, Horn believed "a man can practice [his] religion with seven wives as well as he can with a church full."[86] In the formulation of his theology, Horn, a native of Opelousas, Louisiana, drew from the Bible and saw himself living out the ideals of King Solomon of the Old Testament, who "had seven hundred wives, princesses, and three hundred concubines."[87] Horn, who said he was eighty-four years old when interviewed by LWP employees McKinney, Cherrie, and Lemelle in the late 1930s, professed, "Men ought not work" and "let the woman work and bring the bacon home." Even as women joined Horn's house church and eventually became his "wives," the preacher was mainly interested in leading men "to the right side of the fence," where men were encouraged by God to "have as many wives as Gawd want[ed] them to have." To be converted to the Jeff Horn Spiritual Catholic Church, Horn asserted, "a man must git on his knees and pray in the darkest of the night. He must believe and have faith and be guided by it. Visions will come to a man who believes. They will tell him what to do, and when to do, and with who to do."

Horn preached that men ought not commit themselves to just any woman, but that they must be led by God. Horn, of course, confessed that all his wives came to him through divine inspiration. The two wives who lived with him were Beulah Daniels, or "Saint Mary," and Dora Horn, "Saint Mary 2." Dora told the LWP interviewers, "[Before] I came into this church I asked the prophet to show me a spirit to prove that he was right, and do you know he did." Horn's other five wives did not live with him but "[came] in when he beck[ed] and call[ed]." Horn did not give their names to the LWP workers because some of them were married to other men, and as he put it, "What's the difference? I know them all as Saint Mary. That's the name that I must call 'em." "Saint Mary's job," the LWP interviewers noted, "[was] to look after the house, cook and take care of Jeff while he flings his lazy body from room to room, and while he meditates upon the ways of the world." The Jeff Horn Spiritual Catholic Church, like Prophet Joseph Lyons's Emperor Haile Selassie Nu-Way Ethiopia Mystic Light Baptist and Spiritual and Kingdom Church, met "on the second story of a dingy tenement house at 511S. Derbigny Street." Despite its poor construction, Horn professed that "the Lord comes to it like He goes everywhere else," effectively situating his house church as a legitimate religious institution. This same God showed Horn the Depression before it came. "He showed me by the evening moon," he told the LWP workers, "It was pink; that was the sign . . . the depression was coming!"[88]

Horn theologized and practiced nonmonogamy in his religion and attributed spiritual meaning to each of his relationships with the women in his church. "If you want to mess with the workings of the Lawd you jest mess with these women. These women is Gawd sent women. He sent them to me to be my wives. He sent them in the spirit and then in the flesh. They is good both ways. I done bless these women to make them give up the ways of the world . . . they means something to this neighborhood and to my church. They's good women." Unlike many of the men in prominent organizations and churches like the Universal Negro Improvement Association and the Church of God in Christ, Horn guised his exploitation of women's labor as a celebration of their leadership and professionalization. He encouraged his wives to pursue work outside of the home and to proselytize more followers into the fold to adapt his nontraditional and nonmonogamous sexual politics. He believed that "the Lawd told me that I wasn't supposed to work but I was supposed to see to it that my wives worked and took care of me so that I could keep the spirit working." Deftly attuned to the gender politics of his day and like other male new religious movement leaders such as Father Divine of the Peace Mission, Horn simultaneously rejected and reconfigured traditional gender roles to his liking and for self-serving ends—denouncing the notion that men be providers so that Black women would financially support him during one of the most harrowing economic periods in the history of the United States.[89] With patriarchal flare, Horn's practices mirrored those of other Black men labeled "sex cult" leaders, such as Father Chester Taliaferro in Philadelphia, who was rumored to have fathered twenty-four "Holy Ghost babies" by numerous Black and white women in his religious group.[90]

Although Horn believed that his sexual politics were divinely supported, Louisiana law forbade and criminalized polygamy. Horn declared, "State laws regarding marriage are false" and told the LWP workers that one day a sheriff stopped by his house church and stated, "Say don't you know that you can't have seven women living with you in the same house?" With the threat of arrest prominently in his face, Horn responded, "A prophet never gits scared about nothing about the law which ain't right no how." The sheriff flippantly replied, "If you keep going on like you're doing old man I guess you'll have some smaller saints around here soon." Horn boldly rejected the sheriff's words: "Nope. Needn't worry about that." In another instance, he stated to the LWP, "This is a country of free speech and lets every man, woman and child practice their own religion as they sees fit." Yet Horn, like Lyons, faced incessant police scrutiny, and his religious practices were routinely challenged by state actors. In his attempt to avoid the police, Horn held services "late in the night when the moon is quiet and all is well," with no offering or fee required, resembling the late-night Voudou ceremony so heavily policed by white spectators in the long nineteenth century.

BLACK WOMEN, LOVE, AND BETRAYAL

Given the lack of women's voices in the LWP's interview with Horn—except for one line from Dora—it is difficult to grasp their own interpretations of Horn's theology of nonmonogamy, or whether they found his church to be a space for sexual liberation, sexual oppression, or both. Indeed, as is often the case in the study of Black religions, Black men's voices and experiences are prioritized over and against the perspectives and lived realities of the Black women who filled the pews, or in Horn's case, literally kept his faith healing house church running both day and night.[91] In other LWP interviews, however, there is a surplus of Black women's perspectives concerning love, sex, and marriage in Black religious spaces during the late 1930s.[92] Church women, for instance, talked openly with LWP interviewers about male preachers and their husbands who were unfaithful to their wives in order to highlight how many of these men were in nonmonogamous sexual relationships with women who did not have full awareness of the nature and intentions of those sexual arrangements. Such perspectives help us to further understand how transgressive sexual politics as articulated and understood by many male faith healers and preachers were interpreted by some Black women as sexual transgressions or sinful behaviors that ultimately harmed and exploited women. One of the most extensive of these accounts comes from a woman by the name of Moriath Butler, a seventy-eight-year-old widow who lived at 7418 Garfield Street and was interviewed by LWP worker Robert McKinney on Valentine's Day in 1939. Even though the churchwoman's interview is filled with critiques of Black male religious actors, McKinney observed that she "[didn't] like to talk about religion, as

"DANGEROUS AND SUSPICIOUS"

a rule" and that "religious conversations [saddened] her heart and [caused her to] recall unhappy incidents with her husband, Paul Butler, who is dead but not forgotten."[93] McKinney, a Black man, described Butler in immensely misogynistic terms: "a black, mammy-type woman" who "wears a black head piece most of the time." He continued, "She is arrogant with strangers and submissive with friends. Moriath likes to sing spirituals when she is lonely and go to church when she is happy or [content]." According to McKinney, Butler once stated, "Never go to church less you is content, because if you don't the devil will sho git your mind, and there you is." McKinney told Moriath that he struggled to believe that she was truly seventy-eight given her youthful appearance, to which she responded, "Yes, I'm seventy-eight years old. You know, when Paul was doing his fooling around I was laying low preserving my health. He's gone and I'm still here . . . preserving my health" and "enjoying the fruits of this land."[94]

In her estimation, her husband was a "rock-bottom sinner man . . . who used to always say, 'ain't no need you praying for me. I done seen the Lord and He said I'm bound to go to hell.'" Paul loved whiskey and many women other than his wife. "Mens think about everything to wreck the world, not build it up," she lamented to McKinney while putting her husband's sins in conversation with those of Hitler, Mussolini, and other men promoting violence across the globe in such places as "poor Ethiopia." A country girl from Panchoville, Louisiana, Moriath described to McKinney how her "ma [arranged her] marriage with Paul [even though she] ain't even know him." She remembered how "all she [said] was that he would make you a good husband cause he was older than [she] was and had marrying on his mind." Moriath flippantly observed, "That nigger ain't had no marrying on his mind. He had me on his mind. I was nice and dandy, like the summer flower, ain't been plucked, ain't been plucked at all. He use to see me running around looking good, and that bastard got to thinking." Moriath, who was a member of the Israelite Baptist Church in New Orleans, recalled that "Paul wouldn't pray, he wouldn't go to church, he wouldn't behave himself. [That] bastard got children all over Panchoville and all over this town." Like most men who struggled with infidelity, Moriath noted how Paul often accused her of cheating with her pastor. To her surprise, one preacher tried to take advantage of her dedication to the church and used the widespread news of her husband's unfaithfulness to lure her into his car. She stated to McKinney, "I found it funny that Reverend Charlie Hunter was always telling me that he wanted me to pray with him at his house. One time he took me way, way down a road in his buggy. Had the nerve to stop and come telling me to walk or else. If it wasn't because I hate to walk, I'd beat the hell out of him. A man cracked him over the head with a broom for taking his wife in that old buggy of his. Married in his church." The preacher's predatory sexual behavior starkly resembled those of her husband, to which she recalled, "Man, Paul wouldn't marry me in no church. He just picked me and took me to a preacher friend of his. That old nigger was so anxious to git after me that he ain't never said I do." To Moriath, the men inside of religious institutions were no different from the sinner men outside of them, and for this reason, she only went to church when she felt deeply compelled.

By way of her description of Black men's sexual politics and unethical practices, Moriath also described her own religion-making process as both a church woman and mystic. Her experiences demonstrated how religion making reshaped the interior lives of migrants such that the ways that men and women related in religious spaces was intricately connected to how they engaged in the intimate space of the Black home, and vice versa. A Baptist, Moriath was also deeply attuned to a spiritual world that exceeded the bounds of African American Protestantism. She relayed the following to McKinney toward the end of her interview, "I was never a doubting person. I always [knew] about the Lord. ['Cause] I had to belong to some church. When I was small I used to see spirits. They used to frighten me so. I used to see ghosts, spirits and [natural] mens who was spirits. They would haunt me and stick shovels at me when I was sleeping . . . They left me when I got married, but I had religion when I got married."[95] Moriath described her having dreams and visions as a child and as a young adult as proof of her "having religion," or more specifically, of her "knowing the Lord." Like many Black Southerners, Moriath tapped into a long cultural practice of revering the spiritual significance of dreams. Africana religious studies scholar LeRhonda S. Manigault-Bryant describes the phenomena of discerning spiritual presences at nighttime as "talking to the dead," which "surpasses denominationalism, exceeds the limits of geography, and speaks to the broad use of the custom as a spiritual practice."[96] Manigault-Bryant maintains that talking to the dead has historically represented people of African descent's "pluralistic religious sensibilities," and more specifically, the ways people of African descent have put Christian practice into their own cultural terms by drawing on Black Atlantic folk belief systems.[97] For Moriath, her engagement with the spirit world, specifically her seeing "spirits"—broadly understood as ghosts and natural men who were spirits—and their having negative intent toward her served as a spiritual warning—one that caused her great fear. When she married her husband, Paul, these dreams and

"DANGEROUS AND SUSPICIOUS"   145

visions ceased, perhaps demonstrating her own prophetic insight into her husband's soon-to-come infidelity, excessive drinking, and commitment to "sin" and to "going to hell." Her spiritual gifting, specifically her ability to communicate with spirits, was proof of her "having religion," which confirmed for her that she did not need to regularly participate in the life of a church to be in right standing with her God, even as she believed that she had "to belong to some church."

Moriath's Black Atlantic religion making substantiated her agency around the frequency with which she attended church, her use of cuss words and expletives such as "nigger" in reference to her late husband, Paul, and her enjoyment of certain vices. For instance, in the last lines of her interview, Moriath described participating in the local lottery. "Gimme six, nine and four" she told the numbers man, in front of McKinney. She reasoned, "Son, if them numbers come out I'm going git eighteen dollars . . . That ain't gambling. The Lord says he helps those who helps themselves [and] in these trying times people is got to do something." She concluded by saying that she needed to go off to "dream about them numbers."[98] Moriath's truth telling and her openness to LWP worker Robert McKinney about her failed marriage, her reticence concerning the preachers at her local Baptist church, and her religious experiences replete with dreams, visions, spirits, and numbers confirm the myriad ways that Black New Orleanians negotiated the contested terrain of love, sex, and marriage. These nuances, as confirmed by the LWP archive, also demonstrate the complex religious and sexual politics practiced and debated among religious practitioners of African descent amid Jim Crow policing.

Butler, Horn, Lyons, and informant 864 were all natives to Louisiana, and somehow each found their way to New Orleans or in some form of conversation with the vast religious diaspora of the city. In their efforts to espouse, practice, and theologize their religious, sexual, and everyday experiences as migrants, they each negotiated and encountered the social confinement caused by the white Christian hegemonic state. Whether through literal imprisonment, victimization and misrepresentation in the press, being harassed by the police, or navigating the consequences of Jim Crow and the Great Depression, each of these practitioners articulated their own religion-making discourses. Their claims emphasized the need for religious pluralism, the freedom to practice their own religions, and their own understandings of how their transgressive or nontraditional religious and sexual politics and practices challenged dominant legal structures and the accepted status quo social respectability prominent in many white and

Black mainline Christian institutions. Other religious actors like the storied members of the Universal Negro Improvement Association, the subject of the next chapter, disrupted ideas about social respectability in more forceful ways and called upon African American Protestant clergymen to take seriously the racialized and classed struggles of the urban poor and other migrants from across the African diaspora, using Christian theological hermeneutics in concert with Pan-Africanism, Ethiopianism, Hinduism, and New Thought.

VISITATION 5

ZORA'S UNPUBLISHED SATIRE ON MARCUS GARVEY

"The Emperor Effaces Himself"

As a military genius he had no faith in himself at all. Tho he was Admiralissimo of the "African Navy," Generalissimo of the "African Legions," he frequently expressed a fearful lack of confidence. But these expressions placed side by side with his mighty accomplishments are proof positive of the man's overwhelming modesty....

With rare foresight, he saw that the redeeming of the entire continent of Africa would take time. It would be no easy task to make it safe for the black folk of the world. They must not be too optimistic he told them....

He was a fearless seeker after truth. By scientific investigation, he discovered that The Virgin Mary was a black woman, and that Jesus Christ, a mulatto who has been "passing" these two thousand years. So, what could be fairer than showing them in their true colors? [What] could be darker? Nothing, according to the 1924 edition of his modest little parade.[1]

ZORA NEALE HURSTON

ZORA'S UNPUBLISHED SATIRE ON MARCUS GARVEY

"The Emperor Effaces Himself"

As a military genius he had no faith in himself at all. Tho' he was Admiral-in-chief of the "African Navy," Generalissimo of the "African Legion," he frequently expressed a fearful lack of confidence, but these expressions placed side by side with his mighty accomplishments are not positive of the man's overwhelming modesty.

With rare foresight, he saw that the redemption of the entire continent of Africa would take time. It would be too early yet to make it safe for the black folk of the world. They must not be too optimistic, he told them.

He was a zealous seeker after truth. By scientific investigation, he discovered that The Virgin Mary was a black woman, and that Jesus Christ, a mulatto who has been "passing" these two thousand years. So what could be fairer than showing them in their true colors? What could be clearer? Nothing to the royal edition of the modest little parade.

ZORA NEALE HURSTON

"THE RIGHT IDEA OF GOD"

Sinners and Saints in the New Orleans Division of the Universal Negro Improvement Association

> The Universal Negro Improvement Association is anchored forever, as far as its dignity and honor are concerned, in the city of New Orleans.
>
> MARCUS MOSIAH GARVEY[1]

> It is true that some of us are not church members, neither have we any intention of joining a church until we find a leader who is truly following in the footsteps of Jesus and caring for the hungry and naked children of the poor, as Christians . . . The Universal Negro Improvement Association is our church, our clubhouse, our theater, our fraternal order and our school and we will never forsake it while we live; neither will our men forsake it, but fear has crept into our hearts because of the police's continued interference with our meetings. We are afraid that some night we may have some serious trouble.
>
> WOMEN OF THE NEW ORLEANS DIVISION, Universal Negro Improvement Association[2]

"Some tremble before the blue-eyed God, here and elsewhere, believing that the God of Isaac and of Jacob trembled also before this Son of Belial," exclaimed Barbadian and Universal Negro Improvement Association (UNIA) official Adrian Johnson in a speech delivered to the New Orleans

Division (NOD) in February 1921.[3] "We want the preachers to understand that the UNIA is solidly behind the preachers and the churches who have the right idea of God," he confessed, amid cheers. "What do I mean by the right idea of God?" Johnson asked. "I mean that God created man to enjoy the earth, with unlimited possibilities. He desires man to so unfold the God-like spark in him that when he has accomplished so many wonderful things that will amaze even himself he will, when baffled by the ways of nature, conclude that his Creator is the evident Superior and will be intuitively convicted to worship Him as he should in spirit and truth." Johnson's words, like those of intellectuals E. Franklin Frazier and W. E. B. Du Bois, were a critique of the "jack-legged preachers" of his time who often preached about a blue-eyed, blond-haired white Jesus and "fleeced their flocks."[4] Johnson reasoned, "The preacher who teaches to Negroes that they must not desire silver or gold, but desire only to enter the fold, 'take all this world and give me Jesus,' must go as being spiritually and morally unfit to live as a man created after God's own image." Johnson pleaded with the NOD to "be aware!" and "awake to righteousness and sin not against [God] as being responsible for the race's condition."[5] He believed that the NOD was uniquely charged to spread racial consciousness in the underworld of the Black Atlantic, specifically the unification of all people of African descent across the globe with hopes of eventually returning to the continent of Africa.

A year before Johnson was dispatched from Harlem, New York, by UNIA founder Marcus Mosiah Garvey to lead a membership drive in New Orleans, Alaida (Henry) Robertson, a Nicaraguan, cofounded the NOD in her home on October 12, 1920, in the Eleventh Ward at 621 Dryades Street.[6] Robertson lived with her husband, Sylvester, a native Louisianan and local bank porter; their son, Leon; and her mother, Milwood, a nurse.[7] A revered dressmaker and influential political organizer, Robertson recruited her family and friends into the fold of African redemption as popularized by Garvey and the UNIA. As historian Claudrena Harold has observed, "New Orleans claimed more than four thousand UNIA members by the fall of 1921," thanks to the hard-fought organizing efforts of working-class individuals, such as the Robertsons, Johnson, and secretary Mamie Reason.[8] Historian Mary G. Rolinson similarly notes in *Grassroots Garveyism*, "A huge portion of the UNIA divisions were between or near New Orleans and Baton Rouge right on the river, including eleven in or adjacent to New Orleans. Just south and east of New Orleans were eight more. Southwest of New Orleans were two divisions and moving west and north along the river were twenty-seven UNIA divisions, including seven at Baton Rouge."[9]

"THE RIGHT IDEA OF GOD"

The NOD quickly became one of the largest throughout the US South and circum-Caribbean, due largely to the mass migration of West Indians and Central Americans to the city in the early twentieth century.[10] One reporter observed, "[The UNIA] was a West Indian movement, the first rise of the West Indian peasants."[11] In Black New Orleans during the 1920s and 1930s, the NOD's membership base represented a conglomeration of migrants from the Black Atlantic world.

Garvey, "the Negro Moses," had radicalized people of African descent throughout the British West Indies, and they followed him just as the Israelites had followed the Hebrew prophet Moses. They then migrated from their homelands to such port cities as New Orleans, often immediately searching for UNIA chapters to join as a means of acclimating to the unique racial politics of the United States. On August 12, 1922, for instance, New Orleans residents David J. A. Duncanson, a Jamaican, and Felix H. Britton, a Nicaraguan, wrote to Garvey on behalf of the West Indian Colonies of Louisiana and described him as "the mouthpiece of the living God as Moses was of old."[12] During the 1920s and 1930s, both men were active in the NOD and recruited people from their countries to also join. In March 1922, Britton wrote an opinion editorial in the *Negro World* entitled "The UNIA Is a Religion."[13] By the late 1930s when the NOD began to decline, the two sought out other ways to survive in the underworld. While the sources are unclear about Duncanson's whereabouts by the 1940s, Britton sold numbers, gambled, and was under constant police scrutiny.[14] His struggles with the law, however, were indicative of the incessant policing and criminalization that working-class migrants faced in the era of Jim Crow, especially as they used the black market as a site of employment and survival, and for the cultivation of their own brand of underworld works.[15]

This chapter takes Garvey's observations from the opening epigraph about the NOD's reach and influence along with the NOD's discussions of ritual as a critical opportunity to assess the relationship between religion making and political organizing among migrants of African descent. It draws not only from the political rhetoric in the UNIA's newspaper, the *Negro World*, but also from UNIA opinion editorials about the place and significance of intellectual debate and intracommunal fighting in Black Atlantic religious and political life to argue that people of African descent's religious institutions often materialize by way of principled struggle. Unlike other divisions, it was in New Orleans that Garvey saw this practice of Black Atlantic religion making come together with the UNIA's Afro-Protestantism, specifically the use of scripture, hymns, the Ethiopian National Anthem, and the *Universal Negro Ritual* and the *Universal Negro Catechism*.[16] The NOD was also a stomping ground and an underworld portal to pass through for many notable political organizers and preachers, who took lessons back to the above ground and to their respective divisions and churches after leaving New Orleans.[17] For these reasons, and others related to their disregard for apolitical Black Christianities, as demonstrated by their critiques of Black clergy's frequent misuse of power and exploitation of the poor in New Orleans, the Black press and state entities painted the NOD as "troubled" and aggressively contentious. Moreover, the NOD's insistence on cultivating "the right idea of God" challenged mainline respectability and carved space for those often excluded from actively serving in traditional Afro-Protestant churches. It effectively set itself in direct opposition to anti-Black constructions of the Divine and celebrated Black Atlantic practices—religious, cultural, and otherwise—unique to the city of New Orleans and the Caribbean.

Additionally, the NOD attempted to expand notions of the sacred and to contest understandings of the profane, especially regarding what constituted a "religious" or "sacred" space (i.e., by holding meetings or "church" in fraternity lodges, casinos, bars, homes, etc.) and the disruption of spaces deemed religious or sacred, such as African American Protestant churches, through acts of physical and verbal assault. Without question, the NOD criticized African American religions, more specifically African American Protestant churches, to cultivate their own religious, racial, and political identity and to distinguish themselves from mainline religious, political, and civic organizations, such as the National Association for the Advancement of Colored People (NAACP) and other prominent local entities. The NOD understood errant practices and ways of being demonized by the white American Christian hegemonic state to be sites of the sacred, spaces in which to theorize and theologize its Black religious nationalism. By prioritizing and welcoming conflict, the NOD sacralized long-held notions of the profane and scripturalized its own concept of the sacred. Much of this scripturalization depended on the Bible, whose Africanity the NOD invoked, and the NOD drew parallels between its present-day experiences and those of its African forebears.

The UNIA's political perspectives and tenets were enmeshed with Black Atlantic Christian cultural histories. Thus, partnering with, critiquing, and distancing itself from mainline or more traditional Black Christian formations were central to the UNIA's cultivation of its own "Black religious nationalism," which the historian Tracey E. Hucks aptly describes as being able to "subvert the association of blackness with deified evil and make a deliberate attempt to theologically realign blackness with divine essence," cultivate "new theologies . . . that emphasize the inherent divinity or primordial universality of blackness," and propagate political ideologies in which "Africa is often revalued and historically honored as a sacred source of ancient philosophies and traditions."[18] To develop this strategic grammar for sacred and highly politicized discourse about anti-Blackness in the Americas, the UNIA drew from the very same scriptures that had once been used to dehumanize people of African descent and reinterpreted them. To do so meant that the UNIA could not do away with Black Protestant and Catholic churches but would instead have to encourage those institutions to align theologically with the ethos of Pan-Africanism, especially in places across the diaspora that had only "ended" enslavement in the previous century. In 1929, Garvey posited that the UNIA was "fundamentally a religious institution," and that "instead of attacking the churches of the preachers [the UNIA] should diplomatically get around them and get them to see the virtues of the Organization so that they may fall in line and preach the doctrine of the Universal Negro Improvement Association to their followers." Garvey believed that such a strategy would honor the "religion of [their] fathers" while "harnessing the strongest element on the outside, and in the space of a few years [they] [would] have a Negro idealism of [their] own or any kind of a religion that [would] make [them] strong in [their] faith."[19]

The UNIA's cultivation of a new "Negro idealism," particularly the NOD's Black Atlantic religion making—or put differently, its honoring of some traditions and irreverence toward certain components deemed detrimental to the project of Black liberation—was a significant feature of its underworld work. The *Negro World* noted in 1928, "The Hon. Marcus Garvey is a matchless genius. He knows more about religion than the preacher knows; knows how to apply it better than the preacher [and] in this day and time it behooves every wide-awake Negro to grasp securely the religion of Garveyism."[20] New Orleans's religious culture when combined with Afro-Protestantism deeply shaped and informed the NOD's Black Atlantic religion making, and much of this history is intertwined with New Orleans's long history as an American city home to vice, debauchery, Conjure, rootwork, Voudou, and jazz religion.

This chapter begins with a discussion of the place of religion in the NOD. Then it explores the NOD's inclusion of New Orleans's second line parades and jazz ensembles in its proceedings, which are traditions that hold religious and geographic significance in the region given the influence of Voudou; Black and white Spiritual, Catholic, Pentecostal, and Baptist churches;

FIGURE 5.1. Garvey with New Orleans Division members, December 1927, by Arthur Bedou. Courtesy of Xavier University of Louisiana.

Mardi Gras Indians; and jazz funerals.[21] Next, it examines two cases of clergy murder inside of African American Protestant churches—allegedly involving UNIA (and specifically, NOD) members—in order to examine how infighting (not to be confused with the murders), aided in the cultivation of UNIA and NOD religious, racial, and political identity. Finally, it analyzes the relationship between Garvey's UNIA and Father Divine's Peace Mission through the work of Louisianan Madame Maymie Leona Turpeau de Mena. Here the focus is on how contention and political debate shaped Black religious life in New Orleans in the 1920s and 1930s and ultimately informed migrants' individual practices of Black Atlantic religion making.

RELIGION IN THE NEW ORLEANS DIVISION OF THE UNIVERSAL NEGRO IMPROVEMENT ASSOCIATION

The UNIA was a religious organization with political objectives and a political organization with religious sensibilities. Historian Randall K. Burkett writes, "The religious ethos of the UNIA was pervasive, embracing nearly every facet of its organizational life."[22] Like other divisions, the NOD convened on Sundays, and its meetings simultaneously drew from and critiqued the lexicon and practices of African American Protestantism, using rituals, chants, hymns, scripture readings, and speeches that mirrored sermons. The *Negro World* reported in January 1925 that one such meeting "commenced in the prescribed manner under the chairmanship of Honorable Sylvester V. Robertson, president and commissioner of the States of Louisiana and Mississippi. The hymn 'Shine on, Eternal Light,' written by Arnold Josiah Ford, a Barbadian rabbi, and the musical director at Liberty Hall in Harlem, was sung. The UNIA band rendered a selection and the military units of the division commanded by Colonel C.W. Thompson and Captain Samuel Smith reviewed before the audience."[23] Much like a church announcer, Mr. Phillip Clinton read "the front page of *The Negro World*"; similar to a pastor delivering a fiery sermon, Robertson proclaimed his address; and much like a pastor's wife, Alaida was referred to as Lady Robertson and as the "mother of the division." Indeed, Thomas Anderson, who in 1921 became commissioner of the state of Louisiana for the UNIA, asserted, "We are intensely religious, but the difference between us and the others is that we think."[24]

For the members of the NOD and the UNIA more broadly, "the others" signified African American denominations, such as Baptists, Methodists, and Pentecostals, which Garvey perceived as mainline and more traditional, though of course, as historians of African American religions have shown, many of these same institutions struggled for communal acceptance given their wide-ranging spiritual practices and theological beliefs, especially the "holy-rolling" members of the Sanctified Church. In a 1923 Christmas address at Liberty Hall entitled "Our Religion," Anderson would go on further to describe the need for belief in a Black God among African Americans— a belief that he saw lacking among "the others." "[The negro] must learn to fight; he must believe that God Almighty, the God that he believes in, that he prays to daily, believes also in fighting." He continued, "The black man's conception of God, as I understand it, is a mighty bum conception. He believes in the white man's God." Anderson believed that people of African descent needed to lay down the white man's God, or "a God of jim-crowism, a God of lynching, of burning at the stake, that believes in keeping black folks down." By following a white God, often depicted iconographically in many African American churches as a blue-eyed, blond-haired, white Jesus, the Black man failed "to see God . . . in himself." Anderson's prophetic ruminations incited cheers and laughter, as he also encouraged people of African descent to "celebrate the Birth of Jesus Christ [by setting] a proper conception of God" as a reflection of their own black skin and lived experiences.[25]

As much as the NOD was concerned with the Black liberation struggle and Pan-Africanism, its underworld meetings were contentious sites for the cultivation of Black religious nationalism *and* of sacred space for individuals deemed "sinners" or "heathens" in traditional African American Protestant churches—a mission that differentiated it from such Black transnational denominations as the AME Church. One member boldly proclaimed, "We are not members of the Negro 400 of New Orleans, composed of the class spending their time imitating the rich white, with card parties, eating parties, and studying Spanish as to be able to pass for anything but a Negro. We are not ashamed of the race to which we belong and we feel sure that God made black skin and kinky hair because He desired to express Himself in that type as well as in any other."[26] The emphasis on and theologizing of black skin by UNIA members was largely related to Ethiopianism, or people of African descent's historical and deep spiritual connection with Ethiopia given the biblical "Ethiopian prophecy" from Psalm 68:31, which reads, "Princes shall come forth out of Egypt; Ethiopia shall soon stretch forth her hands unto God."[27] They also saw Ethiopia's emperor Haile Selassie as the chosen prophet given Garvey's words in 1920, "Look to Africa, when a black king shall be crowned, for the day of deliverance is at hand." African American religious actors—for instance, Bishop Henry McNeal Turner and the AME Church and Bishop McGuire and the African Orthodox Church— also saw Liberia, Ethiopia, and continental Africa as God-ordained destinations for oppressed people of African descent across the globe.[28] The NOD's members believed and preached these ideas, often to recruit immigrants. Indeed, people of African descent's use of scripture to convey political ideas has a long history, and the UNIA preached its own Black religious nationalism, which ultimately depended on competing understandings of "nationalism."[29] On the one hand, the UNIA saw itself as re-creating a nation of African-descended peoples across the globe. On the other hand, they were deeply invested in troubling "American" conceptions of "the nation" that undergirded the pillaging, colonization, and invasion of Caribbean, Latin American, and African nations in the late nineteenth and early twentieth centuries. Consider, for instance, the occupation and invasion of Haiti from 1915 to 1934. By appealing to such persons as Haitians, the UNIA's members set themselves in opposition to the United States and to its reach as an empire across the African diaspora. To do so, they utilized transnational networks in conversation with scriptures that supported the work of Black liberation, performing according to a biblical script. Garvey was believed to be a prophet, the UNIA was his flock, and the NOD, like divisions across the United States and the circum-Caribbean, worked to bring members to be shepherded back to Africa.

In the NOD, Black religious nationalism was an organizing principle both within and beyond members' engagement with African American Protestant churches. The NOD, like many of its sister divisions throughout the United States, brought together West Indian, Central American, and African American migrants in African American Protestant churches. In New Orleans, some of these individuals also found themselves transforming African American Catholic churches in the city and throughout Louisiana more broadly.[30] As Sylvester Johnson and Edward Curtis IV have contended, "Black migration from Africa and the Caribbean has been a uniquely important factor in shaping future trends in Black Christianity in the United States. Since the early twentieth century, Black congregations in the United States have included the visible presence of Black immigrants from the Caribbean and Africa (particularly of sub-Saharan nations)."[31] The NOD's relationship to African American Protestantism, albeit contentious, is representative of the historical presence of Caribbean and African immigrants in African American Protestantism, but also of Central Americans and Afro-Latino immigrants in early twentieth-century African American churches, especially in major port cities, such as New Orleans, Louisiana, and Miami, Florida.

In 1917, for example, during his speaking and fundraising tour of New Orleans and other parts of Louisiana, Garvey spoke at several African American Protestant churches. One historian has surmised that "one likely place that Garvey would have spoken at was the radical Tulane Baptist Church," where "most of its members were a part of [the] National Association for the Advancement of Colored People (NAACP), and W.E.B. Du Bois, the editor of the NAACP Magazine the *Crisis*, made an announcement [in] May of 1916 that Garvey would be visiting various cities on a speaking and fundraising engagement."[32] As discussed in chapter 3, Garvey's tour mirrored Booker T. Washington's Louisiana Tour, in much the same way that some of Garvey's political ideology had been informed by Washington.[33] Just as Washington recruited West Indians and Central Americans to attend the Tuskegee Institute, Garvey also recruited them to the UNIA.[34]

In the years following Garvey's tour, several Black New Orleanian clergy members either joined the NOD or invited NOD members to participate in the life of their churches. The *Negro World* observed in 1922, for instance, "Mr. George McWaters, acting president has also contributed favorably to the interest of the UNIA in New Orleans. Mr. McWaters, being a Christian and a prominent church worker, has successfully represented the Universal Negro Improvement Association in the educational and ecclesiastical circle of the Crescent City, so that pastors of note are inviting the Garvey movement to their church for the enlightenment of the church members."[35] McWaters would later become the pastor of the Pleasant Zion Missionary Baptist Church, which he founded on December 26, 1926, just down the road from where one NOD chapter convened. On another occasion, in June 1922, Nicaraguan immigrant Alaida Robertson, commonly referred to as "lady president" and "the pioneer of the work of the UNIA in Louisiana," spoke with force on the part to be played by the women in this great program of a free and redeemed Africa," following a speech by Mrs. E. A. Brown on "The U.N.I.A. in the Light of Theology" inside of the Samuel Israelite Baptist Church.[36] Robertson was widely known in the South and the circum-Caribbean as a great orator who gave lectures "which [were] very much enjoyed and brought much inspiration."[37] One might say that Robertson would have been a preacher had Black women been ordained in many Black mainline denominations.[38] She most certainly preached and brought many souls into the NOD.

Like Robertson, many other NOD members also found ways to preach the gospel of African redemption both inside and outside of African American Protestant churches. The *Negro World* documented several meetings and religious services held at Petty's Chapel AME Zion Church in the city where an immigrant from Georgetown, British Guiana, Reverend Dr. Arthur Clifford Yearwood, pastored.[39] At one such service in September 1925, the honorable J. J. Peters, then-president of the NOD, "filled the pulpit" at Petty's and read from Jeremiah chapter 3, verse 1, with the subject "I am tired of injustice." The *Negro World* reported that he "likened the cry of the bewailing prophet to the cry of the present-day Negro who is being bruised and broken by the road of the 'oppressor.'"[40] In St. Rose, Louisiana, in 1924, the UNIA met at the Fifth African Baptist Church, another church with a radical history, where NOD members delivered speeches.[41] St. Rose division member Samuel Gant observed, "The addresses were full of good advice and inspiration and gave new life to the [St. Rose] members to continue in their good work. The members of this division expect to work harder during the coming year in order that the day of African redemption may be hastened."[42] The following Easter Sunday, Charles W. Jackson, executive secretary of the NOD delivered a "rousing address" before the congregation sang the UNIA's anthem.[43] Although many NOD members were highly critical of African American Protestant churches, many of them found ways to use the pulpit space innovatively to radicalize congregations, teach about African redemption, and stir up a collective interest in the reunification of African peoples across the globe. Intrigued, many congregants would leave their churches and join the NOD. Some, however, struggled to balance a commitment to their local church with one to the NOD.

In a 1928 update to the UNIA, J. J. Peters of NOD 149 wrote in the *Negro World*, "Because the general mass meeting of the U.N.I.A. is being held at the same time in the night when the church is conducting its religious services, hundreds of good citizens and friends of the U.N.I.A. cannot find it convenient to attend our meeting on Sunday night."[44] The NOD changed its meeting time to Sunday at 3:30 p.m. before Sunday-evening church services, demonstrating both the significance and reception of the NOD by some of New Orleans's Black Protestants and their own complicated relationships to the underworld. Their having to choose between traditional church formations and the NOD's church-like programming suggests that there were larger religious implications to the political work that the NOD envisioned itself as doing. Certainly, as Peters emphasized, the NOD did not desire to take African American Protestant churches' place, but its leaders prioritized "usefulness and numerical strength." Yet it is important to also note that many Black New Orleanians continued to consider African American Protestant churches to also be "useful," most evident in the long list of churches open during the period. In the *New Orleans City Guide*, for example, published in 1938 by the Works Progress Administration (WPA), it was reported that "although a recent directory lists 492 churches in the city, it is estimated that there are 600 churches of Negroes alone." In this way, the NOD saw itself in competition with traditional African American Protestants, or what the WPA described as "the major Negro churches," and it sought to recruit members from the "scores of smaller organizations," otherwise referred to as "some negro cults" by the staff of the LWP.[45]

Even as the NOD tried to accommodate traditional Protestant worship styles, its coupling of entertainment with Black religious nationalism offered many a more a holistic faith, which spoke to their spiritual needs but also celebrated members' desire for partying, smoking, and drinking. It also amplified Protestant anxieties about the decline of the "church's influence" and related fears that they would be "eclipsed by the world of entertainments."[46] This anxiety was present within the NOD and in African American Protestant churches in New Orleans, so much so that the NOD strategically sought to ease tensions and forge a way forward for the Christian juke lounge enthusiast who spent many nights in the underworld seeking services and entertainment, albeit under a veil or with a concealed identity. Many of these anxieties related to larger discourses about race, religion, and capitalism, as "a growing variety of popular entertainments such as films, theater, nightclubs, professional sports, and radio programs . . . all marketed specifically to their communities."[47]

The NOD seized this fraught cultural moment and crafted its own marketing and advertising platform, which did not condemn Saturday sinners, but instead readily welcomed them into its meetings on Sunday evenings, a practice that set it apart from theologically and socially conservative Baptists, Methodists, and Pentecostals. The women of the NOD, for instance, once collectively wrote in the *Negro World*, "[The NOD] is our church, our clubhouse, our theater, our fraternal order and our school and we will never forsake it while we live; neither will our men forsake it."[48] In response to these efforts, one NOD member claimed that the NOD "is alive and full of enthusiasm, our Liberty Hall is packed at every meeting, members are joining by the hundred, delinquent members are paying up, some paying six to twelve months back dues, the offerings on meeting night range from $25 to $50." He continued, "This great ship has cast over a Jonah, the sea of dissatisfaction has been calmed and we are now sailing on to success."[49] According to the *Negro World*, the NOD's intentional recruitment efforts and its undoing of the sinner-saint binary so prevalent in African American Protestant church life allowed it to triumph as other religious groups allegedly struggled to keep members, to fill pews, and to appeal to the burgeoning entertainment industry in New Orleans. Rather than set themselves as antagonists to New Orleanian nightlife, the NOD embraced the world of entertainments, jazz, and dancing. As historian Alison Collis Greene has contended regarding the Delta, "The saints danced and played instruments on Sunday mornings, as did the sinners in the juke joints on Saturday nights. Blues singers condemned the preachers, preachers condemned the blues singers, and they all damned the devil."[50] The NOD understood this, condemned the preachers, danced with the sinners, and called white devils out by name.

THE NEW ORLEANS DIVISION, ENTERTAINMENT, AND BLACK RELIGIONS IN THE JAZZ AGE

In 1921, when Marcus Garvey visited New Orleans, he was also captivated by the African diasporic cultural and religious practices of the NOD, in particular New Orleans second line parades and jazz ensembles. Claudrena Harold has contended, "An important cultural center, the New Orleans UNIA provided an institutional space where men and women could listen and dance to the syncopated sounds of the division's jazz band, showcase their various talents, debate the meaning of human existence, laugh and cry over life's joys and pains, and criticize the ways of white folks and the black elite without fear of reprisal."[51] Indeed, Garvey said, "When I arrived in New Orleans I found hundreds of loyal men—good men and true men—who were waiting to receive me through the great work that Johnson had done preparatory to my getting there." He continued, "We had a time in New Orleans. They had a large plaza and they had midnight dances and other amusements. They had music, and they danced all night."[52] Garvey's attention to the uniqueness of New Orleans jazz culture is significant, even as jazz could of course be found in places outside of New Orleans in the 1920s and 1930s. In Harlem, for example, where the UNIA's national headquarters was based, jazz bands were commonly included in the organization's proceedings. One UNIA member reported that in August 1921, "to the strains of jazz music, played as only negro bandsmen can play it, 15,000 negroes [gathered] from all parts of the 'black belt,' as the big negro colony here is known, as a preliminary to the opening of the International Convention of the Negro Races of the World, which [lasted] the month."[53] In January 1922, for instance, "a band played jazz and hymns before the meeting began. Garvey led a prayer, the choir sang, and the meeting began. Uniformed militia of the association, in vivid blue, with swords dangling at just-so-creased and striped trousers, paraded up and down the aisles."[54] Just two years prior, a jazz musician whose parents were from Madagascar, Andy Razaf (otherwise known by his stage name "Razz"), graced Liberty Hall rendering songs entitled "Garvey! Hats Off to Garvey!" and "UNIA." Razz performed and collaborated with celebrated jazz composer Fats Waller and pianist-composer Eubie Blake. The three cowrote lyrics for several popular Black Broadway shows during the 1930s.[55] One historian notes that Garvey and the UNIA partnered with jazz musicians in an effort to recruit members by tapping into the pulse of Black cultural life during the Jazz Age.[56] Yet, even as jazz was commonly invoked across UNIA chapters in the United States, New Orleans was the only place in which Garvey penned a reflection concerning jazz and its religious and political significance in the UNIA.

In the New Orleanian underworld, jazz was inseparable from Black religious culture. In *Gumbo Ya-Ya*, a book published in 1945 by the LWP based on fieldwork from the 1920s and 1930s, the authors took note of the city's Holy Week festivities, writing, "Masquerades and dances still take place in New Orleans and its vicinity [at] night. Many clubs give parties, and most of the Saint Joseph altar-donors terminate the night in dancing. Everyone considers it a joyous intermission in the Lenten season, which is so strictly observed here . . . On South Rampart Street, blacks, browns, and high yellows step high, wide and fancy, and there are numerous balls and dances."[57] What Garvey witnessed when he participated in the NOD's proceedings was the NOD's enmeshment in the larger religious and cultural history of the city of New Orleans. This is evident in how jazz religion was invoked in the division in the years following Garvey's initial visit. On Sunday, April 3, 1927, the NOD held its regular Garvey Day celebration at Liberty Hall at 2919 South Rampart Street. LWP writer Robert Tallant described "jazz [as] the sound of South Rampart Street" such that "it comes from every doorway, from every direction—from juke boxes, from the phonographs in the music stores, wherein the customers seem always to be playing recordings made by Negro bands and artists, from radios in shoeshine stands and barber shops, sometimes from an old-time 'inner player' piano beyond an upstairs window."[58] Indeed, the NOD's celebrations also occurred in the same vicinity as the Saint Joseph's Day and Mardi Gras festivals described by the LWP. One attendee recalled, "The afternoon was spent in a very pleasant manner. We were entertained by two well-known bands of the city, namely, 'The Lions Original Jazz Band' and our band, 'Holy Ghost.'"[59] Out of all of the UNIA chapters, the NOD arguably depended the most on jazz to cultivate a unique identity, rooted in their sacred geospatial location.[60] Garvey was fortunate to bear witness to this, just one year after the NOD was founded.

In the years after, jazz, lavish parties, and dance were particularly quotidian. At one NOD program with jazz as "picturesque as the Garden of Eden," one reporter described the NOD as "surmounting all obstacles and overcoming seeming difficulties. She is eager with a fervent desire to outstrip the very demons of hell and, at last, reach the goal aimed for by the four hundred million Negroes of the world—AFRICA, OUR FATHERLAND."[61] A couple months later, during one of his many visits to New Orleans, the

"THE RIGHT IDEA OF GOD"   163

Rev. James Walker Hood Eason, pastor of the Zion AME Church in New
York and the then-second-highest-ranking official of the UNIA, was "entertained" with jazz by NOD members at the home of Mr. and Mrs. J. W. Jones,
who lived at 917 Joseph Street. "The courses were cocktail appetizer olives,
salad in cucumber cups, creamed crabs on toast, creamed tomatoes, roast
chicken, snap beans, punch, mousse, cream and strawberry sauce." Eason,
"a broad-minded diplomat" explained the aims and objectives of the UNIA,
hoping to impress those there and to recruit more Black New Orleanians.[62]
Eason's words were significant, but perhaps not as essential as the jazz band
and the Joneses' decadent culinary fare.

Even as jazz unified some in the UNIA, it remained largely contentious
for others within the organization, just as it had been for mainline African
American Protestants. In 1936, while Garvey was in London, he scrutinized
Baptists and Pentecostals for their use of "jazz," or a mostly trance-inducing,
enigmatic dance, chanting, and sermonizing. In a letter to Lord John C. W.
Reth, the director of the British Broadcasting Corporation (BBC), Garvey
lambasted Reth for broadcasting a religious service from Washington, DC.
"Anyone who listened to that supposed religious service could have come
to no other conclusion than it was a good circus performance or jazz entertainment," Garvey explained. "There was nothing of RELIGION IN IT except
a shouting of the supposed preacher of the name of 'God' and 'Jesus Christ'
in the midst of a tumult of noise with the rhythmic air of a jazz band. The
stamping of feet and clapping of hands with the boisterous music played do
not coincide with the true religious life of the Negro in the United States."[63]
Garvey had most likely heard the radio broadcast of Elder Solomon Lightfoot Michaux, founder of an independent Church of God congregation in
the district, who had been contracted with the BBC from 1936 to 1938. Felix
Crum, a BBC representative, wrote to Michaux, "The chief thing is to make
the listener in England feel that he is listening—not to a service specially put
on for him—but to a normal Negro gathering . . . In a queer way a service of
this kind, known to be specially arranged, loses authenticity . . . I want my
countrymen at home to realize the power there is in a group singing with
real religious spirit and fervor."[64] Crum and the BBC were titillated by a particular kind of African American religious charisma, and Michaux, who was
known as "the Happy Am I Preacher" for his flamboyant performances and
dramatic sermons, provided them with exactly what they wanted. Moreover,
Michaux's charismatic, conservative evangelical Christianity did not mesh
well with the more left-leaning political rhetoric of Garvey and the UNIA,
especially as Michaux served as what historian Lerone Martin has described

as a "bureau clergyman" under J. Edgar Hoover's tenure as director of the Federal Bureau of Investigation (FBI). In this role, he "laundered information for the FBI" in exchange for "a host of political favors ranging from the all-important Cold War endorsement of the FBI, classified information, and personal favors from the FBI at the expense of taxpayers."[65] The politics at the helm of Michaux's jazz religion incensed Garvey.

Consequently, Garvey expressed his concern with the supposed "religious" practices of the African American charismatic, so much so that he feared that the broadcast was "calculated to be nothing other than a vicious propaganda to discredit the black man before the English public."[66] Despite Garvey's insistence on social respectability and formulism, the NOD, which he had celebrated just fifteen years prior for their use of jazz, regularly blurred the lines between popular notions of the sacred and the secular. The amalgamation of "entertainment" and "religion" as performed and embodied in the New Orleans second line and jazz ensemble disrupted hegemonic categorization and dominant conceptions of "proper" religious and political aesthetics. Garvey, however, overlooked these nuances, notwithstanding the joy he experienced because of it and his having been drawn to its intoxicating elusiveness. As Martin reminds us in *Preaching on Wax*, Garvey, and the UNIA, like other "uplift groups branded these [programs] racist, contrary to bourgeoisie representations of blackness, and therefore a blight to racial progress. Black proponents of middle-class racial uplift believed that the public sphere held the power to shape popular—that is, white— conceptions of [Black people]."[67] Even as the UNIA often criticized other racial uplift groups as acquiescing to whiteness, it also encouraged and practiced bourgeoise respectability. In this way, the UNIA reimagined itself as a church outside of traditional Black Protestantism "by creating alternative forms of commercial entertainment," which were "bourgeois in style" but not bourgeois in the sense that it still appealed to members of the working class.[68]

Much of Garvey's disdain for charismatic religious expression had to do with his association with the Anglican Catholic Church as early as 1908 in Kingston, Jamaica. Historian Colin Grant observes that the emerging leader, then in his early twenties, had "[forged] strong links with the Roman Catholic diocese of Jamaica, and would convert to Catholicism."[69] Prior to his conversion, Garvey and his family were members of local Baptist churches, and he had personally witnessed the revivalist, early Holiness movement take root in Kingston. While the exact reason behind his conversion is unclear, in a 1929 article in the *Blackman*, he wrote, "I have been a Baptist all my life; I have been a Catholic all my life and my fathers before me have been Baptists or Catholics all their lives, and they found no fault with their religion: it is useless if somebody gets up with some new thoughts endeavoring to tell me there is no God, no need to belong to any church, and expect me all in a sudden to give up all the beliefs of my fathers and follow him when he is not a God, when he cannot perform miracles."[70] Garvey was most certainly a Christian, but he had a particular appreciation for more reserved worship, which he found in Catholic devotional culture, and he was particularly distrusting of new religious movement leaders like Michaux, Father Divine, and Daddy Grace for their charismatic services that emphasized loud services and faith healing. Despite his discomfort with such leaders and their worship styles, the irony lay in the UNIA's inclusion of jazz and High Church in its proceedings, even as Garvey criticized those leaders for wearing extravagant attire and preaching and singing a "jazz religion" in urban contexts and across international airwaves. Thus, Garvey promoted a religious conservatism that privileged European classical music—a prominent feature of Catholic devotion—ultimately shedding light on his complicated cultural investments and his opportune use of respectability within Black religious nationalistic discourse.

In this vein, the religion of Garveyism was also fundamentally shaped by Bishop George Alexander McGuire and the African Orthodox Church (AOC), which was founded on September 2, 1921, in New York City, and as its materials stated, the AOC "[held] the Faith as delivered to the Saints and exercise[d] the Apostolic Ministry. It [was] a branch of the One Holy Catholic and Apostolic Church controlled entirely by colored Churchmen."[71] The UNIA routinely used the AOC's *Universal Negro Ritual* and the *Universal Negro Catechism* in its proceedings, even after McGuire broke away from Garvey in 1924 when Garvey refused to designate the AOC the official church of the UNIA. Despite their fraught relationship, UNIA members continued to worship in the spirit of the AOC's Anglican High Church tradition in both devotion and religious regalia, and according to Burkett, some UNIA members left the organization with McGuire.

Nevertheless, Garvey's contention with jazz extended far beyond the UNIA. Jazz was also frowned upon by other African American religious actors, and those who included the troublesome genre in their services and programming were often harshly criticized in the press. In his 1930s writings in the *Blackman* from London, Garvey had actually sided with more prominent, middle-class African American Protestants who looked down on Great Migration–era storefront, Holiness, and Pentecostal churches for their "crazed," "undisciplined" and "unruly" forms of worship.[72] Historian Vaughn Booker has argued, "The 'jazz religion' of charismatic itinerant ministers and emotional displays of worship, each a product of the Great Migration's emerging urban presence of Holiness-Pentecostal preaching and worship styles . . . challenged the reserved, refined, and educated atmosphere that middle-class black Protestants had forged with modern worship and sermonic habits to represent their race's modern propriety."[73] Garvey's recitation of these middle-class African American Protestant ideas serves as yet another example of how the UNIA wrestled with its own religious, racial, and political identity in the early twentieth century, especially as its leader saw himself deeply shaped by both Afro-Protestantism and the Roman Catholic Church such that multiple devotional cultures were critical to UNIA proceedings. As much as the UNIA criticized mainline denominations, it was also challenged by some of the very same debates about what constituted "African American religion" in the Jazz Age. More importantly, Garvey's personal religious biography and its connection to the organization's history suggest that Afro-Protestantism has had an enduring dialectic relationship with Afro-Catholicism, which is also evident in the biographies of others during the period, including but not limited to Billie Holiday.[74]

The NOD's existence in New Orleans is also noteworthy given the prevalence of Hoodoo and Conjure. The NOD, like many of the other UNIA, chapters used a variety of material objects, especially candles, altars, holy water, herbs, and blessed oil, in some of its meetings and also provided advertisement space to local herb and root companies in the pages of the *Negro World*.[75] Although this was common in Black historical newspapers during the period for revenue's sake, the fact that the UNIA also created space for these advertisements and written discussion of these practices demonstrates how they allowed members and those they were recruiting to draw from myriad spiritual traditions in their political work.[76] One sixty-year-old NOD member, D. W. Wood, claimed to "have virtually been made young again by the recently discovered korex compound," a combination of tinctures used by rootworkers to make cough syrup. He told a *Negro World* reporter, "It has brought me back to as good, healthy physical condition as I enjoyed at 35 . . . I am apparently as supple as at 25."[77]

As the sources show, "jazz religion," then, and Garvey's contention with it, was a commentary on the changing religious cultures of many American

"THE RIGHT IDEA OF GOD" 167

cities during the era of the Great Migration and the immigration of Caribbean and Latin American migrants into the United States. Cities like New Orleans became sites for the simultaneous clash and blending of Black Atlantic religious cultures. Jazz, storefront churches, "cults," faith healers, and rootworkers are just a few examples of this dynamic morass of religious and cultural transformation deeply informed by race, class, and various Black nationalisms. While religious diversity often simply caused splits in other religious organizations, in the UNIA disagreement with Garvey's politics and decision-making could lead to a life or death situation. To speak ill of the famed leader, especially from the pulpit of an African American Protestant church, could lead to one's murder.

MARTYRS OR VICTIMS: MURDER, THE PULPIT, AND THE NEW ORLEANS DIVISION

On January 2, 1923, the headline "Negro Preacher Is Shot in Back" appeared in the *Times-Picayune*. The night before, Rev. James Walker Hood Eason, pastor of the Zion AME Church in New York and the former second-highest-ranking official of the UNIA, had been shot at the St. John's Baptist Church in New Orleans on New Year's night. Eason died days later. "I am positive that my assailants were acting on instructions to put me out of the way and prevent my appearing as a witness against Garvey at the trial," Eason asserted before passing. "I have already been threatened several times."[78] Eason described, at length, the intimidation tactics he had experienced by Garvey and the UNIA in the months leading up to his murder.

In the year prior, Eason spent months in New Orleans giving lectures throughout the city and working with local political organizers and clergy.[79] The press described him as "an orator of splendid ability," who spoke masterfully on behalf of the UNIA.[80] However, upon his return to Harlem, Eason and Garvey engaged in fisticuffs when Garvey accused him of trying to disrupt the 1922 UNIA convention.[81] Some divisions, including the NOD, described Eason as trying to "overthrow the work of the UNIA in [New Orleans]" and seeking to take over as president of the NOD, but they reasoned, "It is very evident that the UNIA is firmly established in the State of Louisiana, and especially in the city of New Orleans."[82] Eason, however, claimed to only want to hold Garvey accountable at the 1922 Convention for his recent meeting with Edward Clarke, the assistant grand imperial wizard of the Ku Klux Klan, and for his questionable management of the Black Star Line (BSL), along with his controlling leadership of the UNIA. Garvey, in contrast, ostracized Eason for being an "American" Negro who he felt needed to learn from his West Indian comrades, which essentially meant that Eason should have fallen in line and asked questions later. As Harold notes, Eason was also accused by Garvey's close friend, Thomas Anderson, of "engaging in sexually inappropriate behavior during his recruiting trips across the country" and was consequently expelled from the organization.[83] NOD members Mamie Reason and T. A. Robinson were also dismissed from the UNIA for siding with Eason and joining his offshoot Universal Negro Alliance. Following his expulsion, Eason used his connections throughout the United States and his relationship with the Black press to expose Garvey's misuse of funds raised in the service of the BSL and the UNIA. "I intend . . . to tell the truth to the members of the association as to what has become of the nearly one million dollars collected from the members, with absolutely nothing to show for it."[84] Indeed, much of the tension between Garvey and Eason came from concerns about UNIA funds and alliances, and Garvey ousted all who challenged his leadership decisions.

Following Eason's death, the United States attorney of New York ordered a federal investigation in response to Eason's claims that he had been attacked by Garveyites. The *Times-Picayune* noted, "Rev. Eason was to have left the morning of January 3 for New York, where the Garvey [*sic*] were scheduled to go to trial. He preached in a negro church in New Orleans New Year's night. A block away from the church, two negroes stepped from an alley. Eason turned and they opened fire. One bullet entered the head and the other the back."[85] During his sermon, Eason criticized Garvey and the UNIA publicly. His murderers silenced him, and many Black New Orleanians condemned the act as a "cowardly assassination" of a preacher.[86] Yet the archives of Black Atlantic religious life—specifically long histories of ritual and spiritual killings and harming practices against enemies—evidence the fact that to kill a preacher with whom one did not agree was often a form of Black Atlantic religion making, or a way of getting rid of those who posed a threat to one's own religious or political movement.[87] Robert Elijah Jones, a Black Methodist Episcopal clergyman in New Orleans and the editor of the *Southwestern Christian Advocate*, wrote in 1911, "There are not a few church members who know well how to kill preachers and few preachers who cross their path can withstand their attacks. Preacher killers are well known in all sections and all churches. They do not all work by the same rules. They go for results and usually get them."[88]

Clergy of the Colored Ministers' Alliance were among the most prominent voices decrying Eason's murder in public speeches, including Reverends J. L. Burrell, A. Hubb, P. P. Frampton, T. W. J. Tobias, J. S. Morgan, E. M. Washington, S. A. Duncan, I. E. Perkins, G. C. Rounds, J. A. Granderson, G. H. J. Devore, and L. Brown.[89] In response to these preachers' criticisms of Garvey, the UNIA, and the brutal murder of one of their fellow clergymen, Thomas W. Anderson, Garvey's right-hand man who had been dispatched to New Orleans to "investigate" Eason's murder, lambasted "Negro Baptist ministers," writing, "the vesture of the UNIA remains clean and untarnished and in spite of certain specific efforts on the part of a small group of Negro Baptist ministers, who have been unable to rise above the level of 'camp meeting pulpiteers,' the membership is more loyal than ever." Anderson later continued, "Yet this widow robbing and orphan cheating klan of Negro ministers, vassals of other enemies of the organization, in impotent crocodile fury have left off their offerings to the Christ and are rainbow chasing the [UNIA] because it does not believe in cheating and robbing. So furious have they become here in New Orleans that they do naught at their meetings but legislate enormous fees for burying the dead and stopping Garvey."[90] Anderson's deflection of the ministers' critiques of the UNIA's alleged assassination of Eason further worked to place the UNIA as a bastion of hope for African American Protestants who had given up on traditional churches and Black preachers. He raised a critique against a critique, a "he who is without sin, cast the first stone," in order to represent the UNIA as "clean and untarnished." The members of the Colored Ministers' Alliance were thus scrutinized, and their efforts to vindicate Eason were undermined by their own questionable reputations in the city. Anderson's assessment, however, was nothing other than the UNIA's attempt to frame the clergy as untrustworthy and ultimately did not bring about clarity, answers, or justice for Eason.

The back and forth between the UNIA and mainline African American Protestant churches, however, did not take away from the federal government's investigation into Eason's murder. By the end of January 1923, two Jamaican immigrants, William Shakespeare and Constantine Dyer, were placed on trial under an indictment for manslaughter in connection with Eason's assassination, and by August 1924, the two were acquitted.[91] The NOD organized on behalf of Shakespeare and Dyer and hired a white lawyer named Loys Charbonnet to work in their defense. Following the case, the NOD quickly buried the very recent memory of Eason's assassination by recruiting new members and rebranding the organization with new programming in light of its latest controversy.[92]

Eason's murder, however, would not be the last involving a preacher in the underworld. On March 8, 1928, Laura Adorkor Kofey, founder of the African Universal Church, was murdered in her pulpit in Miami.[93] While Kofey did not live in New Orleans, she spent a significant amount of time in the city, and the NOD often noted that her visits caused many to join the UNIA. One NOD member recalled, "Lady Laura Kofey had been in [our] midst, hundreds have been added to [our] numbers."[94] Garvey, however, became jealous of her growing prominence across the US South and was especially bothered by how she brought to light some of Garvey's suspicious leadership choices. Her death was a pronouncement of Garvey's misogyny and patriarchal commitments.[95]

Kofey's Louisiana tour and her travels throughout the Deep South were not only attempts to spread the gospel of African redemption in her own terms, but she traveled often to keep her enemies at bay. Her followers recounted in a pamphlet following her death, "In the year 1926, the Spirit of her Old Man God then led her to move South by way of New Orleans, through Louisiana, Mississippi and on to Alabama. Making one-night stops in different towns on her way she made her mark and left an indelible impression still remembered by remnants to this day."[96] In other church publications, they narrated her journey as follows: "In less than 18 months in the South, [Kofey] stirred up populations, rallied multitudes of Africa's children to her following in the cities and towns of the States of Louisiana, Mississippi, Alabama, Florida, and Georgia." The writers continued, "Without benefit of news media notices people would line the streets to her meetings long before the opening hour. There would be no standing room inside. Her children declared she radiated divine LOVE . . . in many homes she was a household word and among many the talk of the town."[97] While Kofey's religious biography is fraught with several inconsistencies, historian Richard Newman's account is the most substantive to date.[98] She taught that she was "sent to the United States by her father, King Knesipi of the Gold Coast, to organize Negroes and take them back to Africa" but "in their investigations, Garveyites claimed to discover Laura Kofey to be, in reality, a native of Athens, Georgia, [born Laura Champion], who had worked for the American Red Cross, travelled to New York, England, and Africa, and who had taught school in New Orleans before her advent in Florida."[99] Kofey had also claimed to be raising funds for the Black Star Line and the UNIA but had allegedly pocketed over $19,000 for herself during her southern tour of the United States. Although she visited Garvey in federal prison in Atlanta, Georgia, and gained his support, as he learned of her problematic fundraising practices and alleged misuse of her UNIA affiliation, in October and November 1927 the *Negro World* published notices to all UNIA divisions from Garvey that stated, "No Division or Chapter of the Universal Negro Improvement Association is to entertain one LAURA KOFEY, alias PRINCESS KOFEY and LADY KOFEY, who has for some time been collecting funds from members of the Association in the South under the guise of sending them to Africa, etc. Should she make further appeals, members should have her arrested for fraud."[100] Garvey's warnings about Kofey reached members in the US, Central America, and the West Indies and ultimately ruined her reputation. In the months following these public takedowns, Garvey would be deported from New Orleans in December 1927, leaving Kofey to tend to the African Universal Church and her preaching tour throughout the American South.

With Garvey off United States soil, Kofey refined her religious and political message. Newman has contended, "Laura Kofey's preaching was essentially a blend of Garveyism and religion. She criticized the UNIA for holding dances to raise funds, and advocated prayer meetings in their place."[101] Newman goes on further, "What she added [to Garveyism] was a rather traditional religious dimension, but one that she and her followers transformed into a religious sanction for the black nationalist themes of racial pride, African identification, and community building."[102] Yet Newman mischaracterizes Garveyism as a nonreligion.[103] Understanding Garveyism as an Afro-Protestant religious movement with Afro-Catholic affinities, then, contextualizes Kofey's critiques of Garvey and the UNIA. In effect, Kofey utilized the African Universal Church to institutionalize a Black transnational religious imaginary, which was in conversation with Garveyism but not bound to it. Kofey's hope lay not in a man—Garvey—but rather in the aims and vision of African redemption. In Garvey, she was met with patriarchal silencing tactics. In African redemption, she found a sure foundation. Nonetheless, her assassination, along with Eason's assassination, are examples of how strife animated the religious and political world of the NOD. More importantly, these murders are representative of the challenges that arose in many Black radical organizations in the early twentieth century, especially as they engaged in a world of religion making, or put differently, a world of flight, migration, and movement that necessitated challenging oppressive dynamics in traditional Afro-Protestant settings and making sacred space for those deemed sinners. At times, however, even UNIA members committed grave sins—albeit silencing dissenters or boldly celebrating misogyny.

BLACK MOSES AND (BLACK) GOD IN THE FLESH

To say that Garvey had a contentious relationship with women inside of the UNIA is an understatement.[104] Even as Garvey's patriarchy marginalized women's leadership, some found ways to challenge the leader while homing in and articulating their own political commitments—inside and outside of the UNIA. Louisianan organizer Madame Maymie Leona Turpeau de Mena was one of those women, and she was a bridge between Garvey and Father Divine, specifically between their competing understandings of race, civil rights, and theology. In the aftermath of Garvey's deportation in 1927, she observed, "I believe that the magnetism of Marcus Garvey that gripped all of us as we gazed upon him there in New Orleans; I believe the magnetism of that honorable leader will permeate the entire world, cause people of all nations, of all climes, to rally around the cause and the principles upon which this organization stands."[105] Madame de Mena, who would be brought back to New Orleans just three years later to discuss "Negro nationalism" among clergy and activists, had communicated what many Garveyites felt.[106] This "Negro nationalism" was the religion of Garveyism, and for most of the late 1920s, de Mena championed it, especially as members called for an internationally recognized "negro religion," such that people of African descent might worship "a black Savior."[107] By the 1930s, however, de Mena found affinity with Father Divine, Garvey's rival.[108]

Tensions bubbled to the surface because of Garvey's call for "a black Savior," or the notion that people of African descent should worship a cosmic deity racialized as Black, which significantly differed from the political and theological beliefs of Father Divine, who self-identified as "God" in the flesh. Although Garvey's UNIA was quite influential in New Orleans and the state of Louisiana, Father Divine had also gained a strong following in the region. Although the preacher never lived in or visited New Orleans to my knowledge, the city's residents were fascinated with him and maintained relationships with him. Many residents—Black and white—wrote to Divine and recognized him as "God." Many of these individuals encountered Divine through national newspapers, popular culture, and the field of psychiatry. In 1935, Dr. Lionel L. Cazanavette, veteran specialist in neurology and psychiatry and superintendent of the city hospital for mental diseases in New Orleans, participated in a roundtable called "Psychoses among Followers of Father Divine of New York" at the ninety-first American Psychiatric Association meeting in Washington, DC.[109] In 1936, three *March of Time* short films, sponsored by Time, Inc., were released at the Orpheum Theater in New Orleans featuring Father Divine, and in 1938, one more short film was released, each of which described Divine's spiritual practice, shined light on his religious organization, and labeled him a "lunatic" among many other "cult" leaders. Father Divine also became the archetypal "Negro" cult leader by which all Black faith healers in New Orleans were set in comparison, so much so that one journalist once wrote, "Louisiana has Father Divine" when describing faith healer Bishop Lucien Treadwell of the Church of God in Christ (see chapter 6).[110] By 1947, Bishop A. P. Shaw, editor of the Southwest edition of the *Christian Advocate* (the official organ of the Methodist Church with headquarters in New Orleans), declared Father Divine a "self-styled 'prophet' and 'healer' type of religionist [who racketeered] in religion."[111] Historian Jill Watts has cited one of Divine's followers as saying that "colored people from New Orleans," most likely migrants, attended Divine's services up North, even as Divine proclaimed before a congregation full of Black people, "I don't care anything about colored people. I haven't them in me . . . and cast them out of my consciousness and do not allow them to exist there."[112] Despite Father Divine's negation of a racial analysis amid Jim Crow, the press's unflinching, and at times cynical, focus on him actually caused many people of African descent across the nation to flock to Divine's fold.

Whereas Divine "cast" Black people "out of [his] consciousness," Garvey centered Black people and Africa in his religious and political consciousness, and as a result, the two had a contentious relationship and spoke negatively about the other. Garvey repeatedly emphasized how Divine was not God, and Divine criticized the UNIA's Black nationalist agenda given the Peace Mission's call for racial transcendence. Madame de Mena nonetheless engaged with both of their ideas. Reporting back to the New York division about her travels to New Orleans in 1929, de Mena stated, "I am pleased to note that down in New Orleans where class and color prejudice was so rife and where some professional people were inclined to shun the UNIA, all are now thronging to the Division there, having awakened to the fact that Marcus Garvey, a born leader, had given to the race a broad and substantial program and platform upon which to stand."[113] Just four years later, after being a journalist for the UNIA's *Negro World* up until it ceased publication in 1933, de Mena created her own publication, the *World Echo*, which endorsed Father Divine's teachings about "racial transcendence and charitable works" up until the paper "folded" due to a lack of funding at some point in 1934.[114] In January of that year, the *New York Age*, which followed both Garvey's and Divine's careers closely, published, almost cynically, "We have received the 'World Echo' a new weekly which states that it is owned and published by Mme. LT. DeMena, fiery Garvey leader. But there is no Garvey and no UNIA in it. It is all Father Divine from start to finish, even to the mast-head which carries his picture. Has DeMena renounced the red, black and green or is there a new Emperor of Africa in the making?"[115] De Mena's turn to Divine made sense, however, when one comparatively analyzes the racial and gender politics of Father Divine's Peace Mission and Garvey's UNIA. Moreover, even the *Negro World* took note of the many Garveyites who had become a part of Divine's Peace Mission, the Nation of Islam, the Moorish Science Temple, and Bishop Charles Manuel Grace's United House of Prayer during the 1920s and '30s.[116] Beryl Satter has argued, "Although Garvey denounced as blasphemy Divine's claims to be God, Garvey's own self-presentation as a 'Black Moses' and his suggestion that blacks think of God as dark skinned may have eased the way for some black Americans to accept Father Divine as God."[117] The *World Echo* reflected this. For instance, de Mena included in the *World Echo* a story about a Louisianan man who wanted to confess all his sins following his migration to New York and his subsequent conversion to the Peace Mission. "I am asking You, I know, You are God, Father, to forgive me. Down in Louisiana I took and cut up a man because I thought he bothered my friend, and they arrested me, Father."[118] The *World Echo* was a literary homage to Divine and further glorified him as a Black God in the flesh.[119] De Mena's exclusion of any reference to Garvey and the UNIA suggests that in 1934, she had experienced some sort of political and religious transformation, or what Keisha Blain has otherwise described as a "short stint in Father Divine's Peace Mission."[120] Not only was she a Black transnational organizer, but the pages of the *World Echo* demonstrated her work as a Black religious thinker, and we come to know her as both an intellectual and an organizer in figure 5.2, where she appears to be wearing academic regalia. From January to April 1934, she dedicated her writing to stories about Father Divine, one of the foremost African American religious leaders of the early twentieth century.

When the *World Echo* closed its doors after its last issue on April 14, 1934, de Mena started the *Ethiopian World*, a paper that embodied Black Atlantic religion making as de Mena drew from UNIA proceedings, New Thought discourse, and general information from across the African diaspora.[121] In one issue, de Mena wrote, "If you travel from here to Europe, you will find new truths, new centers of learning, etc. In fact, taking a broad

FIGURE 5.2. Madame M. L. T. de Mena, undated. Robert A. Hill Collection, box PS 22, David M. Rubenstein Rare Book and Manuscript Library, Duke University.

view of the world in general, there is a new outlook. For this reason, the *Ethiopian World* enters a new field of thought: to place and shape the mind of our particular group along successful racial lines." De Mena presented a blending of Garveyism and Divine's racial transcendence. "We are living in a New Day," she exclaimed, echoing the title of Divine's newspaper, the *New Day*, in a paper dedicated to uniting the "children of Ethiopia."[122] One of the paper's objectives encouraged "all serious-minded, forward-looking and progressive men and women of the race to forget their personal animosities, jealousies and squabbles and work together and build a secure future for themselves and their children and children's children." De Mena continued, "Not personalities but programs and planning will help. Let us then concentrate on programs and planning and forget personalities." De Mena saw value in both Divine's and Garvey's political and religious visions, which they peddled within and beyond the bounds of the underworld. She was not a "Garveyite," nor was she a "Divinite," but like many women of African descent during the time period, she was a Black transnational religious thinker pulling together different strands of religious and political thought to carve a path forward for the children of Ethiopia.[123] Oftentimes, de Mena's travels and migrations became the means by which she came to learn of new modes of organizing and of living in the world as a woman of African descent. By 1935, the *Daily Gleaner* publicized her sailing, migrating, and finding love in her new home in Kingston, Jamaica, a port city from which many migrants would also leave for New Orleans during the period.[124]

CONCLUSION

Madame de Mena was just one of many who tried to make sense of Garvey and his complexities. As this chapter has shown, many Southerners certainly had conflicting views of Garvey, of Garveyism, and of the UNIA. New Orleanian Lillie A. Jones, for instance, wrote to the editor of the *Negro World* in June 1927, "Through the Hon. Marcus Garvey our eyes have been opened and we are now able to see the many defects in Christianity as it is practiced by the white man toward the Negro. The bearers of the Christian message have blinded themselves and our people to the powers and virtues of the Negro." Jones lamented, "They have given him religion and have taught him that he needed nothing else in this world."[125] Even as Jones articulated a particular kind of faith and belief in Garvey's message, "Africa for the Africans," she did not explicitly call the UNIA a religious organization or shed light on how Eason's and Kofey's murders may have tainted Garvey's message. Drawing from the words of Jesus in the New Testament, however, Jones stated, "A new day is dawning for the Negro. Let us open our eyes and see the truth which shall make us free."[126] In her letter to the editor, Jones demonstrated how the UNIA, and the NOD specifically, intervened in the larger African American Protestant church life in the city. Jones, and many other Garvey supporters like her, underscored how the NOD mobilized theology, ritual, organization, and activism in ways that were specific to New Orleans and the circum-Caribbean of which it was a part.

The NOD complemented African American Protestant church life in the city, even as the NOD offered substantive criticism of the failures of ministers and churches to support Black self-determination and preach Black religious nationalism. Even as Jones celebrated Garvey and the NOD and lambasted "those Negroes who denounce Marcus Garvey and call his followers 'fools,'" Jones, like many others, did not speak to the culture of infighting, violence, murder, backbiting, and political strife that animated the UNIA and the NOD. Indeed, Jones presented a romanticized picture of Garvey and the organization, or as one *Negro World* reporter put it regarding someone else, she was "inoculated with the spirit of Garveyism." That "spirit," however, caused some Black clergy to die by gun, even as it emboldened many others to embrace their identities as sinner-saints, charging forward toward African redemption.[127] Black journalist and satirist George Schuyler wrote in 1929, "Africa will be redeemed, even if the Garveyites have to kill each other in order to do so."[128] This sentiment was just as much a part of the NOD's religious allegiances as were its commitments to jazz and Anglican High Church. In this way, the conglomeration of jazz, partying, nightlife, fine fare, ritual, theologizing, fighting, and murder within the NOD's underworld community were what made it uniquely positioned as a prominent organization in New Orleans and the circum-Caribbean. Yet it would not be the last religious group to pique the interests of migrants and the many wayward lives of the twentieth-century Black slum.

VISITATION 6

ZORA WORSHIPS WITH THE SANCTIFIED

The Sanctified Church is a protest against the high-brow tendency in Negro Protestant congregations as the Negroes gain more education and wealth. It is understandable that they take on the religious attitudes of the white man which are as a rule so staid and restrained that it seems unbearably dull to the more primitive Negro who associates the rhythms of sound and motion with religion. In fact, the Negro has not been christianized as extensively as it generally believed. The great masses are still standing before their pagan altars and calling old gods by a new name. . . .

So the congregation is restored to its primitive altars under the new name of Christ. Then there is the expression known as "shouting" which is nothing more than a continuation of the African "Possession" by the gods. The gods possess the body of the worshipper and he or she is supposed to know nothing of their actions until the god decamps. This is still prevalent in most Negro protestant churches and is universal in the Sanctified churches. They protest against the more highbrow churches' efforts to stop it. It must be noted that the sermon in these churches is not the set thing that is in the other protestant churches. It is loose and formless and is in reality merely a framework upon which to hang more songs. Every opportunity to introduce a new rhythm is eagerly seized upon. The whole movement of the Sanctified Church is a rebirth of song-making! It has brought in a new era of spiritual-making.[1]

ZORA NEALE HURSTON

FIGURE 6.1. Church of God in Christ, New Orleans, 1930s. Courtesy of State Library of Louisiana.

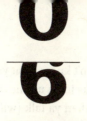

"WE AIN'T SPIRITUALISTS, WE'S THE SANCTIFIED CHURCH"

Black Pentecostals and the Politics of Distinction

> They'll talk to the Lord
> You Know the Lord Jesus Christ
> Is the Biggest Hoodoo Too in the World
> You got to have Him to go along with you to do these things
>
> "First Informant in New Orleans," found in Hyatt, vol. 2, 1624

Mother Brown, the "assistant" of Bishop Lucien H. Treadwell, pastor of the Church of God in Christ of Faith Tabernacle in 1930s New Orleans, told LWP worker Hazel Breaux that she and the other members of Treadwell's church "ain't Spiritualists," as had been assumed, but rather, "we's [the] Sanctified Church." Brown stated, "[There's] no card cuttin', fortune tellin' or readin' in our church an' we don't use no oils." While noting the significance of the laying on of hands, she emphasized, "We only heal [with] our hands [and] if da spirit of da Holy Ghost don't see fit to cure 'em, [they] are not cured." Brown's attentiveness to the centrality of healing among both Spiritualists and the Sanctified Church is undeniable, even as she focused intently on how Treadwell's church had been mocked by outsiders. "Some ignorant people calls us Holy Rollers, but [that's] not so," she said. "When da Holy Ghost takes ya, ya don't know what ya gonna do, sometimes ya roll all over da place. When ya talks in da unknown tongue dats called havin' da gift of tongues and [that] is when ya talk [with] God . . . When [the] spirit come [and] showers ya [that's] Pentecost day, it can be any day, Sunday or Monday." Brown's short-form explanation of Pentecostal belief and practice was then coupled with a self-definition of what anthropologist Judith Casselberry describes as "aesthetic labor," or the "interconnected material and immaterial realms to produce, reproduce, and reconfigure the meanings of the beauty of holiness" through the politics of dress.[1] Unlike Spiritualists, Brown did not wear veils but instead a white band around her hair, and "a long black or white silk robe with large bell sleeves, a small standing collar with a cape attached to the robe [and] a crucifix around her neck hanging from a black ribbon, and around her waist a long white cord with tassels. The cape of the black robe . . . [was] lined with white."[2] In her estimation, this marker was an intentional way to distinguish herself from Spiritualist women, even as her clothes may have resembled those of Catholic nuns. Treadwell similarly wore "a black cap and robe, adorned with a great, big cross," which may have resembled a Catholic priest.[3] Breaux, who described Brown as "a tall, very fat Negress [with] a most interesting face," reasoned, "The Sanctified differ from the Spiritualist in that they don't burn candles or prophesy and they have a band which consists of a drum, cymbals, and tambourines. When the spirit takes the members, they get very lively and besides shouting they dance, some doing the shuffle, others trucking."[4]

To Brown, the differences, however, were vaster—each related to some aspect of material culture, whether dress or spiritual objects. The LWP staff took note, "The line of demarcation between the spiritualistic cult and the sanctified sects is very finely drawn. Sanctified means set aside for holy use. This cult does not burn candles for requests nor prophesy and has a full band for choir."[5] Though the Sanctified did, in fact, prophesy, as was the case with Treadwell and many other prominent leaders in this chapter, the LWP's observation demonstrates how cogently those they interviewed distinguished themselves from the Black Spiritual churches. Moreover, the LWP staff's observation of the Church of God in Christ (COGIC)'s use of particular materials to "come out from among them, and be ye separate, saith the Lord, and touch not the unclean thing" as the scriptures commanded them was representative of how different aesthetic practices and material objects deemed religious could be used to convey unique religious identities.[6] Indeed, if Pentecostals could look and sound different from Spiritualists, they believed that they were relatively close to living true sancti-

"WE AIN'T SPIRITUALISTS, WE'S THE SANCTIFIED CHURCH"   *183*

fied lives. More to this point, if they could emphasize their differences, they
believed that they could refuse confinement to the underworld, a den of
worldliness that they believed was no place for the Sanctified.

Yet despite their own emphasis on the distinction between themselves
and Spiritualists, the similarities between the two were also significant.
Treadwell, for example, was quite often referred to as "Father"—a title used
to revere male Spiritualist leaders and Catholic priests—by congregants, followers, and visitors seeking healing or prophecy.[7] The *Atlanta Daily World*,
for instance, reported in 1932 that one woman came to a revival meeting to be
healed by Treadwell, asking, "Father, won't you put your hand on my throat.
I've a cold." Despite his position as senior "bishop" of the Church of God in
Christ of Faith Tabernacle, which according to some sources split off from
COGIC in 1932 but remained in partnership, Treadwell responded, "Come
on, bless you," and he laid his hands on her. Owing his "gifts" to God through
prayer and fasting for two months, Treadwell's ministry touched "the lame,
the blind, and those otherwise afflicted."[8] Even Brown noted that she "never
missed a service since [she became] a member" in 1934. "I don't wanna open
a church of my own cause everything I have I owe to Bishop Treadwell and
I wouldn't leave him for nothing. I conduct the prayer services which are
every mornin' from nine to twelve."[9] As Anthea Butler contends, however,
"Church mothers formed the backbone of the Church of God in Christ . . .
the church mother in COGIC tradition evolved from an honorary women's
role into something more. Church mothers became a vehicle for women to
remake their religious and social worlds within a framework of piety, devotion, and civic life."[10] Brown's commitment to Treadwell was representative
of her commitment to the church and to living a sanctified life, so much so
that her interview with Hazel Breaux focused less on her own contributions
to COGIC, but on Treadwell's power and prominence throughout Louisiana, and with how Black Pentecostals were unlike Spiritualists, Hoodoo
practitioners, and rootworkers.

While Brown's words emphasized difference, it is significant that the
LWP workers focused on the similarities between the groups. One photo-
graph taken at Treadwell's church that was included in the LWP's files is
captioned "B&W photo, 1930s. Spiritual meeting at Father Treadwell's
Church in New Orleans Louisiana. Possibly Church of God in Christ.
Rev. Lucien H. Treadwell, Pastor."[11] In *Picturing Faith: Photography and the
Great Depression*, historian Colleen McDannell argues that WPA workers
in Chicago made similar "errors," in which they also "[assumed] that one
'Negro Church' was the same as any other 'Negro church.'" She continues,

"Downplaying the significance of religious difference, the photographers followed the lead of the Chicago School and overemphasized class while underestimating denominational history, theology, and ritual."[12] The LWP staff did similarly. Though the subjects self-identified as "Sanctified," such that the LWP workers added "possibly" before "Church of God in Christ," it is probable that the same underestimation took place in New Orleans, or it may have been the case that the religious practices and espoused beliefs at Treadwell's church mirrored those of the Black Spiritual churches that they also visited, such that the workers may have been making honest assessments of what they witnessed. In the same caption, for example, Treadwell is referred to as both "Father" and "Reverend," which suggests that the categories of distinction—as understood by these religious practitioners of African descent—may not have been easily recognizable to outsiders, especially white outsiders who have historically mischaracterized Black religions.

Similarly, the press repeatedly made connections between Treadwell and non-Pentecostal religious leaders in and beyond New Orleans. One writer asserted, "Louisiana has 'Father Divine'" while talking about Treadwell. The same writer also observed "crutches hung on a cross, a Negro 'healer' with a slow deliberate and almost hypnotic voice, surrounded by frantic and shouting Negro men and women." Spectators noted that these revivals occurred daily and nightly at 922 Liberty Street. "Benches up front are occupied by white people, and Treadwell 'cures' white, Negro, halt, lame, blind, children and adults, without discrimination."[13] Another writer from the *Atlanta Daily World* compared Treadwell to Mother Catherine Seals, who founded her Spiritual church as a haven for battered women and children after suffering a paralytic stroke following an abusive marriage and being denied healing by white faith healer Brother Isaiah due to her Blackness. "The daily attendance exceeds several hundred persons of both races." They continued, "His followers bid fair to exceed the number who worshipped at the shrine of Mother Catherine."[14] Despite Mother Brown's self-identification of her church as "[the] Sanctified Church," those enthralled with Treadwell labeled him a divine healer among many Spiritualist and new religious movement leaders. To them, his faith healing style mirrored other underworld workers.

This chapter takes the case of the COGIC and members' insistence on naming how they were different from other religious practitioners of African descent, as a critical entry into exploring a problem that has animated the study of African American religions for quite some time: the erroneous historical and sociological construction of *a monolithic African American religion* and how practitioners of these religions have challenged, compli- cated, and debunked dominant misconceptions concerning them. This chapter attends particularly to Black Pentecostal churches in New Orleans and how they engaged in Black Atlantic religion-making processes depen- dent on understanding the similarities between them while also underlining their respective differences from the Black Spiritual churches and Hoodoo practitioners.[15] Put another way, Pentecostals did not want to be grouped together with Spiritualists, and both did not want to be grouped together with Catholics or Hoodoo practitioners in the larger religious landscape of the city's underworld. As cited in the opening epigraph, some observers nonetheless stressed the similarities between Black Pentecostals, Catholics, and Hoodoo practitioners, in which they described Jesus Christ—the man and deity to whom many practitioners prayed—as "the Biggest Hoodoo in the World."[16] Thus, the LWP's inattention to Pentecostals' differences from Spiritualists also meant that the LWP haphazardly connected Pentecostals to Voudou, Conjure, and rootwork—religious traditions that some Pente- costals viewed as devil worship.[17]

To attend to the differences espoused by this diverse group of Black reli- gious practitioners in New Orleans, this chapter specifically explores the religion-making practices of Black Pentecostals in the city. To date, there is no historical scholarship on Black Pentecostals in New Orleans during the early twentieth century, even as "no other religious group would come to define black religiosity and piety in the modern period as Pentecostals would," as historian Clarence Hardy has argued. "Their influence extended beyond cultural expression to more intellectual domains of how black people thought of themselves, their relations with the larger (white) society, and the divine."[18] Pentecostals used the politics of dress, faith healing, Bible insti- tutes, Bible colleges, convocations, lectures, and new technologies within the Black sacred tradition to cultivate their own unique set of racial politics and their own religious identity. They used these modes of Black Atlantic reli- gion making in the service of maintaining the politics of difference and dif- ferentiation from the Black Spiritual churches and from Hoodoo, Voudou, and Conjure practitioners, partly as a rhetorical device to refuse their rel- egation to the underworld by white spectators and observers. For instance, while the spirits played a significant role in Spiritualist healing practices, it was the Holy Ghost, as Pentecostals underscored in their interviews with the LWP staff, who healed in COGIC. At times, however, these lines blurred. Bishop Charles H. Mason, COGIC's founder, was a conjurer-preacher, who "owned a collection of unusually formed objects including roots, branches, and vegetables that he consulted as 'sources for spiritual revelations,' revisiting the tradition of conjuring charms. Mason would illustrate his sermons by referring to these 'earthly signs' and 'freaks of nature.'"[19]

This chapter takes seriously these complexities and the interconnectedness of these shared religious heritages. The first section of this chapter examines Apostle Elias Dempsey Smith, Bishop J. D. Barber, and the Triumph Church and Kingdom of God in Christ, which embodied Black religious nationalism in its racialization of God, its roots in Louisiana, and its reach throughout the South and eventually to Ethiopia. Next, the chapter discusses two Black Pentecostal denominations in the city and their most prominent leaders: Bishop Lucien H. Treadwell and Elder James Feltus of COGIC and Rev. Dr. James Gordon McPherson of the Watch Tower Worldwide Intercessory Prayer Healing Movement. I historicize their attempts to distinguish themselves from each other and from the Black Spiritual churches and other Black religious practitioners, even though they often "failed" at times, or at the very least refused to underscore obvious similarities. Treadwell, Feltus, church mothers, and their COGIC followers used aesthetic choices to signify religious difference, while McPherson used education, public intellectualism, and American patriotism as a war hero. Each of these individuals used various technologies and modes of differentiation to articulate their own unique religious identities. At the core of the chapter is attention to Black Pentecostals' transnational worldview as part of their religion making and the politics of religious difference embedded in their practices. In this regard, some Pentecostals' Black religious nationalism did, in fact, differ from that of the UNIA, as Hardy has also contended. "Pentecostals' embryonic transnationalism," he writes, "evolved from different cultural networks and a different historical legacy than the transnationalism of Garvey or that of emergent Islamic alternatives."[20] Others, like Smith and Barber, were readily in conversation with Garvey and Ethiopianism. As the sources examined here show, Black Pentecostals embodied varying transnationalisms that took shape on a robust spectrum. Some of their transnationalisms were rooted in Ethiopianism or were recapitulations of Christian missions, respectability, and the demonization of Black Atlantic religions, while others encouraged Pentecostals to see themselves as American citizens and patriots.

BLACK HOLINESS-PENTECOSTALS
FROM NEW ORLEANS TO ETHIOPIA

Black Holiness-Pentecostals have been in New Orleans since the late nineteenth century. While most scholars agree that Pentecostalism did not officially begin until 1906 amid the Azusa Street Revival, the sources in New Orleans and other parts of the Black South suggest that the Pentecostal movement may have, in fact, begun prior to 1906. COGIC, in particular, which was founded in 1897, had been in New Orleans as early as 1903 according to the *Times-Picayune*. One of COGIC's church mothers, Mother Peters, was known "to sing in the African language," and Bishop Mason visited Louisiana regularly to deliver addresses and sermons at several state convocations.[21] Perhaps it is fitting, then, to describe COGIC, prior to Mason's trip to Azusa in 1907, as Black Holiness-Pentecostalism, rather than simply Pentecostalism as several scholars have done, and to also question and take seriously conflicting origin stories among practitioners.[22] As historian David Daniels has observed, "The African American participation in the holiness movement fits the standard narrative only in terms of individuals."[23] Indeed, if we follow Mason's journey in conversation with local Black Holiness-Pentecostal formations in New Orleans, the standard chronology does not entirely hold. Black people in Southern cities and towns were creating their own Pentecostal formations in conversation with white Pentecostals but also necessarily on their own due to the racist violence of Jim Crow. Much of the current literature, however, has emphasized the centrality and interracial components of the Azusa Street Revival as the moment in which the Holiness movement became the Pentecostal movement. Only a few sources take seriously Black religious innovation in the early twentieth century cultivated by Pentecostal people of African descent in their own local communities and churches absent of white people.[24] Much of the historiography on the early Pentecostal movement has also glossed over the effects of white supremacy and poverty for Black Pentecostals. Despite the prevalence of lynching culture and the history of the Anglo-Protestant Ku Klux Klan, historian Grant Wacker has even gone as far as to claim, "I have discovered no evidence that white saints participated in physical violence against blacks, but there is considerable evidence that they participated in the racist assumptions that made such violence possible."[25] Racism and racialized politics, however, were central concerns for Black Holiness-Pentecostals in

New Orleans, and it shaped their religious worldview. Many of them did not engage in interracial worship or tongue talking across the color line. Instead, they envisioned themselves as people of African descent with a sacred connection to the continent of Africa and carved out intentionally all-Black places of worship and political mobilization. For many of them, the late nineteenth to early twentieth century, which historian Wilson Jeremiah Moses has described as "the golden age of black nationalism," was the moment in which these ideas took root.[26]

While many of these individuals had converted from Baptist and Methodist churches during the Holiness movement, and thousands more joined the denomination following Mason's trip to Los Angeles, California, for Azusa, the fact that some of them had already conceived of themselves as Pentecostals prior to Azusa is significant. One of these individuals was Elias Dempsey Smith. A native Mississippian, Smith received visions from God in 1897 and was led to migrate to New Orleans, where he founded his first congregation, Triumph the Righteous Church, in 1902, with headquarters eventually in Baton Rouge, Louisiana. In 1907, Smith partnered with Bishop Mason, and the two eventually split due to theological differences around the question of redemption and interracial cooperation.[27] Mason argued that the Spirit brought the races together. Smith, on the other hand, was committed to Black institutional autonomy. By the end of World War I, Smith's insistence on keeping Black religious spaces Black was further amplified by the leader's engagement with Ethiopianism, Marcus Garvey, and the UNIA. Smith, however, was not alone in his search for a Black religious nationalism within Black Pentecostalism. Several Pentecostal churches "had one or more clergymen who were Garveyites or at least who spoke favorably at local UNIA meetings on behalf of the UNIA."[28] Moreover, COGIC was mentioned explicitly in several issues of the UNIA's *Negro World* between 1931 and 1932 as either hosts or participants in local and national UNIA meetings.[29]

While Pentecostals have historically and historiographically been portrayed as "otherworldly" and unconcerned with the problems of the world in which they lived, many Black Pentecostals who were involved in Black transnational movements theologized their political organizing to be firmly rooted as underworld citizens amid the problems of the anti-Black world.[30] To do so, they often theologized the Divine as Black and on their side and theologized the significance of racial separatism.[31] Smith, who most likely came across Garvey's writings in the *Negro World*, the weekly newspaper of the UNIA that was founded in 1917, certainly did so. As discussed in the previous chapter, the newspaper was a site for the theologizing of Black transnationalism and for religious, philosophical, and political debate among UNIA members and nonmembers who thought favorably of the organization. Smith thought so much of Garvey's political organizing and its significance to Black religious institutions that in 1919, he invited Garvey to give the keynote address at the International Religious Congress of Triumph, held in Chicago, Illinois (see fig. 6.2).

The following year, Smith and Prince J. D. Barber, the church's secretary and Smith's political adviser, journeyed to Abyssinia, Ethiopia, heeding the divine call of Ethiopianism, which had been preached by Garvey and many other leaders of African descent since as early as the nineteenth century.[32] Smith and Barber sought "to effect a closer relation between thee dark races of the Earth."[33] Upon arriving to Ethiopia, the two were given a grand reception by Empress Waizero Zandita and her nephew and coruler, Ras Tafari.[34] In appreciation of the two leaders' warm welcome, Smith planned an elaborate banquet in their honor. During the celebration, however, Smith suddenly fell ill, complained of stomach pains, and died shortly thereafter. In the wake of the Pentecostal leader's death, Barber, his trusted friend and confidant, continued to forge connections with the people of Ethiopia and eventually became more involved with Garvey and the UNIA, serving as a delegate to the 1921, 1924, and 1929 UNIA conventions and eventually becoming a widely sought after UNIA speaker.[35] In 1921 poet Ethel Trew Dunlap, a Black woman from Los Angeles, penned the following about Barber and his influence on the UNIA in the *Negro World*:

Since J.D. Barber crossed the sea
And grasped the Crown Prince's hand,
We know just why you try to keep
Us in this hoodlum land.
The lions didn't eat him up—
He came back looking fine!
Black men, we've been fools long enough—
Let's take the Black Star Line.
Some Negroes say they never lost
A thing across the sea,
But some things here that we have found
Don't look so good to me.
You say America's your home,
But if it is I dare
For you to make yourself at home

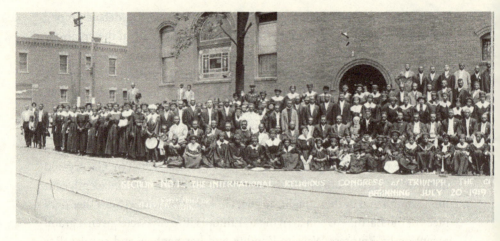

FIGURE 6.2. The International Religious Congress of Triumph, Chicago, 1919. Library of Congress, LC-USZ62-107501.

>   Or take a parlor chair.
>   Good-bye, America, good-bye!
>   We cannot wait to be
>   The President since Barber saw
>   That Queen across the sea!
>   Good-bye, America, good-bye![36]

Dunlap's poetry deftly characterized how Smith's having traveled to Ethiopia—the Promise Land for Garveyites and all people of African descent—set him apart in the service of African redemption. Barber used his experience in Ethiopia to garner followers for both Triumph and the UNIA. In 1922, the *Negro World* reported, "Rev. J.D. Barber furnished a wealth of information regarding the government of Abyssinia, which he said was already founded and was recognized by other governments all over the world, having at its shrine British, French, Russian, Turkish, Japanese legations. Abyssinia, he thought, was the most logical and fertile field for the [UNIA], from which they could strike out to reach the natives in other parts of Africa."[37]

At another UNIA meeting the same year, Barber and other prominent leaders debated "The Future Religious Faith and Belief of the Negro," in which they collectively reasoned, "It was not the desire . . . of the [UNIA] to dictate any one's religious faith or religious belief, that was to say, we were not assuming to tell anyone to become a Catholic or Baptist or Episcopalian

or Seventh Day Adventist or Holy Roller or anything else." The *Negro World* article continued, "The idea was to bring the Negro a scientific understanding of religion. What was desired was one great Christian confraternity without regard to any particular denomination, believing ourselves to be religious Christians."[38] Despite the paper's summarization of this particular meeting, Barber was nonetheless committed to his Pentecostal roots, as he took over Smith's role as the senior bishop of Triumph the Church and Kingdom of God in Christ in 1921. As bishop, Barber believed it was his duty to bring Pentecostals into the fold of African redemption. "The eyes of the preacher should be opened, he should not be fought, the preachers were not to blame for they were in the majority of cases mere creatures of a system," he stated at the 1924 convention of the UNIA.[39]

To Barber, the true churches of God in Christ would need to open their eyes to the joint struggles of people of African descent throughout the United States and the globe. Speaking of his time in Ethiopia, he commented, "The condition of the Negro race in Africa was vile, and the heads of the church should be made to realize that Negroes were alive to the suffering of their brethren throughout the world."[40] In his organizing with Pentecostal pastors and church leaders, Barber also led the charge in appealing to Catholic and other Protestant churches. In August of 1924, for instance, Barber chaired a committee within the UNIA which "[drafted] an appeal to His Holiness the Pope of Rome, His Grace the Archbishop of Canterbury, and the heads of the Christian churches, as leaders of Christianity, for an honest and human settlement of the problems of humanity, especially as such problems affect the Negro."[41] By 1925, Barber was referred to as "Bishop of the Triumph Church" by the *Negro World*, in which the preacher told UNIA members, "The Negro race should be original in all things. We should do away with the white man's religion, his science and his literature and think for ourselves."[42] Just two years later, in 1927, the UNIA referred to the leader as "Bishop J.D. Barber of Triumph, the Church of the New Age, and Ambassador of Abyssinia, Africa."[43] In 1929, Barber preached before the New York division of the UNIA, "I do not believe that Jesus was white. Some time ago He was pictured to us as being identified with the black race. I see Him as a righteous invisible spirit. I see Him coming in a black body. The hatred of the white man is universal." He continued, again harkening back to Ethiopia,

> I realize if redemption must come it must come through righteousness among us. We need a new day, we need a new theology, to help to put the program over. It was my good pleasure in 1920 to visit the court of a country of five hundred thousand square miles. I met a black queen of twenty-five million black folks and eight million soldiers. A kingdom that boasts she has never been conquered. If you turn to God in righteousness and Garvey in spirit we shall never be defeated. It is the white man's propaganda to make fun of us.[44]

Barber's call for a "new theology" was not only a call for UNIA members to continue theologizing their Black transnational political vision, but it was also a call for Black Christians, especially the Black Pentecostals that he pastored and led as bishop, to tear down iconographies of white Jesus and to effectively replace them with images and a theology that said that Jesus was Black.

To blacken his Pentecostal theology or unearth Pentecostalism's African roots within COGIC—both in terms of its theological content and its geographical orientation—Barber continued to draw upon his own experiences in Ethiopia.[45] For example, in his address on January 4, 1931, in New York City, Barber preached, "The Redemption of Africa is a fixed principle and must be fulfilled. Abyssinia is destined to play her part in history. Ras Tafari, Emperor of Ethiopia and of the tribe of the Lion of Judah, has come forth in all his Majesty as King of Kings." He continued, "We should be creating employment for ourselves and our posterity. Before we can have a government, we must be able to operate big business, and fields and industry. Our boys and girls should be learning Arabic and African dialects, so that whenever you return home, you would not be a stranger among your own people."[46] In order to continue bridging connections among Triumph, the UNIA, and Ethiopia, the preacher made several voyages back and forth to Abyssinia from 1920 to the early 1930s, and upon each return, he gave riveting sermons, telling the story of "the rise of ancient Ethiopia," with "the chariot and royal blood ascending."[47]

Barber's brand of Pentecostalism rooted in Black religious nationalism and Ethiopianism was, in effect, a homage to the Africanisms of the denomination.[48] One might say that Barber embodied much of what Zora Neale Hurston captured in her writings in the early twentieth century about Black Pentecostals throughout the US South. For instance, on March 20, 1940—amid her time as a staff member of the WPA's archival and documentation efforts—Hurston worshipped with and studied the "ritualistic expression from the lips of the communicants of the Seventh Day Church of God" in Beaufort, South Carolina. She wrote, "Its keynote is rhythm. In this church they have two guitars, three symbols, two tambourines, one pair of rattle goers, and two washboards. Every song is rhythmic as are their prayers and their sermons." Focusing in on the sonic resonances of the Sanctified Church, Hurston continued, "The unanimous prayer is one in which every member of the church prays at the same time but prays his own prayer aloud, which consists of exotic sentences, liquefied by intermittent chanting so that the words are partly submerged in the flowing rising and falling chant." Initially intrigued by the church's ritualistic similarities with Black Atlantic religions, Hurston then described "the form of prayer"—with its Africana soteriological orientation—"like the limbs of a tree, glimpsed now and then through the smothered leaves. It is a thing of wondrous beauty, drenched in harmony and rhythm."[49] In the paragraph before Hurston's analysis of Black Pentecostal sonic choreography and its Africana genealogical roots, however, she wrote explicitly, "To the Interviewer this church seems to be a protest against the stereotype form of Methodist and Baptist churches among Negroes. It is a revolt against the white man's view of religion, which has been so generally accepted by the literate Negro and is therefore a version to the more African form of expression."[50] While there is no definitive way to measure or quantify Africanisms, individuals like Smith, Barber, and Hurston understood Pentecostalism to be a Black Atlantic religion, and for Barber in particular, such a characterization necessitated that Black Pentecostals and all people of African descent reconnect with the continent of Africa.

Barber's vision, however, did not extend to all factions of COGIC. Even though Triumph had spread from Louisiana throughout the United

States—to such places as Montgomery, Pittsburgh, Indianapolis, and Chicago by the mid-1930s and well into the 1940s—the religious organization that Smith and Barber had a hand in founding in New Orleans and Baton Rouge would take a turn.[51] Rather than continuing the Black transnational work as conceived by its two forerunners, Triumph, like many other COGIC churches, became more invested in respectability politics and aesthetic practices of distinction undergirded by classism, which they imagined as being able to set them apart from the underworld workers in their very neighborhoods. In the New Orleans church, in particular, Triumph was categorized in much the same way as other Sanctified churches, and the political rhetoric and Black religious nationalism of Barber, in particular, did not resemble the rather conservative and socially restrictive theologies espoused in Triumph's storefront church located at 3431 Loyola Street. "The sect is a typical Negro holiness body of the second-blessing type," wrote Elmer T. Clark in *The Small Sects in America*. "It stresses the second coming of Christ and 'the baptism by fire.'"[52] Similarly, the US Bureau of the Census wrote, "Triumph the Church and Kingdom of God in Christ teaches that Jesus shed His blood for the complete cleansing of the justified believer from all indwelling sin, and from its pollution subsequent to regeneration; and that entire sanctification is an instantaneous, definite second work of grace obtained by faith on the part of the fully consecrated believer. It believes in the second coming of Christ and the baptism by fire as a definite Scriptural experience obtainable by faith. All doctrines contrary to God's revealed word are severely opposed."[53] The last sentence cemented Triumph's opposition to the underworld, despite how Black Pentecostals had been confined there just like the people they had opposed.

LWP writers similarly wrote of Triumph in the late 1930s, "Members of this church, like the spiritualists, are forbidden the use of coffee, tobacco, wine, and whiskey. 'To be clean inside you must also be clean outside,' hence the refraining from alcoholic drinks and smoking. There is no communion or water baptism here. There is only the baptism of the Holy Ghost." Not only did Triumph's New Orleans branch denounce smoking and drinking—two "vices" that were commonly enjoyed in the underworld and at the UNIA meetings that Barber attended and preached at—but the New Orleans church also allowed white people to be leaders, something on par with other COGIC churches but nonetheless a diversion from Barber's and Garvey's insistence on pro-Black and all-Black leadership. "There is a white Evangelist, known as the Shepherd, who visits the numerous churches and conducts revivals," wrote LWP writers. "The one they had died recently . . . and they are looking for another, but as yet have been unsuccessful in finding anyone to take his place." The group did, however, continue to use "Prince" for male members—a title given to Barber when he served as adviser and secretary to Triumph's founder, Apostle Elias Dempsey Smith.[54]

By the time of the LWP's report on Triumph, the extent of COGIC's Black transnationalism could solely be found in its missionary efforts. Even as Barber viewed sanctification and Black religious nationalism as coconstitutive for the moral uplift of people of African descent, many of the churches under his care perceived the two as diametrically opposed, ultimately privileging the former, while demonizing non-US Black religionists. As historian Calvin White has contended, "COGIC missionaries dedicated their lives to uplifting blacks whom they believed still lived under a veil of heathenism. Driven by the theory of sanctification and their growing acceptance of middle-class values, COGIC missionaries reproduced paternalistic views toward Africans with whom they worked."[55] COGIC's missionary efforts in Africa eventually spread to the West Indies. These projects asserted COGIC's belief in American exceptionalism and privileged Christianity over and against Black Atlantic religions, which were already being heavily policed by the white American Christian hegemonic state on US soil and in occupied territories across the globe. While missionaries articulated these ideals in their preaching and teaching to Africans and West Indians, saving "heathen nations" was not the sole focus of COGIC inside of its churches in the United States. In New Orleans, faith healing and the politics of dress were its actual priorities.

FAITH HEALING AND THE POLITICS OF DRESS

According to the 1941 *Directory of Churches and Religious Organizations in New Orleans*, compiled by the WPA staff in Louisiana, COGIC had gained a significant following throughout the state and specifically in New Orleans by the late 1930s and early 1940s. Bishop Lucien H. Treadwell was the state convocation moderator and head bishop, and under his care were five COGIC jurisdictions, including Triumph.[56] Treadwell, however, was the most popular in the press and in LWP documents, along with Elder James Feltus, one of the leaders charged to Treadwell's care. Both men were known for their preaching and faith healing styles and for how their members dressed themselves and embodied their vision of the beauty of holiness. In each of their respective churches, church mothers and other women were especially responsible for upholding and maintaining the aesthetic politics of religious difference in and beyond COGIC. The LWP said of Triumph, "Although not as colorful, the services at this Sanctified church are practically the same as those at Bishop Treadwell's."[57] Treadwell and his church set the standard.

Following his migration to New Orleans in 1918 from Fayetteville, North Carolina, by way of Memphis, Tennessee, Treadwell's powerful ministry began in the Crescent City the same year.[58] The LWP staff observed, "He was ordained bishop because of his ability to cure any kind of ill, but his knowledge of the Bible also had some influence on his elevation to this rank" in COGIC. "There is nothing in a man he can do but to live that God can do through him," Treadwell often exclaimed.[59] Despite Treadwell's emphasis on his power coming from God, which he gained by "[having] to fast twenty-one solid days, and even fasting, meditation, and long periods of prayer," the press continued to characterize him as a "Spiritualist," a "cult leader," and a "Hoodoo." Treadwell, however, "openly avowed that he [was] no Hoodoo, and that is why the Hoodoos of New Orleans and Algiers are so determined to run him out of town."[60] Nonetheless, one reporter from the *Louisiana Weekly* attended Treadwell's revivals and mischaracterized him as a "magic healer."

> Hearing so much about the "miracle man" of New Orleans, the Reverend Father Treadwell, the Religious Editory of the Weekly could not resist the temptation to drop everything before him and go and see what it was all about. And, lo! when he got on the scene and studied the magic healer at close range, he was so impressed with what he saw and heard that he found himself precisely baffled with the conflicting questions that perplexed the resplendent Queen of Sheba, who being swept off her feet on the occasion of her visit to Solomon of old, exclaimed "The half has never been told." Yes, that's it. "The half has never been told." No matter what you hear, or rumor has to say about this Reverend Father Treadwell you have to go there for yourself if you wish to get the full unadulterated benefit of his miraculous performance. Furthermore, it will not suffice to drop in and run out. You must stay around, with eyes, ears, and mouth open. If you bat an eye or turn your head you are bound to miss something, for mind you, there is something doing all the time, for when Father Treadwell swings into action and gets right down to business all kinds of things happen.[61]

Despite the reporter's mischaracterization of Treadwell as "magic healer," they underscored not only Treadwell's "marvelous and dramatic personality," but his magnetism and pull. "His technique is well planned," the reporter observed. "For every colored person singled out for treatment, a white person follows; one white, one colored, or one colored, one white; that is the method of procedure." Not only did Treadwell's faith healing cross the color line of the 1930s South, but it also crossed denominational lines. "People and I mean church people are there from all denominational families: the Baptists, the Methodists, the Catholics—those of all creeds and no creed. And they are there from far and near. An old Indian from the plains of Oklahoma, has been camping around the Treadwell sanctuary for some three months. Being a complete cripple, he believes that Father Treadwell can bring him around."[62] Treadwell was not only rumored to be a healer, but many testified at his services, in letters, and in newspaper articles about the efficacy of his spiritual practice—their blind eyes were opened, deaf ears unstopped, and disabled bodies healed.

Treadwell, however, was not the only preacher within COGIC to garner a significant following. Elder James Feltus, Sr., Louisiana state overseer, also drew massive crowds and spread COGIC in New Orleans and in the surrounding towns.[63] In 1914, Feltus expanded COGIC throughout Louisiana with Bishop Mason's blessing and with the support of his brother, Henry. The two brothers had been leading Pentecostal services in the Sixth Street Holiness Church, which they founded in 1907, and through connections and travels to Memphis, the two formed an alliance with Mason and other COGIC leaders. The Feltus brothers along with Mason grew COGIC in Louisiana to more than two hundred churches, according to the state jurisdiction's history.[64] Over time, James emerged as state overseer in the region, and was reelected several times, up until he passed away in 1946. When interviewed and photographed by the LWP in the late 1930s, Feltus noted, "I've been head of the Church of God in Christ since Elder Johnson died. Elder Johnson was the one who brought 'the light' to the dark streets of New Orleans. He founded this very church in 1905. And, from this tree has been spread the seeds of the fruit of God. Throughout the state we have churches. They come under different districts. There are six in all: Baton Rouge, New Orleans, Alexandria, Monroe, Shreveport, and Lake Charles. Each one is headed by a district superintendent."[65] Feltus's children, especially his sons, aided him in his evangelizing efforts.

To trace a genealogy between his 1930s church and the Holiness-

Pentecostal movement of the late nineteenth century, Feltus went on to draw connections, for the LWP worker, between New Orleans COGIC and Memphis, the birthplace of COGIC. "Then, there's Senior Bishop, Elder C.H. Mason. He's from Memphis you know." Feltus would then go on to describe the hierarchy of the denomination under Mason. "And, of course, just like the men are divided into districts the women have districts, too, under Mother McInnis."[66] It is significant that these male leaders not only were interviewed alongside church mothers, but that they spoke their names and expressed quite explicitly their influence throughout the denomination and the state.

Mother Eliza (Holland) McInnis, who was originally from Pine Bluff, Arkansas, was "state mother" in Louisiana who "[ran] all the women's organizations" in COGIC, and she and Feltus were two prominently featured individuals in the LWP's papers.[67] They were so influential that COGIC members from other Louisianan towns and other Southern cities came to New Orleans to join their churches. For example, one sister from Baton Rouge and another brother from Houston, Texas, spoke passionately about the need to be one with the church in New Orleans. Mother McInnis, who claimed she "had the Christian spirit all [her] life," told an LWP worker, "Well, I've been with the saints since this church was founded in 1905. The women's group have charge of the missionaries and the other women's auxiliaries in all the districts . . . There are about one hundred and twenty churches we have in Louisiana."[68] Under Mother McInnis, Black women of all ages were healed and encouraged to grow in their spiritual gifting, even as COGIC did not allow women to be ordained as preachers. As scholars have long contended, women's auxiliaries afforded Black women leadership roles, voting power, and a collective voice in Black Pentecostal denominations where a patriarchal theological culture required that women be submissive to men. Mother McInnis, for example, often spoke at the "ministers' Bible Institute for the training of negro ministers and church workers," in which she drew on her strength as a Bible study teacher, prayer band leader, and church mother.[69] McInnis's dress, as shown in figure 6.3, also resonated with the sartorial choices espoused by Mother Brown, such that the women's auxiliary became a site for COGIC to distinguish itself from the Black Spiritual churches through the politics of dress, and more specifically, by way of Black women's bodies. As Butler has also argued, "Dress, hairstyle, and bodily discipline became important in navigating the nexus between body and belief. One's body had to manifest the beliefs of sanctification and appear pure,

FIGURE 6.3. Mother Eliza McInnis. Courtesy of State Library of Louisiana.

unlike the urban bodies that were sculpted to fit the new urban lifestyle" common among urban migrants.[70]

For COGIC members in New Orleans and Louisiana more broadly, modest dress worn by Black women was a means by which they differentiated themselves not only from "the world," but more specifically, from Spiritualists who, given their practices, were also considered "otherworldly." COGIC members feared that Spiritualists' "otherworldliness," however, had eclipsed their own but in unsanctioned ways. Thus, to confirm their holy living, Black Pentecostal women's clothes, and by extension the policing of their bodies in those clothes, ironically became a fertile ground for the denomination to articulate its own aesthetic politics in the long struggle to counteract mischaracterizations of COGIC in relation to Spiritualism and Hoodoo. Thus, Black women's bodies were, yet again, the spiritual battleground for race-based respectability politics and the denomination's religion making, even as Black women were not officially ordained as preachers.[71]

A similar dynamic existed in the NOD of the UNIA, through the Universal African Black Cross Nurses, a Black women's organization designed after the American Red Cross that offered medical and educational services to people of African descent.[72] Like the Women's Department of COGIC, religious motivation was also central to how Black Cross Nurses organized themselves. In 1929, for example, they hosted "Negro Health Week" in New Orleans, in which they "[gave their] full quota of service to the great service of Hygeia—the goddess of health."[73] Bishop Barber of Triumph, who was known to speak often about the "nobility of women," often praised the Black Cross Nurses, stating, "It is indeed a pleasure . . . to compliment the Black Cross Nurses and the Legion Staff on their wonderful hospital demonstration as shown here. Much has been said of the Red Cross Nurses and we expect much of our Black Cross Nurses."[74]

The Black Cross Nurses' dress aided their organizing efforts and helped them cultivate their own humanitarianism using a Black transnational religious ethos. "Not the wanton Jezebels of white imagination," writes historian Barbara Bair, "the nurses were instead angels of charity and mercy, holy sisters united in purity and devotion to their own community and its redemption."[75] Black Cross Nurses were acutely aware of how the politics of dress, as Casselberry again reminds us in *The Labor of Faith*, could be used to subvert hegemonic and oppressive constructs about Black womanhood in and outside of African American religions (see fig. 6.4).[76] For example, Mrs. Beulah McDonald, president of the Black Cross Nurses, often spoke throughout Louisiana while wearing her nurses' habit in order to recruit women into the NOD, and she was heralded by reporters as a champion who did "some noble pioneering work."[77] A prolific speaker, in November 1927, she asked the NOD "to use every effort to keep the association intact until [Garvey] returns."[78] In December of the same year, she told them, "In the UNIA, there is room for improvement for all."[79] Black Cross Nurses, like McDonald, actively worked to bring healing to the UNIA, and much of their organizing emphasized an ethic of care, deeply informed by the UNIA's Black religious nationalism. Black Cross Nurses also carved out intentional spaces within the UNIA to question internal injustices, often initiated and exacerbated by men. As Anthea Butler has argued, Black Pentecostal women employed similar methods on the altar as intercessors and in Bible studies as teachers, asserting spiritual authority and challenging male dominance and patriarchy.[80]

Despite the undeniable labor of Black women in religious organizations like COGIC and the UNIA, men often took credit for building these institutions. The "bald-headed Rev. James [Feltus]," for example, like many Black Pentecostal men of his time, believed that he was the one to whom the Spirit had entrusted a uniquely powerful spiritual gift, thus attracting his huge

FIGURE 6.4. Spotlight on Universal Black Cross Nurses, New Orleans, *National Times*, June 1, 1940. Robert A. Hill Collection, box PS 21, David M. Rubenstein Rare Book and Manuscript Library, Duke University.

"flock" and defending COGIC's honor as a true religion in the eyes of the white American Christian hegemonic state. Speaking of his experiences in his hometown Centreville, Mississippi, in the 1920s before "[getting] a feelin' for [New Orleans]" where he moved to make more money and have a larger following, Feltus boasted about "running them Baptist preachers out of town," because "their religion [was] based on Baptism and [his was] based on faith and the spirit." During COGIC Holy Convocation on April 12, 1940, in New Orleans, Feltus recounted these things to an LWP worker as follows:

> I got to turnin' and a-turnin' around Centreville and fore you know it I was the talk of the town. I had everybody gettin' religion. I had done [heard] about that new [religion] way up in the north part of Mississippi and I says I want to try it. I was a Baptist at first and so was everybody else, but I wanted to git away from that mess and try that new kind of

[religion], the Church of God in Christ. Its [like] the Sanctified. I always [like] to shout and this [religion] gives you plenty nuff time, and room. Everybody on the farms [likes] to shout. Well sir, when I came out with that new [religion], the Church of God in Christ, I had all them farm hands shouting and dancin' till they couldn't no mo'. Fore I knowed it everybody was havin' a good time who was in my church, and they all started joinin', too.[81]

Feltus brought his religious fervor to New Orleans, where he did garner more followers. Yet his reach and influence did not exceed that of Treadwell. In fact, the press followed Treadwell more closely than Feltus, and people traveled near and far, risking their lives to be touched by the former.

Notwithstanding Treadwell's widespread fame and the acclaimed efficacy of his spiritual practice, one failed healing would haunt the leader's career up until he died. In the context of the spiritual marketplace of 1930s New Orleans, which was full of "fakes," "quacks," and "crooks," successful healings were a critical site for distinguishing "real" religious practitioners from the "fakes." Moreover, successful healings were used as examples of which traditions—Pentecostalism, Spiritualism, and Hoodoo—should be considered legitimate in the eyes of the state and among Black New Orleanians who would ultimately depend on these faith healers. It was important to followers of these traditions that they not be conjured, Hoodooed, or spiritually harmed by a leader to whom they willingly gave their trust.[82] In 1932, Joseph Randolph, forty-nine, like the thousands of others who attended Treadwell's daily and nightly revivals, entrusted the faith healer with his sick body. Randolph, however, would not be physically healed, nor would he even survive the revival.

The day after the African American man's tragic death in the church, the *Times-Picayune* published the headline "Invalid Seeking Faith Cure Dies During Services: Stricken as He Leaves Altar after Asking for 'Healer's' Aid." Randolph, who was from Thibodaux, a town about sixty miles from New Orleans, "had suffered from heart trouble for many years," and his cardiovascular condition most likely affected his mobility. Treadwell heard the man's pleas for mercy and healing and prayed for him. Yet Randolph's extensive travels to New Orleans added an additional strain on his already weakened heart. While standing at the altar for prayer, the man fainted but not in the sense of being overcome by the Spirit. One can surmise from various newspaper clippings that Treadwell discerned something of a different sort, something far more nerve-racking.[83] The situation was so dire that

Treadwell called upon the other elders and preachers to help him pray for the man. Even the LWP staff had recorded in their notes, "Bishop Treadwell's coworkers are unable to heal, but they are no less interesting than their leader."[84] Yet Treadwell broke his own rule. The situation demanded it. One of the leaders he called upon was another famed revivalist, Rev. Dr. James Gordon McPherson. As the two faith healers prayed alongside R. H. Lee, "hundreds of negroes in the church sang hymns." After an hour of prayer and singing—hoping for divine intervention—the police and physicians from Charity Hospital, which had a record of denying Black patients, were called to the scene. "But Randolph died before their arrival. The body was removed to the morgue and the 'healer' continued his services."[85]

And that he did. In the years following Randolph's death, Treadwell continued to lead revivals and was continually reelected as senior bishop of the Church of God in Christ of Faith Tabernacle in New Orleans. In 1940, for example, he held the eighth national convocation for the tabernacle—which seemed to have split from COGIC in 1932, the same year of Randolph's unfortunate death inside of Treadwell's church. Despite the discomfort that circulated around Treadwell's revivals, many of his followers seemed to blame the cause of Randolph's death on his heart failing, rather than on Treadwell's faith healing abilities. Even Bishop Charles H. Mason attended the 1940 convocation in New Orleans, suggesting that he had probably heard of Randolph's death but nonetheless still trusted and believed in Treadwell's ministry.[86] In the years following, Treadwell continued to serve COGIC and his own denomination, up until he died in April 1946 at the age of fifty-nine.[87] His ministry, however, would not be the last to make a mark on Black Pentecostalism in the city of New Orleans. His colleague and friend, Rev. Dr. James Gordon McPherson, who had helped Treadwell pray for Randolph, would also make his own mark.

NEW ORLEANS'S BLACK BILLY SUNDAY

While COGIC in New Orleans and throughout the United States pivoted toward missionary efforts as its own form of Black transnationalism and concerned itself mainly with sartorial choices as a form of respectability and differentiation from Spiritualists and Hoodoo practitioners during the 1930s and 1940s, other Pentecostals and Pentecostal-adjacent leaders in the city envisioned themselves as world citizens and patriotic contributors to the American nation-state. One such person was the Rev. James Gordon McPherson, the founder of the Watch Tower Worldwide Intercessory Prayer Healing Movement. A native of New Orleans, McPherson was born about 1869 and was a war veteran who served in the Spanish-American War after enlisting in the Twenty-Fourth United States Infantry.[88] A highly respected and gifted orator, McPherson pursued theological training and earned a doctor of divinity degree in the late 1890s from the Guadalupe College (or College of the Guadalupe Baptist Association) in Sequin, Texas, a Baptist institution for African Americans, and became a well-known preacher and faith healer, traveling throughout the nation on a decades-long revival tour. The historian Nicole Myers Turner has contended, "Theological education for ministers became de facto kind of gender training for black men. Available only to recognized leaders of black churches, theological education reinforced the ministry as a male domain."[89] McPherson was certainly a part of this cadre of Black male preachers whose entry into the ministry was made possible by his alliances with what Turner describes as "white co-religionists." Ordained a Baptist minister by a council of white Baptists in 1901 and appointed the Field Evangelist for the National Baptist Convention (unincorporated), McPherson eventually found affinity with Pentecostals, in which his revivals included "an old-fashioned Holy Ghost and Fire Daybreak prayer meeting" and the "riches of the blessings of Christian Healing."[90]

In contemporary parlance, McPherson was an early twentieth-century Baptist-Pentecostal, or "Bapticostal," whose long-standing itinerant career, like that of many preachers and gospel singers in the early twentieth century, afforded him the space to oscillate and cross over between various Protestant denominations, bringing together Black and white Pentecostals and Baptists, and even Methodists.[91] In 1916, McPherson held a revival attended by both Black and white people at the Duarte AME Church in Pasadena, California, in which "the religious fervor is said to [have run] high at each service, with a shouting time and the regular, old-fashioned Holy Ghost fire and brimstone type of ceremony together with songs reminiscent of the big camp meetings in the old South."[92] He brought revivals to Colorado, Wyoming, Texas, and other states such that he had "an enviable reputation that [was] nationwide as one of the greatest negro preachers in America."[93] In 1918, the *Nashville Globe* reported that the famed preacher held a "big union revival meeting ... at a monster Gospel Tabernacle, corner of Grande and Texas avenue, right in the very heart of the city" which was attended by three thousand people. The article continued, "'Black Billy' is one of the most forceful evangelists of the race ... because of the immense mixed throngs that gather at his meetings in every section of the country, and here in the South thousands of both races."[94] McPherson's revivals were largely attended by "thousands of Negro religious workers, along with many of the leading ministers representing every denomination [including] members of the Black Billy Sunday Evangelistic Committee." Though aesthetically Black Pentecostal in its emphasis on "Holy Ghost and fire," McPherson's revivals were both interracial and interdenominational, and it was his remarkable speaking ability coupled with widespread news of his miracle working and faith healing that drew the masses, near and far, in New Orleans and beyond.[95] The press, for instance, commonly described him as follows: "'Prophet' McPherson is said to be one of the outstanding faith healers and is reported to have cured thousands of many diseases."[96]

Among all of his many attributes, however, McPherson's time in the military informed his Black Pentecostal theological viewpoint the most. Unlike COGIC's Bishop Mason, who opposed World War I "and [advised] negroes to resist the draft," McPherson boasted about his having served on behalf of the US government and encouraged war participation as a true form of American patriotism.[97] According to the *New Orleans States*, "The members of the Church of God in Christ do not believe in bloodshed or war. The negroes are advised they may join military forces as non-combatants, and many of them are doing so."[98] A Bapticostal preacher, McPherson took a different stance. The *Salt Lake Tribune* reported in 1917, "Evangelist McPherson was formerly a member of the Twenty-Fourth United States Infantry that was stationed at Fort Douglas, and went from [Salt Lake City, Utah,] to Cuba in 1898, where he took part in the Battle of San Juan Hill, afterwards serving as a volunteer nurse in the Yellow Fever Pest Hospital at Siboney de Cuba."[99] The preacher once said, "I was there. I was in the second set of four's that marched to the foot of San Juan Hill and we charged clean to the top, sir, and stayed there till we were ordered back. I was a sinful man in those days, but the Lord spared me. Men dropped to the right of me and to the left of me, shot dead and wounded, but I never got a scratch, sir."[100] In his preaching ministry, McPherson regularly drew upon his experiences in the Spanish-American War, so much so that he was also referred to as "patriot-preacher" by the press, especially as he often raised funds for foreign missions throughout Latin America and the Caribbean.[101] Other writers described him as "an evangelist with an enviable war record, 'the Fighting Parson,'" and "hero of the Yellow fever camps of Cuba."[102]

During each of his ministry trips, McPherson would preach and also lecture on "the privations experienced by the negro troops in the army" in

Cuba.[103] Other times he would gather groups of Black men to discuss "civic betterment in the battle for moral uplift."[104] In one of his revivals in Austin, Texas, McPherson lectured on "The Daring Charge of the Fighting Black Troopers at the Battle of San Juan Hill," and the press observed that religious services included "a sacred concert by a double chorus of colored singers in a program replete with sweet old Southern melodies, plantation jubilee songs and patriotic selections."[105] Notwithstanding the racialized and racist depictions of African American religions in the press, McPherson's services most certainly embodied what sociologist W. E. B. Du Bois described as "the preacher, the music, and the frenzy" of the African American Protestant church experience in *The Souls of Black Folk*. McPherson, however, not only connected the character of his revivals to the Spirit or the Holy Ghost as did most of the individuals in Du Bois's study, but he owed the peculiar and charismatic aspects of his revivals to his time in war. He once stated, "No man knows the terrible mental and moral struggle through which the soul goes as it comes in contact with the groan of the dying and the shot of the gun and the piercing of the bayonet as he who has been in the midst of a mighty conflict."[106] McPherson's close proximity to the dead and dying undergirded his theological conviction, and he adapted a holiness or hell message that prioritized sanctification. In 1915, for instance, he preached "Quit Your Cussedness and Come on the Lord's Side" during "a big revival in a tent on the Colored Y.M.C.A. grounds" in Los Angeles, in the waning days of the Azusa revival.[107]

Nonetheless, during the late 1920s and early 1930s McPherson's ministry underwent a significant transformation influenced by the spiritual marketplace of New Orleans, where Pentecostals, Spiritualists, Hoodoo practitioners, and other religious leaders competed for followers and business. Despite the sense of competitiveness in New Orleans during the period, McPherson's intellectual performances distinguished him from other members of the Sanctified Church, in which he held "the record of attracting the largest crowds of any Negro revivalist in the world."[108] In the edits for their report on the "fanatic cults," even the LWP staff noted, for example, "Rev. [James] Gordon McPherson—'The Black Billy Sunday'—when [the official report is] written will fit in between the Holy Rollers and the Baptists making the bridge from the fanatic to the legitimate religion," symbolizing how the white American Christian hegemonic state privileged middle-class markers of intellectualism.[109] The irony, however, lies in the fact that McPherson was not only a revivalist and lecturer but also an underworld worker and faith healer who practiced rootwork. The LWP staff observed, "Dr. McPherson

"WE AIN'T SPIRITUALISTS, WE'S THE SANCTIFIED CHURCH"

had found it necessary to include healing in his program, probably because of competition, he now found it practical to add herbs to his healing."[110] On December 22, 1928, the *Louisiana Weekly* also published an advertisement for the preacher, most likely written and submitted by McPherson himself:

> Dr. J. Gordon McPherson, a regular ordained Baptist minister with strange power to help suffering afflicted humanity, Christian herbalist healer of so-called incurable diseases, by the power of prayer, herbs, barks, roots, flowers of the fields and the forest gathered from Nature's great botanical laboratory. Why use poisonous drugs when our heavenly Father in His divine wisdom and beneficence has provided a vegetable cure for most of the ills of afflicted and suffering humanity? When all else has failed to give you relief, and your physician holds out no hope for you, don't despair and give up, for there is hope as long as there is life. Why not come across the river to Algiers and see the Creole Wonder Herb Remedy Man, whose herb treatments wrought almost miraculous cures when all other treatments had failed. Our terms are reasonable. Consultation free.
>
> Treatment Parlors
> 1015 Vallette Street,
> Algiers, Louisiana[111]

In his embrace of Pentecostal faith healing and with his deep appreciation for intellectualism, McPherson also found affinity with rootwork—a tradition that has historically and historiographically been deemed a poor, unlearned person's religion.[112] Moreover, his drawing from multiple Black Atlantic religious traditions in his cultivation of his own religious practice was his own embodied form of religion making, and as the archive suggests, McPherson was acutely aware of the times, and like many of his peers, he sought out inventive ways to survive the Depression. Unlike Mother Brown and Bishop Treadwell's church, it was not just the Holy Ghost that healed in McPherson's ministry. Yet like COGIC's Bishop Mason, McPherson, too, was a conjurer-preacher.

Outside of the church, McPherson was active in several social organizations. Most notably, he was a member of one of the many Masonic lodges in New Orleans—the Improved Benevolent Protective Order of Elks of the World—and his participation in that space was due largely to "the spirit of harmony between black fraternal orders and black churches," as historian John M. Giggie has observed, given "what the two institutions had in common: their leaders, members, buildings, rites, ethics, and appellations."[113] Giggie further argues that "lodges provided opportunities for black men to experiment with ideas about southern African American manhood and black civic culture. Fraternal orders gave members new means of achieving a level of financial and emotional stability otherwise nearly impossible during Jim Crow."[114] These Black men often joined together to discuss the problems of their raced, classed, and gendered positions and did so with hopes of bettering their own condition. In July 1926, for example, McPherson cowrote a letter on behalf of his lodge, with four of his brothers—Aaron A. B. Chatters, chairman, and W. H. Mitchell, secretary of the YMCA, and A. J. Llopis and Joseph Geddes—in which the men wrote, "We are going after the 1927 Grand Lodge Session, and a large delegation should make the trip in order to assist in place before the members of the Session the advantages of New Orleans as a Convention City. Let our slogan be 'New Orleans, in 1927.'"[115] To their credit, the men were able to bring the convention to New Orleans, and several important conversations were had in the city. One Dr. William J. Thompkins of Kansas City noted the grave health disparities common about Negroes: "Throughout the country the percentage of tuberculosis deaths, largely because of neglect, is seven times higher among negroes than among the whites."[116] Four years later, in 1931, McPherson "[made] the principal patriotic address" at a flag ceremony in Audubon Park conducted by New Orleans Lodge No. 30, Order of Elks, and Crescent City Post No. 125 of the American Legion, in which "negro veterans of the World War and the Spanish American War" presented a salute to the flag.[117] Indeed, many of the men that McPherson participated in Masonic activities with were veterans, and this particular community actively supported his ministry.

Above all, McPherson was a Holiness preacher, a patriotic war veteran, and a lecturer, whose theological reflections on war and civil rights set him apart as a public intellectual. In 1922, he was awarded his second doctorate, this time in psychology, by the Chicago School of Psychology, and "the following year he became pastor of the First Baptist Church of Hansboro, Miss., although he continued to conduct successful revivals throughout the nearby states. People began to call him 'Black Billy Sunday,' and many of those who heard him acclaimed him a better speaker than the white edition."[118] McPherson, like Reverend Calvin P. Dixon in historian Lerone Martin's *Preaching on Wax*, also "adopted the nickname 'Black Billy Sunday' in honor of famed white revivalist Billy Sunday." Martin contends, "Beginning in the late nineteenth century until his death in 1935, Billy Sunday barnstormed the country championing a muscular Christianity and moral crusades against the urban 'vices' of drinking, dancing, and gambling." Black Protestant preachers like McPherson and Dixon "used the phonograph to trumpet [their] voice across the country and establish [themselves] both as reviver[s] of traditional black Protestantism and progenitor[s] of modern black church work."[119] Martin further contends, "The pioneers of phonograph religion attempted to utilize the medium of black popular entertainment as a means to sway the habits and practices of modern culture toward traditional Protestant piety and beliefs."[120] Between 1930 and 1931, McPherson recorded four sermonettes for Paramount Records in Grafton, Wisconsin: "Red Horse and Its Rider," "Chickens will Come Home to Roost," "Quit Your Meanness," and "This Old World's in a Hell of a Fix."[121] These recordings led the LWP staff to describe him as "not having lost the simplicity that is the natural heritage of his race."[122] In their estimation, McPherson's commitment to keeping the spirituals in his services were a homage to the plantation church, and these songs drew the white masses to his revivals and prompted listening audiences to purchase his records.

In his preaching, McPherson emphasized the evils of the world in which he lived and encouraged his eager listeners to take heed to the scriptures and to give their lives over to sanctification and holy living. These stern warnings were a direct response to the supposed evils of urban cities, where vices and the world of entertainments were said to draw all toward sin. McPherson's charisma, however, attracted sinners and made them saints. His fiery presence coupled with his own brand of religion making, however—specifically his blend of Pentecostal faith healing, sanctification theology, rootwork commercialism, and intellectualism rooted in American patriotism—had inspired the likes of white American playwright Marc Connelly in the development of his 1930 play, *The Green Pastures*. The play had been adapted from Roark Bradford's 1928 collection of stories, *Ol' Man Adam an' His Chillun*, and Warner Bros. turned it into a film in 1936.[123] In the 1930s, journalists had observed, "It was the Rev. Mr. McPherson's emotional sermons, based on a literal belief in the Bible which first inspired Roark Bradford to write 'Ol Man Adam and His Chillun.' When Connelly decided to write his famous play he traveled to New Orleans and with Bradford attended the pastor's revival meetings and drew the character of 'De Lawd' in the play from the Rev. Mr. McPherson. The Negro preacher is proud of the part which he played in bringing the play into being and is equally proud and at the same time modest about his healing power."[124] Not only were both Bradford and Connelly inspired by a wide array of Black churches in New Orleans, but the press noted that they had been especially influenced by McPherson. Regarding their visits, McPherson is quoted as saying, "Many white folks visit negro churches to hear vibrant spirituals."[125] While white spectators visited Black churches for many other reasons, including but not limited to social scientific purposes, and in the case of Bradford and Connelly, for artistic inspiration, McPherson and other faith healers like him were keenly aware of the white gaze and the implications of that gaze. This is particularly evident in the fact that Bradford and Connelly became friendly with McPherson and "visited the negro preacher at his residence, 2314 New Orleans Street," in which McPherson "was very happy over the success of his inspiration."[126] That inspiration would, undoubtedly, draw more followers to his revivals throughout the country.

The play-turned-film was set in Louisiana and depicted scenes from the Old Testament as seen and understood through the eyes of a young Black child. One writer described it as follows: "'The Green Pastures' is a stage presentation of the story of creation and sacred history [throughout] the ages to the dawn of our era, as conceived by the unsophisticated plantation negroes of the South, abounding in naïve humor yet also filled with poignant tragedy, and spectacular [throughout]."[127] In the opening montage of the film, the following words fill the screen: "God appears in many forms to those who believe in Him. Thousands of Negroes in the Deep South visualize God and Heaven in terms of people and things they know in their everyday life." In this way, God or "De Lawd" was depicted as a Black man, and the angels, though dressed in white, had Black skin. In fact, the film, as Judith Weisenfeld notes, featured an all-Black cast, though to be clear, "Connelly's decision to have his characters refer to the God character in the play and in the film most frequently as 'De Lawd' also provides the opportunity for viewers to distance themselves from fully imagining the God of the Bible as a black man. This character becomes, instead, simply the God of black people."[128] What is striking, however, is that the film did include a variety of signs and symbols related to African American religious traditions, including Conjure and Masonry.[129] Given McPherson's own religious and social involvement, Connelly most likely sought to bring to the screen Black Atlantic religious practices that resonated with the likes of McPherson and his faithful followers, especially as the film uses New Orleans as its main setting and "locates sin in urban contexts."[130] Indeed, McPherson's theology, his attention to the problems affecting African Americans in New Orleans, and his charisma as a public intellectual are all over *The Green Pastures*, especially as "Connelly offered his work as authentic African American Protestant theology, a view from the inside."[131]

It is no surprise, then, that in 1936, when McPherson died at age sixty-seven from complications of a stroke and pneumonia, the *Santa Rosa Republican* publicized his death with the headline, "McPherson, Black Billy Sunday Gone to Green Pastures." The newspaper noted that McPherson "went to his own green pastures—the Elysian fields he preached about for forty years, and which, indirectly, inspired Marc Connelly's play."[132] Before he died, he said, "Wrap me in old glory, lay my bible on my breast, and bury me in Chalmette National Cemetery at New Orleans with the other veterans, for I was a soldier and fought for Uncle Sam just as hard as I fought Satan and sin."[133] In another instance, he murmured, "I always tried to preach simple faith and goodness to my people. I fought sin hard. I knew they slipped, for I slipped myself. But that's where the mercy and the forgiveness of the Lord comes in."[134] The preacher's tombstone read "Rev. Dr. J. Gordon McPherson. Spiritual Therapeutist," suggesting that McPherson, like Father Divine, engaged the New Thought movement, which emerged in the nineteenth century and taught mental healing or the power of the mind to bring purity, self-restraint, and physical health.[135] To be clear, the term "Spiritual Therapeutist" has origins in this movement. For example, one New Thought leader wrote in 1911, "What we need is the light of the divine idea which shall disperse the darkness of error. A receptive patient is particularly open to such illumination. The Therapeutist is the friendly lamp-bearer who guides the way through the dark journeyings of the soul."[136] The fact that the term made its way onto McPherson's tombstone suggests that his family affirmed the Bapticostal preacher's religious and philosophical commitments to New Thought and implies that his practice was widely known. Even in death, he was memorialized according to the religion making he conjured in life—not just as a successful preacher or even as patriotic veteran, but as a "Spiritual Therapeutist" and underworld worker in and beyond the four walls of the traditional church, across racial, class, and denominational lines.

CONCLUSION

Black Pentecostals like McPherson, along with Bishop Treadwell, Elder Feltus, Mother Brown and the Women's Department, and Apostle Elias Dempsey Smith and Bishop J. D. Barber, each made sense of the world in which they lived on deeply spiritual terms and through their lived experiences as migrants of African descent in New Orleans. Some of them theologized Black religious nationalism, and others focused on Christian missions, Bible studies, prayer bands, and the politics of dress. Yet with all their respective differences and disagreements; their varying racial, gender, and class politics; and their intentional and strategic modes of distinguishing themselves from Black Spiritualists and Hoodoo practitioners, they each made up "the Sanctified Church." Without question, their differences, and the politics of those differences, were integral to their Black Atlantic religion making, or how they made up the great gathering of the saints. This chapter has underscored their differences—within COGIC and adjacent denominations—to work against how the white American Christian hegemonic state has historically collapsed Black religious practitioners' articulation of their unique identities. Pentecostals in and beyond New Orleans have been caricatured by the press and arguably within African American religious historiography as "otherworldly" and unconcerned with the problems of the world. Yet the actors in this chapter tell us something different. "[They] tell great stories," contends Arlene M. Sánchez-Walsh. "How they tell their stories, why they tell their stories, and how their stories affect others help craft their success globally."[137] If we take Mother Brown seriously when she said, "We ain't spiritualists. We's da Sanctified Church," we must diligently sit with, and perhaps tarry with, what the Sanctified Church was and how it constructed its own religious identity in relation to the underworld workers orbiting around its storefront churches and tent revivals.[138] In their attempts to navigate the anti-Black world of Jim Crow and the debilitating effects of the Great Depression, Pentecostals and all the other actors in the religious landscape of the city sought out inventive ways to set themselves apart, and to truly "not conform to the ways of this world" that viewed all Negroes and their churches the same—a site for the consumption of religious fanaticism and racist hyperbole, which would only be further commodified in the tourist economy, in Hollywood, and in the academy.[139]

CODA

Black New Orleans on the Move

The Black Atlantic religious practitioners discussed in *Underworld Work* illuminate how Black New Orleanians circumvented the policing of largely non-Christian and quasi-Christian Black Atlantic religious practices by the white American Christian hegemonic state and its allies, while simultaneously creating and engineering their own Black Atlantic religions in the face of Jim Crow racial-sexual terrorism and anti-Blackness. Members, clients, and followers of these religious actors affirmed the intentional religion making strategies of their leaders who healed them of ailments and guided them into spiritual truth. Members, clients, and followers, however, did not just partake in the fruits of their leaders' religion making; they also cultivated their own Black Atlantic religion making strategies, often by negotiating where they would worship, with whom they would consult for plant medicine and rootwork tinctures, and how they would either associate or disavow traditional religious and cultural institutions in Black Atlantic communities.

Following the demise of the Louisiana Writers' Project in the 1940s, some Black Atlantic religious practitioners in the city of New Orleans would also use this shifting religious landscape and the crosscurrents of the Great Migration to take their Black Atlantic religion making to new cities outside of the Crescent City. One such person was King Louis Herbert Narcisse, most likely of Haitian descent, who was born in 1921 in Gretna, just across the Mississippi River from New Orleans, and moved to the city after his father (whom he never knew) died in a shipyard accident. In a 1963 *Ebony* feature on Narcisse, journalist Louie Robinson noted, "In New Orleans, where superstitions abound, it was considered good luck to touch a child who never saw his father. People came and touched Louis."[1] Historian Martha C. Taylor has likewise observed, "Narcisse moved to New Orleans where he was steeped in Roman Catholicism and the cult of voodoo."[2] As a teenager he joined the Mount Zion Baptist Church choir, and his singing talents won him five radio auditions.

In New Orleans, the young singer most certainly encountered the vast array of Black Atlantic religious practitioners in the city doing their underworld works, such as Mother Catherine Seals and the Temple of the Innocent Blood down in the Lower Ninth Ward, or perhaps he caught wind of the New Orleans Division of the Universal Negro Improvement Association and their ruminations on Black religious nationalism at the Pythian Temple, fraternity lodges, or local bars. He undoubtedly heard the sanctified sounds of the Church of God in Christ, which had a faithful following in the city, and whose music and sermonizing had influenced the likes of fellow New Orleanian Mahalia Jackson, with whom Narcisse—the uncle of renowned Black gospel singer Bessie Griffin, a member of the Southern Revivalists of New Orleans and later, the Caravans—would later collaborate on several of his music projects, after Jackson met Griffin in 1951 and took her under her wing.[3] Given his proximity to Griffin, and specifically Jackson, who often reflected on her "Aunt Duke's gifts of herbal healing" in New Orleans, Narcisse had assuredly heard or witnessed the work of conjurers, Hoodoo practitioners, and other spiritual merchants selling their gospel and peddling new ideas about race, religion, and sexuality in the city's vibrant center and out by the banks of the river.[4] Indeed, his own religion making was shaped by the world of religion making around him.

After he registered for the World War II draft on February 16, 1942, he finally joined the scores of African Americans who migrated west during the period.[5] As Taylor has observed, "With an African American population of about eighty-five hundred in 1940, Oakland saw about thirty-seven thousand more settle there by 1945."[6] Narcisse was one of these newcomers. Like Mahalia Jackson, Narcisse was raised a Baptist in New Orleans, and in 1945 he founded the Mount Zion Spiritual Temple in the Black enclave of West Oakland and modeled it after his childhood church except with a Spiritualist bent. During his first few years in his new city, however, Narcisse had been hired as a musician at the local Providence Baptist Church and worked at the naval shipyard, like his deceased father, on Mare Island.[7] The preacher-musician declared throughout Oakland, "It's nice to be nice, and let others know you are nice." Within his church, Narcisse espoused several significant theological beliefs and emphasized the importance of ritual. He told *Ebony* in 1963, "1) 'We should worship the Spirit of God every day, not on just a special day;' 2) 'The burning of incense in the home will drive out evil spirits;' 3) 'There is a blessing in oils and holy waters;' and 4) 'I believe if you are pure and right, good will always conquer.'"[8] In turn, Robinson observed that his church was "built around a strange mixture of Catholic ritual, Protestant practice, [and] Holy Roller jubilation."[9] In addition, Narcisse's theological beliefs and the spiritual efficacy of his practice—evidenced by the scores of followers who claimed that he had effectively healed them—attracted many poor and working-class migrants looking for financial prosperity. He laid his hands on them, and his followers believed that that they would be just as blessed as he was.

In this way, Narcisse resembled Father Divine of the Peace Mission and Daddy Grace of the United House of Prayer, and he was most certainly as flamboyant as Detroit's Prophet Jones, as he also flaunted himself in capes, crowns, jewels, and lived in a mansion with a Rolls Royce.[10] Narcisse even said himself, "Father Divine fed people, gave them decency. Father (Prophet) Jones gave people the benefit of prophecy. Daddy Grace had a power of God that he passed on to people."[11] Yet, like Jones in particular, there was some speculation surrounding Narcisse's (queer) sexuality, and these suspicions and rumors seemed to be supported by his collaborations with gospel and rock 'n' roll singer Little Richard, who once identified as homosexual and bisexual and whose career began in the Sanctified Church, and the fact that the Hawkins Brothers (also rumored to be gay) attended his services.[12] *Ebony* even included an image of a male follower of Narcisse on bended knee kissing his hand (see fig. C.1), and characterized the wealthy faith healer and musician as the "be-ringed king with long, feminine finger nails [with] conspicuous consumption wearing three rings, three gold bracelets, gold watch and pendant."[13] The *Oakland Tribune* similarly insinuated that Narcisse was gay by calling attention to his "occasional, perfectly timed handclaps and his gestures"—signifiers of his queer-gendered performance—and "the jewels and long fingernails that adorned his hands."[14] Another writer has outrightly argued, "From a sexual standpoint, The King was thought to be gay, a preference which did not seem to bother anyone, black or white."[15]

Accordingly, Narcisse's "queerness" as it related to his "strange" religious practices had drawn the masses, which was the case with so many of his forebears in the city of New Orleans that I have discussed in *Underworld Work*, including but certainly not limited to the Council of God members, Prophet Joseph Rajah Lyons, and Mother Catherine Seals. Black New Orleanians who "said they were unemployed and hope[d] to find jobs in Oakland" were also drawn to Narcisse's particular brand of Black Atlantic religion making,

FIGURE C.1. Louis H. Narcisse kissed by a male follower, from *Ebony*, July 1963.

and he told the press that "a welcoming committee [had been] formed and urged other groups to help the migrants."[16] The faith healer's relationship to New Orleans persisted throughout his spiritual career in Oakland. In 1965, for instance, Narcisse claimed that "by Christmas Day four truckloads of clothes, blankets and food will reach needy flood victims in New Orleans."[17] His enduring relationship with the city that had initially nurtured his own Black Atlantic religion making crystallized the New Orleans-to-Oakland migratory patterns of so many people of African descent during the midcentury and ultimately served as a recruitment strategy for his church.[18] Once they joined Mt. Zion, migrants would take on different roles within the religion's hierarchy and based on their own spiritual strengths—temple mothers, nurses, musical directors, and so on—and they were expected to wear vestments resembling the Roman Catholic Church. As figure C.2 also

In "Palace" courtyard, Narcisse delivers pep talk to high ranking members of religious order. Various costumes denote different ranks. "I walk on a red carpet and I live royally," holy monarch explains, "because I am a leader and I must stay above my people. Those I cannot lead, I must follow," he adds with cryptic change of pace.

FIGURE C.2. Narcisse with members of the Mount Zion Spiritual Temple, from *Ebony*, July 1963.

shows, women were his most faithful followers and the "chief source of [the] sect's strength."[19]

Narcisse's influence reached far and wide. In one service in 1952, the *Oakland Tribune* observed, "The 30-year-old bishop, the youngest bishop of his church, is asking many of the churches of Oakland to dismiss their evening services today so that all may hear his message."[20] And many of those churches did oblige the well-liked leader, as his preaching and faith healing attracted Californians from across the state, many of whom squeezed into the main temple in Oakland, which held more than three hundred persons at a time. Robinson noted, "The flock is primed for the main event with services conducted by temple functionaries before the King arrives. Shortly after his grand entrance, he heightens the mood by leading the congregation in song with his rather pleasant tenor voice." Soon after, the people began "pacing jerkily back and forth," running around the temple, quickening, screaming, praising, and dancing, and Robinson observed, "the singing [grew] in intensity as religious lyrics, accompanied by staccato handclapping, [were] fused with rock 'n' roll."[21] By the 1960s, Narcisse boasted "two and-half million followers in California, Arizona, Texas, Tennessee, Louisiana, and other states, as well as Germany and the Scandinavian countries."[22]

Individuals like Narcisse animate a robust portion of African American religious historiography even as they have often been eclipsed by the privileging of largely heterosexual male clergymen. By devoting critical attention to the respective religion-making strategies of marginalized figures, I have demonstrated in *Underworld Work* that Black Atlantic religion making in the Americas from the long postemancipation period to the mid-twentieth century was always context based, uniquely orchestrated, strategic, and specific to the geographical space in which the practitioners were located. Even as white supremacy loomed large and despite the pernicious underbelly of policing encircling Black people and their religious communities, practitioners and migrants cultivated and created intentional modes of making religions that were conducive to their lived experience and recognized their whole personhood with all its complexities and contradictions. It is no surprise, then, that these religions were enmeshed with a robust racialized sexual discourse that countered the sexualized race making of white supremacists during the period. It is also fitting that Black Atlantic practitioners deified themselves as Black gods in the face of systems of domination that rendered them animals and fanatics beholden to "voodooism," and fit for sacrifice by white supremacists on the American cross and the lynching tree. In their cultivation of their own Black Atlantic religions, which caught the eye of people like anthropologist Zora Neale Hurston, the practitioners surveyed—conjurers, church mothers, sex workers, queer faith healers, and street preachers—joined together, fought and debated each other, emphasized their differences, made sense of the underworld in which they lived, and utilized Black Atlantic religion making to survive on their own terms. With underworld work as the modus operandi of their salvation, late nineteenth- and early twentieth-century practitioners shine the light of freedom on the paths of those longing for their own individualized and uniquely crafted religious practices in the contemporary anti-Black world and its underworld and in the worlds here and elsewhere to come.

ACKNOWLEDGMENTS

Books come to be in community, and I am overflowing with gratitude for all who came together to support me in the researching and writing of this book. I am especially grateful to the intellectual and archival ancestors whose theories, interventions, and stories fill each chapter. I am deeply honored to have been granted access to their interior lives by way of a process of rigorous archival mediumship, and I am even more humbled by the gift of being trusted with their secrets, survivalisms, and Black religious ways of knowing, seeing, and thinking in the afterlife of chattel slavery and in the face of gratuitous state-sanctioned terror and policing.

The ideas in this book first materialized while I was a graduate student at Princeton University, but they had long been in my mind while I was studying at Williams College under the mentorship of Rhon Manigault-Bryant, who introduced me to the study of religion as an undergraduate through the interdisciplinary ethos of Africana studies. These ideas and questions continued to germinate in the courses of James Manigault-Bryant, Joy James, Leslie Brown, Neil Roberts, David Smith, Gretchen Long, and many others. At Princeton, where I attended graduate school in the Department of Religion, I benefited greatly from the immense support and enthusiasm of my adviser, Judith Weisenfeld, who shepherded me through a tumultuous time in my personal and professional journey and encouraged me with academic kindness and an intellectual generosity that is unmatched. A sacred conversation with the late, pathbreaking historian of African American religion, Albert J. Raboteau, in the lounge in 1879 Hall charged me with the weight of the task at hand, and conversations with Wallace Best, Eddie Glaude, Seth Perry, Jessica Delgado, Keeanga-Yamahtta Taylor, Imani Perry, Reena Goldthree, Wendy Belcher, Joshua Guild, and my graduate school colleagues in the Departments of Religion and African American Studies sharpened and deepened my thinking and questions.

I am especially grateful to Nyle Fort, Candace Jordan, Kelsey Moss, KB Dennis Meade, Alyssa Maldonado-Estrada, Leslie Ribovich, Eden Consenstein, Andrew Walker-Cornetta, Madeline Gambino, Kris Wright, Mélena Laudig, Kim Akano, Michael Baysa, Caroline Matas, William Stell, Emma Thompson, Beth Stroud, Kimberly Bain, Kessie Alexandre, and Janet Kong-Chow. I am also appreciative of the support and friendship of my writing partner, Ambre Dromgoole, along with the camaraderie of James Hill Jr., Cori Tucker-Price, Eziaku Nwokocha, Whitney Baisden-Bond, Candace Simpson, Shawn Torres, Kevin Lawrence Henry, Jathan Martin, Jalen Parks, Ellen Louis, Jared Loggins, George Aumoithe, Pablo José López Oro, Jeremy O'Brien, Shatavia Wynn, Paul Anthony Daniels II, Ralph Craig III, Quincy James Rhineheart, Brandon Thomas Crowley, Alix Chapman, Darnell Moore, Imani Uzuri, Olivia Polk, Alexis Pauline Gumbs, Aishah Shahidah Simmons, Farah Tanis, Amita Swadhin, Chelsea Yarborough, Brenton Miles Brock, Christopher Mathis, Hari Ziyad, Henry Love, Aman Gabe, Biko Caruthers, Jallicia Jolly, Brieanne Adams, Anika Wilson-Brown, Regina Langley, Charise Barron, La Marr Jurelle Bruce, VaNatta Ford, Shakira King, Mia Michelle McClain, Jordan Mulkey, Ahmad Washington, Jeremy Williams, Nikia Robert, Will Pruitt, Chelsea Frazier, Elle Hearns, the late Janisha Gabriel, and the late Devon Tyrone Wade, among many others.

I have also benefited greatly from conversations with Kathryn Lofton (who encouraged me to submit this book to the Class 200 series), Vaughn Booker, J. T. Roane, Jarvis Givens, Alisha Lola Jones, Alexis Wells-Oghoghomeh, Nicole Myers Turner, Axelle Karera, Eboni Marshall Turman, Leonard McKinnis, Laura McTighe, Jamil Drake, Todne Thomas, Melva Sampson, Alexia Williams, N. Fadeke Castor, Braxton Shelley, Matthew Harris, Anthony Petro, and Matthew Cressler. Other senior colleagues have mentored me and offered encouraging words over the years: Khalil Muhammad, Anthea Butler, Yvonne Chireau, Barbara Savage, Rachel Harding, Anthony Pinn, Victor Anderson, Dianne Stewart, Juan Floyd-Thomas, Saidiya Hartman, Keri Day, Joseph Winters, Jeffrey McCune, Calvin Warren, Josef Sorett, Kelly Brown Douglas, Celia Naylor, Judith Casselberry, Monique Moultrie, Margarita Simon Guillory, Tamura Lomax, Michael Brandon McCormack, Heath Carter, Mark Lewis Taylor, the late David Daniels III, Monica Coleman, Kimberly Russaw, Obery Hendricks, Cheryl Townsend Gilkes, Valerie Bridgeman, Almeda Wright, and others in the Society for the Study of Black Religion. Please forgive me for any mistakenly omitted names; as the adage goes in the Black church tradition: "Charge my head, and not my heart."

In addition, the drafts of several chapters were greatly improved with the aid of feedback and generative questions and critiques from colleagues in the Religion in the Americas subfield and the Center for the Study of Religion at Princeton, the Africana Religious History Working Group, the Black Religious Studies Working Group through the Crossroads Project, and the Afro-American Religious History Unit at the American Academy of Religion. I also appreciate feedback on working drafts and conference papers presented at the Organization of American Historians, the American Society of Church History, and the American Studies Association.

A number of individuals and institutions have made the research for this book possible. I owe many thanks to Lisa C. Moore and the staff at the Amistad Research Center at Tulane University for our email exchanges about relevant source materials. I am also thankful for Mary Wernet and Sharon Wolff at the Cammie G. Henry Research Center at Northwestern State University of Louisiana for sending hundreds of scans my way from the Federal Writers' Project Collection, which have been a foundational source of material for my project. Huge thanks to John Kennedy, an archivist at Dillard University, who sent me newspaper clippings related to Haile Selassie's visit to New Orleans in 1954. I am also especially grateful to Kathleen Shoemaker and Randall K. Burkett for their advice and assistance sorting through the rich collection of materials related to African American religious history at Emory University. In this vein, I am also appreciative of the archival staff at New Orleans Public Library, the Historic New Orleans Collection, the Schomburg Center for Research in Black Culture, and Duke University, who were immensely helpful during my many visits to their research collections. I would also like to thank the archivists at Xavier University of Louisiana, who graciously allowed me to use several significant images from their excellent collections.

This book is also the product of generous institutional support and research funding. I received external grants from the New Orleans Center for the Gulf South at Tulane University, the American Society of Church History Research Fellowship, the Mellon Mays Undergraduate Fellows Travel and Research Grant, and the SSRC Predoctoral Research Development Grant. At Princeton University, I received funding from the Dr. Laurence C. Morse *80 African Studies Graduate Fellowship, the Religion and Culture Fellowship and the Religion and Public Life Fellowship from the Center for the Study of Religion, the Dissertation Research Grant from the Department of African American Studies, the Summer Dissertation Research Grant in American Studies, and the Dean's Grant Research Award and President's Fellowship. My work was also supported by a yearlong fellowship while on the faculty at Northwestern University in the Departments of African American Studies and Religious Studies. I owe special thanks to Mary Pattillo, Martha Biondi, Marquis Bey, E. Patrick Johnson, kihana miraya ross, Nitasha Sharma, Nikki Spigner, Tracy Vaughn-Manley, Alex Weheliye, and Kennetta Hammond Perry.

Research sabbaticals and generous research funding support as a faculty member at Harvard Divinity School made the last leg of writing possible. I am grateful to former dean David Hempton, associate dean David Holland, and current dean Marla Frederick for allowing me the time and resources to complete this book as a junior faculty member. Many thanks to my colleague Mayra Rivera, who read an earlier version of chapter 3 and invited me to participate in the Colloquium of Coloniality, Race, and the Study of Religion at HDS. I am especially appreciative of the support and mentorship of Tracey E. Hucks, who facilitated a book manuscript workshop in my first semester at Harvard, which included outside readers Sylvester Johnson, Leslie Harris, Pablo Gómez, and Elizabeth Pérez, each of whom diligently read the manuscript and offered feedback that made each chapter far better than I could have made it on my own. Thank you. Other colleagues including but not limited to Janet Gyatso, Amy Hollywood, David Lamberth, Diane Moore, Catherine Brekus, Charles Stang, Annette Yoshiko Reed, and Jacob Olupona have indulged me in conversation about my research, and I am grateful for their insights. I am also thankful for Raymond Carr, who, while a visiting fellow at Harvard, consistently reminded me of the significance of Charles Long's theorizing for the study of Black religion.

I also thank my editor, Kyle Wagner, and the great team at the University of Chicago Press for all their work to bring this book into being.

Long before all of the scholarly research and writing, my blood and chosen family were an anchor. My maternal grandmothers, to whom this book is dedicated, nurtured my intellectual curiosity as a precocious child while sitting at our kitchen table. I am grateful for my mother, who encouraged me to find sanctuary at the library and whose tenacity and love are unmatched. I am thankful, too, for my stepfather, who shares my love of books; all the church mothers who prayed for me; my many, many aunties; my godmother Debra; my uncle Kevin; and so many other family members who helped raise me. Without my village, I would not be. I am also thankful for my beloved friends, more like family—Sevonna Brown, Maurissa Walls, Tavyen Williams, Torren Grace, Wesley Dixon, Shay Myrick, Arielle Steele, Darius Lee, and a host of others who keep me grounded and covered in love and radical honesty. Most of all, I give thanks to Almighty God and to my ancestors. I submit this book as an offering in recognition that I could never have written it in my own strength.

NOTES

INTRODUCTION

1. *Evansville Courier and Press*, February 7, 1960, 5.
2. Saidiya V. Hartman, *Wayward Lives, Beautiful Experiments: Intimate Histories of Social Upheaval* (New York: W. W. Norton, 2019).
3. Zora Neale Hurston, *Mules and Men* (Bloomington: Indiana University Press, 1978), 193.
4. Hurston, *Mules and Men*, 210–11, 201.
5. Dianne M. Stewart and Tracey E. Hucks, "Africana Religious Studies: Toward a Transdisciplinary Agenda in an Emerging Field," *Journal of Africana Religions* 1, no. 1 (2013): 28–77; Aisha M. Beliso-De Jesús, "A Hieroglyphics of Zora Neale Hurston," *Journal of Africana Religions* 4, no. 2 (2016): 291.
6. Hurston, *Mules and Men*, 209.
7. Katrina Hazzard-Donald, *Mojo Workin': The Old African American Hoodoo System* (Champaign: University of Illinois Press, 2012), 32; Jessica Marie Johnson, "Black New Orleans Is the Center of the World," *Journal of African American History* 103, no. 4 (September 1, 2018): 641–51.
8. Carla Kaplan, *Zora Neale Hurston: A Life in Letters* (New York: Anchor Books, 2002), 124.
9. Kaplan, *Zora Neale Hurston*, 150.
10. Kaplan, 154.
11. Solimar Otero, *Archives of Conjure: Stories of the Dead in Afrolatinx Cultures* (New York: Columbia University Press, 2020), 41; also, gratitude to the anonymous reviewer who gifted me this language.
12. Richard Brent Turner, "The Haiti-New Orleans Vodou Connection: Zora Neale Hurston as Initiate Observer," *Journal of Haitian Studies* 8, no. 1 (2002): 112–33. Here, I am conversant with the brilliant and expansive theoretical scaffolding offered by the historian J. T. Roane in *Dark Agoras: Insurgent Black Social Life and the Politics of Place* (New York: New York University Press, 2023), in which Roane theorizes "Black queer urbanism" or what he characterizes as "a critical approach that views nonnormative forms of Black social-geographic life and the distinctive and often discredited knowl-

edge produced in dark agoras [or "insurgent Black working-class migrant formulations of social and geographic connection"] as the conceptual resources and bases for an alternate vision for the future of urban life." See Roane, *Dark Agoras*, 4, 9.

13. Roane, *Dark Agoras*, 9.

14. Jennifer L. Freeman Marshall, *Ain't I an Anthropologist: Zora Neale Hurston beyond the Literary Icon* (Urbana: University of Illinois Press, 2023).

15. Harry Middleton Hyatt, *Hoodoo—Conjuration—Witchcraft—Rootwork in Five Volumes: Beliefs Adopted by Many Negroes and White Persons These Being Orally Recorded Among Blacks and Whites*, Memoirs of the Alma Egan Hyatt Foundation (Cambridge: Western Publishing, 1978), 2:1010.

16. Hyatt, *Hoodoo—Conjuration—Witchcraft—Rootwork*, 2:1010. For more on Collins and others like her in their use of Hindu in their Hoodoo, see, for example, Philip Deslippe, "The Hindu in Hoodoo: Fake Yogis, Pseudo-Swamis, and the Manufacture of African American Folk Magic," *Amerasia Journal* 40, no. 1 (2014): 35–56.

17. Hyatt, *Hoodoo—Conjuration—Witchcraft—Rootwork*, 1:1–2.

18. Thomas Heise, *Urban Underworlds: A Geography of Twentieth-Century American Literature and Culture* (New Brunswick: Rutgers University Press, 2010), 16.

19. Sylvester A Johnson, *African American Religions, 1500–2000: Colonialism, Democracy, and Freedom* (New York: Cambridge University Press, 2015).

20. Hartman, *Wayward Lives, Beautiful Experiments*, 32.

21. *Oxford English Dictionary*, s.v. "underworld, n.," July 2023.

22. Gunnar Myrdal, *An American Dilemma: The Negro Problem and Modern Democracy* (New York: Harper & Brothers, 1944), 330.

23. Heise rightly cautions, "To think of the underworld as holding a wholly negative cultural value then is to miss how this vital, though not officially recognized, sector of the urban economy helped men and women on both sides of the divide discover and remake their identities." See Heise, *Urban Underworlds*, 16.

24. Outside of New Orleans, the Black "underworld" also became an object of discourse in the early twentieth century throughout the Caribbean and Latin America due to the influence of Italian criminologist Cesare Lombroso and Malthusian theories of social evolution. It also proliferated due to state and legal prohibitions against religious practices and cultural performances deemed excessive along with the expansion of the black market, gangs, drug addiction, and narcotics sales in back alleys and on street corners. Most relevant among the texts that conceptualized these projects was former police informant Fernando Ortiz's 1906 *Hampa afro-cubana: Los negros brujos*, the first book to popularize the term "afrocuban" and detail different types of Afro-Cuban "cults" in a semiscientific way, in which he leaned heavily upon police and surveillance technologies as material for sociological inquiry. In general, though, Afro-Caribbean and Afro-Latin religions came to be known during this period through the investigations of police officers (sometimes in concert with social scientists), such as in the example of Raphael Roche y Monteagudo's *La Policia y Sus Misterios* (1908). See Alejandra Bronfman's *Measures of Equality: Social Science, Citizenship, and Race in Cuba, 1902–1940* (Chapel Hill: University of North Carolina Press, 2004) and "En Plena Libertad y Democracia': Negros Brujos and the Social Question, 1904–1919," *Hispanic American*

NOTES TO PAGES 5–9

Historical Review 82, no. 3 (2002): 549–88. In newspapers from the Black Atlantic world, reporters also drew upon this criminological impulse and spread word of an underworld "on the run," wreaking havoc throughout Afro-Caribbean and Afro-Latin urban communities.

25. Daniel J. Crowley, "The Traditional Masques of Carnival," *Caribbean Quarterly* 4, no. 3–4 (1956): 196–97.

26. In the same issue as Crowley's article, Munro S. Edmonson published "Carnival in New Orleans," *Caribbean Quarterly* 4, no. 3–4 (1956): 233–45.

27. Zora Neale Hurston, *The Sanctified Church* (Berkeley, CA: Turtle Island, 1983), 26.

28. See Elizabeth Pérez, "Spiritist Mediumship as Historical Mediation: African-American Pasts, Black Ancestral Presence, and Afro-Cuban Religions," *Journal of Religion in Africa* 41, no. 4 (January 1, 2011): 330–65. For more on "work" and "working" in Black religions, see Joseph M. Murphy, *Working the Spirit: Ceremonies of the African Diaspora* (Boston: Beacon, 1994), 7; Sharla M. Fett, *Working Cures: Healing, Health, and Power on Southern Slave Plantations* (Chapel Hill: University of North Carolina Press, 2002); Judith Casselberry, *The Labor of Faith: Gender and Power in Black Apostolic Pentecostalism* (Durham, NC: Duke University Press, 2017).

29. Hyatt, *Hoodoo—Conjuration—Witchcraft—Rootwork*, 5:ii.

30. Hyatt, 5:ix.

31. Otero, *Archives of Conjure*, 17.

32. Robert Orsi, *History and Presence* (Cambridge, MA: Belknap Press of Harvard University Press, 2018), 250.

33. Stephen C. Finley, Margarita Guillory, and Hugh Page Jr., eds., *Esotericism in African American Religious Experience: "There Is a Mystery . . ."* (Boston: Brill, 2015).

34. Hortense J. Spillers, "Mama's Baby, Papa's Maybe: An American Grammar Book," *diacritics* 17, no. 2 (1987): 65–81.

35. The term "white race makers" derives from Judith Weisenfeld's *New World A-Coming: Black Religion and Racial Identity during the Great Migration* (New York: New York University Press, 2016), in which she writes about how people of African descent confronted "white people's agency in race making" even as race making was a recurring "maintenance event" used to enforce and uphold white supremacy and racial dominance. See Weisenfeld, 6, 281–82.

36. *The Negro in Louisiana*, p. 5, Marcus Christian Collection, Earl K. Long Library, University of New Orleans.

37. Tracey E. Hucks, *Obeah, Orisa, and Religious Identity in Trinidad*, vol. 1, *Obeah: Africans in the White Colonial Imagination* (Durham, NC: Duke University Press, 2022), 16.

38. See, for example, Saidiya V. Hartman, *Scenes of Subjection: Terror, Slavery, and Self-Making in Nineteenth Century America* (New York: Oxford University Press, 1997); Frank B. Wilderson, *Red, White, and Black: Cinema and the Structure of U.S. Antagonisms* (Durham, NC: Duke University Press, 2010); Jared Sexton, "The Social Life of Social Death: On Afro-Pessimism and Black Optimism," *Tensions* 5 (2011): 1–47; Calvin L. Warren, *Ontological Terror: Blackness, Nihilism, and Emancipation* (Durham, NC: Duke University Press, 2018); Joseph R. Winters, "Nothing Matters: Black Death, Repetition, and an Ethics of Anguish," *American Religion* 2, no. 1 (Fall 2020): 1–4.

39. June Jordan, "Black Studies: Bringing Back the Person," in *New Perspectives on Black Studies*, ed. John W. Blassingame (Urbana: University of Illinois Press, 1971), 29.

40. Ida Bell Wells-Barnett, *Mob Rule in New Orleans: Robert Charles and His Fight to the Death* (Chicago, 1900).

41. There is an abundance of significant scholarship on colonial New Orleans, and colonial Louisiana more broadly, and that literature has extensively charted the region's connection to the larger Atlantic world, especially with regard to colonialism, slavery, and dispossession. This book begins in the late nineteenth century and builds on earlier studies. See, for example, Gwendolyn Midlo Hall, *Africans in Colonial Louisiana: The Development of Afro-Creole Culture in the Eighteenth Century* (Baton Rouge: Louisiana State University Press, 1992).

42. Saidiya V. Hartman and Frank B Wilderson, "The Position of the Unthought," *Qui Parle* 13, no. 2 (2003): 183–201; Tomoko Masuzawa, *The Invention of World Religions, or, How European Universalism Was Preserved in the Language of Pluralism* (Chicago: University of Chicago Press, 2005).

43. Marla Frederick, *Colored Television: American Religion Gone Global* (Stanford, CA: Stanford University Press, 2015), 5.

44. On this point, see an excellent discussion in Josef Sorett, *Black Is a Church: Christianity and the Contours of African American Life* (New York: Oxford University Press, 2023).

45. Letter from Zora Neale Hurston to W. E. B. Du Bois, June 11, 1945, W. E. B. Du Bois Papers (MS 312), Special Collections and University Archives, University of Massachusetts Amherst Libraries.

46. Letter from W. E. B. Du Bois to Zora Neale Hurston, July 11, 1945.

47. See Beliso-De Jesús, "Hieroglyphics of Zora," 293.

48. Zora Neale Hurston, "Hoodoo in America," *Journal of American Folklore* 44, no. 174 (1931): 319.

49. LeRhonda S. Manigault-Bryant, *Talking to the Dead: Religion, Music, and Lived Memory among Gullah/Geechee Women* (Durham, NC: Duke University Press, 2014). In my use of the term "critical Black religious studies," I build on Axelle Karera's notion of "critical Black philosophies," which "consider black suffering to be a crucial site of interrogation [and] question what it means to inhabit a structural position whereby the black philosopher is always already forced to align herself with exclusionary terms in order to register anti-black violence as violence." See Karera, "Blackness and the Pitfalls of Anthropocene Ethics," *Critical Philosophy of Race* 7, no. 1 (2019): 32–56.

50. Alice Walker, "Looking for Zora," in *In Search of Our Mothers' Gardens: Womanist Prose* (San Diego: Harcourt Brace Jovanovich, 1983), 404.

51. Christina Sharpe, *In the Wake: On Blackness and Being* (Durham, NC: Duke University Press, 2016), 10.

52. Sharpe, 21.

53. See also PBS's 2013 documentary *Homegoings*; Karla F. C. Holloway, *Passed On: African American Mourning Stories: A Memorial* (Durham, NC: Duke University Press, 2002); Suzanne E. Smith, *To Serve the Living: Funeral Directors and the African American Way of Death* (Cambridge, MA: Harvard University Press, 2010).

54. Hartman, *Scenes of Subjection*, 139; on Black religion, maps, and freedom, see Nicole

NOTES TO PAGES 13–16

Myers Turner, *Soul Liberty: The Evolution of Black Religious Politics in Postemancipation Virginia* (Chapel Hill: University of North Carolina Press, 2020).

55. For more on the uses of the "Exodus" narrative in African American religious historiography, see Eddie S. Glaude, *Exodus!: Religion, Race, and Nation in Early Nineteenth-Century Black America* (Chicago: University of Chicago Press, 2000); Albert J. Raboteau, "African Americans, Exodus, and the American Israel," in *Down by the Riverside: Readings in African American Religion* (New York: New York University Press, 2000), 20–25; Clarence E. Hardy, "From Exodus to Exile: Black Pentecostals, Migrating Pilgrims, and Imagined Internationalism," *American Quarterly* 59, no. 3 (2007): 737–57; Herbert Robinson Marbury, *Pillars of Cloud and Fire: The Politics of Exodus in African American Biblical Interpretation* (New York: New York University Press, 2015). For a critique of this historiography, see Judith Weisenfeld, "'A Rare Human Document': LoBagola's African American Humbug Religion," *American Religion* 1, no. 1 (2019): 30.

56. W. E. B. Du Bois, *Black Reconstruction in America* (New York: Harcourt, Brace, 1935), 30.

57. Ronnie W. Clayton, *Mother Wit: The Ex-Slave Narratives of the Louisiana Writers' Project* (New York: P. Lang, 1990), 38.

58. Clayton, *Mother Wit*, 39.

59. Clayton, 66.

60. Paul C. Johnson, "Vodou Purchase: The Louisiana Purchase in a Caribbean Perspective," in *New Territories, New Perspectives: The Religious Impact of the Louisiana Purchase*, ed. Richard J. Callahan (Columbia: University of Missouri Press, 2008), 146–67.

61. Calvin Warren, *Ontological Terror: Blackness, Nihilism, and Emancipation* (Durham, NC: Duke University Press, 2018), 15.

62. Warren, *Ontological Terror*, 15.

63. Charles H. Long, *Significations: Signs, Symbols, and Images in the Interpretation of Religion* (Aurora, CO: Davies Group Publishing, 1986), 191.

64. Long, *Significations*, 191.

65. See, for example, Albert J. Raboteau, *Slave Religion: The "Invisible Institution" in the Antebellum South* (New York: Oxford University Press, 2004); Jason R. Young, *Rituals of Resistance: African Atlantic Religion in Kongo and the Lowcountry South in the Era of Slavery* (Baton Rouge: Louisiana State University Press, 2007); Tracey E. Hucks, *Yoruba Traditions and African American Religious Nationalism* (Albuquerque: University of New Mexico Press, 2012); Ras Michael Brown, *African-Atlantic Cultures and the South Carolina Lowcountry* (Cambridge: Cambridge University Press, 2013); Alexis Wells-Oghoghomeh, *The Souls of Womenfolk: The Religious Cultures of Enslaved Women in the Lower South* (Chapel Hill: University of North Carolina Press, 2021). For more on the necessity of locating New Orleans in these early American religious histories, see Charles H. Long, "New Orleans as an American City: Origins, Exchanges, Materialities, and Religion," in *Ellipses: The Collected Writings of Charles Long* (New York: Bloomsbury, 2018), 25–38.

66. Brendan Jamal Thornton, "Refiguring Christianity and Black Atlantic Religion: Representation, Essentialism, and Christian Variation in the Southern Caribbean," *Journal of the American Academy of Religion* 89, no. 1 (March 1, 2021): 60.

67. See, for example, Milton C. Sernett, *Bound for the Promised Land: African American Religion and the Great Migration* (Durham, NC: Duke University Press, 1997); Wallace D. Best, *Passionately Human, No Less Divine: Religion and Culture in Black Chicago, 1915–1952* (Princeton, NJ: Princeton University Press, 2005); Weisenfeld, *New World A-Coming*; Matthew J. Cressler, *Authentically Black and Truly Catholic: The Rise of Black Catholicism in the Great Migration* (New York: New York University Press, 2017).

68. E. Franklin Frazier, "Recreation and Amusement among American Negroes," 1940, Carnegie-Myrdal Study of the Negro in America Research Memoranda Collection, Sc Micro F-13242, Schomburg Center for Research in Black Culture, Manuscripts, Archives and Rare Books Division, New York Public Library. Thank you to J. T. Roane who scanned copies of this file and sent them to me.

69. The full quote is "There is a new Negro, just as there is a new South." See "Negro Migration as the South Sees It," *Survey* 38 (August 11, 1917): 428. It is important to note that the phrase/concept "new South" has a historiography dating back to at least C. Vann Woodward's *The Origins of the New South, 1877–1913* (Baton Rouge: Louisiana State University Press, 1951). However, I am interested in the notion of a "new South" that emerges with African Americans, West Indians, and Central Americans in central view considering their mass migration to/from multiple Souths.

70. Winston James, *Holding Aloft the Banner of Ethiopia: Caribbean Radicalism in Early Twentieth-Century America* (New York: Verso, 1997); Lara Putnam, *Radical Moves: Caribbean Migrants and the Politics of Race in the Jazz Age* (Chapel Hill: University of North Carolina Press, 2013); Glenn A. Chambers, *From the Banana Zones to the Big Easy: West Indian and Central American Immigration to New Orleans, 1910–1940* (Baton Rouge: Louisiana State University Press, 2019).

71. Joseph R. Roach, *Cities of the Dead: Circum-Atlantic Performance* (New York: Columbia University Press, 1996); J. Lorand Matory, *Black Atlantic Religion: Tradition, Transnationalism and Matriarchy in the Afro-Brazilian Candomblé* (Princeton, NJ: Princeton University Press, 2005), 274. See also Elizabeth Pérez, *Religion in the Kitchen: Cooking, Talking, and the Making of Black Atlantic Traditions* (New York: New York University Press, 2016); Aisha M. Beliso-De Jesús, *Electric Santería: Racial and Sexual Assemblages of Transnational Religion* (New York: Columbia University Press, 2015).

72. Hurston, "Hoodoo in America," 318.

73. See, for example, Lara Putnam, "Rites of Power and Rumors of Race: The Circulation of Supernatural Knowledge in the Greater Caribbean, 1890–1940," in *Obeah and Other Powers: The Politics of Caribbean Religion and Healing*, ed. Diana Paton and Maarit Forde (Durham, NC: Duke University Press, 2012), 243–67.

74. "Phases of Mediumship (Negro)," 1–2, Fanatic Cults, folder 36, Federal Writers' Project Papers, Northwestern State University of Louisiana.

75. Some white practitioners faced policing and criminalization, but they were not as scandalized as Black practitioners. White individuals like New Orleans's Brother Isaiah, for example, was generally able to heal freely by the levee.

76. "Voodoo—Suppression, Mayoralty of New Orleans, City Hall, May 12, 1897," Lyle Saxon Papers, Manuscripts Collection 4, Louisiana Research Collection, Howard-Tilton Memorial Library, Tulane University.

NOTES TO PAGES 19–24

77. Markus Dressler and Arvind-pal Singh Mandair, eds., *Secularism and Religion-Making* (New York: Oxford University Press, 2011), 3.

78. Dressler and Mandair, 21.

79. Hyatt, *Hoodoo—Conjuration—Witchcraft—Rootwork*, 2:1669.

80. Pablo F. Gómez, *The Experiential Caribbean: Creating Knowledge and Healing in the Early Modern Atlantic* (Chapel Hill: University of North Carolina Press, 2017), 13–14.

81. For more on "Blackened" sentient beings and "antiblack metaphysics," see Zakiyyah Iman Jackson, *Becoming Human: Matter and Meaning in an Antiblack World* (New York: New York University Press, 2020), 119.

82. *The Negro in Louisiana*, p. 5, Marcus Christian Collection. See also Joan Redding, "The Dillard Project: The Black Unit of the Louisiana Writers' Project," *Louisiana History* 32, no. 1 (Winter 1991): 47–62.

83. Marcus Christian, "Voodooism and Mumbo-Jumbo," in *The Negro in Louisiana*, Marcus Christian Collection.

84. Christian substantively engages Benjamin Elijah Mays and Joseph W. Nicholson's 1933 book, *The Negro's Church*.

85. See, for example, Hurston, "Hoodoo in America"; Robert Tallant, *Voodoo in New Orleans* (Grenta, LA: Pelican, 1946); Carolyn Morrow Long, "Perceptions of New Orleans Voodoo: Sin, Fraud, Entertainment, and Religion," *Nova Religio* 6, no. 1 (2002): 86–101; Jessie Ruth Gatson, "The Case of Voodoo in New Orleans," in *Africanisms in American Culture*, ed. Joseph E. Holloway, 2nd ed. (Bloomington: Indiana University Press, 2005), 111–51; Martha Ward, "Where Circum-Caribbean Afro-Catholic Creoles Met American Southern Protestant Conjurers: Origins of New Orleans Voodoo," in *Caribbean and Southern: Transnational Perspectives on the U.S. South*, ed. Helen A. Regis (Athens: University of Georgia Press, 2006), 124–38. In *Voodoo and Power: The Politics of Religion in New Orleans, 1881–1940*, for example, historian Kodi A. Roberts argues, "Voodoo was synonymous with New Orleans," and that Black religious practitioners in New Orleans engaged in "the ritual technology of Voodoo [which] essentially played off social technologies of difference that marked race and gender as unchangeable categories" (4, 11). For critiques of this phenomenon, see Stephan Palmié, "Conventionalization, Distortion and Plagiarism in the Historiography of Afro-Caribbean Religion in New Orleans," in *Creoles and Cajuns: French Louisiana—La Louisiane Française*, ed. W. Binder (Frankfurt: Peter Lang, 1998), 315.

86. Tallant, *Voodoo in New Orleans*, 247.

87. Zora Neale Hurston, "Reviewed Work(s): Voodoo in New Orleans by Robert Tallant," *Journal of American Folklore* 60, no. 238 (1947): 436–38.

88. Charles M. Melden, "Religion and the Negro," in *Progress of a Race*, William Henry Crogman, James Lawrence Nichols, and John William Gibson, eds. (Naperville, IL, J. L. Nichols), 309.

89. Claude F. Jacobs, "Folk for Whom? Tourist Guidebooks, Local Color, and the Spiritual Churches of New Orleans," *Journal of American Folklore* 114, no. 453 (2001): 309–30; Jonathan Mark Souther, *New Orleans on Parade: Tourism and the Transformation of the Crescent City* (Baton Rouge: Louisiana State University Press, 2006). Judith Weisenfeld also discusses this period and the emergence of the Black religious "imposter" as a site

NOTES TO PAGES 24–31

for white voyeurism in the 1930s. See "'A Rare Human Document': LoBagola's African American Humbug Religion," *American Religion* 1, no. 1 (2019): 27–48.

90. Federal Writers' Project of the Works Progress Administration for the City of New Orleans, *New Orleans City Guide*, American Guide Series (Boston: Houghton Mifflin, 1938), x.

91. "Phases of Mediumship (Negro)," 1.

92. Hurston, "Hoodoo in America," 357. For more on the institutionalization of Black religious practitioners deemed mentally ill, see Judith Weisenfeld, *Black Religion in the Madhouse: Race and Psychiatry in Slavery's Wake* (New York: New York University Press, 2025).

93. For more on engaging state documents as source material in African American religious history, see, for example, Sylvester A. Johnson, *African American Religions, 1500–2000: Colonialism, Democracy, and Freedom* (New York: Cambridge University Press, 2015), 273–400; Weisenfeld, *New World A-Coming*; Sylvester A. Johnson and Steven Weitzman, *The FBI and Religion: Faith and National Security Before and After 9/11* (Berkeley: University of California Press, 2017); Lerone Martin, "Bureau Clergyman: How the FBI Colluded with an African American Televangelist to Destroy Dr. Martin Luther King, Jr.," *Religion and American Culture* 28, no. 1 (2018): 1–51.

94. Saidiya V. Hartman, "Venus in Two Acts," *Small Axe* 26 (2008): 1–14; see also Ahmad Greene-Hayes, "Discredited Knowledges and Black Religious Ways of Knowing," *J19: The Journal of Nineteenth-Century Americanists* 9, no. 1 (2021): 41–49.

95. Sharpe, *In the Wake*, 113–30.

96. "BTW Beginnings," box 37, folder 11, Tom Dent Papers, Amistad Research Center, Tulane University.

97. Beliso-De Jesús, "Hieroglyphics of Zora"; Otero, *Archives of Conjure*, 41.

VISITATION 1

1. Zora Neale Hurston, *Tell My Horse: Voodoo and Life in Haiti and Jamaica* (New York: J. B. Lippincott, 1938), 114–15.

2. Zora Neale Hurston, "Hoodoo in America," *Journal of American Folklore* 44, no. 174 (1931): 318.

CHAPTER 1

1. Paul Christopher Johnson, "An Atlantic Genealogy of 'Spirit Possession,'" *Comparative Studies in Society and History* 53, no. 2 (2011): 395.

2. Zora Neale Hurston, *The Sanctified Church* (Berkeley, CA: Turtle Island, 1981), 103.

3. Throughout the book, I invoke the term "spirit possession" to refer to a conglomeration

NOTES TO PAGE 32

of Black Atlantic religious experiences related to the occupation of practitioners' bodies by *the Spirit*, as in the Holy Spirit, or *the spirits*, such as the Orisa, in which practitioners perform deeds, declare utterances, dance, or are in trance under the power of spirit. Of course, this looks different in varying contexts, and I rely on practitioners' own words when describing spirit possession or what some scholars now refer to as "spirit manifestation." On the "shared possessions" of African American Protestants and other Black Atlantic religious practitioners, see, for example, Teresa L. Reed, "Shared Possessions: Black Pentecostals, Afro-Caribbeans, and Sacred Music," *Black Music Research Journal* 32, no. 1 (2012): 5–25, https://doi.org/10.5406/blacmusiresej.32.1.0005.

4. Carl A. Brasseaux and Glenn R. Conrad, eds., *The Road to Louisiana: The Saint-Domingue Refugees, 1792–1809* (Lafayette: Center for Louisiana Studies, University of Southwestern Louisiana, 1992); Nathalie Dessens, *From Saint-Domingue to New Orleans: Migration and Influences* (Gainesville: University Press of Florida, 2007).

5. For more on this historical framing and its complexities, see Michel-Rolph Trouillot and Sidney Mintz, "The Social History of Haitian Vodou," in *Sacred Arts of Haitian Vodou*, ed. Donald Cosentino (Los Angeles: UCLA Fowler Museum of Cultural History, 1995), 123–47. See also Ronnie W. Clayton, *Mother Wit: The Ex-Slave Narratives of the Louisiana Writers' Project* (New York: P. Lang, 1990), 74–75. On Vodou and "work," see Elizabeth McAlister, *Rara!: Vodou, Power, and Performance in Haiti and Its Diaspora* (Berkeley: University of California Press, 2002).

6. Charles Dudley Warner, *Studies in the South and West, with Comments on Canada* (New York: Harper & Brothers, 1889), 64. See also Newbell Niles Puckett, "Folk Beliefs of the Southern Negro" (Chapel Hill: University of North Carolina Press, 1926), 181–96.

7. Kate Ramsey, *The Spirits and the Law: Vodou and Power in Haiti* (Chicago: University of Chicago Press, 2011). Other scholars have noted at length the policing of African diasporic religions during the colonial period and in slavery throughout the Black Atlantic world, in such places as Trinidad, Jamaica, and Brazil. See, for example, Rachel E. Harding, *A Refuge in Thunder: Candomblé and Alternative Spaces of Blackness* (Bloomington: Indiana University Press, 2003); Dianne M. Stewart, *Three Eyes for the Journey: African Dimensions of the Jamaican Religious Experience* (Oxford: Oxford University Press, 2005); Tracey E. Hucks, *Obeah, Orisa, and Religious Identity in Trinidad*, vol. 1, *Obeah: Africans in the White Colonial Imagination* (Durham, NC: Duke University Press, 2022); Danielle N. Boaz, *Banning Black Gods: Law and Religions of the African Diaspora* (University Park: Pennsylvania State University Press, 2021).

8. For an extensive discussion of the distinction between the two, see Emily Suzanne Clark, "Nineteenth-Century New Orleans Voudou: An American Religion," *American Religion* 2, no. 1 (2020): 131–55. I follow Clark's lead in using the spelling "Voudou" regarding the religion in Louisiana to align with sources from the period.

9. Federal Writers' Project, A161, folder 7, Louisiana Religion, p. 17, WPA Records, Library of Congress. See also Nicole Myers Turner, *Soul Liberty: The Evolution of Black Religious Politics in Postemancipation Virginia* (Chapel Hill: University of North Carolina Press, 2020), 13, 18–20; Ramsey, *Spirits and the Law*.

10. The original source uses the language of "refugee slaves," and I find the phrasing to be

historically inaccurate and have changed it to "refugees" to align more closely with the important work of the Freedmen's Bureau. See Federal Writers' Project, A161, folder 7, Louisiana Religion, p. 17, WPA Records, Library of Congress.

11. Emily Suzanne Clark, *A Luminous Brotherhood: Afro-Creole Spiritualism in Nineteenth-Century New Orleans* (Chapel Hill: University of North Carolina Press, 2016), 168–75.

12. *Evening Post* (Charleston, SC), March 23, 1900, 6.

13. William Wells Newell, "On the Field and Work of a Journal of American Folk-Lore," *Journal of American Folklore* 1, no. 1 (1888): 3. The Louisiana Association's efforts were similar to, yet distinct from, the Hampton Folk-Lore Society, the first African American folklore society, at the Hampton Normal Industrial Institution due mainly to its all-white, largely elite membership. For more on Hampton, see Yvonne P. Chireau, *Black Magic: Religion and the African American Conjuring Tradition* (Berkeley: University of California Press, 2006), 132–36.

14. Jamil W. Drake, *To Know the Soul of a People: Religion, Race, and the Making of Southern Folk* (New York: Oxford University Press, 2022), 39, see also 63–64.

15. Lindsay V. Reckson, *Realist Ecstasy: Religion, Race, and Performance in American Literature* (New York: New York University Press, 2020), 5, 17.

16. Calvin Warren, *Ontological Terror: Blackness, Nihilism, and Emancipation* (Durham, NC: Duke University Press, 2018).

17. Sarah Haley, *No Mercy Here: Gender, Punishment, and the Making of Jim Crow Modernity* (Chapel Hill: University of North Carolina Press, 2016), 11.

18. Brian Hochman, *Savage Preservation: The Ethnographic Origins of Modern Media Technology* (Minneapolis: University of Minnesota Press, 2014), xiii. For his discussion of Cable and New Orleans, see 73–114.

19. Jeroen Dewulf, *From the Kingdom of Kongo to Congo Square: Kongo Dances and the Origins of the Mardi Gras Indians* (Lafayette: University of Louisiana at Lafayette Press, 2017).

20. Henry Rightor, *Standard History of the New Orleans, Louisiana* (Chicago: Lewis, 1900), 629.

21. Rightor, 630.

22. Richard D. E. Burton, *Afro-Creole: Power, Opposition, and Play in the Caribbean* (Ithaca, NY: Cornell University Press, 1997), 156–263.

23. For a comprehensive discussion of this history and its philosophical underpinnings, see J. Lorand Matory, *The Fetish Revisited: Marx, Freud, and the Gods Black People Make* (Durham, NC: Duke University Press, 2018). The term "long postemancipation period" is inspired by Jacquelyn Dowd Hall, "The Long Civil Rights Movement and the Political Uses of the Past," *Journal of American History* 91, no. 4 (2005): 1233–63.

24. "The Voudou Dance," *Times-Picayune*, June 22, 1891, 3.

25. See James B. Bennett, *Religion and the Rise of Jim Crow in New Orleans* (Princeton, NJ: Princeton University Press, 2005).

26. John W. Blassingame, *Black New Orleans, 1860–1880* (Chicago: University of Chicago Press, 1973), 15; see also Jessica Marie Johnson, *Wicked Flesh: Black Women, Intimacy, and Freedom in the Atlantic World* (Philadelphia: University of Pennsylvania Press, 2020), 121–232.

NOTES TO PAGES 36–39

27. Michelle Y. Gordon, "'Midnight Scenes and Orgies': Public Narratives of Voodoo in New Orleans and Nineteenth-Century Discourses of White Supremacy," *American Quarterly* 64, no. 4 (2012): 779–80.

28. Ann Taves reminds us that similar concerns emerged in the eighteenth century regarding the revivals of the First and Second Great Awakenings, in which Christians "shouted" and were "possessed." See Taves, *Fits, Trances, and Visions: Experiencing Religion and Explaining Experience from Wesley to James* (Princeton, NJ: Princeton University Press, 1999), 76–117. Historian Hilary Sparkes also addresses this concern: "Much of the discomfiture about African-Caribbean spiritual practices expressed by late postemancipation ethnographers appears to stem from the inclusion in those faiths of inducing possession as a means of contact with the spirit world." See Sparkes, "Minds Overwrought by 'Religious Orgies': Narratives of African-Jamaican Folk Religion and Mental Illness in Late Nineteenth-Century and Early Twentieth-Century Ethnographies," *Journal of Africana Religions* 9, no. 2 (2021): 242.

29. Johnson, "Atlantic Genealogy," 405.

30. Elizabeth Pérez, *Religion in the Kitchen: Cooking, Talking, and the Making of Black Atlantic Traditions* (New York: New York University Press, 2016), 114. See also J. Lorand Matory, *Sex and the Empire That Is No More: Gender and the Politics of Metaphor in Oyo Yoruba Religion* (Minneapolis: University of Minnesota Press, 1994), 228–29.

31. Henry C. Castellanos, *New Orleans as It Was: Episodes of Louisiana Life* (New Orleans: L. Graham & Son, 1895), 100.

32. Castellanos, 100; see also Kathleen M. Brown, *Good Wives, Nasty Wenches, and Anxious Patriarchs: Gender, Race, and Power in Colonial Virginia* (Chapel Hill: University of North Carolina Press, 2012).

33. Hortense J. Spillers, "Mama's Baby, Papa's Maybe: An American Grammar Book," *Diacritics* 17, no. 2 (1987): 68.

34. See, for example, Nora E. Jaffary, *False Mystics: Deviant Orthodoxy in Colonial Mexico* (Lincoln: University of Nebraska Press, 2004); Joan Cameron Bristol, *Christians, Blasphemers, and Witches: Afro-Mexican Ritual Practice in the Seventeenth Century* (Albuquerque: University of New Mexico Press, 2007); Carole A. Myscofski, *Amazons, Wives, Nuns, and Witches: Women and the Catholic Church in Colonial Brazil, 1500–1822*, vol. 32 (Austin: University of Texas Press, 2013); Alexis Wells-Oghoghomeh, *The Souls of Womenfolk: The Religious Cultures of Enslaved Women in the Lower South* (Chapel Hill: University of North Carolina Press, 2021).

35. See, for example, Deborah Gray White, *Ar'n't I a Woman?: Female Slaves in the Plantation South*, 1st ed. (New York: Norton, 1985); Tera W. Hunter, *To 'joy My Freedom: Southern Black Women's Lives and Labors after the Civil War* (Cambridge, MA: Harvard University Press, 1997); Stephanie M. H. Camp, *Closer to Freedom: Enslaved Women and Everyday Resistance in the Plantation South* (Chapel Hill: University of North Carolina Press, 2004); Johnson, *Wicked Flesh*; Wells-Oghoghomeh, *Souls of Womenfolk*.

36. It is important to note that these "anxieties" function as an affective feature of demonization, in that the demonizers or white race makers create their own religion of whiteness whereby anxiety functions as both a conduit for demonization's hegemonic reach and a symptom of the powerful, colonial trope of the Negro as diabolical.

37. Ordinance No. 3847 (April 7, 1858), reel 7, Robert Tallant Papers, New Orleans Public Library.

38. "Unlawful Assemblies," *Times-Picayune*, July 31, 1850, 2.

39. "Voudou Meeting Broken Up," *Times-Picayune*, July 31, 1863, 2.

40. "Fetish Rites and Voudou Mysteries," *New York Day-Book*, October 3, 1863, 3.

41. *Morning Herald*, February 24, 1899, 6; "George W. Cable," *Chicago Saturday Record*, August 3, 1895, 8.

42. George Washington Cable, "Creole Slave Songs," *Century Magazine* 31, no. 6 (1886): 820.

43. George Washington Cable, "The Dance in Place Congo," *Century Magazine* 31, no. 4 (1886): 518.

44. Cable, "Dance in Place Congo," 527.

45. Cited in Rosan Augusta Jordan and Frank De Caro, "'In This Folk-Lore Land': Race, Class, Identity, and Folklore Studies in Louisiana," *Journal of American Folklore* 109, no. 431 (1996): 41.

46. Cable, "Creole Slave Songs," 818.

47. Cable, 815.

48. Cable, "Dance in Place Congo," 519.

49. Haley, *No Mercy Here*, 40.

50. Camp, *Closer to Freedom*, 128.

51. Wells-Oghoghomeh, *Souls of Womenfolk*, 226.

52. Cable, "Dance in Place Congo," 523.

53. Cable, 525. Daina Ramey Berry also addresses this issue in her discussion of "soul values" in *The Price for Their Pound of Flesh: The Value of the Enslaved, from Womb to Grave, in the Building of a Nation* (Boston: Beacon Press, 2017). On Black religion, interiority, and slavery, see Albert J. Raboteau, *Slave Religion: The "Invisible Institution" in the Antebellum South* (New York: Oxford University Press, 1978); Wells-Oghoghomeh, *Souls of Womenfolk*.

54. W. E. B. Du Bois, *The Souls of Black Folk: Essays and Sketches* (Chicago: A. C. McClurg, 1903), 190–91.

55. James A. Manigault-Bryant, "Reimagining the 'Pythian Madness' of Souls," *Journal of Africana Religions* 1, no. 3 (2013): 327, https://doi.org/10.5325/jafrireli.1.3.0324.

56. Cable, "Creole Slave Songs," 819.

57. Paul Christopher Johnson argues that "Spirit possession as a conceptual apparatus of the West descended from the nomenclature of Christian demonology, beginning with the New Testament and peaking from the fifteenth to the first half of the seventeenth century." See Johnson, "Atlantic Genealogy," 398.

58. See Pablo F. Gómez, *The Experiential Caribbean: Creating Knowledge and Healing in the Early Modern Atlantic* (Chapel Hill: University of North Carolina Press, 2017).

59. On harming practices, see Yvonne P. Chireau, *Black Magic: Religion and the African American Conjuring Tradition* (Berkeley: University of California Press, 2006), 59–89; Wells-Oghoghomeh, *Souls of Womenfolk*, 173–93, 209–10.

60. All quotes regarding this story included in this paragraph are from James W. Buel, *Mysteries and Miseries of America's Great Cities* (St. Louis: Historical, 1883), 540.

61. Buel, 542.

62. Wells-Oghoghomeh, *Souls of Womenfolk*, 205.

NOTES TO PAGES 44–51

63. See also Clark, *Luminous Brotherhood*, 123.
64. Cable, "Creole Slave Songs," 820.
65. Ahmad Greene-Hayes, "Hair, Roots, and Crystal Balls: Archival Viscerality, Black Conjuring Traditions, and the Study of American Religions," *Journal of the American Academy of Religion*, 2024, lfae029, https://doi.org/10.1093/jaarel/lfae029.
66. George Washington Cable, *The Grandissimes: A Story of Creole Life* (New York: Charles Scribner's Sons, 1880), 231.
67. Cable, *Grandissimes*, 235.
68. Clayton, *Mother Wit*, 35.
69. Louisiana Association of the American Folklore Society, Minutes, 1892–96 typescript, p. 5, Louisiana Research Collection, Howard-Tilton Memorial Library, Tulane University.
70. Rosan Augusta Jordan, "Folklore Study in New Orleans' Gilded Age: The 'Louisiana Association,'" *Louisiana Folklore Miscellany* 7 (1992): 2.
71. Jordan, 1.
72. Jordan, 12.
73. Jordan and De Caro, "'In This Folk-Lore Land,'" 42.
74. Jordan and De Caro, 43.
75. Johnson, "Atlantic Genealogy," 396.
76. Katherine McKittrick, "Plantation Futures," *Small Axe* 17, no. 3 (42) (2013): 1–15.
77. Johnson, "Atlantic Genealogy," 400.
78. This is just one example in a larger constellation of cases, in which entire careers, fields, and associations were developed through the unethical, harmful, and nonconsensual study of Black people by white Americans. See, for example, Harriet A. Washington, *Medical Apartheid: The Dark History of Medical Experimentation on Black Americans from Colonial Times to the Present* (New York: Doubleday Books, 2006); Rana A. Hogarth, *Medicalizing Blackness: Making Racial Difference in the Atlantic World, 1780–1840* (Chapel Hill: University of North Carolina Press, 2017); Deirdre Cooper Owens, *Medical Bondage: Race, Gender, and the Origins of American Gynecology* (Athens: University of Georgia Press, 2017).
79. The American Folklore Society was modeled after the Folk-Lore Society in England, founded in 1878, with a similar purpose. See "[The Credit of Originating the Term 'Folk-Lore']," *Journal of American Folklore* 1, no. 1 (1888): 79–81.
80. William W. Newell, "Myths of Voodoo Worship and Child Sacrifice in Hayti," *Journal of American Folklore* 1, no. 1 (1888): 16–30.
81. Alcée Fortier, "Customs and Superstitions in Louisiana," *Journal of American Folklore* 1, no. 2 (1888): 136–37.
82. Fortier, 138.
83. Fortier, 138–39.
84. W. W. Newell, "Reports of Voodoo Worship in Hayti and Louisiana," *Journal of American Folklore* 2, no. 4 (1889): 42, 47.
85. Stewart Culin, "Reports Concerning Voodooism," *Journal of American Folklore* 2, no. 6 (1889): 232–33.
86. Louisiana Association of the American Folklore Society, Minutes, 1892–96 typescript, p. 5.

NOTES TO PAGES 51–60

87. "Folk-Lore Studies," *Times-Picayune*, March 22, 1892, 7.

88. Louisiana Association of the American Folklore Society, Minutes, 1892–96 typescript, p. 22–24.

89. Jordan, "Folklore Study in New Orleans," 14.

90. Jordan and De Caro, "'In This Folk-Lore Land,'" 47.

91. For more on this rich history, see Ina J. Fandrich, *The Mysterious Voodoo Queen, Marie Laveaux: A Study of Powerful Female Leadership in Nineteenth Century New Orleans* (New York: Routledge, 2005); Carolyn Morrow Long, "Marie Laveau: A Nineteenth-Century Voudou Priestess," *Louisiana History* 46, no. 3 (2005): 262–92; Carolyn Morrow Long, *A New Orleans Voudou Priestess: The Legend and Reality of Marie Laveau* (Gainesville: University Press of Florida, 2007); Martha Ward, *Voodoo Queen: The Spirited Lives of Marie Laveau* (Jackson: University Press of Mississippi, 2009); Kodi A. Roberts, *Voodoo and Power: The Politics of Religion in New Orleans, 1881–1940* (Baton Rouge: Louisiana State University Press, 2015), 15–44; Johnson, *Wicked Flesh*, 230, 298.

92. *The Picayune's Guide to New Orleans*, revised and enlarged, 4th ed. (New Orleans: Picayune, 1900), 62.

93. *Picayune's Guide*, 15.

94. *Picayune's Guide*, 64.

95. *Picayune's Guide*, 64.

96. Claude F. Jacobs, "Folk for Whom? Tourist Guidebooks, Local Color, and the Spiritual Churches of New Orleans," *Journal of American Folklore* 114, no. 453 (2001): 309–30; Jonathan Mark Souther, *New Orleans on Parade: Tourism and the Transformation of the Crescent City* (Baton Rouge: Louisiana State University Press, 2006).

97. For images of some of the ex-slaves at Melrose Plantation, see Clayton, *Mother Wit*, 227–30.

98. Clayton, 231–37.

99. Hurston, "Hoodoo in America," 317.

100. Clayton, *Mother Wit*, 4–5.

VISITATION 2

1. Hurston letter to Countee Cullen, March 5, 1943, Amistad Research Center, Tulane University.

CHAPTER 2

1. Catherine Dillon, "The Council of God," 3, Folklore, Fanatic Cults, Mother Catherine, folder 91, Federal Writers' Project Papers, Northwestern State University of Louisiana.

2. Zora Neale Hurston, *The Sanctified Church* (Berkeley, CA: Turtle Island, 1981), 103.

3. Nicole Myers Turner, *Soul Liberty: The Evolution of Black Religious Politics in Postemancipation Virginia* (Chapel Hill: University of North Carolina Press, 2020), 13.

NOTES TO PAGES 60–62

4. "Madam McNairdee-Moore," *Colored American*, July 19, 1903, 7.

5. See, for example, Richard S. Newman, *Freedom's Prophet: Bishop Richard Allen, the AME Church, and the Black Founding Fathers* (New York: New York University Press, 2008); J. Gordon Melton, *A Will to Choose: The Origins of African Methodism* (Lanham, MD: Rowman & Littlefield, 2007); Carol V. R. George, *Segregated Sabbaths: Richard Allen and the Emergence of Independent Black Churches, 1760–1840* (New York: Oxford University Press, 1975).

6. James B. Bennett, *Religion and the Rise of Jim Crow in New Orleans* (Princeton, NJ: Princeton University Press, 2005), 71–100.

7. Brendan Jamal Thornton, "Refiguring Christianity and Black Atlantic Religion: Representation, Essentialism, and Christian Variation in the Southern Caribbean," *Journal of the American Academy of Religion* 89, no. 1 (March 1, 2021): 42.

8. It was widely believed that this church underwent several name changes before its final name, "Council of God"; those names included Christ Hebrew Church, the Christian Jewish Church, and Christ's Council. See Dillon, "Council of God," 3. Jacob S. Dorman, *Chosen People: The Rise of American Black Israelite Religions* (New York: Oxford University Press, 2016), 5.

9. Catherine Dillon, "Council of God," 7.

10. See, for example, Eddie S. Glaude, *Exodus!: Religion, Race, and Nation in Early Nineteenth-Century Black America* (Chicago: University of Chicago Press, 2000); Albert George Miller, *Elevating the Race: Theophilus G. Steward, Black Theology, and the Making of an African American Civil Society, 1865–1924* (Knoxville: University of Tennessee Press, 2003); Michele Mitchell, *Righteous Propagation: African Americans and the Politics of Racial Destiny after Reconstruction* (Chapel Hill: University of North Carolina Press, 2004); Laurie F. Maffly-Kipp, *Setting down the Sacred Past: African-American Race Histories* (Cambridge, MA: Belknap Press of Harvard University Press, 2010).

11. Tracey E. Hucks, *Yoruba Traditions and African American Religious Nationalism* (Albuquerque: University of New Mexico Press, 2012), 44.

12. Dianne M. Stewart explores the multivalences of "nation" in Africana religions in *Obeah, Orisa, and Religious Identity in Trinidad*, vol. 2, *Orisa: Africana Nations and the Power of Black Sacred Imagination* (Durham, NC: Duke University Press, 2022).

13. Yvonne P. Chireau, "Black Culture and Black Zion: African American Religious Encounters with Judaism, 1790–1930, an Overview," in *Black Zion: African American Religious Encounters with Judaism*, ed. Nathaniel Deutsch and Yvonne P. Chireau (New York: Oxford University Press, 1999), 21.

14. Dillon, "Council of God," 8.

15. Judith Weisenfeld, *New World A-Coming: Black Religion and Racial Identity during the Great Migration* (New York: New York University Press, 2016), 6–7.

16. Sylvester A. Johnson, "The Rise of Black Ethnics: The Ethnic Turn in African American Religions, 1916–1945," *Religion and American Culture* 20, no. 2 (2010): 127, https://doi.org/10.1525/rac.2010.20.2.125.

17. Dillon, "Council of God," 5.

18. Albert J. Raboteau, "African Americans, Exodus, and the American Israel," in *Down by the Riverside: Readings in African American Religion* (New York: New York University

Press, 2000), 20–25; Glaude, *Exodus!*; Herbert R. Marbury, *Pillars of Cloud and Fire: The Politics of Exodus in African American Biblical Interpretation* (New York: New York University Press, 2015).

19. Dillon, "Council of God," 5.
20. Dillon, 5. For more on ethnic Jews in New Orleans, see Barry Stiefel and Emily Ford, *The Jews of New Orleans and the Mississippi Delta: A History of Life and Community along the Bayou* (Charleston, SC: History, 2012), 77–109; Bobbie Malone, *Rabbi Max Heller: Reformer, Zionist, Southerner, 1860–1929* (Tuscaloosa: University of Alabama Press, 1997), 37–55; Catherine C. Kahn and Irwin Lachoff, *The Jewish Community of New Orleans* (Charleston, SC: Arcadia, 2005), 75–104.
21. Malone, *Rabbi Max Heller*, 34.
22. Tudor Parfitt, *Black Jews in Africa and the Americas* (Cambridge, MA: Harvard University Press, 2013), 66–101.
23. Stiefel and Ford, *Jews of New Orleans*, 86.
24. Stiefel and Ford, 94–97.
25. Stiefel and Ford, 99.
26. Dillon, "Council of God," 4.
27. *Times-Picayune*, October 20, 1907, 7.
28. Dillon, "Council of God," 3–4. One book that the Rev. Antoine and his followers could have read was the work of Pandit C. R. Srinivasa Sastrigal of Chidambaram, India, who was also the author of the 1891 book *Transmigration of Souls: An Important Doctrine of Hinduism* and editor of *Brahma Vidya Patrika*, a Tamil-Sanskrit fortnightly magazine devoted to philosophy and religion. See "BRAHMAVIDYA' PUBLICATIONS," in *Theosophist* 14, no. 11 (August 1893): 694.
29. Dillon, "Council of God," 10, 27; *Daily Picayune*, October 21, 1907, 5. While I am interested in these individuals as persons who were a part of the COG, further inquiry into the details of their lives yielded little results beyond where they lived and the kinds of jobs they had in New Orleans. For details regarding members' addresses, see *St. Tammany Farmer*, October 26, 1907; for additional names, see *Times-Picayune*, October 20, 1907, 7.
30. Weisenfeld, *New World A-Coming*, 91.
31. Dillon, "Council of God," 9.
32. See, for example, Kenneth C. Barnes, *Anti-Catholicism in Arkansas: How Politicians, the Press, the Klan, and Religious Leaders Imagined an Enemy, 1910–1960* (Fayetteville: University of Arkansas Press, 2016).
33. *St. Mary Banner*, September 19, 1908.
34. Dillon, "Council of God," 4–5.
35. *Times-Picayune*, October 20, 1907, 4.
36. *Times-Picayune*, October 20, 1907, 4; see also Dillon, "Council of God," 12–13.
37. See Christopher B. Strain, *Pure Fire: Self-Defense as Activism in the Civil Rights Era* (Athens: University of Georgia Press, 2005); Charles E. Cobb, *This Nonviolent Stuff'll Get You Killed: How Guns Made the Civil Rights Movement Possible* (New York: Basic Books, 2014).
38. See also Ahmad Greene-Hayes, "'A Very Queer Case': Clementine Barnabet and the

NOTES TO PAGES 66–70

Erotics of a Sensationalized Voodoo Religion," *Nova Religio* 26, no. 4 (2023): 58–84, https://doi.org/10.1525/nr.2023.26.4.58.

39. Seth Perry, *Bible Culture and Authority in the Early United States* (Princeton, NJ: Princeton University Press, 2018), 67.

40. Tina M. Campt, *Listening to Images* (Durham, NC: Duke University Press, 2017), 59.

41. Saidiya V. Hartman, *Wayward Lives, Beautiful Experiments: Intimate Histories of Social Upheaval* (New York: W. W. Norton, 2019), 18.

42. Yvonne P. Chireau, *Black Magic: Religion and the African American Conjuring Tradition* (Berkeley: University of California Press, 2006), 59–89.

43. Zora Neale Hurston, "Hoodoo in America," *Journal of American Folklore* 44, no. 174 (1931): 390.

44. Dillon, "Council of God," 7.

45. Dillon was born around 1888 and was married to Lawrence Dittmar in 1907. Her parents were native Louisianans, and her grandparents were Mississippians, most likely of Irish Catholic origins. See New Orleans Ward 1, Orleans, Louisiana, Enumeration District 0001, *1910 United States Federal Census*, Ancestry.com. Prior to working for the LWP, Dillon's writings had been included in a citywide art exhibit; see "125 Art Pupils to Show Work," *New Orleans Item*, May 2, 1926, 29. She was also a writer for the *New Orleans States*; see, for example, July 15, 1928; March 1, 1931; April 10, 1932. For a brief feature on Dillon and other WPA writers, see *Times-Picayune*, September 19, 1938, 33.

46. This book engages LWP records all throughout. The COG files appear to be the only ones in which there is not a final copy included with revisions. That said, the revisions and their archival reality are what are examined here. Weisenfeld similarly examines Hall Johnson's editing of the King James Bible to show how the composer was transformed by Christian Science. See Judith Weisenfeld, "'The Secret at the Root': Performing African American Religious Modernity in Hall Johnson's *Run, Little Chillun*," *Religion and American Culture* 21, no. 1 (2011): 56–60.

47. In my consultation of many of these historical newspapers, upon which Dillon depended heavily for information about the COG, I found that she plagiarized a significant portion of the LWP report from "Officer Cambias' Martyrdom Averted a Greater Tragedy," *Daily Picayune*, October 21, 1907, 5.

48. Dillon, "Council of God," 6.

49. Matthew J. Cressler, "Centering Black Catholic Religio-Racial Identity, Revealing White Catholicism," *Journal of the American Academy of Religion* 88, no. 2 (May 23, 2020): 322–23.

50. See, for example, Stephen J. Ochs, *Desegregating the Altar: The Josephites and the Struggle for Black Priests, 1871–1960* (Baton Rouge: Louisiana State University Press, 1990); Matthew J. Cressler, *Authentically Black and Truly Catholic: The Rise of Black Catholicism in the Great Migration* (New York: New York University Press, 2017).

51. Carolyn Morrow Long, "Perceptions of New Orleans Voodoo: Sin, Fraud, Entertainment, and Religion," *Nova Religio* 6, no. 1 (2002): 86–101.

52. Dillon, "Council of God," 6; *Times-Picayune*, October 20, 1907, 7.

53. Michel-Rolph Trouillot, *Silencing the Past: Power and the Production of History* (Boston: Beacon, 2015), 72.

54. *Cincinnati Enquirer*, October 20, 1907, 9.

55. Dillon, "Council of God," 2–3.

56. Dillon, 7.

57. For more on "free love" in new religious movements, see Lawrence Foster, *Religion and Sexuality: Three American Communal Experiments of the Nineteenth Century* (New York: Oxford University Press, 1981).

58. "Officer Cambias' Martyrdom," 5.

59. *Times-Picayune*, October 20, 1907, 7.

60. Ahmad Greene-Hayes, "Wayward Negro Religions in the Twentieth-Century Slum," *Journal of African American History* 106, no. 1 (Winter 2021): 117–21, https://doi.org /10.1086/712022.

61. Dillon, "Council of God," 3.

62. Dillon, 3.

63. Dillon, 7–9.

64. *Times-Picayune*, October 20, 1907, 7.

65. *Daily Picayune*, May 2, 1850, 2, column 5.

66. Dillon, "Council of God," 13.

67. *Times-Picayune*, October 20, 1907, 7.

68. Dillon, "Council of God," 11.

69. Dillon, 3, 10.

70. Dillon, 4.

71. Dillon, 8a.

72. Dillon, 35.

73. "Homicide in New Orleans, 1898–1913, of the New Orleans Police Department," v. 10, 1907, Louisiana Division, City Archives, New Orleans Public Library. Available through the Criminal Justice Research Center at Ohio State University: https://cjrc.osu.edu /research/interdisciplinary/hvd/united-states/new-orleans.

74. "Homicide in New Orleans."

75. "Homicide in New Orleans."

76. "'Council of God' Caused the Riot," *Atlanta Constitution*, October 20, 1907, C6.

77. Dillon, "Council of God," 18.

78. Dillon, 19.

79. *Times-Picayune*, October 20, 1907, 4.

80. *Times-Picayune*, October 20, 1907, 4.

81. *Times-Picayune*, October 20, 1907, 4.

82. *Courier-Journal*, October 21, 1907, 4.

83. *Indianapolis Star*, October 22, 1907, 2.

84. *St. Tammany Farmer*, October 26, 1907.

85. *Nashville Tennessean*, October 23, 1907, 4.

86. Dillon, "Council of God," 15, 23.

87. *Boston Globe*, October 20, 1907, 24.

88. Dillon, "Council of God," 15.

89. "Officer Cambias' Martyrdom," 5; Dillon, "Council of God," 8a.

90. Dillon, 25.

NOTES TO PAGES 78–81

91. *St. Helena Echo*, January 22, 1897, 1, col. 3.

92. Grace Elizabeth Hale, *Making Whiteness: The Culture of Segregation in the South, 1890–1940* (New York: Pantheon Books, 1998), 229.

93. There is a rich body of scholarship on armed self-defense; see, for example, Christopher B. Strain, *Pure Fire: Self-Defense as Activism in the Civil Rights Era* (Athens: University of Georgia Press, 2005); Cobb, *This Nonviolent Stuff*; Nicholas Johnson, *Negroes and the Gun: The Black Tradition of Arms* (Amherst, NY: Prometheus Books, 2014).

94. Ida B. Wells-Barnett, "Lynch Law in All Its Phases," February 13, 1893, https://awpc.cattcenter.iastate.edu/2017/03/09/lynch-law-in-all-its-phases-february-13-1893/.

95. Matthew Frye Jacobson, *Whiteness of a Different Color: European Immigrants and the Alchemy of Race* (Cambridge, MA: Harvard University Press, 1998).

96. Dillon, "Council of God," 2.

97. Dillon, 1.

98. Dillon, 23.

99. "Officer Cambias' Martyrdom," 5.

100. Dillon, "Council of God," 24.

101. "Benefit for Family of Patrolman Cambias," *New Orleans Item*, October 27, 1907, 21. See also "Wheatley's Record for Courage," *Herald*, October 1911, for similar valorization by the white press of another New Orleans police officer, Sergeant Wheatley, who was shot during the raid of Edward Honore's house.

102. Only one source notes the possibility of Black Catholic engagement. See *New Orleans Item*, October 29, 1907, 5.

103. "Police Slaughter by the Council of God," *Daily Picayune*, October 24, 1907, 5, c. 1, in Louisiana Works Progress Administration, Digital Collection, State Library of Louisiana.

104. John W. Blassingame, *Black New Orleans, 1860–1880* (Chicago: University of Chicago Press, 1973), 155–56.

105. Walter F. Pitts, *Old Ship of Zion: The Afro-Baptist Ritual in the African Diaspora* (New York: Oxford University Press, 1993), 29. See also Evelyn Brooks Higginbotham, *Righteous Discontent: The Women's Movement in the Black Baptist Church, 1880–1920* (Cambridge, MA: Harvard University Press, 1993).

106. "Crush the Serpents," *New Orleans Item*, October 29, 1907, 5.

107. The alliance's words were presented by Rev. S. J. Channell, DD, presiding elder of Baton Rouge District, AME Church; seconded by Rev. D. Burrell, pastor of Morris Brown AME Church; and further discussed by Rev. G. B. Hill, DD, presiding elder of the New Orleans District; Rev. Joseph W. Washington, pastor of the St. James AME Church; and Rev. James R. Campbell, pastor of Smith Chapel.

108. "Denounced by Alliance," *New Orleans Item*, October 23, 1907.

109. *Times-Picayune*, October 23, 1907, 5.

110. "Denounced by Alliance," 7.

111. "Dr. Edwards Preaches on the Recent Riot," *Times-Picayune*, October 21, 1907, 5.

112. *Times-Picayune*, October 20, 1907, 7.

113. "Big Negro Mass Meeting Denounces the Fanatics," *Times-Picayune*, October 29, 1907, 12.

114. Dillon, "Council of God," 25.
115. Lerone Martin, "Bureau Clergyman: How the FBI Colluded with an African American Televangelist to Destroy Dr. Martin Luther King, Jr.," *Religion and American Culture* 28, no. 1 (2018): 24.
116. Bennett, *Religion and the Rise*, 59.
117. See, for example, Donald E. DeVore, *Defying Jim Crow: African American Community Development and the Struggle for Racial Equality in New Orleans, 1900–1960* (Baton Rouge: Louisiana State University Press, 2015), 62–91.
118. Dillon, "Council of God," 1, 2, 4.
119. For a more robust discussion of theological education in the postemancipation period, see Myers Turner, *Soul Liberty*, 81–105.
120. "Theological Instructor: To Be Sent through the South to Instruct Negro Preachers," *Afro-American*, January 4, 1902, 1.
121. Dillon, "Council of God," 7.
122. "Police Slaughter by the Council of God," *Daily Picayune*, October 24, 1907, 5, c. 1.
123. *St. Landry Clarion*, September 18, 1908.
124. *St. Mary Banner*, September 19, 1908.
125. "Why Divinity Student Became a Hangman," *Washington Post*, October 18, 1909, 4.
126. James H. Cone, *Black Theology and Black Power* (New York: Seabury, 1969); James H. Cone, *A Black Theology of Liberation* (Philadelphia: Lippincott, 1970); James H. Cone, *The Cross and the Lynching Tree* (Maryknoll: Orbis Books, 2011); Donald G. Mathews, "The Southern Rite of Human Sacrifice: Lynching in the American South," *Mississippi Quarterly* 61, no. 1/2 (2008): 27.

VISITATION 3

1. Zora Neale Hurston, *The Sanctified Church* (Berkeley: Turtle Island, 1983), 23–24.

CHAPTER 3

1. "New Orleans Gets Dancing Religion," *Chicago Defender*, November 15, 1924, A1; Federal Writers' Project of the Works Progress Administration for the City of New Orleans, *New Orleans City Guide*, American Guide Series (Boston: Houghton Mifflin, 1938), 199.
2. *New Orleans City Guide*, 199.
3. Margarita Simon Guillory, *Spiritual and Social Transformation in African American Spiritual Churches: More Than Conjurers* (London: Routledge, Taylor & Francis, 2018), 39–40.
4. Alecia P. Long, *The Great Southern Babylon: Sex, Race, and Respectability in New Orleans, 1865–1920* (Baton Rouge: Louisiana State University Press, 2004), 137.
5. *New Orleans City Guide*, 199; Zora Neale Hurston, *The Sanctified Church* (Berkeley: Turtle Island, 1983), 23.

NOTES TO PAGES 91–95

6. Edward Laroque Tinker, "Mother Catherine's Castor Oil," *North American Review* 230, no. 2 (August 1930): 149.
7. *New Orleans City Guide*, 199–202.
8. Guillory, *Spiritual and Social Transformation*, 39–66; Danny Ryan Gray, "Effacing the 'Imagined Slum': Space, Subjectivity, and Sociality in the Margins of New Orleans" (PhD diss., University of Chicago, 2012), 68–116; and D. Ryan Gray, "A Manger in a Sea of Mud: Material Legacies and Loss at the Temple of the Innocent Blood," *Archeological Papers of the American Anthropological Association* 26, no. 1 (2015): 105–21.
9. Christina Simmons, "African Americans and Sexual Victorianism in the Social Hygiene Movement, 1910–40," *Journal of the History of Sexuality* 4, no. 1 (1993): 53.
10. Saidiya V. Hartman, *Wayward Lives, Beautiful Experiments: Intimate Histories of Social Upheaval* (New York: W. W. Norton, 2019), 224.
11. Tinker, "Mother Catherine's Castor Oil," 148.
12. Hurston, *The Sanctified Church*, 27.
13. Simmons, "African Americans," 58.
14. Francis J. White, "The Sainted Cult of Catherine," *Times-Picayune*, August 31, 1924, 56.
15. Tinker, "Mother Catherine's Castor Oil," 152.
16. "Physicking Priestess," *Time* 17, no. 16 (April 20, 1931), 63–64.
17. "Physicking Priestess," 63.
18. Tinker, "Mother Catherine's Castor Oil," 152.
19. Cited in Guillory, *Spiritual and Social Transformation*, 42.
20. For more on Mother Leafy Anderson and her legacy in New Orleans, see Jason Berry, *The Spirit of Black Hawk* (Jackson: University Press of Mississippi, 1995), 55–122; Guillory, *Spiritual and Social Transformation*, 9–38; Kodi A. Roberts, *Voodoo and Power: The Politics of Religion in New Orleans, 1881–1940* (Baton Rouge: Louisiana State University Press, 2015), 45–64.
21. Cited in Guillory, *Spiritual and Social Transformation*, 41.
22. "Negro Woman Healer Plans Retreat for Life," *New Orleans Item*, March 26, 1922, 30.
23. "Negro Woman Healer Plans Retreat for Life," 30.
24. "Catherine Seals," New Orleans, Orleans, Louisiana, p. 26A, Enumeration District 0150, FHL microfilm: 2340542, *1930 United States Federal Census*, Ancestry.com.
25. "Negro Woman Healer Plans Retreat for Life," 30.
26. White, "Sainted Cult of Catherine."
27. "Mother Catherine Seals," reel 9, Robert Tallant Papers, New Orleans Public Library.
28. Catherine Dillon, "The Manger of True Light," Folklore, Fanatic Cults, Mother Catherine, folder 91, Federal Writers' Project Papers, Northwestern State University of Louisiana.
29. Tinker, "Mother Catherine's Castor Oil," 153.
30. Hurston, *The Sanctified Church*, 25–26.
31. Hurston, 24.
32. Hurston, 26.
33. Mac Rebennack and Jack Rummel, *Under a Hoodoo Moon: The Life of the Night Tripper*, illus. ed. (New York: St. Martin's Griffin, 1995), 160; Guillory, *Spiritual and Social Transformation*, 46–47.
34. Hurston, *The Sanctified Church*, 1981, 28.

35. Hurston, 25.

36. Hurston, 28.

37. On Vodou *drapo*, see Patrick Arthur Polk, *Haitian Vodou Flags* (Jackson: University Press of Mississippi, 1997). For more on Arthur Bedou's photography in New Orleans, see Michael Bieze, *Booker T. Washington and the Art of Self-Representation* (New York: Peter Lang, 2008), 75–82; Shawn Michelle Smith, "Unfixing the Frame(-up): A. P. BEDOU," in *Pictures and Progress: Early Photography and the Making of African American Identity*, ed. Shawn Michelle Smith and Maurice O. Wallace (Durham, NC: Duke University Press, 2012), 267–73; Shawn Michelle Smith, "Booker T. Washington's Photographic Messages," *English Language Notes* 51, no. 1 (Spring/Summer 2013): 137–46. The image is available in the holdings at Xavier University of Louisiana in the Archives Photographs Collection, and archivists confirm that the exact photographer and the date the photograph was taken are unknown, but it is highly likely that the photograph was taken by Bedou. One archivist originally emailed me that "we presently only hold 4 photographs of Mother Catharine Seals, which you can see in our Digital Archives. Those photographs, although taken by Mr. Bedou, are part of the Archives Photograph Collection, which is a separate collection from the Arthur P. Bedou Photograph Collection." He later clarified that he was unsure if the photograph had, in fact, been taken by Bedou. Yet several clues suggest that it was.

38. Bieze, *Booker T. Washington*, 76.

39. Smith, "Booker T. Washington's Photographic Messages," 143. I am grateful to Elizabeth Pérez for making mention of this idea as conceived by Chad Seales, who has forthcoming work on the business suit in religious studies. See also Chad Seales, "Spatial Constructions of the American Secular," in *Oxford Research Encyclopedia of Religion*, Oxford University Press, February 26, 2018, https://doi.org/10.1093/acrefore/9780199340378.013.78; Guillory, *Spiritual and Social Transformation*, 58.

40. Hurston, *The Sanctified Church*, 27.

41. "Physicking Priestess."

42. Hurston, *The Sanctified Church*, 28.

43. Tinker, "Mother Catherine's Castor Oil," 150.

44. Dillon, "Manger of True Light."

45. For a description of her artistry and for an image of Mother Catherine's statue, see Lyle Saxon, Edward Dreyer, and Robert Tallant, eds., *Gumbo Ya-Ya: A Collection of Louisiana Folk Tales* (Cambridge, MA: Riverside Press, 1945), 207–11, 248.

46. Marguerite Young, "Mother Catherine's Manger," *New Orleans Item*, December 25, 1927, 47.

47. For more on autobiographical "oral narrations" of "spiritual formations" in Black Atlantic religions, see, for example, Elizabeth Perez, "Willful Spirits and Weakened Flesh: Historicizing the Initiation Narrative in Afro-Cuban Religions," *Journal of Africana Religions* 1, no. 2 (2013): 151–93.

48. Hartman, *Wayward Lives, Beautiful Experiments*, 228.

49. Hurston, *The Sanctified Church*, 28.

50. "Booker Washington—Coming Here to Talk to the Colored People," *Times-Picayune*, November 5, 1899.

51. James Creelman, "The Effect of Booker T. Washington's Atlanta Speech," described in

NOTES TO PAGES 100–106

the *New York World*, September 19, 1895, Daniel Murray Pamphlet Collection, Library of Congress.

52. "Pointing the Way to Negro Progress," *Times-Picayune*, November 11, 1899.

53. Michael Bieze and Marybeth Gasman, eds., *Booker T. Washington Rediscovered* (Baltimore: Johns Hopkins University Press, 2012), 3.

54. See Ahmad Greene-Hayes, "Booker T. Washington's Protestant Coloniality in the Afterlife of the Plantation" (forthcoming in the *Harvard Theological Review*). Some of the analysis here is further explored in this essay.

55. For more on Washington's Protestant work ethic and his theological training at Wayland Seminary in DC, see Kenneth M. Hamilton, *Booker T. Washington in American Memory* (Springfield: University of Illinois Press, 2017).

56. Farah Jasmine Griffin, "Zora Neale Hurston's Radical Individualism," in *African American Political Thought: A Collected History*, ed. Melvin L. Rogers and Jack Turner (Chicago: University of Chicago Press, 2020), 314.

57. Hurston, "The Negro in the United States," *Encyclopedia Americana*, 1947.

58. Hurston, *The Sanctified Church*, 26.

59. "Pointing the Way to Negro Progress," *Times-Picayune*, November 11, 1899.

60. "Pointing the Way to Negro Progress."

61. Booker T. Washington, "A Protest against the Burning and Lynching of Negroes," *Birmingham Age-Herald*, February 29, 1904, Daniel Murray Pamphlet Collection, Library of Congress.

62. *Times-Picayune*, December 21, 1900; *Times-Picayune*, September 21, 1902; "Apostle of Industrial Education," *Southwestern Christian Advocate*, April 18, 1895; "Loosening Up Louisiana," *Survey*, June 19, 1915.

63. Booker T. Washington, "The Religious Life of the Negro," *North American Review* 181, no. 584 (1905): 20.

64. See Tomoko Masuzawa, *The Invention of World Religions, or, How European Universalism Was Preserved in the Language of Pluralism*, Invention of World Religions (Chicago: University of Chicago Press, 2005).

65. Hurston, *The Sanctified Church*, 25.

66. Cited in Berry, *Spirit of Black Hawk*, 73.

67. Kristina Kay Robinson, "Assemblages and Inheritances," *Art in America*, December 6, 2021, https://www.artnews.com/art-in-america/features/assemblage-and-inheritance -new-orleans-1234612426/.

68. Saxon, Dreyer, and Tallant, eds., *Gumbo Ya-Ya*, 211.

69. White, "Sainted Cult of Catherine."

70. *New Orleans City Guide*, 200.

71. *New Orleans City Guide*, 200. For more on the archaeology and construction of the Manger, see Gray, "Effacing the 'Imagined Slum,'" 68–87; Gray, "A Manger in a Sea of Mud."

72. "Mrs. G. LeGallais," May 1940, in "Mother Catherine Seals," reel 9, Robert Tallant Papers.

73. Guillory, *Spiritual and Social Transformation*, 44.

74. Alice Walker, "Womanist" (1983) in Layli Phillips, ed., *The Womanist Reader* (New York: Taylor & Francis, 2006), 19; Alice Walker, "Looking for Zora," in *In Search of Our*

Mothers' Gardens: Womanist Prose (San Diego, CA: Harcourt Brace Jovanovich, 1983), 395–411.

75. White, "Sainted Cult of Catherine."

76. Louis R. Harlan, Raymond W. Smock, and Barbara S. Kraft, eds., *Booker T. Washington Papers, Volume 5: 1899–1900* (University of Illinois Press, 1976), 519.

77. See, for example, Gail Bederman, *Manliness and Civilization: A Cultural History of Gender and Race in the United States, 1880–1917* (Chicago: University of Chicago Press, 1995); Marlon B. Ross, *Manning the Race: Reforming Black Men in the Jim Crow Era* (New York: New York University Press, 2004).

78. Roderick A. Ferguson, "Of Our Normative Strivings: African American Studies and the Histories of Sexuality," *Social Text* 23, no. 3–4 (December 1, 2005): 92.

79. Ferguson, 92.

80. "Negro Urban League Near Organized in New Orleans," *Times-Picayune*, November 25, 1919, 14.

81. "Negroes to Organize," *Times-Picayune*, November 24, 1919, 15.

82. "Committee Approves Negro Urban League Plans," *New Orleans Item*, November 25, 1919, 2.

83. See LaKisha Michelle Simmons, *Crescent City Girls: The Lives of Young Black Women in Segregated New Orleans* (Chapel Hill: The University of North Carolina, 2015).

84. Hurston, *The Sanctified Church*, 24.

85. Tinker, "Mother Catherine's Castor Oil," 150; *Oxford English Dictionary*, s.v. "holt (n.2), sense 3," December 2023, https://doi.org/10.1093/OED/4203396485.

86. J. Lorand Matory, "The 'Cult of Nations' and the Ritualization of Their Purity," *South Atlantic Quarterly* 100, no. 1 (2001): 190.

87. While Walter F. Pitts draws a connection between white dress worn by Afro-Baptists and Orisha devotees, I find that Pitts and many scholars after him do not contend with the anti-Africanness of many Black Protestant churches despite their semblances with non-Christian and quasi-Christian African diasporic religions. See, for instance, Pitts, *Old Ship of Zion: The Afro-Baptist Ritual in the African Diaspora* (New York: Oxford University Press, 1993), 103, 110, 157.

88. See Booker T. Washington, ed., *A New Negro for a New Century* (Chicago: American Pub. House, 1900), 410; Rosalyn Terborg-Penn, *African American Women in the Struggle for the Vote, 1850–1920* (Bloomington: Indiana University Press, 1998), 91–92, 116; Nicolle Muller Dunnaway, "Flowers in Their Beauty: The Phyllis Wheatley Club of New Orleans," *ProQuest Dissertations and Theses* (master's thesis, Southeastern Louisiana University, 2011).

89. Fannie Barrier Williams, "Club Movement among Negro Women," in *The Colored American from Slavery to Honorable Citizenship*, John W. Gibson and William H. Crogman, eds. (Naperville, IL: J. L. Nichols, 1902c., 1903), 207.

90. See Evelyn Brooks Higginbotham, *Righteous Discontent: The Women's Movement in the Black Baptist Church, 1880–1920* (Cambridge, MA: Harvard University Press, 1993), 167.

91. "Veteran Teacher Dies After 51 Years Service," *New York Age*, August 27, 1921, 7; "Delegates to Chicago Meeting—National Association of Colored Women," *Southwestern Christian Advocate*, August 10, 1899, 8.

92. "Colored Statistics: The Progress of a Race in Louisiana," *Times-Picayune*, September 29, 1892, 3.

93. Mrs. Sylvanie Francoz Williams, "The Social Status of the Negro Woman," *Voice of the Negro* 1, no. 7 (July 1904): 298–300.

94. Hurston, *The Sanctified Church*, 29.

95. See, for example, Hunter, *To 'joy My Freedom: Southern Black Women's Lives and Labors after the Civil War*; Carole Emberton, "'Only Murder Makes Men': Reconsidering the Black Military Experience," *Journal of the Civil War Era* 2, no. 3 (2012): 369–93.

96. Williams, "Social Status," 299.

97. Hurston, *The Sanctified Church*, 1983, 27.

98. Higginbotham, *Righteous Discontent*, 15, 44.

99. Booker T. Washington, "Making Religion a Vital Part of Living," in *Putting the Most into Life* (New York: Thomas L. Crowell, 1906), 27.

100. Fannie Barrier Williams, "The Club Movement among Colored Women of America," in *A New Negro for a New Century*, Booker T. Washington, ed. (Chicago: American Publishing House, 1900), 379, 382.

101. Darlene Clark Hine, "'We Specialize in the Wholly Impossible': The Philanthropic Work of Black Women," in *Hine Sight: Black Women and the Re-construction of American History* (Bloomington: Indiana University Press, 1994), 109–28.

102. Margaret Murray Washington (Mrs. Booker T. Washington), "Social Improvement of the Plantation Woman," *Voice of the Negro* 1, no. 7 (July 1904): 288, 290. See also Hartman, *Wayward Lives, Beautiful Experiments*.

103. Hurston, *The Sanctified Church*, 25.

104. Mrs. Sylviane F. Williams, "An Open Letter to Mothers of the Race," *Southwestern Christian Advocate*, April 20, 1911.

105. Similar strategies to prevent and fight crime among people of African descent were used by Black northern social reformers during the period. See, for example, Khalil Gibran Muhammad, *The Condemnation of Blackness: Race, Crime, and the Making of Modern Urban America* (Cambridge, MA: Harvard University Press, 2010), 146–225.

106. Booker T. Washington, "Negro Crime and Strong Drink," *Journal of the American Institute of Criminal Law and Criminology* 3, no. 3 (September 1912), 384–92.

107. W. E. B. Du Bois, "Alcohol and the American Negro," 1928, W. E. B. Du Bois Papers (MS 312), Special Collections and University Archives, University of Massachusetts Amherst Libraries.

108. Sarah Haley, *No Mercy Here: Gender, Punishment, and the Making of Jim Crow Modernity* (Chapel Hill: University of North Carolina Press, 2016), 123.

109. Hurston, *The Sanctified Church*, 26.

VISITATION 4

1. Zora Neale Hurston, *Mules and Men* (Bloomington: Indiana University Press, 1978), 195, 200–201.

2. Carla Kaplan, *Zora Neale Hurston: A Life in Letters* (New York: Anchor Books, 2002), 156.

CHAPTER 4

1. Harry Middleton Hyatt, *Hoodoo—Conjuration—Witchcraft—Rootwork in Five Volumes: Beliefs Adopted by Many Negroes and White Persons These Being Orally Recorded Among Blacks and Whites*, Memoirs of the Alma Egan Hyatt Foundation (Cambridge: Western Publishing, 1978), 2:1670.

2. "Peddlin' Jerry," folder 1024, Federal Writers' Project Papers #3709, Southern Historical Collection, Wilson Library, University of North Carolina at Chapel Hill.

3. *Clarion-News*, March 3, 1938.

4. *Daily Picayune*, June 18, 1912, in reel 9, Robert Tallant Papers, New Orleans Public Library.

5. According to the New Orleans Public Library, the New Orleans Police Department arrest records, specifically "the volumes for 1881–1947 are unavailable due to condition issues." http://archives.nolalibrary.org/~nopl/inv/nopd/nopdarrests.htm.

6. "Hoodoo Doctor Held," *Times-Picayune*, September 11, 1915, 9.

7. Ignatius Reilly, protagonist in John Kennedy Toole's *A Confederacy of Dunces*, cited in Rebecca Solnit and Rebecca Snedeker, *Unfathomable City: A New Orleans Atlas* (Berkeley: University of California Press, 2013), 42.

8. LaShawn Harris, *Sex Workers, Psychics, and Numbers Runners: Black Women in New York City's Underground Economy* (Urbana: University of Illinois Press, 2016), 30–31.

9. Saidiya V. Hartman, *Wayward Lives, Beautiful Experiments: Intimate Histories of Social Upheaval* (New York: W. W. Norton, 2019).

10. "Father Albert to Give Sermon on Hoodooism Sunday," *Crowley Daily Signal*, January 26, 1924.

11. Tisa Joy Wenger, *Religious Freedom: The Contested History of an American Ideal* (Chapel Hill: University of North Carolina Press, 2017), 188–231. To understand these practices and rituals within a larger religious and cultural context, I respond in this chapter to religious studies scholar Megan Goodwin's call for "scholars of new, marginal, and minority religions to think critically about sex," given the ways "mainstream cultures often interpret unconventional religious beliefs or practices as evidence of sexual transgression" and in light of how "[new religious movements] often deploy transgressive sexual practices and gender norms to distance themselves from and correct mainstream culture." See Megan Goodwin, "Sex and New Religions," in *The Oxford Handbook of New Religious Movements: Volume II*, ed. James R. Lewis and Inga Tøllefsen (New York: Oxford University Press, 2016).

12. Hartman, *Wayward Lives, Beautiful Experiments*, 227.

13. I raise these concerns in my roundtable essay, "Wayward Negro Religions in the Twentieth-Century Slum," *Journal of African American History* 106, no. 1 (Winter 2021): 117–21, https://doi.org/10.1086/712022. Hartman responded, "Many of those in

NOTES TO PAGES 123–127

Wayward Lives expressed a belief in God, but the cabaret or the private party provided the milieu of their ecstatic experience rather than the church." Although she leaves religion out of her account, she also notes here that many of the women joined Spiritualist churches. See Saidiya Hartman, "Intimate History, Radical Narrative," *Journal of African American History* 106, no. 1 (January 1, 2021): 127–35, https://doi.org/10.1086 /712019. See also J. T. Roane, *Dark Agoras: Insurgent Black Social Life and the Politics of Place* (New York: New York University Press, 2023).

14. Zora Neale Hurston, *The Sanctified Church* (Berkeley: Turtle Island, 1983), 103.

15. Hyatt, *Hoodoo—Conjuration—Witchcraft—Rootwork*, 1:i.

16. Hyatt, 2:1676.

17. See, for example, C. Riley Snorton, *Black on Both Sides: A Racial History of Trans Identity* (Minneapolis: University of Minnesota Press, 2017); Marquis Bey, *Cistem Failure: Essays on Blackness and Cisgender* (Durham, NC: Duke University Press, 2022); Marlon Bryan Ross, *Sissy Insurgencies: A Racial Anatomy of Unfit Manliness* (Durham, NC: Duke University Press, 2022).

18. This literature is extensive. See, for example, Mary Ann Clark, *Where Men Are, Wives and Mothers Rule: Santería Ritual Practices and Their Gender Implications* (Gainesville: University Press of Florida, 2005); Elizabeth Pérez, *Religion in the Kitchen: Cooking, Talking, and the Making of Black Atlantic Traditions* (New York: New York University Press, 2016), 111–40; Roberto Strongman, *Queering Black Atlantic Religions: Transcorporeality in Candomblé, Santería, and Vodou* (Durham, NC: Duke University Press, 2019).

19. David H. Brown, *Santería Enthroned: Art, Ritual, and Innovation in an Afro-Cuban Religion* (Chicago: University of Chicago Press, 2003), 102–8.

20. Alexis Wells-Oghoghomeh, *The Souls of Womenfolk: The Religious Cultures of Enslaved Women in the Lower South* (Chapel Hill: University of North Carolina Press, 2021), 162.

21. Wells-Oghoghomeh, 162.

22. Mary A. Owen, "Among the Voodoos" (paper presented at the Second International Folk-lore Congress, 1891), 231. Source cited in Yvonne P. Chireau, *Black Magic: Religion and the African American Conjuring Tradition* (Berkeley: University of California Press, 2006), 162, 20n.

23. Chireau, *Black Magic*, 22.

24. Ellen Samuels, "Examining Millie and Christine McKoy: Where Enslavement and Enfreakment Meet," *Signs* 37, no. 1 (September 1, 2011): 56.

25. Hyatt, *Hoodoo—Conjuration—Witchcraft—Rootwork*, 2:1676.

26. Claude F. Jacobs and Andrew J. Kaslow, *The Spiritual Churches of New Orleans: Origins, Beliefs, and Rituals of an African-American Religion* (Knoxville: University of Tennessee Press, 1991).

27. Hyatt, *Hoodoo—Conjuration—Witchcraft—Rootwork*, 2:1677.

28. Hyatt, 2:1677.

29. Katrina Hazzard-Donald, *Mojo Workin': The Old African American Hoodoo System* (Champaign: University of Illinois Press, 2012); LeRhonda S. Manigault-Bryant, "'I Had a Praying Grandmother': Religion, Prophetic Witness, and Black Women's Herstories," in *New Perspectives on the Black Intellectual Tradition*, ed. Keisha N. Blain, Christopher

Cameron, and Ashley D. Farmer (Evanston: Northwestern University Press, 2018), 115–30, https://doi.org/10.2307/j.ctv7tq4rv.11.

30. Hyatt, *Hoodoo—Conjuration—Witchcraft—Rootwork*, 2:1678.

31. Hyatt, 2:1681.

32. Albert J. Raboteau, *Slave Religion: The "Invisible Institution" in the Antebellum South* (New York: Oxford University Press, 1978), 288.

33. Hyatt, *Hoodoo—Conjuration—Witchcraft—Rootwork*, 2:1681.

34. Hyatt, 2:1686.

35. Hyatt, 2:1683.

36. Kodi A. Roberts describes other instances of this in *Voodoo and Power: The Politics of Religion in New Orleans, 1881–1940* (Baton Rouge: Louisiana State University Press, 2015), 103–37.

37. Hyatt, *Hoodoo—Conjuration—Witchcraft—Rootwork*, 2:1682.

38. Hyatt, 2:1683.

39. Roberts, *Voodoo and Power*, 104.

40. Harris discusses the threat of violence many women and queer sex workers experienced at the hands of men and how they counteracted these threats in the early twentieth century. See *Sex Workers*, 42–53.

41. WWII Draft Card (1945), digital images, Fold3, https://www.fold3.com/image/607419475; "The Emperor Haile Selassie Nu-Way Ethiopia Mystic Light Baptist and Spiritual and Kingdom Church," reel 9, Robert Tallant Papers.

42. For more on the crossover between Hindu and Hoodoo in African American religions, see Philip Deslippe, "The Hindu in Hoodoo: Fake Yogis, Pseudo-Swamis, and the Manufacture of African American Folk Magic," *Amerasia Journal* 40, no. 1 (2014): 35–56, https://doi.org/10.17953/amer.40.1.a21442914234450w.

43. Judith Weisenfeld, *New World A-Coming: Black Religion and Racial Identity during the Great Migration* (New York: New York University Press, 2016), 6.

44. James B. Bennett, *Religion and the Rise of Jim Crow in New Orleans* (Princeton, NJ: Princeton University Press, 2005).

45. "The Emperor Haile Selassie," Robert Tallant Papers.

46. See Theodore M. Vestal, *The Lion of Judah in the New World: Emperor Haile Selassie of Ethiopia and the Shaping of Americans' Attitudes toward Africa* (Santa Barbara, CA: Praeger, 2011).

47. Haile Selassie I, "Appeal to the League of Nations," June 1936, https://www.mtholyoke.edu/acad/intrel/selassie.htm.

48. Keisha N. Blain, *Set the World on Fire: Black Nationalist Women and the Global Struggle for Freedom* (Philadelphia: University of Pennsylvania Press, 2018).

49. Hazel V. Carby, *Race Men: The W. E. B. Du Bois Lectures* (Cambridge, MA: Harvard University Press, 1998), 68, 113.

50. In *Hard, Hard Religion: Interracial Faith in the Poor South* (Chapel Hill: University of North Carolina Press, 2017), historian John Hayes argues that during the early twentieth century, "a grassroots religious culture became the basis of a sense of class commonality. The grassroots religious culture brought a different imaginative vision than the ideology of white supremacy, fostering identification outside the categories of white

NOTES TO PAGES 131–134

and black" (9). While Hayes's focus is primarily Protestant Christianity, the interracial relationships forged in non-Protestant religious formations in New Orleans—such as in Lyons's church—are also worthy of critical reflection. Kodi Roberts argues similarly in *Voodoo and Power*, 67–102.

51. "The Emperor Haile Selassie," Robert Tallant Papers; see also Wallace D. Best, *Passionately Human, No Less Divine: Religion and Culture in Black Chicago, 1915–1952* (Princeton, NJ: Princeton University Press, 2005), 35–70; Deidre Helen Crumbley, *Saved and Sanctified: The Rise of a Storefront Church in Great Migration Philadelphia* (Gainesville: University Press of Florida, 2012).

52. Federal Writers' Project of the Works Progress Administration for the City of New Orleans, *New Orleans City Guide*, American Guide Series (Boston: Houghton Mifflin, 1938), 199–211.

53. For a discussion of the anti-Blackness embedded in these social scientific and government-sponsored projects, see Curtis J. Evans, *The Burden of Black Religion* (Oxford: Oxford University Press, 2008).

54. On "rats" in African American history, literature, and culture, see Joshua Bennett, *Being Property Once Myself: Blackness and the End of Man* (Cambridge, MA: Harvard University Press, 2020), 18–65.

55. Colleen McDannell, *Picturing Faith: Photography and the Great Depression* (New Haven, CT: Yale University Press, 2004).

56. "The Emperor Haile Selassie," Robert Tallant Papers.

57. Roberts, *Voodoo and Power*, 128.

58. Don Romesburg, "'Wouldn't a Boy Do?': Placing Early-Twentieth-Century Male Youth Sex Work into Histories of Sexuality," *Journal of the History of Sexuality* 18, no. 3 (2009): 368.

59. See, for example, Richard Godbeer, *Sexual Revolution in Early America* (Baltimore: Johns Hopkins University Press, 2002); Zeb Tortorici, *Sins against Nature: Sex and Archives in Colonial New Spain* (Durham, NC: Duke University Press, 2018).

60. Alecia P. Long, *The Great Southern Babylon: Sex, Race, and Respectability in New Orleans, 1865–1920* (Baton Rouge: Louisiana State University Press, 2004).

61. Colleen McDannell, *Material Christianity: Religion and Popular Culture in America* (New Haven, CT: Yale University Press, 1995), 57.

62. McDannell, 57.

63. Roberts, *Voodoo and Power*, 139.

64. Jeffrey Q. McCune Jr., *Sexual Discretion: Black Masculinity and the Politics of Passing* (Chicago: University of Chicago Press, 2014), 74, 157. See also C. Riley Snorton, *Nobody Is Supposed to Know: Black Sexuality On the Down Low* (Minneapolis: University of Minnesota Press, 2014); Alisha Lola Jones, "'Are All the Choir Directors Gay?': Black Men's Sexuality and Identity in Gospel Performance," in *Issues in African American Music: Power, Gender, Race, Representation*, ed. Portia K. Maultsby and Mellonee V. Burnim (New York: Taylor & Francis, 2016), 216–36.

65. See Gillian Frank, Bethany Moreton, and Heather White, eds., *Devotions and Desires: Histories of Sexuality and Religion in the Twentieth-Century United States* (Chapel Hill: University of North Carolina Press, 2018).

66. Kevin J. Mumford, *Interzones: Black/White Sex Districts in Chicago and New York in the Early Twentieth Century* (New York: Columbia University Press, 1997), 86; Harris, *Sex Workers*, 145.

67. George Chauncey, *Gay New York: Gender, Urban Culture, and the Makings of the Gay Male World, 1890–1940* (New York: Basic Books, 1994), 348–49. For more on vice crackdowns in New Orleans, see Ryan Prechter, "Gay New Orleans: A History" (Atlanta: Georgia State University, 2017), 24–31, https://scholarworks.gsu.edu/history_diss/60.

68. In E. Patrick Johnson's oral history *Sweet Tea: Black Gay Men of the South* (Chapel Hill: University of North Carolina Press, 2008), one interviewee by the name of George Eagerson (otherwise known as "Countess Vivian") came of age during the 1920s and 1930s in New Orleans and describes how gays and lesbians—both Black and white— reimagined various urban spaces to articulate their own unique religious and sexual identities. See Johnson, 474–94.

69. "Voodooism and Mumbo-Jumbo," in *The Negro in Louisiana*, p. 58, Marcus Christian Collection, Earl K. Long Library, University of New Orleans.

70. Richard D. White, Jr., *Kingfish: The Reign of Huey P. Long* (New York: Random House, 2006), 3–4.

71. "Voodooism and Mumbo-Jumbo," p. 58.

72. "The Emperor Haile Selassie," Robert Tallant Papers.

73. See Henrik Bogdan, *Western Esotericism and Rituals of Initiation* (Albany: State University of New York Press, 2007), 207, 68n. Lyons's contemporary, N. H. Hobley, who was interviewed in New Orleans in June 1941 by Zoe Posey as an "ex-slave," also engaged in Hoodoo practices while reading *The Great Book of Magical Art, Hindu Magic and Indian Occultism* (1915) by L. W. de Laurence. It is likely that Lyons may have also read this text. See Ronnie W. Clayton, *Mother Wit: The Ex-Slave Narratives of the Louisiana Writers' Project* (New York: P. Lang, 1990), 117.

74. Aisha M. Beliso-De Jesús, *Electric Santería: Racial and Sexual Assemblages of Transnational Religion* (New York: Columbia University Press, 2015), 2, 42–43.

75. Andrew H. Apter, *Black Critics and Kings: The Hermeneutics of Power in Yoruba Society* (Chicago: University of Chicago Press, 1992), 99. See also the role of electricity as a metaphor in Hermione Harris, *Yoruba in Diaspora: An African Church in London* (New York: Palgrave Macmillan, 2006), 99; Peter Probst, *Osogbo and the Art of Heritage: Monuments, Deities, and Money* (Bloomington: Indiana University Press, 2011), 143–44; William Elison, *The Neighborhood of Gods: The Sacred and the Visible at the Margins of Mumbai* (Chicago: University of Chicago Press, 2018).

76. "The Emperor Haile Selassie," Robert Tallant Papers.

77. Weisenfeld, *New World A-Coming*, 152.

78. *Pittsburgh Courier*, October 1, 1938, 24; *Pittsburgh Courier*, September 30, 1939.

79. "National Council for a Permanent FEPC Holds Two Day Conference," *Postal Alliance* (Washington, DC: National Alliance of Postal Employees, July 1945), 18–19; "Executive Order 8802: Prohibition of Discrimination in the Defense Industry (1941)," Record Group 11, National Archives, Washington, DC.

80. WWII Draft Card (1945), digital images, Fold3, https://www.fold3.com/image /607419475.

NOTES TO PAGES 139-144

81. *Afro-American*, June 21, 1952, 2.

82. *Chicago Defender*, May 11, 1957, 1. See also David K. Johnson, *The Lavender Scare: The Cold War Persecution of Gays and Lesbians in the Federal Government* (Chicago: University of Chicago Press, 2009).

83. *Baltimore Sun*, January 1, 1972.

84. "The Emperor Haile Selassie," Robert Tallant Papers.

85. Hartman, *Wayward Lives, Beautiful Experiments*, 143.

86. "The Jeff Horn Spiritual Catholic Church," reel 9, Robert Tallant Papers.

87. 1 Kings 11:3 (NKJV).

88. For more on these "spiritual awakenings," see Alison Collis Greene, *No Depression in Heaven: The Great Depression, the New Deal, and the Transformation of Religion in the Delta* (New York: Oxford University Press, 2017), 51–65.

89. Beryl Satter, "Marcus Garvey, Father Divine and the Gender Politics of Race Difference and Race Neutrality," *American Quarterly* 48, no. 1 (1996): 43–76.

90. See, for example, "Taliaferro Sent to Asylum," *New Journal and Guide*, February 6, 1935; "Discharge of 'Holy Ghost' Babies into Custody of Their Mothers Saves County Money," *Norfolk Journal and Guide*, March 2, 1935, 20; "Freedom Coming for Taliaferro, 'Holy Ghost Dad,'" *Pittsburgh Courier*, July 6, 1935, 4.

91. For more on this in African American women's religious history, see Evelyn Brooks Higginbotham, *Righteous Discontent: The Women's Movement in the Black Baptist Church, 1880–1920* (Cambridge, MA: Harvard University Press, 1993); Cheryl Gilkes, *If It Wasn't for the Women—: Black Women's Experience and Womanist Culture in Church and Community* (Maryknoll, NY: Orbis Books, 2001); Anthea D. Butler, *Women in the Church of God in Christ: Making a Sanctified World* (Chapel Hill: University of North Carolina Press, 2007); Bettye Collier-Thomas, *Jesus, Jobs, and Justice: African American Women and Religion*, 1st ed. (New York: Alfred A. Knopf, 2010); Judith Weisenfeld, "Invisible Women: On Women and Gender in the Study of African American Religious History," *Journal of Africana Religions* 1, no. 1 (2013): 133–49; Casselberry, *Labor of Faith*.

92. Roberts, *Voodoo and Power*, 103–37.

93. "McKinney, Robert (interviewer), 'How I Got Religion,' Moriath Butler, 14 February 1939," folder 1024, Federal Writers' Project Papers #3709, Southern Historical Collection, Wilson Library, University of North Carolina at Chapel Hill.

94. According to the 1940 census, where her name is incorrectly listed as "Martha," she was born around 1869 and was seventy-one at the time of collection. She also lived with her daughter Rebecca Butler and her nephew Oscar Jackson. See *1940 United States Federal Census*, Louisiana, New Orleans, Orleans, Enumeration District No. 36-434, Ancestry .com. In her interview with McKinney, she stated that she was born "Moriath Jones" in Panchoville, Louisiana, to Henry and Henrietta and that her mother "worked in the fields. Yes, she was a slave."

95. "McKinney, Robert (interviewer), 'How I Got Religion,' Moriath Butler, 14 February 1939."

96. LeRhonda S. Manigault-Bryant, *Talking to the Dead: Religion, Music, and Lived Memory among Gullah/Geechee Women* (Durham, NC: Duke University Press, 2014), 116.

97. Manigault-Bryant, 131.

98. "McKinney, Robert (interviewer), 'How I Got Religion,' Moriath Butler, 14 February 1939."

VISITATION 5

1. Zora Neale Hurston, *You Don't Know Us Negroes and Other Essays*, ed. Margaret Genevieve West and Henry Louis Gates (New York: Amistad, 2022), 174, 176, 180–81.

CHAPTER 5

1. Robert A. Hill, ed., *The Marcus Garvey and Universal Negro Improvement Association Papers, Vol. III: September 1920–August 1921* (Berkeley: University of California Press, 1984), 694.
2. *Negro World*, March 24, 1923. The signatories were Mrs. G. D. Dans, RN, Mrs. Octavia Franklin, Mrs. Essie Hathaway, and Miss Florence Watterhouse of the Voluntary Committee of the UNIA. See also *New York Age*, March 10, 1923; *Appeal*, March 17, 1923; *Afro-American*, March 21, 1923.
3. In the Hebrew Bible, the term "Belial" is used to speak of the "devil."
4. Barbara Dianne Savage, *Your Spirits Walk Beside Us: The Politics of Black Religion* (Cambridge, MA: Harvard University Press, 2009), 20–67; Lerone A. Martin, *Preaching on Wax: The Phonograph and the Shaping of Modern African American Religion* (New York: New York University Press, 2014).
5. *Negro World*, April 2, 1921. By 1924, Garvey articulated his own desire for "faith in Black God." More specifically, he was quoted as saying, "God tells us to worship a God in our own image. We are black, and to be in our image God must be black. Our people have been lynched and burned in the South because we have been worshipping a false god . . . We must create a god of our own and give this new religion to the negroes of the world" (*New York Times*, August 4, 1924).
6. *Negro World*, February 19, 1921. "Alaida" is the spelling used in the *Negro World* and has subsequently been used by scholars. However, the spelling "Alada" is found in government records and in other newspapers. I use the former for historiographical consistency.
7. *1910 United States Federal Census*, Louisiana, New Orleans, Orleans, Enumeration District No. 190, Family No. 142, Ancestry.com.
8. Claudrena N. Harold, *The Rise and Fall of the Garvey Movement in the Urban South, 1918–1942* (New York: Routledge, 2007), 31.
9. Mary G. Rolinson, *Grassroots Garveyism: The Universal Negro Improvement Association in the Rural South, 1920–1927* (Chapel Hill: University of North Carolina Press, 2012), 232, 60n. For the sake of clarity, in this chapter, I am less concerned with distinguishing each individual subdivision of the New Orleans Division and will use "NOD" to refer

NOTES TO PAGE 151

to them as a conglomeration of people who met together regularly in various parts of New Orleans and Louisiana.

10. Glenn A. Chambers, *From the Banana Zones to the Big Easy: West Indian and Central American Immigration to New Orleans, 1910–1940* (Baton Rouge: Louisiana State University Press, 2019).

11. "Negroes Seek All Africa for Home," *Christian Science Monitor*, August 4, 1920.

12. *Negro World*, August 12, 1922. See also *Negro World*, October 11, 1919; Truman Hughes Talley, "Marcus Garvey—The Negro Moses?" *World's Work* 7, no. 1 (December 1920–January 1921); "A Negro Moses and His Plans for an African Exodus," *Gleaner*, April 15, 1921; Edmund David Cronon, *Black Moses: The Story of Marcus Garvey and the Universal Negro Improvement Association* (Madison: University of Wisconsin Press, 1955). According to the 1930 Census, Duncanson was born in Jamaica around 1882 and entered the United States in 1905. See *1930 United States Federal Census*, Louisiana, New Orleans, Orleans, Enumeration District No. 36-11, Family No. 419, Ancestry .com. Britton was born on October 14, 1896, in Bluefields, Nicaragua, a major Central American port city, and migrated to New Orleans in 1910. See *1930 United States Federal Census*, Louisiana, New Orleans, Orleans, Enumeration District No. 36-11, Family No. 170, Ancestry.com; *Times-Picayune*, February 25, 1960.

13. *Negro World*, March 18, 1922.

14. In 1949, he "was charged for being a lottery agent after he was found allegedly selling plays" (*Times-Picayune*, April 17, 1949). By 1953, he was recognized as an official gambling stamp holder by the Internal Revenue Service (*Times-Picayune*, August 30, 1953; *Times-Picayune*, August 3, 1954). In 1954, he was arrested again for "operating lottery shops, acting as [a] lottery agent, and [for] possessing lottery paraphernalia" (*Times-Picayune*, August 12, 1954). Britton died six years later at the age of sixty-three (*Times-Picayune*, February 24, 1960).

15. Duncanson and Britton were just two of the many West Indian and Central Americans who migrated to New Orleans and joined forces with African Americans in the city. For example, Archibald Francis, a Jamaican, wrote to the *Negro World* in 1925, just two years after he immigrated to New Orleans, stating, "The program of the UNIA ought to bring comfort to the heart of every well-thinking Negro" (*Negro World*, June 6, 1925). Garvey's wife, Amy Jacques Garvey, a Jamaican who visited the NOD on August 20, 1925, described in full Garvey's efforts to recruit Black people around the world: "He lived and worked for many years in Central America and parts of South America, observing the awful conditions under which West Indians worked, and advantages taken of them, he published leaflets and small newspapers putting forth their grievances, but he was dubbed an Agitator and had to leave Republic after Republic"; see Amy Jacques Garvey, "Notes on Marcus Garvey," box PS 4, Robert A. Hill Collection, David M. Rubenstein Rare Book and Manuscript Library, Duke University; *Negro World*, September 5, 1925; Ula Yvette Taylor, *The Veiled Garvey: The Life and Times of Amy Jacques Garvey* (Chapel Hill: University of North Carolina Press, 2003). While it is true that Garvey's rhetoric drew people like Duncanson, Britton, and Francis, the recruitment efforts of local Black New Orleanian activists, especially Black women like NOD cofounder Alaida Robertson and secretary Mamie Reason cannot be denied. See Keisha N. Blain, *Set the World*

on Fire: Black Nationalist Women and the Global Struggle for Freedom (Philadelphia: University of Pennsylvania Press, 2018). See also "Our Women and What They Think," *Negro World*, February 14, 1925; "Women's Clubs Score Lynching," *Negro World*, February 21, 1931; "Women in UNIA," box AM 10, Robert A. Hill Collection.

16. Here I am in conversation with Randall K. Burkett, *Garveyism as a Religious Movement: The Institutionalization of a Black Civil Religion* (Metuchen, NJ: Scarecrow Press, 1978). While Burkett names Garveyism a "Black Civil Religion" (drawing from Robert N. Bellah's 1967 essay, "Civil Religion in America") and Garvey a "Black theologian," I am interested in the ways the NOD rejected notions of "religion" as propagated and defined by mainline denominations and utilized the profane and irreverent practices as a site of religion making.

17. Historian Claudrena Harold writes, "Strong believers in the principle of self-determination, [NOD members] asserted their right to develop their own locally-based programs, maintain autonomy over the movement at the local level, and determine for themselves their relationship with other racial advocacy organizations." See Harold, *Rise and Fall*, 30.

18. Tracey E. Hucks, *Yoruba Traditions and African American Religious Nationalism* (Albuquerque: University of New Mexico Press, 2012), 44–45.

19. *Blackman*, August 31, 1929, box J20, Robert A. Hill Collection.

20. *Negro World*, February 11, 1928.

21. Richard Brent Turner, *Jazz Religion, the Second Line, and Black New Orleans* (Bloomington: Indiana University Press, 2009).

22. Burkett, *Garveyism as a Religious Movement*, 37; see also Randall K. Burkett, ed., *Black Redemption: Churchmen Speak for the Garvey Movement* (Philadelphia: Temple University Press, 1978).

23. *Negro World*, January 10, 1925. For more on Arnold Josiah Ford, see *The Universal Negro Ethiopian Hymnal* (New York: Beth B'nai Abraham Publishing Co., 1922), digitized in Yale Collection of American Literature, Beinecke Rare Book and Manuscript Library, Yale University. For more on gender and religious titles and honorifics, see Cheryl Gilkes, *If It Wasn't for the Women—: Black Women's Experience and Womanist Culture in Church and Community* (Maryknoll, NY: Orbis Books, 2001); Anthea D. Butler, *Women in the Church of God in Christ: Making a Sanctified World* (Chapel Hill: University of North Carolina Press, 2007); and Judith Casselberry, *The Labor of Faith: Gender and Power in Black Apostolic Pentecostalism* (Durham, NC: Duke University Press, 2017). On women in the UNIA, see, for example, Barbara Bair, "'Ethiopia Shall Stretch Forth Her Hands Unto God': Laura Kofey and the Gendered Vision of Redemption in the Garvey Movement," in *A Mighty Baptism: Race, Gender, and the Creation of American Protestantism*, ed. Susan Juster and Lisa MacFarlane (Ithaca, NY: Cornell University Press, 1996), 44–49.

24. *Negro World*, October 14, 1922.

25. Cited in Burkett, *Garveyism as a Religious Movement*, 130–31.

26. *Negro World*, March 24, 1923. The invocation of "Spanish" here is odd given that the UNIA regularly included articles in the *Negro World* in both French and Spanish and highlighted the organizing efforts of its West Indian and Central American chapters in

NOTES TO PAGES 156–158

each issue of the newspaper. What the writer here seems to be suggesting, however, is that the NOD saw itself having a different set of politics from Spanish-speaking Creoles and Creoles of color, who have historically distanced themselves from Black-identified people of African descent in Louisiana.

27. Roy Kay, *The Ethiopian Prophecy in Black American Letters* (Gainesville: University Press of Florida, 2011).

28. Michele Mitchell, *Righteous Propagation: African Americans and the Politics of Racial Destiny after Reconstruction* (Chapel Hill: University of North Carolina Press, 2004); Judith Weisenfeld, *New World A-Coming: Black Religion and Racial Identity during the Great Migration* (New York: New York University Press, 2016); Blain, *Set the World on Fire*; Vaughn A. Booker, *Lift Every Voice and Swing: Black Musicians and Religious Culture in the Jazz Century* (New York: New York University Press, 2020), 109–36.

29. Gayraud S. Wilmore, *Black Religion and Black Radicalism: An Interpretation of the Religious History of African Americans*, 3rd ed. (Maryknoll, NY: Orbis Books, 1998); Eddie S. Glaude, *Exodus!: Religion, Race, and Nation in Early Nineteenth-Century Black America* (Chicago: University of Chicago Press, 2000); Laurie F. Maffly-Kipp, *Setting down the Sacred Past: African-American Race Histories* (Cambridge, MA: Belknap Press of Harvard University Press, 2010).

30. Burkett, *Garveyism as a Religious Movement*; Stephen J. Ochs, *Desegregating the Altar: The Josephites and the Struggle for Black Priests, 1871–1960* (Baton Rouge: Louisiana State University Press, 1990).

31. Edward E. Curtis IV and Sylvester A. Johnson, "The Transnational and Diasporic Future of African American Religions in the United States," *Journal of the American Academy of Religion* 87, no. 2 (June 2019): 337.

32. Jahi U. Issa, "The Universal Negro Improvement Association in Louisiana: Creating a Provisional Government in Exile" (PhD diss., Howard University, 2005), 89, 2n.

33. Charles Vincent, "Booker T. Washington's Tour of Louisiana, April, 1915," *Louisiana History* 22, no. 2 (1981): 189–98; David H. Jackson, *Booker T. Washington and the Struggle against White Supremacy: The Southern Educational Tours, 1908–1912* (New York: Palgrave Macmillan, 2008).

34. Frank Guridy, *Forging Diaspora: Afro-Cubans and African Americans in a World of Empire and Jim Crow* (Chapel Hill: University of North Carolina Press, 2010), 17–60.

35. *Negro World*, February 18, 1922.

36. *Negro World*, June 17, 1922.

37. *Negro World*, January 22, 1927.

38. See Evelyn Brooks Higginbotham, *Righteous Discontent: The Women's Movement in the Black Baptist Church, 1880–1920* (Cambridge, MA: Harvard University Press, 1993); Butler, *Women in the Church*. By 1927, Robertson and her husband had migrated to Cleveland, Ohio, where they became active members of the UNIA division there, at which they both spoke at almost every meeting. For instance, in May 1927, Robertson was the principal speaker, and her subject was "The Awakened Souls." Following her speech, the meeting closed with the singing of the Ethiopian National Anthem (*Negro World*, May 7, 1927). Members of the Cleveland division expressed how she was a "very strong and able exponent of the doctrines of the Universal Negro Improvement Asso-

ciation," often "[speaking] very eloquently and [closing] amid loud applause" (*Negro World*, July 2, 1927). UNIA reporter Louise Edwards observed, "She is the star of Ohio, and is accomplishing much among the women, not only in the Cleveland Division, but throughout the entire State of Ohio" (*Negro World*, July 16, 1927). In 1929, the Robertsons, along with other UNIA members like Madame Maymie L. T. de Mena, boarded the SS Celba from the Honduras-Nicaragua border and sailed to New York (*Kingston Gleaner*, September 12, 1929). By 1930, Robertson had assumed one of the highest ranks offered to women in the UNIA as "officer-in-charge," with which she presided over meetings and, on one occasion, "reminded the newly-elected officers of the seriousness of the obligations that they were about to assume" (*Negro World*, February 15, 1930).

39. *Negro World*, June 13, 1925; *Negro World*, September 19, 1925. See also Archie Ebenezer Perkins, *Who's Who in Colored America* (Baton Rouge, LA: Douglas Loan Co., 1930), 97. Yearwood was born on October 14, 1888. According to the US World War I Draft Registration of 1917–18, he lived in Redding, Shasta County, California and pastored in the AME Zion Church, and according to California State Court naturalization records, he was naturalized in Fresno, California, on May 15, 1918. By 1925, he had migrated to New Orleans and continued preaching.

40. *Negro World*, September 19, 1925.

41. *Negro World*, April 2, 1921.

42. *Negro World*, January 19, 1924.

43. *Negro World*, April 19, 1924.

44. *Negro World*, September 8, 1928.

45. Federal Writers' Project of the Works Progress Administration for the City of New Orleans, *New Orleans City Guide*, American Guide Series (Boston: Houghton Mifflin, 1938), 83, 199–211.

46. Judith Weisenfeld, *Hollywood Be Thy Name: African American Religion in American Film, 1929–1949* (University of California Press, 2007), 136.

47. Weisenfeld, 136.

48. *Negro World*, March 24, 1923.

49. *Negro World*, October 28, 1922.

50. Greene, *No Depression in Heaven*, 47.

51. Harold, *Rise and Fall*, 37.

52. Robert A. Hill, ed., *The Marcus Garvey and Universal Negro Improvement Association Papers, Volume XI: The Caribbean Diaspora, 1920–1921* (Durham, NC: Duke University Press, 2014), 365.

53. Robert A. Hill, ed., *The Marcus Garvey and Universal Negro Improvement Association Papers, Volume IX: Africa for the Africans, June 1921–December 1922* (Berkeley: University of California Press, 1995), 139–40.

54. Robert A. Hill, ed., *The Marcus Garvey and Universal Negro Improvement Association Papers, Volume IV: 1 September 1921–2 September 1922* (Berkeley: University of California Press, 1985), 353.

55. See Robert A. Hill, *The Marcus Garvey and Universal Negro Improvement Association Papers, Volume II: 27 August 1919–31 August 1920* (Berkeley: University of California Press, 1983), 230–38.

NOTES TO PAGES 162–166

56. See Nicholas L. Gaffney, "Mobilizing Jazz Communities: The Dynamic Use of Jazz as a Political Resource in the Black Liberation Struggle," 1925–1965" (PhD diss., University of Illinois at Urbana-Champaign, 2012), 77.

57. Lyle Saxon, Edward Dreyer, and Robert Tallant, eds., *Gumbo Ya-Ya: A Collection of Louisiana Folk Tales* (Cambridge, MA: Riverside Press, 1945), 99–100.

58. Robert Tallant, *Voodoo in New Orleans* (Grenta, LA: Pelican, 1946), 3.

59. *Negro World*, April 16, 1927.

60. Turner, *Jazz Religion, the Second Lines*.

61. *Negro World*, March 25, 1922.

62. *Negro World*, May 27, 1922.

63. Robert A. Hill, ed., *The Marcus Garvey and Universal Negro Improvement Association Papers, Volume VII: November 1927–August 1940* (Berkeley: University of California Press, 1991), 714.

64. Cited in Lillian Ashcraft Webb, *About My Father's Business: The Life of Elder Michaux* (Westport, CT: Greenwood, 1981), 45–46.

65. Lerone Martin, "Bureau Clergyman: How the FBI Colluded with an African American Televangelist to Destroy Dr. Martin Luther King, Jr.," *Religion and American Culture* 28, no. 1 (2018): 3–4.

66. Hill, *Marcus Garvey and UNIA Papers, Vol. VII*, 714.

67. Martin, *Preaching on Wax*, 46.

68. Martin, 50.

69. Colin Grant, *Negro with a Hat: The Rise and Fall of Marcus Garvey* (New York: Oxford University Press, 2008), 18.

70. *Blackman*, August 31, 1929, box J20, Robert A. Hill Collection.

71. See first page of monthly publication of the *Negro Churchman* in "African Orthodox Church," box 11, folder 10, Universal Negro Improvement Association, Central Division, New York Records, Schomburg Center for Research in Black Culture, New York Public Library.

72. Wallace D. Best, *Passionately Human, No Less Divine: Religion and Culture in Black Chicago, 1915–1952* (Princeton, NJ: Princeton University Press, 2005).

73. Booker, *Lift Every Voice*, 26.

74. Tracy Fessenden, *Religion around Billie Holiday* (University Park, PA: Pennsylvania State University Press, 2018); Matthew J. Cressler, *Authentically Black and Truly Catholic: The Rise of Black Catholicism in the Great Migration* (New York: New York University Press, 2017); James B. Bennett, *Religion and the Rise of Jim Crow in New Orleans* (Princeton, NJ: Princeton University Press, 2005).

75. See also the *Universal Negro Ritual* and *Universal Negro Catechism*.

76. Chireau has observed, "The press played an important role in publicizing Conjure and its practitioners. Between 1903 and 1933 an explosion of print advertisements crowded the pages of major black newspapers. Initially, such advertisements were simple offerings for alternative doctoring and medical treatment." See Yvonne P. Chireau, *Black Magic: Religion and the African American Conjuring Tradition* (Berkeley: University of California Press, 2006), 141.

77. *Negro World*, June 9, 1923.

78. *Times-Picayune*, January 2, 1923.

79. "American Leader Takes New Orleans by Storm," *Negro World*, June 10, 1922.

80. *New Journal and Guide*, April 5, 1922; *Negro World*, June 10, 1922; *New Orleans Item*, October 9, 1922.

81. *New Journal and Guide*, August 26, 1922.

82. *Negro World*, October 14, 1922.

83. *Negro World*, September 2, 1922.

84. Cited in Harold, *Rise and Fall*, 40.

85. *Times-Picayune*, January 14, 1923.

86. *Times-Picayune*, January 19, 1923.

87. See, for example, Chireau, *Black Magic*, 59–89; Pablo F. Gómez, *The Experiential Caribbean: Creating Knowledge and Healing in the Early Modern Atlantic* (Chapel Hill: University of North Carolina Press, 2017), "kill/ing" on 279; Alexis Wells-Oghoghomeh, *The Souls of Womenfolk: The Religious Cultures of Enslaved Women in the Lower South* (Chapel Hill: University of North Carolina Press, 2021).

88. "Preacher Killers," January 19, 1911, box 3, folder 9, item 1, Robert Elijah Jones Papers, Amistad Research Center, Tulane University.

89. *Times-Picayune*, January 19, 1923.

90. *Negro World*, March 10, 1923.

91. *New Orleans States*, January 30, 1923; *Times-Picayune*, August 1, 1924.

92. Harold, *Rise and Fall*, 45.

93. Portions of this discussion of Kofey first appeared in Ahmad Greene-Hayes, "Black Religious Studies, Misogynoir, and the Matter of Breonna Taylor's Death," *Religions* 12, no. 8 (2021), https://doi.org/10.3390/rel12080621.

94. *Negro World*, February 12, 1927.

95. Bair, "'Ethiopia Shall Stretch Forth,'" 59.

96. *African Messenger*, undated, box PS14, Robert A. Hill Collection.

97. "A Self-Help Project of the Missionary African Universal Church, Inc.," undated, box PS 14, Robert A. Hill Collection.

98. Richard Newman, "'Warrior Mother of Africa's Warriors of the Most High God': Laura Adorkor Kofey and the African Universal Church," in *This Far by Faith: Readings in African-American Women's Religious Biography*, ed. Judith Weisenfeld and Richard Newman (New York: Routledge, 1996), 110–23.

99. Newman, 111.

100. *Negro World*, October 22, 1927; *Negro World*, November 5, 1927; *Negro World*, November 12, 1927.

101. Newman, "'Warrior Mother,'" 113.

102. Newman, 113.

103. Burkett, *Garveyism as a Religious Movement*.

104. Anthea D. Butler, "Women and Garveyism," in *Encyclopedia of Women and Religion in North America*, ed. Rosemary Skinner Keller, Rosemary Radford Ruether, and Marie Cantlon, vol. 3 (Indianapolis: Indiana University Press, 2006), 1076–81.

105. "Speech by E.B. Knox, Personal Representative of Marcus Garvey," in Hill, *Marcus Garvey and UNIA Papers, Vol. VII*, 16.

NOTES TO PAGES 172–179

106. *New Orleans Item*, December 7, 1930: 9.

107. *New York Times*, August 20, 1929.

108. Jill Watts, *God, Harlem USA: The Father Divine Story* (Berkeley: University of California Press, 1992), 113–17.

109. "Proceedings of Ninety-first Annual Meeting of the American Psychiatric Association and Committee Reports," *American Journal of Psychiatry* 92 (September 1935): 451; "Will Address Psychiatrists," *New Orleans Item*, April 29, 1935: 12. A journal article of the same title appeared in the *Journal of Nervous and Mental Disease* in April 1938 by Lauretta Bender MA, MD, and Zuleika Yarrell, MD.

110. *Pittsburgh Courier*, November 5, 1932, A10. This was also the case with Michaux, Daddy Grace, and others.

111. "'Prophets' and 'Healers' Called Religious 'Racketeers' by Bishop," *Los Angeles Sentinel*, May 22, 1947, 6.

112. Watts, *God, Harlem USA*, 89.

113. *Negro World*, January 12, 1929.

114. Courtney Desiree Morris, "Becoming Creole, Becoming Black: Migration, Diasporic Self-Making, and the Many Lives of Madame Maymie Leona Turpeau de Mena," *Women, Gender, and Families of Color* 4, no. 2 (September 14, 2016): 186–87.

115. *New York Age*, January 27, 1934: 5.

116. *Negro World*, September 10, 1927; *Negro World*, April 15, 1933.

117. Beryl Satter, "Marcus Garvey, Father Divine and the Gender Politics of Race Difference and Race Neutrality," *American Quarterly* 48, no. 1 (1996): 45.

118. *World Echo*, March 31, 1934.

119. Clarence E. Hardy, "'No Mystery God': Black Religions of the Flesh in Pre-War Urban America," *Church History* 77, no. 1 (2008): 128–50.

120. Blain, *Set the World on Fire*, 106–7.

121. For more on New Thought in Father Divine's Peace Mission, see R. Marie Griffith, "Body Salvation: New Thought, Father Divine, and the Feast of Material Pleasures," *Religion and American Culture* 11, no. 2 (2001): 119–53.

122. "D' Ye Hea' Me Talkin' to U," *Ethiopian World*, May 26, 1934.

123. "Greetings! Children of Ethiopia," *Ethiopian World*, May 26, 1934. See also Mitchell, *Righteous Propagation*.

124. Morris, "Becoming Creole, Becoming Black," 187.

125. *Negro World*, June 4, 1927.

126. *Negro World*, June 4, 1927.

127. *Negro World*, October 14, 1922.

128. *Pittsburgh Courier*, July 6, 1929, box OW9, Robert A. Hill Collection, David M. Rubenstein Rare Book and Manuscript Library, Duke University.

VISITATION 6

1. Zora Neale Hurston, *The Sanctified Church* (Berkeley: Turtle Island, 1983), 103–4.

CHAPTER 6

1. Judith Casselberry, *The Labor of Faith: Gender and Power in Black Apostolic Pentecostalism* (Durham, NC: Duke University Press, 2017), 153.
2. "Mother Brown," May 7, 1937, p. 1, reel 9, Robert Tallant Papers, New Orleans Public Library.
3. "Divine Healer Curing Lame, Halt, Blind," *Louisiana Weekly*, June 24, 1933, in Folklore, Fanatic Cults, Mother Catherine, folder 91, Federal Writers Project Papers, Northwestern State University of Louisiana (hereafter FWP Papers).
4. "Mother Brown," 1–2.
5. "Triumph and Truck," folder 91, FWP Papers.
6. 2 Corinthians 6:17 (KJV). This scripture is often used within Holiness-Pentecostal theology. Colleen McDannell argues similarly about religion and material culture in American history in *Material Christianity: Religion and Popular Culture in America* (New Haven, CT: Yale University Press, 1995).
7. Butler contends, "Familial roles also found their way into the everyday relationship between church mothers and pastors [in COGIC]. Because of the use of the term 'church mother,' pastors, and in particular C. H. Mason, were sometimes referred to as 'fathers,' or, in the case of Mason, 'Dad Mason.'" See Anthea D. Butler, *Women in the Church of God in Christ: Making a Sanctified World* (Chapel Hill: University of North Carolina Press, 2007), 48.
8. "Hundreds, Yea Thousands Are Being Healed Daily by Prayers of Holy Man," *Atlanta Daily World*, November 19, 1932, 1. In 1940, however, Bishop Charles H. Mason, COGIC founder, attended a convocation in New Orleans led by Treadwell. See "Convocation Announced by Father Treadwell," *Pittsburgh Courier*, September 14, 1940, 14.
9. "Mother Brown," 1.
10. Butler, *Women in the Church*, 12.
11. "Spiritual Meeting at Father Treadwell's Church in New Orleans, Louisiana in the 1930s," Louisiana Works Progress Administration, Digital Library, State Library of Louisiana.
12. Colleen McDannell, *Picturing Faith: Photography and the Great Depression* (New Haven, CT: Yale University Press, 2004), 232.
13. "Louisiana Has 'Father Divine,'" *Pittsburgh Courier*, November 5, 1932, A10.
14. "And They Left Their Crutches and Canes Behind," *Atlanta Daily World*, Nov. 19, 1932, 1.
15. For more on Black Spiritualist beliefs in New Orleans, see, for example, "Doctrines of The Divine Spiritualist Church of the Southwest," reel 9, Robert Tallant Papers.
16. One scholar has observed that such criticism was due largely to the exceptionalization of the city and its religious practitioners in early guidebooks published by the LWP, in which "writers misrepresented the Spiritual churches as a part of Louisiana folk culture associated with voodoo." See Claude F. Jacobs, "Folk for Whom? Tourist Guidebooks, Local Color, and the Spiritual Churches of New Orleans," *Journal of American Folklore* 114, no. 453 (2001): 314.
17. Yvonne P. Chireau, *Black Magic: Religion and the African American Conjuring Tradition*

NOTES TO PAGES 185–187

(Berkeley: University of California Press, 2006), 113. This chapter necessarily revisits questions invoked by anthropologists Claude F. Jacobs and Andrew J. Kaslow in their foundational 1991 text, *The Spiritual Churches of New Orleans*, in which they asked, "How are the Spiritual churches similar to Pentecostal churches? Do they have any connection to Spiritualism? How do we talk about voodoo?" While much has been written about the Spiritual churches and their connection to Catholicism since these questions were raised, there is rather scant attention to the relationship, if any, between Black Pentecostals and the Black Spiritual churches in African American religious historiography. See Claude F. Jacobs and Andrew J. Kaslow, *The Spiritual Churches of New Orleans: Origins, Beliefs, and Rituals of an African-American Religion* (Knoxville: University of Tennessee Press, 1991); Hans A. Baer, *The Black Spiritual Movement: A Religious Response to Racism* (Knoxville: University of Tennessee Press, 2001); Emily Suzanne Clark, *A Luminous Brotherhood: Afro-Creole Spiritualism in Nineteenth-Century New Orleans* (Chapel Hill: University of North Carolina Press, 2016); and Margarita Simon Guillory, *Spiritual and Social Transformation in African American Spiritual Churches: More Than Conjurers* (London: Routledge, Taylor & Francis, 2018). In Jacobs and Kaslow's study, one interviewee, Rev. Jules Anderson, described the Black Spiritual churches as "a *sanctified* Catholic church," to which Jacobs and Kaslow assumed an inherent commonality between Spiritualists, Catholics, and Pentecostals (16). Yet, in their anthropological focus, the two overemphasized the "syncretic" methods that have historically likened these religions in communities of African descent, arbitrarily overlooking the clear-cut distinctions articulated by practitioners of Black Atlantic religions during the 1920s and well into the 1940s in New Orleans (3–7, 82–87). For instance, Jacobs and Kaslow contended, "No hard lines of distinction can be drawn to separate the churches' spiritual advisors from 'workers' and people who are more deeply rooted in occult or Hoodoo practices" (37). The individuals discussed in this book, however, would have taken offense to such a statement. To their credit, however, Jacobs and Kaslow did maintain that the Spiritual churches—that were "influenced by Catholicism, Pentecostalism, Spiritualism, and voodoo"—"constructed a belief system of their own" (92).

18. Hardy, "'No Mystery God,'" 131.

19. Chireau, *Black Magic*, 111.

20. Clarence E. Hardy, "Fauset's (Missing) Pentecostals: Church Mothers, Remaking Respectability, and Religious Modernism," in *The New Black Gods: Arthur Huff Fauset and the Study of African American Religions*, ed. Edward E. Curtis IV and Danielle Brune Sigler (Indianapolis: Indiana University Press, 2009), 25.

21. See *Times-Picayune*, August 3, 1924; *Times-Picayune*, March 24, 1932.

22. Vinson Synan, "The African-American Pentecostals," in *The Holiness-Pentecostal Tradition: Charismatic Movements in the Twentieth Century* (Grand Rapids, MI: Eerdmans Publishing Company, 1971), 167–86; William Clair Turner, "The United Holy Church of America: A Study in Black Holiness-Pentecostalism" (PhD diss., Duke University, 1984); Cheryl J. Sanders, *Saints in Exile: The Holiness-Pentecostal Experience in African American Religion and Culture* (New York: Oxford University Press, 1996); John Michael Giggie, *After Redemption: Jim Crow and the Transformation of African*

264   NOTES TO PAGES 187–190

American Religion in the Delta, 1875–1915 (New York: Oxford University Press, 2008), 165–93.

23. David Douglas Daniels, "The Cultural Renewal of Slave Religion: Charles Price Jones and the Emergence of the Holiness Movement in Mississippi" (PhD diss., Union Theological Seminary, 1992), 2.

24. See, for example, Butler, *Women in the Church*; Calvin White, *The Rise to Respectability: Race, Religion, and the Church of God in Christ* (Fayetteville: University of Arkansas Press, 2012); Deidre Helen Crumbley, *Saved and Sanctified: The Rise of a Storefront Church in Great Migration Philadelphia* (Gainesville: University Press of Florida, 2012).

25. Grant Wacker, *Heaven Below: Early Pentecostals and Early American Culture* (Cambridge, MA: Harvard University Press, 2009), 226.

26. Wilson Jeremiah Moses, *The Golden Age of Black Nationalism, 1850–1925* (New York: Oxford University Press, 1978).

27. Estrelda Y. Alexander, ed., *The Dictionary of Pan-African Pentecostalism, Volume I: North America* (Eugene, OR: Cascade Books, 2018), 380–81.

28. Randall K. Burkett, *Garveyism as a Religious Movement: The Institutionalization of a Black Civil Religion* (Metuchen, NJ: Scarecrow Press, 1978), 182.

29. See, for example, *Negro World*, December 26, 1931; *Negro World*, January 9, 1932; *Negro World*, January 16, 1932.

30. See Clarence E. Hardy, "From Exodus to Exile: Black Pentecostals, Migrating Pilgrims, and Imagined Internationalism," *American Quarterly* 59, no. 3 (2007): 737–57; Keri Day, *Azusa Reimagined: A Radical Vision of Religious and Democratic Belonging* (Stanford, CA: Stanford University Press, 2022).

31. Hardy has contended, "In their quest to escape (white) man-made divisions, black religionists reached for the world beyond the nation's borders. In the wake of mass migrations after World War I, black activists and religionists reconceived the separatism that had animated the rise of black independent denominations in the decades immediately after slavery." See Hardy, "Fauset's (Missing) Pentecostals," 26.

32. See Michele Mitchell, *Righteous Propagation: African Americans and the Politics of Racial Destiny after Reconstruction* (Chapel Hill: University of North Carolina Press, 2004); Judith Weisenfeld, *New World A-Coming: Black Religion and Racial Identity during the Great Migration* (New York: New York University Press, 2016), 244–48; Dorman, *Chosen People*, 113–51.

33. *Youngstown* (Ohio) *Triumph*, September 25, 1919. Cited in Robert A. Hill, ed., *The Marcus Garvey and Universal Negro Improvement Association Papers, Volume III: September 1920–August 1921* (Berkeley: University of California Press, 1984), 653. Barber also often visited the Youngstown UNIA division according to *Negro World*, May 7, 1927, 8; *Negro World*, April 19, 1930, 2.

34. "The Beginning," Triumph, accessed March 4, 2020, http://www.triumphthechurchband25.org/Creed.htm.

35. *Negro World*, September 3, 1921, 12; see also Hill, *Marcus Garvey and UNIA Papers, Vol. III*, 652–53.

36. "Going Back into the Land of Ham," *Negro World*, December 31, 1921, 10.

37. *Negro World*, August 19, 1922, 7.

NOTES TO PAGES 191–195

38. *Negro World*, September 2, 1922, 12.

39. *Negro World*, August 16, 1924, 14.

40. *Negro World*, August 16, 1924, 3.

41. *Negro World*, August 23, 1924, 9.

42. *Negro World*, July 11, 1925, 6; *Negro World*, October 17, 1925, 6.

43. *Negro World*, May 28, 1927, 8.

44. *Negro World*, April 27, 1929, 2.

45. For more on "Precedents in Early Charismatic Movements, 1900–1960s" in Africa, see Ogbu Kalu, *African Pentecostalism: An Introduction* (New York: Oxford University Press, 2008), 1–83.

46. *Negro World*, January 10, 1931, 4.

47. *Negro World*, January 17, 1931, 2; *Negro World*, February 14, 1931, 8.

48. To be clear, my use of the term "Africanisms" differs from that of Black literary scholar and Black studies foremother Toni Morrison in her conception of "American African-isms," which she defines through her "investigation into the ways in which a nonwhite, African-like (or Africanist) presence or persona was constructed in the United States, and the imaginative uses this fabricated presence served." She continues, "I use it as a term for the denotative and connotative Blackness that African peoples have come to signify, as well as the entire range of views, assumptions, readings and misreadings that accompany Eurocentric learning about these people." See Morrison, *Playing in the Dark: Whiteness and the Literary Imagination* (Cambridge, MA: Harvard University Press, 1992), 6–7. In my conception of "Africanisms," I am specifically referring to Afri-can retentions, or the cultural remnants of an African past among people of African descent in the Americas in the wake and in the afterlife of chattel slavery. Here, I draw from Zora Neale Hurston, Lawrence Levine, Albert Raboteau, et al. There is a robust discussion of this concept and the scholarly debates surrounding it in the following anthologies in religious studies: Joseph E. Holloway, ed., *Africanisms in American Cul-ture*, 2nd ed. (Bloomington: Indiana University Press, 2005); *Africas of the Americas: Beyond the Search for Origins in the Study of Afro-Atlantic Religions* (Boston: Brill, 2008).

49. Zora Neale Hurston, "Ritualistic Expression from the Lips of the Communicants of the Seventh Day Church of God, Beaufort, South Carolina," March 20, 1940, box C5, folder 13, Papers of Margaret Mead, Library of Congress.

50. Hurston.

51. See, for example, "News of the Churches," *Chicago Defender*, July 12, 1919; "Church News: Triumph the Church and Kingdom of God in Christ," *Atlanta Daily World*, January 11, 1940; Elliott Ferguson, "'Store Front' Churches in Pittsburgh: God Fearing People Attend These Little Temples of Worship," *Pittsburgh Courier*, March 29, 1941.

52. Elmer T. Clark, *The Small Sects in America* (New York: Abingdon-Cokesbury, 1949), 129.

53. T. F. Murphy, ed., *Religious Bodies: 1936, Volume II, Part 2* (Washington, DC: United States Government Printing Office, 1941), 1274.

54. "Triumph the Church and Kingdom of God in Christ (Sanctified)," reel 9, Robert Tal-lant Papers.

55. White, *Rise to Respectability*, 93–94.

266   NOTES TO PAGES 195–197

56. Louisiana Historical Records Survey, Community Service Programs, Works Progress Administration, *Directory of Churches and Religious Organizations in New Orleans* (Department of Archives, Louisiana State University, 1941), 34.

57. "Triumph the Church," Robert Tallant Papers.

58. The pastor came from humble beginnings. Lucien Herbert Treadwell was born on February 1, 1874, in Fayetteville, North Carolina. In 1896, Lucien married Julia Lloyd, and just four years later, in 1900, they welcomed their first child, Lucy B. Treadwell, into the world. Working hard to support his family, Treadwell lived and worked as a driver in Wilmington, North Carolina, from 1902 to 1905. By 1909, city records note that Treadwell had become a preacher and was pastoring a "Sanctified church" back in Fayetteville, located at 246 Williams Street. That same year, his son Leroy Treadwell was born. Two years later, in 1911, the Treadwells welcomed their second daughter, Lillian, who was born on October 10 in Fayetteville. Storefront in nature, Treadwell relocated his "Holy Church" to 10 Simmons Avenue in Fayetteville in 1913, perhaps to be able to maintain a sustainable rent cost. (It is unsurprising that Treadwell's Holiness/Pentecostal ministry began in North Carolina, given its rich history of Black Holiness-Pentecostalism reaching back to the nineteenth century, as noted in Turner, "The United Holy Church of America."). A mechanic and driver by training, Treadwell tried to honor his call to the preaching ministry while earning a livable wage to support his growing family. In 1914, for instance, he listed his "Old Reliable Electric Shoe Shop" for sale in the *Fayetteville Index*, citing his reason for selling as "haven't time to devote to it" and signing, "Rev. L. H. Treadwell" (*Fayetteville Index*, September 16, 1914). Following the death of their infant son in 1915, the Treadwells moved to Memphis, where L. H. was introduced to Mason and COGIC (for discussion of Memphis, see White, *Rise to Respectability*, 97–98). By September 1918, the family moved to New Orleans, where they resided at 2022 Flood Street.

59. Treadwell, "Fanatic Cults," folder 91, FWP Papers.

60. Treadwell, "Fanatic Cults."

61. "Divine Healer Curing Lame," FWP Papers.

62. "Divine Healer Curing Lame."

63. The press and the LWP staff commonly misspelled his last name as "Felkus." I have chosen to use "Feltus" in accordance with the way the preacher recorded his own name on his World War I draft registration card. James was born in Centreville, Mississippi on June 4, 1884 (*U.S., World War II Draft Registration Cards, 1942*, Ancestry.com). In 1905, James married his wife, Lillie Packnett Feltus. The two welcomed thirteen children within twenty years—a son Alfred in 1909, another son Joseph in 1910, a daughter Lucinda in 1913, another son Ellion in 1915, a daughter Clara Mae in 1917, a son Julius in 1919, a daughter Lillie in 1919, a son James Feltus Jr. in 1921, and another daughter Ruth in 1925. The other four children's names are not listed in the census, but in James Feltus Jr.'s obituary, he says he had twelve siblings (*U.S., World War II Draft Registration Cards, 1942*, Ancestry.com; *1930 United States Federal Census*, Louisiana, New Orleans, Orleans, Enumeration District No. 36-174, Ancestry.com; *U.S., Social Security Applications and Claims Index, 1936–2007*, "Lillie Feltus Walker" SSN: 438981377, Ancestry

NOTES TO PAGES 197–203

.com; see obituary for "Bishop James Feltus, Jr." [1921–2016]). By 1930 and well into the 1940s, most of the Feltus children lived with their mother and father at the family home at 2619 S. Galvez Street in New Orleans along with a granddaughter, Elizabeth, who was born in 1932 (*1940 United States Federal Census*, Louisiana, New Orleans, Orleans, Enumeration District No. 36-315, Ancestry.com).

64. The *Times-Picayune*, however, reported on March 23, 1939, "Rev. James Feltus . . . said that five new churches had been established in the state during the year, bringing the total to 113, and that 500 new members had been added."

65. "Elder James Felkus [Feltus]," reel 9, Robert Tallant Papers.

66. "Elder James Felkus [Feltus]."

67. *Times-Picayune*, March 30, 1938; *Times-Picayune*, March 31, 1938; *Times-Picayune*, March 24, 1939.

68. "Elder James Felkus [Feltus]," Robert Tallant Papers.

69. "Institute Formed to Train Ministers," *Times-Picayune*, March 29, 1938.

70. Butler, *Women in the Church*, 69.

71. For a discussion of the theology and scriptural interpretation undergirding the politics of dress among women in Black Pentecostalism, see Sanders, *Saints in Exile*, 68–69; Deidre Helen Crumbley, "'Dressed as Becometh Holiness': Gender, Race, and the Body in a Storefront Sanctified Church," in *Spirit on the Move: Black Women and Pentecostalism in Africa and the Diaspora*, ed. Judith Casselberry and Elizabeth A. Pritchard (Durham, NC: Duke University Press, 2019), 89–105. For a discussion of unordained Black preaching women in Pentecostalism, see Wallace D. Best, "'The Spirit of the Holy Ghost Is a Male Spirit': African American Preaching Women and the Paradoxes of Gender," in *Women and Religion in the African Diaspora: Knowledge, Power, and Performance*, ed. Barbara D. Savage and R. Marie Griffith (Baltimore: John Hopkins University Press, 2006), 101–27.

72. Natanya Duncan, "The 'Efficient Womanhood' of the Universal Negro Improvement Association" (PhD diss., University of Florida, Gainesville, 2009), 125–60.

73. *Negro World*, March 9, 1929.

74. *Negro World*, April 27, 1929, 2; *Negro World*, April 26, 1930, 2.

75. Bair, "'Ethiopia Shall Stretch Forth,'" 41.

76. Casselberry, *Labor of Faith*.

77. *Negro World*, October 31, 1925.

78. *Negro World*, November 12, 1927.

79. *Negro World*, December 3, 1927.

80. Anthea D. Butler, "Women and Garveyism," in *Encyclopedia of Women and Religion in North America*, ed. Rosemary Skinner Keller, Rosemary Radford Ruether, and Marie Cantlon, vol. 3 (Indianapolis: Indiana University Press, 2006); Butler, *Women in the Church*.

81. "Elder James Felkus [Feltus]," Robert Tallant Papers.

82. Chireau, *Black Magic*, 59–89.

83. *Times-Picayune*, November 15, 1932, 22; *Atlanta Daily World*, November 19, 1932, 1, 3.

84. "Sanctified—Treadwell," folder 91, FWP Papers.

85. *Times-Picayune*, November 15, 1932, 22.

86. *Pittsburgh Courier*, September 14, 1940, 14.

87. *New Orleans, Louisiana, Death Records Index, 1804–1949, Orleans Death Indices 1937–1948*, vol. 222, p. 2690, Ancestry.com.

88. *Items-Tribune*, May 5, 1930, in "Black Billy Sunday," folder 91, FWP Papers; for McPherson's enlistment, see "Register of Enlistments in the U.S. Army, 1798–1914," National Archives Microfilm Publication M233, 81 rolls, Records of the Adjutant General's Office, 1780's–1917, Record Group 94, National Archives, Washington, DC.

89. Nicole Myers Turner, *Soul Liberty: The Evolution of Black Religious Politics in Postemancipation Virginia* (Chapel Hill: University of North Carolina Press, 2020), 105.

90. "Black Billy Sunday," folder 91, FWP Papers; "Black Billy Sunday," *Nashville Globe*, December 27, 1918.

91. There is a rich historiography in the study of Black gospel music on "crossover" as it relates to Black Baptists and Black Pentecostals. See Anthony Heilbut, *The Gospel Sound: Good News and Bad Times* (New York: Simon and Schuster, 1971); Teresa Reed, *The Holy Profane: Religion in Black Popular Music* (Lexington: University of Kentucky, 2003); Jerma Jackson, *Singing in My Soul: Black Gospel Music in a Secular Age* (Chapel Hill: University of North Carolina Press, 2004); Robert Darden, *People Get Ready!: A New History of Black Gospel Music* (New York: Continuum, 2004); Wallace D. Best, *Passionately Human, No Less Divine: Religion and Culture in Black Chicago, 1915–1952* (Princeton, NJ: Princeton University Press, 2005); Gayle Wald, *Shout, Sister, Shout!: The Untold Story of Rock-and-Roll Trailblazer Sister Rosetta Tharpe* (New York: Beacon, 2007); Mark Burford, *Mahalia Jackson and the Black Gospel Field* (New York: Oxford University Press, 2019). For more on the historical relationship between Black Pentecostalism and other Black Protestant denominations, especially Black Baptists and Methodists in the American South, see David Douglas Daniels, "The Cultural Renewal of Slave Religion: Charles Price Jones and the Emergence of the Holiness Movement in Mississippi" (PhD diss., Union Theological Seminary, 1992), 18–95.

92. *Monrovia Daily News*, July 21, 1916.

93. *Ogden*, July 12, 1917.

94. "Black Billy Sunday," *Nashville Globe*, December 27, 1918.

95. "Black Billy Sunday."

96. "'Prophet' Is Here," *Brooklyn Times Union*, September 16, 1933.

97. "Mississippi Blacks Get German Cash," *New Orleans States*, April 1, 1918.

98. "Denies Church Is Helping Germany," *New Orleans States*, April 2, 1918.

99. *Salt Lake Tribune*, July 10, 1917.

100. *Items-Tribune*, May 5, 1930, in "Black Billy Sunday," folder 91, FWP Papers.

101. *Items-Tribune*. McPherson, like many African American men, were drafted during the period, and many of them also drew upon their experiences in their theologizing and in their construction of Black masculinities in the late nineteenth and early twentieth centuries. For a rich discussion of this, see Albert George Miller, *Elevating the Race: Theophilus G. Steward, Black Theology, and the Making of an African American Civil Society, 1865–1924* (Knoxville: University of Tennessee Press, 2003), 119–39; Adriane Lentz-Smith, *Freedom Struggles: African Americans and World War I* (Cambridge, MA: Harvard University Press, 2009), 80–108. Lentz-Smith describes this process as "the

NOTES TO PAGES 205–210

making and the unmaking of black manhood," in which African American men relied upon Victorian ideals of men as providers and protectors and engaged in social and religious discourses to lay claim to manhood, citizenship, military service, and national belonging.

102. *Denver Star*, May 19, 1917.

103. *El Paso Herald*, August 11, 1917.

104. *Houston Post*, November 11, 1917.

105. *Austin American-Statesmen*, November 29, 1917.

106. *Houston Post*, October 26, 1917.

107. *Los Angeles Evening Express*, May 11, 1915; *Los Angeles Evening Express*, May 17, 1915.

108. *Denver Star*, May 19, 1917.

109. "Black Billy Sunday," folder 91, FWP Papers.

110. "Black Billy Sunday."

111. *Louisiana Weekly*, December 22, 1928, in "Black Billy Sunday," folder 91, FWP Papers.

112. Evelyn Brooks Higginbotham, *Righteous Discontent: The Women's Movement in the Black Baptist Church, 1880–1920* (Cambridge, MA: Harvard University Press, 1993), 44.

113. Giggie, *After Redemption*, 67.

114. Giggie, 67.

115. "Annual Grand Lodge Session, Improved Order B.P.O.E. of the World," folder 1, James Gordon McPherson Collection, 1926–1933, Amistad Research Center, Tulane University.

116. "Negro Health Conditions 'Worst Ever,'" *New Orleans Item*, August 27, 1927.

117. "Flag Ceremonies Planned Tuesday," 1931, James Gordon McPherson Collection.

118. "Black Billy Sunday," folder 91, FWP Papers.

119. Martin, *Preaching on Wax*, 63.

120. Martin, 73.

121. "J. Gordon McPherson," Paramount Records Discography, Mills Music Library Digital Collections, University of Wisconsin–Madison.

122. "Black Billy Sunday," folder 91, FWP Papers.

123. Weisenfeld has observed, "Connelly visited Bradford in New Orleans and spent the summer in black churches and 'barrelhouse dives' while reworking the first draft of the play. He recalled that he came away from that summer with a sense of some variety of theological orientation within what he called 'fundamentalist Negro churches,' 'indicating differences as definite as the deep water and the sprinkling forms of baptism.'" See Weisenfeld, *Hollywood Be Thy Name*, 58. See also "The Religious and Cultural Meaning of *The Green Pastures*" in Curtis J. Evans, *The Burden of Black Religion* (Oxford: Oxford University Press, 2008), 203–21.

124. "Negro Revivalist Heard Here Was 'De Lawd' Original," *Brooklyn Daily Eagle*, September 18, 1933.

125. "Black Billy Sunday," folder 91, FWP Papers.

126. "Black Billy Sunday."

127. *Pomona Progress Bulletin*, June 7, 1932, 2.

128. Weisenfeld, *Hollywood Be Thy Name*, 71.

129. Weisenfeld, 76.

130. Weisenfeld, 79.

131. Weisenfeld, 53.

132. *Santa Rosa Republican*, April 10, 1936.

133. "Outstanding Negro Evangelist Is Dead," *Bristol Herald Courier*, April 11, 1936, 8.

134. *Chattanooga Daily Times*, April 10, 1936, 13.

135. *Santa Rosa Republican*, April 10, 1936; *Times Dispatch*, April 10, 1936, 11. For more on the history of African Americans in the New Thought movement, see R. Marie Griffith, "Body Salvation: New Thought, Father Divine, and the Feast of Material Pleasures," *Religion and American Culture* 11, no. 2 (2001); Darnise C. Martin, *Beyond Christianity: African Americans in a New Thought Church* (New York: New York University Press, 2005).

136. "Spiritual Therapeutist" is used in an earlier section of the article, and "Therapeutist" is used as shorthand. See "An Estimate of the New Thought," *New-Church Review* 18, no. 2 (April 1911): 168.

137. Arlene M. Sánchez-Walsh, *Pentecostals in America* (New York: Columbia University Press, 2018), 103.

138. "Mother Brown," 1–2.

139. Romans 12:2 (KJV).

CODA

1. Louie Robinson, "The Kingdom of King Narcisse," *Ebony*, July 1963, 115–16.

2. Martha C. Taylor, *From Labor to Reward: Black Church Beginnings in San Francisco, Oakland, Berkeley, and Richmond, 1849–1972* (Eugene, OR: Wipf & Stock, 2016), 126.

3. Alan Young, *Woke Me Up This Morning: Black Gospel Singers and the Gospel Life* (Jackson: University Press of Mississippi, 1997), 196; Mark Burford, *Mahalia Jackson and the Black Gospel Field* (New York: Oxford University Press, 2019), 33–97.

4. Johari Jabir, "On Conjuring Mahalia: Mahalia Jackson, New Orleans, and the Sanctified Swing," *American Quarterly* 61, no. 3 (2009): 649–69.

5. Oakland, California, City Directory, 1951, *U.S., City Directories, 1822–1995*, Ancestry .com.

6. Taylor, *From Labor to Reward*, 92.

7. Taylor, 122, 126.

8. Robinson, "Kingdom of King Narcisse," 114.

9. Robinson, 112.

10. "Narcisse Displays Vocal Prowess," *Oakland Tribune*, August 20, 1962, 10; Robinson, "Kingdom of King Narcisse"; Tim Retzloff, "'Seer or Queer?': Postwar Fascination with Detroit's Prophet Jones," *GLQ: A Journal of Lesbian and Gay Studies* 8, no. 3 (2002): 271–96.

11. Robinson, "Kingdom of King Narcisse," 116.

12. Taylor, *From Labor to Reward*, 126. In "Black Church Rumor: Sexual Violence and Black (Gay) Gospel's Rev. James Cleveland," *GLQ: A Journal of Lesbian and Gay Studies* 28,

no. 1 (2022): 115–44, I discuss the Hawkins Brothers and rumors about queerness in African American religious life and culture using rumors that also circulated around the Rev. James Cleveland.

13. Robinson, "Kingdom of King Narcisse," 115.

14. "Narcisse Displays Vocal Prowess," 10.

15. Opal Louis Nations, "'It's So Nice to Be Nice': The Story of 'His Grace' King Louis H. Narcisse," http://www.opalnations.com/files/King_Louis_Narcisse_Blues_Rhythm _150_June-July_2000.pdf.

16. *Oakland Tribune*, May 1, 1962, 1.

17. "Gifts for Needy of New Orleans," *Oakland Tribune*, December 20, 1965, 20.

18. See forthcoming work by Cori Tucker-Price examining Black religion in California during the era of the Great Migration.

19. Robinson, "Kingdom of King Narcisse," 114.

20. *Oakland Tribune*, March 30, 1952, 30.

21. Robinson, "Kingdom of King Narcisse," 118.

22. Robinson, 114.

INDEX

Page numbers in italics refer to figures.

abuse, 91, 93, 113, 184

African identities: Afro-Creole, 10, 17, 32–49, 53–54, 80, 96, 99, 120; West African, 10, 55. *See also* Black Israelites; Blackness; Caribbean; *and other nations of the African diaspora*

African Methodist Episcopal Church, 21–22, 60, 80, 156, 158; Duarte AME Church, 204; Union Chapel AME Church, 90

African Methodist Episcopal Zion Church, 21

African Orthodox Church (AOC), 156, 165

African Universal Church, 170–71

Afropessimism, 14–15

agnosticism, 95–96

Albert, Father, 122

alcohol, 5, 31, 35, 45, 114–15, 121, 128, 143, 194

Allen, Richard, 60

altars, 29, 31, 40, 87, 123, 128, 133, 162, 166, 179, 200, 202

American Folklore Society (AFS), 33, 48–52; Louisiana Association of the American Folklore Society, 33, 47–48, 51–55

ancestors: African, 102; archival, 2, 6; and Carnival, 5; communication with, 4, 7, 12, 28, 31; knowledges, 25, 127; Lucumí, 125; and religion, 20; and slavery, 10, 15; veneration of, 7, 12, 35; white, 64, 78, 113; wisdom, 38

Anderson, Leafy, 93–95, 103, 126

Anderson, Thomas W., 155, 168–69

Anglican Catholic Church, 164

Anglican High Church, 3, 165, 177, 191

Antoine, Albert Leon (Abaline Antoine), 59–63, 71–74, 82. *See also* Council of God (COG)

archives: of Hurston, 2–3; and innovation, 20–21; institutional, 12; police records, 14, 25, 26, 120–21; and underworld work, 4, 6, 10–13, 24, 27; violence of, 25–26

Asia, 10

Augustin, Marie, 51

baptisms, 8, 130, 194, 201

Baptist groups: Bapticostals, 204; and Moriath Butler, 144–45; and class, 79, 82; and club women, 112; and COG, 72, 81; and COGIC, 197, 201; Colored Baptist Ministers' Conference, 80; Emperor Haile Selassie NuWay Ethiopia Mystic Light Baptist and Spiritual and Kingdom Church, 129, 134–35, 140; Fifth African Baptist Church, 158; First Baptist Church of Hansboro, 208; First Baptist Church of New Orleans, 81; Guadalupe College, 204; Hebrew-Baptist congregation, 72; Israelite Baptist Church, 143; London Baptist Missionary Society, 50; Mount Zion Baptist Church, 214; and Narcisse, 214; National Baptist Convention (NBC), 110, 204; and Pentecostals, 189–93, 206–7; Pleasant Zion Missionary Baptist, 158; Providence

274 INDEX

Baptist groups (*continued*)
    Baptist Church, 214; and Reconstruc-
    tion, 32; Samuel Israelite Baptist Church,
    158; and Seals, 94, 112, 114; Southern
    Baptists, 130; Spiritual Baptists, 60; St.
    John's Baptist Church, 167; Tulane Baptist
    Church, 157; and UNIA, 153–60, 163–65,
    169, 189–96
Barbados, 149, 155
Barber, J. D., 186, 189–95, 200, 211
Bedou, Arthur, 96–99, 107–8, *109*, *154*
Behrman, Martin, 62–63
Bethune, Mary McLeod, 82
Beugnot, Aimée, 51
Bible: and Black Atlantic religions, 61, 212; and
    COG, 61, 64–67, 71; and COGIC, 198, 200;
    colleges, 185; Exodus, 13; and fundamen-
    talism, 43; and *The Green Pastures*, 210–11;
    Hebrew, 64–67, 72, 138; and informant
    864, 126; and Long, 135; and Lyons, 138,
    140; and McPherson, 209; New Testa-
    ment, 43, 67, 111, 138, 177; Old Testament,
    140, 210; and Seals, 98, 106; and Treadwell,
    196; and UNIA, 152, 156–57; and white
    supremacy, 76
Black Atlantic religions: and the Bible, 61, 212;
    and class, 4, 167, 184; commodification of,
    8, 24, 44, 212; defined, 18–20; demonized,
    7, 17, 20–21, 40, 65, 70, 92, 103, 113, 115, 152,
    186, 195; differentiation in, 19–20; as dirty,
    132; and faith healing, 110, 115–16, 213, 218;
    hypersexualization of, 32–39, 42, 71–74, 85,
    100, 102, 218; and Jim Crow, 3, 18, 20, 22–
    23, 27, 43; and lynching, 6, 8, 10, 24, 27–28,
    56, 123, 218; as mysterious fetish worship,
    54; policing of, 6–8, 14, 17–18, 20–28, 213,
    218; and queerness, 10, 24, 27; in relation
    to African American religions, 15–16;
    and ritual, 6, 8, 18, 23, 29. *See also specific*
    religions and organizations
Black Israelites, 27, 61–62, 67
Black Methodist Episcopal Church, 168
Blackness: anti-Blackness, 4–10, 14–15, 25, 65,
    110, 128, 152–53, 188, 212–13, 218; Black
    God, 155, 172–76; Black gods, 218; and

    nationalism, 62, 64, 67, 130, 152, 156–59,
    165, 167, 171–73, 177, 186–89, 193–95, 200,
    212, 214; pathologization of Black people,
    4, 115; policing of Black Atlantic religions,
    21–22, 70, 81–82, 122–23; and separatism,
    61, 78, 188; and suffering, 9, 13
Black Spiritual churches, 93, 182–86, 198;
    Guiding Star Spiritual Church, 103
Boas, Franz, 2
bootleggers, 4, 6, 128
Botkin, Benjamin A., 54–55
Boyd, Ferdinand (Prophet Joel), 64
Boyd, Henry (Father Abraham), 64
Boyd, Lottie (Sister Rhodia), 64
Bradford, Roark, 209–10
Breaux, Hazel, 181–83
British Guiana, 158
Britton, Felix H., 151
Brown, E. A., 158
Brown, L., 169
· Brown, Marie, 46–47
Brown, Mother, 181–84, 198, 207, 211–12
Buddha, 96
Buel, James W., 43–44
Burrell, J. L., 169
Burroughs, Nannie Helen, 111
Butler, Henrietta, 13–14
Butler, Moriath, 142–45
Butler, Paul, 143, 145

Cable, George Washington, 33, 40–49, 52–53;
    "Creole Slave Songs," 40–41, *41*, 45–46,
    46, 49–50
Cambias, Robert J., 75–79, 84
candles, 2, 29, 31, 45, 126, 128, 166, 182
cards, 17–18, 181
Caribbean: and colorist politics, 79; missions
    to, 205; and race in New Orleans, 10; and
    religion, 15–17, 22, 35, 61, 77, 129; sexualiza-
    tion of, 38; and sex work, 122; and UNIA,
    151–52, 156–58, 167, 177
Carnival, 5, 35
Castellanos, Henry C., 37–38
Cazanavette, Lionel L., 172
cemeteries, 11–13, 53, 101, 211

INDEX   275

Central America, 22, 63, 122, 151, 157, 171

ceremonies. *See* rituals

chants, 31, 155, 163, 193

Charbonnet, Loys, 169

charisma, 63, 163–66, 206, 209–10

Chatters, Aaron A. B., 208

Christ Hebrew Church, 72

Christian, Marcus, 8, 21–22, 135

Christianity: Christianization, 15, 32, 46, 59, 62, 113, 179; church mothers, 20, 183, 186–87, 196, 198, 218; and non-Christian Black Atlantic religions, 14, 17–22, 27, 32, 36, 39, 43, 54, 59, 61, 65, 69, 74, 79–80, 85, 92, 101, 112–13, 119, 213; orthodoxy, 60, 81, 93; and quasi-Christian Black Atlantic religions, 14, 17–19, 22, 27, 59, 61, 69, 85, 92, 101, 112–13, 119–20, 213

Christian Jewish Church, 72

Christian Science, 131

Christ's Council, 72

Church of God in Christ (COGIC): and Black Pentecostals, 185–88, 192; divisions within, 193–95; and dress, 195–202; Holy Convocation, 201–2; and LWP, 182–84; and naming, 184. *See also* Barber, J. D.; Mason, Charles H.

Church of God in Christ of Faith Tabernacle, 181, 183, 203–4

Civil War, 48, 111

clairvoyants, 18, 36, 60

clapping, 31, 163, 215, 217

Clark, Elmer T., 194

Clarke, Edward, 167

class: and COG, 61, 63, 70; and COGIC, 194–95; and fraternal orders, 208; and interracial politics, 100; middle, 23, 72, 82, 90, 92, 107, 110–14, 164, 166, 195, 206; and Pentecostalism, 21, 211–12; planter, 43–44, 49; and racialization, 101; and UNIA, 167, 173; upper, 156; working, 23, 70–72, 79–80, 92, 96, 101, 106, 110, 113, 114, 146, 150–51, 215. *See also* sex: and Victorianism

Clinton, Phillip, 155

coffee, 87, 128, 194

COG. *See* Council of God (COG)

COGIC. *See* Church of God in Christ (COGIC)

Coleman, Jerry, 119

Collins, Madame, 4

Colored Methodist Episcopal, 21, 80

Colored Ministers' Alliance, 169

Congo, 45

Congo Square, 27, 32, 46, 52–53, 56, 59

Congregational Church, 21, 80–81

conjuring, Conjure: and Black Atlantic religions, 2, 4, 18, 22, 52, 92, 120; and Black slums, 122; and COG, 69; and COGIC, 185–86, 202, 207; and Haiti, 50; and healing, 55; as "highest development," 17; Hurston on, 2; and informant 864, 126–27; as knowledge making, 20; and Narcisse, 214; and Pentecostals, 185, 210; and respectability politics, 27, 112; and Seals, 98, 101; and sex, 113, 115, 124, 126; and underworld work, 6–7, 28, 218; and UNIA, 153, 166; and wake work, 13

Connelly, Marc, 209–11

Cooper, Anna Julia, 82

Coptic Christianity, 130

Council of God (COG): in Algiers, 61, 63; alternative names for, 72; creed, 65–72; demonized, 75, 81, 84; feast days, 62; listed as Baptist, 72; and LWP, 69–74; and police, 79–85; as queer, 61–69; religio-racial self-fashioning, 129; temple, 76. *See also* Antoine, Albert Leon (Abaline Antoine); Cambias, Robert J.

Crawley, Daniel J., 5

creeds, 17, 32, 65–72, 94, 135, 197

Creelman, James, 99

creoles: "Creole Slave Songs," 40–41, *41*, 45–46, *46*, 49–50; creolization, 10, 61

Cuba, 16, 205–6

Culin, Stewart, 50

cult(s): Black policing of, 82; COG as, 61, 76–77, 81, 83; Negro, 16, 18, 21, 24, 70, 91, 100, 131, 159, 173, 206; and reform, 27; Sanctified Church as, 182, 196; sex, 71, 141; and underworld work, 3, 16, 21–22, 93, 167

Daddy Grace, 165, 174, 215

dancing: Africana, 7, 31–32, 59; *bamboula*, 31, 91; calinda, 31; carabiné, 31; and COG, 63; and COGIC, 202; congo, 31; and Hoodoo, 117; and jazz, 160–63; juba, 31; and Narcisse, 217; and Pentecostalism, 202, 209; and queer relationships, 134; ring shout, 31, 59; and Sanctified Church, 182; and UNIA, 171; and Voudou, 35, 39–41, 46–47, 52, 89

Daniels, Beulah (Saint Mary), 140

Davis, Samuel E. (High Priest Aaron), 64, 75

de Mena, Madame Maymie Leona Turpeau, 154, 172–76

Dent, Thomas, 27

devils: and COG teachings, 60, 64–67; and discourse on COG, 73, 75, 81, 84; and discourse on Voudou, 35, 43, 46, 53–54; and jazz, 162; and Pentecostalism, 211; white, 60, 64–67, 160; worship of, 185

Devore, G. H. J., 169

diabolical, the, 10, 28, 38, 54, 73, 81

Dillard History Unit. *See* Louisiana Writers' Project (LWP)

Dillon, Catherine, 69–84, 94; and anti-Voudou sentiment, 56, 81–84; and Cambias, 75–78; and COG, 61, 64–65, 69–74; as Irish Catholic, 61; and Seals, 94; and tourism, 54

disability, 93, 184, 197

dress: and class, 105, 110; politics of, 182, 185, 195–200, 212; religious, 96

drugs, 115, 121, 128, 207

drums, 31, 46, 50, 59, 89, 91, 117, 182

Du Bois, W. E. B., 11–13, 42–43, 82, 101, 115, 150, 157, 206

Duncan, S. A., 169

Duncanson, J. A., 151

Dunlap, Ethel Trew, 189–90

Duvernet, Roland, 8–10

Dyer, Constantine, 169

Eason, James Walker Hood, 163, 167–71, 177

Edwards, C. V., 81

electricity, 136–38

Emperor Haile Selassie NuWay Ethiopia Mystic Light Baptist and Spiritual and Kingdom Church, 129, 134–35, 140

English language, 36, 47–48, 79, 164

Episcopalianism, 124, 190

Ethiopia, 16, 129, 143, 151, 156, 176, 186–93

Ethiopianism, 20, 130, 132, 146, 156, 186–89, 193; and Abyssinia, 189–93

ethnography, 1–3, 12–13, 33–34, 42, 50–55, 68, 96, 101, 124, 136; salvage, 12, 27, 34, 40, 44, 53–55

Europe, 10–11, 25, 35, 49, 55, 63, 84, 92, 165, 174

exorcism, 34, 43–44, 44, 46. *See also* spirit possession

fanaticism, 3, 19, 21, 72–77, 80–83, 138, 206, 212, 218

Father Divine, 130, 136–38, 141, 154, 165, 172–76, 184, 211, 215

Federal Bureau of Investigation (FBI), 81, 164

Feltus, Henry, 197

Feltus, James, Sr., 186, 195–202, 211

Fletcher, Rebecca, 14

Flower, Walter Chew, 18, 100

folklore: *Journal of American Folklore*, 12–13, 23; and queerness, 125; and tourism, 52–55; and Voudou, 27, 33–35, 47–52; white, 33, 51, 54. *See also individual folklorists*

Ford, Arnold Josiah, 155

Fortier, Alcée, 47–52

Fortier, Louise, 51

fortune tellers, 6, 17–18, 24, 36, 117, 181

Frampton, P. P., 169

France, 5, 10, 36, 47, 78–79, 120, 136, 190

fraternal orders, 149, 160, 207–8

Frazier, E. Franklin, 16, 150

freaks, 10, 95, 103, 124, 126, 186

Freedman's Bureau, 32

freedom, 7–8, 13–14, 48, 61–62; of religion, 122, 145, 218

Froude, J. A., 48–49

fundamentalism, 43, 60, 79

gambling, 4, 6, 115, 120–21, 145, 151, 209

Gammon, R. E., 50

INDEX

Gant, Samuel, 158

Garvey, Marcus Mosiah: on Africa for the Africans, 176–77; and Barber, 189–94; and British West Indies, 151; and de Mena, 175–77; deported, 162, 171–72, 200; and Eason's murder, 167–69; and Ethiopia, 156; and Father Divine, 173–75; Hurston on, 147; at International Religious Congress of Triumph, 189, *190*; and jazz, 161–67; and Kofey, 170–71; at Protestant churches, 157–58; and Elias Smith, 188–89; and transnationalism, 186; and women, 170–72. *See also* Universal Negro Improvement Association (UNIA); Universal Negro Improvement Association's New Orleans Division (NOD)

Gaspar, Joseph (Prophet Amos), 64

Geddes, Joseph, 208

gender: and class, 107–8, 114–15; and criminalization, 134; and Father Divine, 141, 174; and fraternal orders, 208; intersex, 124, 128; and Jim Crow, 34; mutability, 126; nonbinary, 124–29; nonconforming, 24, 27, 115, 122, 125–28; queer-gendered performance, 215; and reform movements, 27; roles, 141; and Sanctified Church, 212; and theological education, 204; ungendering, 38; and Voudou, 38–39

Germany, 143, 217

Grace, Charles Manuel (Daddy Grace), 165, 174, 215

Granderson, J. A., 169

Graves, Mamie (Sister Eve), 64

Great Britain, 113, 190

Great Depression, 25, 116, 134–35, 138, 141, 145, 207, 212

Great Migration, 16, 62, 166–67, 213

Green Pastures, The (Connelly), 209–11

Griffin, Bessie, 214

hair, 96, 98, 119, 126, 150, 155–56, 182, 198

Haiti: and *bamboula*, 31, 91; Baptist Missionary Society in, 50; Code Pénal, 32; Haitian Revolution, 32; Hurston on, 1, 29; Narcisse from, 213; refugees from, 32; and UNIA,

156; United States Minister Resident to Haiti, 50; and Voudou, 29, 32, 35, 40, 48–50, 96

Hampton Normal and Agricultural Institute, 102, 125–26

Hawkins Brothers, 215

healing: and Black Atlantic religions, 110, 115–16, 213, 218; and Black slums, 122, 128–29; and Moriath Butler, 142–43; and COGIC, 184–85; and Father Divine, 138, 173; and Garvey, 165; and Horn, 142; and informant 864, 126; and laying on of hands, 28, 94–96, 181; and Lyons, 119–20, 129–33, 139–40; magic, 196–97; and Narcisse, 214–17; and politics of dress, 195–203; and "quacks," 202; and Sanctified Church, 181; and Seals, 5, 91–103, 106, 115; and Spiritualist churches, 183; as underworld work, 6–7, 19–20, 28; and UNIA, 167; and Voudou, 43–45; and Watch Tower Worldwide Intercessory Prayer Healing Movement, 186, 204–11

Henry, Cammie, 54–55

herbs, 8, 29, 55, 120, 128, 166, 207, 213–14

Herron, Leonora, 126

heteropatriarchy, 96, 98, 107

heterosexuality, 3, 111–15, 133–34, 218

Hinduism, 27, 61, 64, 129, 146

Holiness movement, 164, 166, 188, 194, 197, 208

Holiness-Pentecostal movement, 61, 166, 187–88, 197–98

Holy Ghost, 141, 162, 181, 182, 185, 194, 204–7

Honore, Edward (Chief Butler), 64–65, 73–76, 83–84

Honore, Marie (Mother Superior), 64, 75–76

Hoodoo: and Black Atlantic religions, 17–22, 92, 122; called Voudou, 41; and criminalization, 119–23; and dance, 46; doctors, 2, 24, 55, 77, 117–20, 126; and healing, 214; "Hindu weed" in, 4; Hurston and, 12, 17, 29, 87, 95, 117, 179; Jesus Christ as "Biggest Hoodoo," 181, 185; and New Orleans, 1–2, 22–28; and Pentecostals, 183, 185, 196, 199, 202–3, 206; practice, 4, 20, 27, 125–28, 183,

Hoodoo (*continued*)

185, 203, 206, 212, 214; and respectability politics, 115, 203; and Roman Catholicism, 6, 24, 127, 185; and sex work, 124–29; and underworld work, 6; and UNIA, 166. *See also* informant 864; Sanctified Church

Horn, Dora (Saint Mary 2), 140, 142

Horn, Jeff, 140–42, 145; Jeff Horn Spiritual Catholic Church, 140

hospitals, 76, 172, 200, 203, 205

Hubb, A., 169

Hughes, Langston, 2, 118

Hunter, Charlie, 143

Hurston, Zora Neale: as agnostic, 95–96; call for Black cemetery, 11–13; as daughter of Baptist preacher, 1; and Eatonville, 1, 13; as ethnographer, 1–3, 12, 55, 59, 69, 96, 101, 123; five psychic experiences of, 2; on Garvey, 147; and Hoodoo, 17, 23–24, 27, 117; in *Journal of American Folklore*, 12–13, 23; on lynching, 57; and method, 1–3, 218; and Pentecostals, 193; and salts, 87–88, 95, 108; and Sanctified Church, 179; and Seals, 95–98, 101, 103, 106, 108, 112, 114; as underworld worker, *xii*, 3–6, 12, 27; on "Voodoo," 29

Hyatt, Harry Middleton, 3–6, 19, 119, 124, 126, 128, 181

immigration, 25, 34, 63, 84, 92, 156–58, 167, 169

India, 129

indigeneity, 15–16, 34–35, 51, 93, 102

informant 864, 124–29, 145

International Convention of the Negro Races of the World, 161

intersex people, 124, 128

Isaiah, Brother, 93, 95, 184

Islam, 96, 174, 186

Italy, 128, 130, 143

Jackson, Charles W., 159

Jackson, Mahalia, 214

Jamaica, 16, 151, 164, 169, 176

Japan, 190

jazz, 103, 113, 127, 153–54, 160–67, 177

Jewish people, 17, 23, 72, 92; and anti-Semitism, 63; Black Jews, 62, 66, 70, 74, 84; and Hebrew Bible, 64–67, 138; and Hebrews, 62–63, 68; and Judaism, 20, 62–63, 67

Jim Crow: and Black Atlantic religions, 3, 18, 20, 22–23, 27, 43; Black Codes, 33; and class, 82, 102, 108; and COG, 61; and colonialism, 130; and Father Divine, 173; and fraternal orders, 208; grammars, 10, 43, 124; laws, 18, 139; and LWP, 24–25, 55, 84, 145; and Lyons, 130–31, 135, 139; and Methodism, 60; modernity, 10–11, 15, 23, 34, 47, 54, 120, 126; and Pentecostals, 187, 212; segregation, 6, 20, 60–61, 67, 82, 90, 131; and sex work, 123–24, 127–28; surveillance, 68; and survival, 69; and underworld, 4–15; and UNIA, 151, 155; and Victorianism, 96. *See also* lynching; terrorism

Johnson, Adrian, 149–50, 161

Johnson, Elder, 197

Johnson, John, 77–78

Johnston, Frank E., 83–84

Joiner, Arch, 77–78

Jones, J. W., 163

Jones, Lillie A., 176–77

Jones, Prophet, 215

Jones, Robert Elijah, 168

Joseph, Henrietta (Madame Joseph), 127, 129

Kofey, Laura Adorkor (Laura Champion), 170–71, 177

Ku Klux Klan, 8, 64, 77, 168, 187

Lamar, Aurora (Obá Tolá, Ibae), 125

Latimore, Daniel (Apostle Paul), 64

Laveau, Marie, 2, 40–41, 46, 53, 98

Lee, R. H., 203

Lee, Tom, 120

LeGallais, Mrs. G., 104

Lemelle, 131–32, 135–40

Lévi, Eliphas, 136

Liberia, 156

Little Richard, 215

Llopis, A. J., 208

Long, Huey P., 135

lotteries, 145

Louisiana Writers' Project (LWP): and Black Atlantic religions, 22–25, 213; and Moriath Butler, 142, 145; and COG, 61, 69–74, 83–84; and COGIC, 182–85, 195–98, 201–3; documenting white violence, 8; and faith healing, 195; and Father Divine, 130, 138; *Gumbo Ya-Ya*, 8–9, *9*, 162; and Lyons, 131–32, 135, 138–42; and McPherson, 206, 209; *The Negro in Louisiana*, 21, 135; as part of WPA, 24; and police records, 14, 26; and Reconstruction, 32; and Sanctified Church, 181; and Seals, 91, 94, 97, 104; and Triumph Church, 194–95; and UNIA, 159, 162; and Voudou, 46, 54–55. *See also individual workers*

Lucumí, 125

lynching: antilynching activism, 102; and Black Atlantic religions, 6, 8, 10, 24, 27–28, 56, 123, 218; of COG members, 61, 70, 73, 76–78, 83–84; Hurston on, 57; and Italian Army in Ethiopia, 130; and Pentecostals, 187; UNIA against, 155; and Voudou, 45–46; and white Christianity, 21

Lyons, Joseph Rajah: conception of church, 136; and faith healing, 119–20, 129–33, 138–40; and police surveillance, 142; and sex politics, 129–39, 145, 215

Madagascar, 161

magic, 6, 55, 95, 136, 196–97

Major, David (Prophet Melanchia), 64, 76

Manson, Thomas (Apostle Peter), 64

maps, 8–10, 13

Mardi Gras: festival, 162; Indians, 35, 154

marriage, 38, 71, 111, 115, 140–45, 184; and non-monogamy, 141–42; and polygamy, 71, 141

Mason, Charles H., 185–88, 197–98, 203, 205, 207

Masonry, 136, 207–10

McCarthy, Joseph R., 139

McGuire, George Alexander, 165

McInnis, Eliza Holland, 198, *199*

McKinney, Robert, 17, 20, 24, 119, 131–32, 135–45

McNairdee-Moore, Madam, 60

McPherson, James Gordon, 186, 203–11

McWaters, George, 158

Mediterranean, 10

mediums, 18, 27, 36

Melden, Charles M., 23

Methodism: and Antoine, 59–61, 72; and *Christian Advocate*, 102, 168, 173; and class, 79–80; and COG, 59–61, 72, 79–82; and COGIC, 193, 197; and Pentecostals, 188, 204; and Reconstruction, 32; and Seals, 114; and UNIA, 155, 160. *See also specific denominations*

Michaux, Lightfoot Solomon, 81, 163–65

missionaries, 49–50, 60, 68, 83, 102, 113, 186, 195, 198, 203, 205, 212

Mitchell, W. H., 208

modernity, 19, 34, 47–48, 102, 107, 130, 136, 166, 185, 209; Jim Crow, 10–11, 15, 23, 34, 47, 54, 120, 126

Mohammed (founder of Islam), 96

Mohammed Ally Christian Catholic Church, 130

Moorish Science Temple, 174

morality, 23, 82, 91–92, 102, 106–7, 111–15, 119, 195, 206, 208–9

Morgan, J. S., 169

Morris, Althea, 17–20, 24

mothers: church, 20, 183, 186–87, 196, 198, 218; unwed, 89, 112

Mount Zion Baptist Church, 214

Mount Zion Spiritual Temple, 214, *217*

murder, 13, 74–78, 84, 102, 113, 120, 154, 167–71, 177

music: and Black churches, 206–7; classical, 165; "Creole Slave Songs," 40–41, *41*, 45–46, *46*, 49–50; hymns, 8, 151, 155, 161, 203; and Narcisse, 214–16; Negro spirituals, *9*, 132, 143, 209–10; singing, 44, 64, 89, 91, 103, 114, 143, 155, 159–65, 187, 203–6, 214–17; songs, 39, 134, 179, 193, 204, 206, 209,

music (*continued*)
217; and UNIA, 155, 163; and Voudou, 41, 46. *See also* jazz
mystics, 7, 28–29, 39, 122, 144

Narcisse, King Louis Herbert, 213–18
National Association for the Advancement of Colored People (NAACP), 152, 157
National Association of Colored Women (NACW), 92, 110–15
National Council for the Fair Employment Practice Committee (FEPC), 139
National Urban League (NUL), 107–10
Nation of Islam, 174
Native Americans, 10, 34, 93, 197; Mardi Gras Indians, 35, 154
Negro spirituals, 9, 132, 143, 209–10
Newell, William Wells, 33, 48–52
New Orleans Division. *See* Universal Negro Improvement Association's New Orleans Division (NOD)
new religious movements, 27, 62, 70–72, 94, 133, 141, 165, 184. *See also specific groups*
New Thought, 20, 27, 61, 64, 146, 174, 211
Nicaragua, 16, 150–51, 158
numerologists, 6

oils, 28–29, 75, 97, 166, 181, 215; castor, 92, 95; snake, 119

paganism, 2, 29, 102, 123, 179
Pan-Africanism, 20, 146, 153, 156
Pentecostalism: and Azusa Street Revival, 187–88, 206; Bapticostals, 204; and charisma, 63, 166; diversity within Black, 185–86, 212; early history of in New Orleans, 187–88; and faith healings, 202, 209; Holiness-Pentecostals, 61, 166, 187–88, 197–98; Holy Rollers, 21, 94, 155, 181, 191, 206, 215; and jazz, 153, 163, 166; as patriotic, 186, 203–11; and Sanctified Church, 182–83, 212; and sensory experiences, 28; and UNIA, 155, 160, 188–94; and women, 198–200. *See also* Church of God in Christ (COGIC); McPherson, James Gordon

Perkins, I. E., 169
Peters, J. J., 158–59
Peters, Mother, 187
phonograph, 34, 162, 209
Phyllis Wheatley Club, 92, 110
Pierre, Jacques (Prophet Ezekiel), 64, 83–84
Plessy v. Ferguson, 33, 36, 61
police: and Black Atlantic religions, 6–8, 14, 17–18, 20–28, 213, 218; Black Protestant collusion with, 79–85, 163–65; characterizing Black people as dangerous, 120; and COG, 60–61, 65, 69–80; and COGIC, 195, 199, 203; and faith healing, 119–20; protection from interference of, 14, 60; records, 3, 14, 25, 26, 120–21; and respectability, 100, 114–16; and Seals, 89, 92; and sex, 122–23; and sex work, 124, 132, 135, 138, 142, 145; and UNIA, 149, 151; and Voudou, 32–34, 39–42, 54, 59. *See also* Cambias, Robert J.
pornography, 12, 121, 132–35
Portugal, 10, 36
Posey, Zoe, 14, 46
poverty, 1, 6, 65, 67, 85, 103, 115, 120, 128, 135, 187
Presbyterians, 80–81
primitivism, 32, 34, 102, 179
prison: avoidance of, 20, 47, 123; and Cambias's murder, 76; and class, 114; and COG, 68–69, 71, 75–76, 81, 84; and faith healers, 120–21; Garvey in, 170–71; and Hoodoo, 119, 124; and policing, 8, 145
Protestantism: Afro-Protestantism, 43, 151–53, 166, 171; Anglo-Protestantism, 64, 70, 187; mainline, 80, 89, 146, 152, 155, 158, 163, 166, 169
pulpits, 3, 158–59, 167–70

queerness: of being "worked up," 132–34; and Black Atlantic religions, 10, 24, 27; and COG, 61–69, 71, 74; cross dressing, 124–26; on down low (DL), 134–35; and faith healers, 120, 218; homosexuality, 133–34, 215; and informant 864, 124–28; and Jamèt people, 5; and jazz, 163; and Lyons, 134–35,

INDEX

139; and Narcisse, 215; and police records, 120–21; and Seals, 112; and sex, 123–24; and sex work, 5, 27; and underworld, 3; and Voudou, 42, 53. *See also specific queer individuals*

race making: and COG, 64; white, 7, 21, 28, 32, 35–40, 48, 62, 65, 70, 76, 84, 111, 113–16

radio, 135–36, 160–63, 214

Randall, Sarah (Mother Seriah), 64

Randolph, A. Philip, 139

Randolph, Joseph, 202–3

Rastafarianism, 136

Razaf, Andy "Razz," 161

Reason, Mamie, 150, 168

Reconstruction, 13, 32, 34, 48, 82

reform, 27, 91–92, 96, 99–105, 108–16

religion: Black Atlantic religions, 1, 3, 5, 18–22, 25, 28, 100, 218; and Moriath Butler, 144–45; COG, 60–61, 64, 70, 73, 79; COGIC, 199; and informant 864, 126; and Lyons, 132–33, 136–40; and Narcisse, 213–16; Sanctified Church, 185–86, 207–12; and Seals, 94, 106, 112; and sex, 123; in slavery and unfreedom, 7–15, 32–33, 50, 60; and UNIA, 151–54, 168, 171, 174; and women, 105

religio-racial identity, 62, 64, 129, 139

Rightor, Henry, 35

rituals: and birthing, 110; and Black Atlantic religions, 6, 8, 18, 23, 29; and COG, 61–64, 77; and COGIC, 184; criminalized, 18; and fiction, 117; funerary, 74; healing, 28; and Hoodoo, 117, 124; and informant 864, 126–28; to keep police away, 14; and lynching, 84; and Lyons, 135–36; and Narcisse, 214; as "orgies," 32; and Pentecostalism, 193, 204; policing, 8; Roman Catholic, 95, 132, 215; and Seals, 89–90, 95; and sex, 123; Spiritualist, 105, 132; and UNIA, 151, 155, 168, 177; *Universal Negro Ritual* and *Universal Negro Catechism*, 152, 165; and Voudou, 2, 8, 27–28, 31–45, 48–49, 53–54, 59, 74, 89–90, 142; white ritual violence, 8–9; as work, 6; Yorùbá, 136

Robertson, Alaida (Henry), 150, 158

Robertson, Sylvester V., 155

Roman Catholicism: and anti-Catholicism, 64, 82; Blessed Sacrament Catholic Church, 110; and COG, 64; and creeds, 197; and Europeans, 92; and Garvey, 164–65; and government leaders, 17–18; and Haitian Revolution, 32; and Hoodoo, 6, 24; Irish Catholicism, 61, 64; and Long, 135; and Lyons, 136; and Narcisse, 214, 216; nuns, 182; and oil, 29; and policing of Black Atlantic religions, 21–22, 70, 81–82, 122–23; popes, 62, 191; priests, 83, 122, 182–83; and racial hierarchy, 18; rituals, 215; Saint Joseph's Day, 162; saints, 2, 29, 127, 132; and Seals, 93, 95; and sex, 133; St. Teresa's Colored Catholic Church, 122; and UNIA, 153, 157, 164–66, 171, 190–91; and Voudou, 32; and white supremacy, 84. *See also individual Roman Catholics*

rootwork: and Black Atlantic religions, 4–8, 18–22, 69, 92; and COG, 69–70; and COGIC, 191–93; doctors, 13, 55; and faith healing, 119–22, 129, 206–7; informant 864's grandmother and, 128; and Pentecostals, 183–88, 206–9; and reform, 113, 115; tinctures, 19, 41, 128, 166, 213; and UNIA, 153, 166–67

Rosicrucianism, 136

Rounds, G. C., 169

Rouquette, Adrienne, 40

Russia, 88, 190

salts, 87–88, 91, 95, 108

Salvador C., 128

Sanctified Church: defined, 182; and faith healing, 184, 202; and Hurston, 2, 179, 193; and Little Richard, 215; and LWP, 21, 181–83; and McPherson, 206; self-definition of, 181–84, 212; sonic culture of, 193, 214; and Triumph, 194, 196; and UNIA, 155. *See also* Pentecostalism

Santería, 123

Saxon, Elizabeth Lyle, 54–55

Saxon, Lyle, 9, 54

Seals, Mother Catherine: and Black Hawk, 93; "come just as you are" refrain of, 112; early life of, 93–94; and Hurston, 87–88, 95, 108; industrialism of, 99–106; and meaning making, 5–6; and mothering, 93–99; and Narcisse, 214; possible connection to informant 864's grandmother, 126; and queerness, 215; and respectability politics, 111–14; and resurrection, 115–16; Treadwell compared to, 184; as trombonist, 103, *104*; and underworld work, 89–92. *See also* Temple of the Innocent Blood

second line parades, 153, 161, 164

sects, 6, 16, 18, 32, 49, 70–72, 80–82, 89, 100, 182, 194

Selassie, Haile, 129–31, 134–35, 140, 156

Seventh Day Adventist, 191

Seventh Day Church of God, 193

sex: and the archive, 24; and Black brute trope, 74, 107; and Black club women, 110–16; and Moriath Butler, 142–44; and commandment to be fruitful, 67; ethics, sexual, 64, 67, 125; and free love, 67, 71; hypersexualization of Black Atlantic religions, 32–39, 42, 71–74, 85, 100, 102, 218; and immigration, 92; interracial, 36, 77, 92, 100, 187–88, 205; and Jim Crow, 23, 34; liberation, sexual, 142; morality, sexual, 133; and Narcisse, 214–15; "negro cult" as sexualized category, 18, 21; oppression, sexual, 142; passion, sexual, 85, 114, 127; in prison, 120; and religio-racial identity, 64; and UNIA, 168; unrestrained Black sexuality, 5; and urban purity, 106–10; and Victorianism, 23, 74, 85, 91–92, 96, 106–16; and violence, 95, 113–14, 123. *See also* marriage; terrorism: racial-sexual

sex work: criminalization of, 122–23, 126, 141, 145; and Horn, 141–42; and immigration, 92; and Jamèt people, 5; as knowledge making, 20; and Lyons, 131–35, 138–40; male, 132, 139; New Orleans bans on, 133; queer, 132; and red-light district, 90; as religious commerce, 27–28, 129; and Seals's ministry, 89–93, 103, 108–10; and

segregation, 90; spiritualized, 7; and underworld, 4, 6, 13, 124, 128. *See also* informant 864

Shakespeare, William, 169

Shaw, A. P., 173

Slaughter, Robert (Prophet Daniel), 64

slavery: and COG, 59–62, 65–68, 73, 84; and "Creole Slave Songs," 40–41, *41*, 45–46, *46*, 49–50; and faith healing, 125; and migration, 122; and planters, 18, 36, 38, 43–49, 65, 113; religion in afterlives of, 3, 6–10, 13–15, 18, 32, 59, 92, 129; and respectability, 23, 102–3, 112–14; and Seals's religion, 98; and sex, 126; and slavecatchers, 78; and survival, 5; and UNIA, 153; and Voudou, 33–39, 51–55

Smith, Elias Dempsey, 186–95, 211

Smith, Samuel, 155

social science, 1–3, 6–8, 20–21, 24–25, 84, 210

Spanish-American War, 186, 204–8

Spanish language, 10, 36, 156

spells, 8, 50, 128

spirit possession, 31, 34–39, 41–45, 48, 54, 59, 73, 90, 96, 179; mounting, 31, 36–37, 40, 48

Spiritualist churches: dietary codes of, 194; and dress, 199; and faith healing, 28, 185, 202; and Hurston, 2; and informant 864, 126–27; and Lyons, 130; and Narcisse, 214; and reform, 105, 206; and Roman Catholicism, 132, 182; and Sanctified Church, 181–84, 203, 212; and Seals, 93; and Treadwell, 196; and underworld work, 6, 17–20, 184–85; and UNIA, 27; and Voudou, 32. *See also* *individual practitioners*

storefront churches, 8, 19, 59, 131, 166–67, 194, 212

street preachers, 19, 73, 83, 122, 218. *See also* *individual preachers*

surveillance: and Black Atlantic religions, 6, 8, 10, 17, 22, 24, 27–28; and class, 115, 120–21; and COG, 60–61, 65, 68–69, 75; of queer sexuality, 134; of Voudou, 27, 35, 37, 42, 45

Taliaferro, Chester, 141

Tallant, Robert, *9*, 23, 94, 162

teachers, 80–83, 108, 113, 125, 131, 198, 200

Temple of the Innocent Blood, 5, 88–98, 103–12, 116, 214

Terrell, Mary Church, 111

terrorism: COG identified with, 67; Italian aggression in Ethiopia as, 130; ontological, 14–15; racial, 15, 18, 77; racial-sexual, 8, 25, 60, 103, 123, 213; and Voudou, 38, 45, 49

Thomas, Jessie O., 107–8

Thompson, C. W., 155

Thompson, Samuel, 24

tinctures, 19, 41, 128, 166, 213

Tinker, Edward Laroque, 90–91, 95, 97, 108

Tobias, T. W. J., 169

tongues, speaking in, 31, 182, 188

tourism: and commodification of Black Atlantic religions, 8, 24, 44, 212; and *New Orleans City Guide*, 24, 91, 104, 131, 159; and performativity, 44; and *Picayune's Guide to New Orleans*, 33, 52–54; and Voudou, 52–56

transgender people, 124–28; transphobia, 124

Treadwell, Lucien H., 173, 181–86, 195–97, 202–3, 207, 211

Trinidad, 5

Triumph the Church and Kingdom of God in Christ (Triumph the Righteous Church), 186–96, 200

Turkey, 190

Turner, Henry McNeal, 156

Turner, Leon, 2

Turner, Luke, 117

Turner, Nat, 12, 32, 60

Tuskegee Normal and Industrial Institute, 92, 96, 99, 102, 105–7, 113, 157

underworld work: and antichurch or unchurched individuals, 6; and archives, 4, 6, 10–13, 24, 27; defined, 4; as Hoodoo work, 6; Hurston as underworld worker, *xii*, 3–6, 12, 27; and Jim Crow, 4–15; and lynching, 3, 16, 21–22, 93, 167; and sex work, 4, 6, 13, 124, 128; under/worlding as method, 3

Universal Negro Improvement Association (UNIA): Afro-Protestantism of, 151–53, 166, 171; anchored in New Orleans, 149; and Black Star Line, 168, 170, 189; as religio-political organization, 153–55. *See also* Universal Negro Improvement Association's New Orleans Division (NOD)

Universal Negro Improvement Association's New Orleans Division (NOD): and Eason's murder, 167–71; and entertainment, 161–67; religion in, 149–54, 176–77; and Universal African Black Cross Nurses, 199–200, *201*; and women, 172–76

US Census, 3, 25, 64, 69, 94, 194

violence: anti-Black, 4, 6, 65, 187; and archives, 25; and authenticity, 20; Black people identified with, 78; and colonialism, 143; and creolization, 10; and faith healing, 128; and freedom, 14; intimate partner, 91–93; and religion making, 7; sexual, 95, 113–14, 123; and slavery, 49; state, 6, 72, 115; and UNIA, 177; and white Christianity, 61–62; white ritual, 8, 73; and xenophobia, 63. *See also* Jim Crow; lynching; white supremacy

Voodoo, Voudou, Vodou: and anti-Voudou sentiment, 23, 77, 84; and Black Atlantic religions, 22–28; and "blood of the dragon" discourse, 77; and COG, 59, 70, 73–76, 77, 82; commodification of, 70; demonization of, 40, 43, 49, 70, 92, 113; *drapo*, 96; and folklore, 47–52; and Haiti, 32, 40, 48; and Hurston, 2, 13, 29, 95, 117; and jazz, 113, 153; and Lyons, 130–31, 138; and masks, 5, 35; misrepresentations of, 18, 22–23, 33–39, 40–41, 45–52, 54–55, 123, 218; and Narcisse, 214; and Pentecostals, 185; perceived dangers of, 49–50; policing of, 33–34, 61; resisting Christianization, 32; and respectability, 112; and ritual, 2, 8, 27–28, 31–45, 48–49, 53–54, 59, 74, 89–90, 142; and Seals, 89, 90, 91, 98; and sex, 123; and Spiritualism, 17; and tourism, 52–56;

Voodoo, Voudou, Vodou (*continued*)
as unlawful assembly, 39; vanishing and
transformation of, 34, 40–52; as *Veaudeau*,
55; votaries, 91; and white race makers, 32.
See also spirit possession; tourism

Walker, Alice, 13, 106
Warner, Charles Dudley, 32
Washington, Booker T., 80, 92, 96, 99–107,
110–15, 157. *See also* Tuskegee Normal and
Industrial Institute
Washington, E. M., 169
Washington, Margaret Murray, 92, 99, 113
Watch Tower Worldwide Intercessory Prayer
Healing Movement, 186, 204–11
Watkins, Doctor Green, 120
Wells, Emma, 138
Wells-Barnett, Ida Bell, 10, 25, 78, 102
West Indies, 22, 42, 63, 151, 157, 168, 171, 195
Whidden, Benjamin F., 50
white supremacy: and Black Atlantic religion
making, 13, 122, 218; COG protesting, 64–
65, 67, 69, 73–78, 83; and criminalization
of Black community, 115; and interracial
relationships, 36; and LWP, 69, 84; and
method, 25; and Methodists, 60; and Pen-

tecostals, 187; Seals against, 103; terrorism,
18; violence, 83; and Voudou critiques, 32;
and white Christianity, 4, 10, 20–22, 32–33,
65, 70, 72, 75, 77, 79, 81, 84, 93, 120–23, 131,
145, 152, 195, 201, 206, 212–13

Williams, Fannie Barrier, 110–14
Williams, Gus, 77
Williams, Sylvanie Francoz, 92, 110
Wood, D. W., 166
Woods, Louise, 64
Works Progress Administration (WPA), 24,
26, 159, 183, 193, 195; and *New Orleans
City Guide*, 24, 91, 104, 131, 159. *See also*
Louisiana Writers' Project (LWP)
World War I, 186, 188, 205–8
World War II, 24, 139, 214

Yearwood, Arthur Clifford, 158
Yorùbá, 36, 136
Young, Marguerite, 98
Young Men's Christian Association (YMCA),
208

Zandita, Waizero (empress), 189
Zenon, Alfred (Prophet Job), 64
Zion AME Church, 163, 167